Relational Family Therapy

Relational Family Therapy introduces a cutting-edge family and couple therapy model that synthesizes relational theories and integrates object relations theory with interpersonal psychoanalysis and self-psychology. The model holds that individuals deal with conflicts rooted in the frustrated and threatening environment they grew up in by later forming intimate relationships that are comparable to the core experiences from their primary family systems. The book outlines the three levels of experience—systemic, interpersonal, and intrapsychic—and provides concrete ways for the therapist to address client problems and promote affect regulation. Chapters include transcripts of actual family therapy sessions as well as genograms so readers can see the model in action.

Christian Gostečnik, OFM, PhD, is a professor in the Family Studies and Marriage and Family Therapy programs at the University of Ljubljana. He is also a Franciscan priest, clinical psychologist, and practicing marriage and family therapist.

Relational Family Therapy

The Systemic, Interpersonal, and Intrapsychic Experience

CHRISTIAN GOSTEČNIK

Routledge
Taylor & Francis Group
NEW YORK AND LONDON

First published 2017
by Routledge
605 Third Avenue, New York, NY 10017

and by Routledge
2 Park Square, Milton Park, Abingdon, Oxon, OX14 4RN

Routledge is an imprint of the Taylor & Francis Group, an informa business

First published in Slovenian by Založba brat Frančišek & Frančiškanski družinski inštitut & Teološka fakulteta as Inovativna relacijska družinska terapija

Library of Congress Cataloging in Publication Data
A catalog record for this book has been requested

ISBN: 978-1-138-68618-2 (hbk)
ISBN: 978-1-138-68619-9 (pbk)
ISBN: 978-1-315-54274-4 (ebk)

Typeset in Minion
by Apex CoVantage, LLC

Contents

Introduction

The contemporary psychotherapeutic approach to families has had a strong impact on systemic studies and research and, in particular, on systemic family therapy, which emerged from this research. This new concept of treatment and studying families continues to consider individuals as an integral part of the family in which they grew up: the family of origin or primary family. This is also the basis of the current contribution, which substantially completes the initial *Relational Family Therapy* edition. Studying the family unit this way has become a widely accepted psychological paradigm on the basis of which contemporary authors research family dynamics, the causes of mental illness, and emotional and behavioral disorders (Catherall, 2004; Cummings & Davies, 2010; MacFarlane, 2004; Maroda, 2010; McCormack, 2000; Robins, 2010; Slipp, 1988, 1993, 1996; Solomon, 1992, 2009). The most prevalent models in this vast and variegated field are the so-called strategic (Haley, 1987), structural (Minuchin & Fishman, 1981), intergenerational (Framo, 1992), contextual (Boszormenyi-Nagy, Grunebaum, & Ulrich, 1991; Boszormenyi-Nagy & Krasner, 1986), and Bowen (1978) models. All of these psychotherapeutic models emerged from the new epistemological foundation composed of systems theory and the theory of cybernetics (Bitter, 2014; Gehart, 2016; White, Klein, & Martin, 2015).

The focus is on actual and evident, as well as covert, pathological transactions and transfers of unresolved and often painful mental content to a particular individual, who is unconsciously or involuntarily forced to accept this content, identify with it, and thus becomes the identifying patient or "scapegoat" in the family system. In this context, it is possible to see how behavioral, affective, and cognitive models are reawakened and repeated generation after generation. Sometimes, as research of abuse (Fonagy, Gergely, Jurist, & Target, 2007; Main & Goldwin, 1996; Schore, 2003, 2012; Siegel, 2009, 2011) and clinical implications increasingly evidence, the affective complications only fully reveal themselves in subsequent generations. So, for example, spouses who have been emotionally, mentally, physically, or sexually abused are able to create a fairly functional relationship, while their children become addicted to the affects of abuse and ultimately demonstrate a wide array of symptomatology (Repič, 2008). These symptoms are often the result of the abuse suffered by their parents, the symptomatic responses having been suppressed only to reawaken in the next generation.

A similar process occurs in the case of trauma: traumatic experience is recorded in the neurobiological and somatic structure of an individual's psychic construct where it remains. This is especially true of children who were exposed to trauma, and nobody in the family system was able to help them deal with the trauma and to process and regulate the related affects. In such cases, the traumatic experience or preserved stressful experiences not only persist through an individual's life but live on in subsequent generations as well. Thus the consequences can be truly catastrophic as members of subsequent generations are not even aware of what is happening to them or why. Consequently, research on the family systems theory has intensified in recent decades, as various authors of systems theory began to integrate analytical theories that take into account past generations and thus respond to the increasing complexities encountered in clinical practice. Here we are referring to the new integrative models that link intrapsychic and interpersonal mechanisms with systems dynamics.

These approaches understand that deep-rooted intrapsychic and interpersonal experiences from childhood are transferred to the interpersonal level and are manifested in current family relationships. These models attempt to trace the affects and the somatic content that is reawakened and influences current relationships. They attempt to discern the meaning of such content in current relationships and how the content is conveyed. In other words, these authors integrate family systems theory with theories that address a variety of perspectives concerning intrapsychic and interpersonal dynamics. What is being created is a new approach to considering the individual as well as the couple as parts of a system within the context of the entire family system. Contemporary authors focus on integrating intrapsychic mechanisms with interpersonal and systemic dynamics: for example, self-psychology with systems theory (Siegel & Solomon, 2013; Solomon, 1992, 1994, 2009), object relations theory with systems theory (D. E. Scharff, 1992; J.S. Scharff & Scharff, 1994, 2006, 2014; Slipp, 1988, 1996), self-psychology with object relations and systems theory (Pinsof, 1995; Pinsof & Lebow, 2005), and attachment theory with systems theory (Johnson, 2014; Johnson & Whiffen, 2003). The goal is to create a new approach to the intricacies and complexities of clinical practice as well as to systemic family research.

The innovation of relational family therapy lies in the integration of the relational model developed by Mitchell (1988, 1993, 2000, 2002), with the interpersonal model (Cummings & Davies, 2010), systems theory (Catherall, 2004; MacFarlane, 2004; J.S. Scharff & Scharff 2006, 2014), and psycho-organic dynamics (Fishbane, 2013; Fonagy et al., 2007; Poulton, 2013; Schore, 2003, 2012; Siegel, 2010, 2011; Solomon, 2009). Relational family therapy has integrated these intricate dynamics and complexities into a psycho-organic paradigm and applied it to our understanding of the individual, who is also an integral part of the family system. This psycho-organic paradigm provides the basis for the integrative therapeutic approach, combining intrapsychic dynamics with interpersonal mechanisms and a systems theory perspective, thus providing a more efficient psychotherapeutic and scientific approach to contemporary family therapy. Relational family therapy seeks to provide clarification and pragmatic resolutions to painful traumatic and pathologic problems that repeatedly and unconsciously intrude into new relationships and circumstances.

This book will first focus on the basic elements of relational family therapy and then follow with a review of systems theory. The focus will be on relational concepts that are otherwise implicitly included in systems theory but are not specifically defined. The two main relational mechanisms are projective and introjective identification and repetition compulsion. Although many proponents of systems theory do not explicitly apply these concepts, they do describe the dynamics of a system and implicitly apply them in their theories and clinical practice. We will lay out the design of the relational family therapy model, and the approach to couples and family therapy that integrates intrapsychic, interpersonal, and systemic mechanisms. The fundamental premise of this integrative model is that every relationship is founded on a certain core affect, somatic memory or emotion, which has an organic basis and dictates, through interpersonal dynamics, the formation of a specific relational pattern. This means that real change occurs in therapy at a conscious level as the core affects that the therapist and individual experience undergo transformation. The goal is to portray the affective experiencing of the therapeutic approach, which is the very foundation of our model.

Only by reaching the level of affect regulation that drives, manages, and orients the entire system of relationships, experiencing, and making connections with new people—in this case with the therapist—can the therapist access the essence of dysfunctional and pathological attachments that created the affective psychic construct with which family members defend themselves from distress. We will break down these theories and models, find their organic foundations that manifest in a myriad of sensations and present them in the integrated form of the entire family system. Without such integration, which is the essence of this psycho-organic model, our understanding of marital and family relationships would be insufficient. Only a complex relational family model can fully describe the system and relational dynamics at the level of the individual's, couple's, and family's life. This model also enables a comprehensive and holistic approach to the theoretical research of the individual, the couple, and the family as well as of clinical practice in general.

1 Fundamentals of Relational Family Therapy

As stated in the introduction, relational family therapy is an innovative psycho-organic model that is based on three basic levels of experiencing: systemic, interpersonal, and intrapsychic. These levels are further divided into cognitive-mental and somatic parts. Because the family is an organic psychosocial unit and each individual within it is an organic psychological entity, combined they form an organic and social family system. These three levels are based on five dynamic principles: projective and introjective identification, repetition compulsion, core affect, affective psychic construct, and affect regulation, which fundamentally constitute the innovative psycho-organic paradigm. The relational family model is founded on the premise that recurrent patterns of relationships in the human experience—early childhood experiences, physical sensations, and especially the core affects that they generate—are constantly recreated at all three levels of experiencing.

In this context, we often refer to the satisfaction of the basic needs for preservation, continuity, connection, and belonging to a personal world of relationships and the familiarity offered by known forms of relationships (Fonagy et al., 2007; Mitchell, 1988, 2002; Poulton, 2013; Ringstrom, 2014; Schore, 2003, 2012; Stern, 2010). These represent the primary constitutive affective relationships that make up the mental and/or organic structure of a human being and that all people continually seek to recreate. These affective relationships, and the cognitive-mental and somatic parts that are connected to them and preserved in physical sensations, are expressed through relational mechanisms such as projective and introjective identification and repetition compulsion, both of which are constitutive elements and preservation mechanisms of the human mental structure. These are the fundamental tendencies of human experiencing in which feelings of the-self-in-connection-with-the-other have extraordinary significance on the intrapsychic, interpersonal, and systemic levels. Relational family therapy is therefore oriented toward all three aspects: systemic or family, interpersonal or marital, and intrapsychic or individual. In therapy, all three levels and their various aspects are explored for psychological traumas and an attempt is made to resolve any traumas that are discovered. At the same time, therapy will attempt to resolve the affective psychic constructs that function as defense mechanisms and establish various dynamics of affect regulation that serve to preserve both functional and dysfunctional dynamics in the system on all three levels.

In relational family therapy, we refer to the so-called progressive process of discovering core affects and the affective psychic constructs that are connected to them, because relational family therapy takes into account all the levels of a person's experience: that is, all three levels of interaction. If, for example, it is not possible to find a solution on the systemic level, the therapist can attempt to resolve psychological traumas on the interpersonal and, finally, the intrapsychic level, because, as we shall see, there is a similar configuration of relationships, affects, and affect regulation on all three levels. These configurations comprise the relational space between individuals in the family, or the system of affective psychic constructs, which serves as the basis for the regulation of difficult or unacceptable affects. The progressive approach might be compared to an archeological excavation that goes gradually deeper and deeper until true treasure is unearthed. The relational therapist works in a similar fashion, first attempting to solve a problem on the systemic level or on the level of family organization, then looking for solutions between the spouses and in their mental space, and finally digging down to the unconscious level: that is, to the level of the somatic, organic content of implicit organic memory.

All three levels and the affective content that creates the interpersonal relational space between them compose the integrated family system and all the categories that are contained in a particular family system. Relational family consciously explores and reveals on which level a given problem has its roots, determines the cause of specific regulation functions and attempts to find a way forward that will suggest concrete solutions. It is important that the core affect is discovered and addressed by the therapist on the intrapsychic level, and then discovered and addressed on the interpersonal and systemic levels, as only this will enable the individual and the whole system to improve functionality in terms of behavior, emotion and cognition. Relational family therapy is also a model geared toward uncovering the primary affective psychic construct and resolving it on all three levels. This construct maintains very specific patterns of relationships, which in turn precipitate certain problematic behavior through which the individual, couple or entire system regulate painful affects.

1.1 The Systemic Level

As already stated, the relational family therapist attempts to resolve problems generated and preserved in the systemic and organizational dynamics of the family (Pinsof, 1995; Pinsof & Lebow, 2005). Viewed at the level of the family system, a problem might be seen as a compromise formed in order to conceal deeper affects—such as fear, anger, sadness, etc.—with which family members cannot yet cope. One of the family members, the identified patient, becomes the carrier of the family affective distress or affective psychic construct, and at the same time becomes the regulator and maintainer of systemic balance or homeostasis. This affective psychic construct may be expressed in many forms, through poor behavior at school, decadence or dissipation, illness, etc. The concept of mutual or circular causality plays an essential role in this regard because, without it, it would be almost impossible to describe the family as a system (Bitter, 2014; Gehart, 2016; Gurman & Kniskern, 1991; Haley,

1976). This is not to say that each individual in the family system should not be viewed as a separate entity, but rather that each individual can and does influence others in the system and vice versa. The systemic point of view emphasizes circular as opposed to linear causality. Furthermore, the individual's mental, emotional, and behavioral processes constitutively influence the overall context of the family and its members (Carlson & Sperry, 2010; McCormack, 2000) who collectively co-create and maintain the family homeostasis or status quo. In the coming pages, we will first review the general systemic rules that govern and organize the family system in both its functional and dysfunctional aspects (Bitter, 2014; Cummings & Davies, 2010; McCormack, 2000; White et al., 2015). The relational family therapist first approaches the question of affect regulation, which enables dysfunctional behavior, and therefore must be explored carefully. Only the main themes and dynamics will be put forth in this section. Subsequent sections will address the various systemic theories that contribute to the relational family therapy model.

1.1.1 Systemic Homeostasis

At the outset of the development of systemic theory, research focused more on how balance was preserved in a system and less on how to change that balance (Bitter, 2014; Gurman & Kniskern, 1991). In other words, while researchers looked at certain kinds of feedback that cause change—that is positive feedback—they didn't research this area as intensely as might be expected (Bitter, 2014; Hecker & Wetchler, 2003) given that all living systems are in a state of constant change. Changes are necessary and adaptations to new conditions are one of the most essential dynamics of each life opus (Pinsof, 1995; Pinsof & Lebow, 2005). For example, each family or family system experiences chronological developments—the family cycle—that influence both individuals and the family system as a whole (Guttman, 1991; White et al., 2015). Included in the family cycle are events that transform everyday life (such as birth, marriage, and death), and events that fundamentally change the life of specific individuals and consequently the entire family system (such as illness, unemployment, etc.). Just as individuals must adapt to these kinds of events, so too must family systems. In systemic terminology, these events are initiators or agents of deviation. In other words, they are events that activate the positive feedback mechanism. The family system must react in some way to them: by changing structure, rebalancing power, or introducing new rules that will regulate the family system (Dallos & Draper, 2005; Gehart, 2016; Gurman & Kniskern, 1991; Hecker & Wetchler, 2003). In response, a family system can either change definitively or strive to return to the primary condition, causing negative feedback that reduces deviation. In this context, system theorists (Dallos & Draper, 2005) refer to changes of the first and second order. A change of the first order takes place when a system is inclined to return to the primary condition or seek a renewed balance, which doesn't allow for change and preserves the system in a stable state. This means that while there may have been a change in the relationships between certain individuals in the system, the basic rules and fundamental balance have been preserved. A change of the second order takes place when there is a more radical response to a given challenge from the environment or from the system itself (Pinsof, 1995; Pinsof & Lebow, 2005). Rules and roles are essential to maintaining the balance of a given system, and when there is a change in the rules, there will also be a change in interpersonal relationships in the system (Hecker & Wetchler, 2003). It is also possible that one of the members of the family will manifest both inclinations: toward change and toward the status quo. For example, a young person may continually rebel against certain rules of the family that seem unacceptable, and in this way be the agent of positive feedback in the family system. At the same time, this same person can be a carrier of negative feedback that encourages the family to maintain a static method of organization (Cummings & Davies, 2010; Gurman & Kniskern, 1991; McCormack, 2000).

Changes of the second order represent changes in the rules that determine the proximity or distance of individual subsystems in the family system as a whole (Bitter, 2014; Haley, 1976). For example, a chronically ill member of the family will initiate or force change in the family system, while at the same time resisting change. On the one hand, the family must respond to the family member's illness, having to care for that member or at least take his or her condition into account. On the other hand, precisely the health status of this family member prevents real change by not allowing and even actively preventing the family system from changing the rules that make it possible for them to provide the needed care (Gurman & Kniskern, 1991; McCormack, 2000; Siegel & Solomon, 2013). In such cases, we often observe a vicious cycle in which the family system becomes entangled and from which it cannot extricate itself. Such a situation can last a very long time and is more painful and acute in family systems where violence and addiction are present. What is observable in such extreme cases is how the family system resists changes in behavior and actively strives to preserve the differentness that is a consequence of family crises.

The process of change is complicated in all families. It is never simple to introduce change into a system: that is, to adapt to and accept new information that demands alterations in the family system. It is important to understand that there are many different kinds of systems: from open, to relatively closed, to impermeable. It is extremely difficult, sometimes virtually impossible, for closed systems to accept new information, while open systems offer a good possibility that information will reach its goal, although it is not always clear how. What is clear is that there are systemic forces that reduce deviation and stem from the internal, often unspoken rules of the system that lead, direct, and regulate the system's functioning. Therefore, any input or positive feedback must be sufficiently strong to cause a deviation or a denial of the previous rules that are deeply embedded and serve to preserve the status quo or systemic homeostasis (Gehart, 2016; Guttman, 1991; Hecker & Wetchler, 2003). One such input is the growth or maturation of members of the family. This applies, for example, to maturing children and their increasing abilities and growing independence. Such inputs do not come from the family alone, but also from the external environment including new ideas, convictions, standards, and rules that enter the family through "outsiders" such as friends and acquaintances who become part of the family, as well as through other social environments and institutions such as work and school (Gurman & Kniskern, 1991; Pinsof, 1995; Pinsof & Lebow, 2005).

New input or information must be sufficiently powerful, either as negative or positive feedback, to change the system. The family system can be very selective when it comes to new information, especially when this new information engages the capability and willingness to accept something new. Each family system tends toward preserving its own fundamental structure and organization. In stark contrast to homeostasis is systemic flight, which means that the entire system experiences a sudden and total transformation (Guttman, 1991; Pinsof, 1995; Pinsof & Lebow, 2005). This can happen, for example, if parents divorce and the children remain with one or the other—in other words, if there is a permanent division among the members of the system. Then we no longer discuss a single-family system with the previous form and format, but rather a radically different system with entirely new rules (Dallos & Draper, 2005; Hecker & Wetchler, 2003).

1.1.2 Constitutive Elements of the System

It is of enormous importance for the relational family therapist to discover and define the fundamental constitutive elements of a system, for example, of a family structure that is made up of precisely defined methods or patterns of behavior, emotions, and cognition. It is also essential for the relational family therapist to discover the organization of family members and how this organization prevents resolution to problems that arise from dysfunctional patterns of interaction. This organization can be of an emotional or rational nature, but it generally plays out in the arena of interpersonal family relations. The relational family therapist looks at the family as if at a corporation and strives to organize it in such a way that it will eventually be capable of solving its own problems. Each family has an unspoken structure or plan that dictates who is at the head, who manages, and the responsibilities of each member. The family structure also dictates the patterns of family communication and determines who is in a position of leadership on a daily basis and in specific situations, and who speaks with whom when things are going well and when they are not (Gehart, 2016; Gurman, 2008; Haley, 1976; Hecker & Wetchler, 2003; Pinsof, 1995; Pinsof & Lebow, 2005). For instance, parents are usually responsible for the establishment of boundaries and the rules that apply to the family whereas children may only participate in certain conversations, such as family outings, holidays, etc.

For this reason, it is essential that the relational family therapist trained in systems theory or family therapy first discern how the family organizes itself as it solves various problems. This enterprise will include questions of whether problems are successfully solved, whether family members can speak directly about emerging problems, whether the family is sufficiently flexible to introduce essential changes, whether others who do not necessarily belong in the system are included in such conversations, whether problems persist because a system of family secrecy and taboos prevail, and thus not only are family members incapable of solving problems but others are prevented from assisting as well (Gehart, 2016; Minuchin & Fishman, 1981). The answers to all of these questions are essential as they reveal the character and strength of the family organization. Based on this assessment of structure, the therapist can develop a plan of therapy as well as related interventions intended to help the family.

In general, families use different structures and methods to solve problems in various situations (Bitter, 2014; Cummings & Davies, 2010; Minuchin & Fishman, 1981; White et al., 2015). For example, children cooperate much more actively with the mother on family matters that relate to everyday activities if the father is excluded because he is frequently away. Such a situation becomes more difficult in cases where the father is an addict because the children must take on more functions. If the mother is also an addict, then the situation is worse still. In such cases, the children become the primary victims, taking on virtually all of the parental functions. If the mother and father are successfully treated, for example, for addiction or alcoholism, then the roles must be reversed again. This can also be a very difficult task because the family at such a juncture will need a complete reconstruction of the rules and roles, and this can place an enormous, sometimes unsustainable burden on a family system. For instance, a basic mistrust can occur when a system has created an entirely new structure in order to survive and the newly created system is not flexible enough to suddenly change once again when new circumstances are introduced (Bitter, 2014).

Hierarchy is also an important element in the conceptualization of the family system. It plays a special role in defining the family organization and also in the development of family therapy. The founding fathers of systemic theory (Bitter, 2014; Haley, 1976; Minuchin & Fishman, 1981; Sexton, Weeks, & Robbins, 2003) began by describing the above hierarchical dynamics: namely that different family members have different ways of supervising other members and some play a more dominant role in defining the rules than others. Whenever the prevailing hierarchy is toppled, fundamental changes take place in the family system that can be more or less destructive and painful, but, in general, the family system will react by striving to reestablish equilibrium. While in healthy families it is the duty of the parents to reestablish order, in a family where the mother and father are dysfunctional, one of the children will take on the role of primary caretaker. If that does not occur and there is no suitable solution, then the entire system will search for new solutions, and this can manifest, for example, in one of the children becoming ill, engaging in inappropriate behavior, dissipation, alcohol, drugs, etc.

The concept of hierarchy refers to the boundaries that divide the leadership subsystem from other members of the family. Structural family therapy assumes that for a group or family to function, and especially to solve problems, someone must take on the leadership role (Bitter, 2014; Dallos & Draper, 2005; Minuchin & Fishman, 1981). Members of the leadership subsystem must have more powers and responsibilities in decision-making processes than other members of the family. For instance, the parents of small children decide when the children will go to bed, when and how long they will watch television, play, use the computer, etc. Of course, the children also have their opinions on these matters, and those opinions may be respected to a degree, but the parents have the final word (Minuchin & Fishman, 1981; White et al., 2015). The hierarchical organization in a family therefore refers to specific boundaries that determine parental responsibilities in the upbringing of children. In this process, it is essential that the entire family, and especially the parental leadership subsystem, have structures in place for achieving goals in the different situations it may find itself. In other words, it needs various hierarchical arrangements to fulfill its role in accordance with the responsibilities that are assigned to individual family members in specific situations and to accomplish specific tasks (Hecker & Wetchler, 2003; Robins, 2010; Sexton et al., 2003).

1.1.3 Systemic Structure

In keeping with its organizational approach, systems theory and therapy divides the family into various subsystems or groups of family members that carry out specific roles (Colapinto, 1991; Hecker & Wetchler, 2003; Kerr & Bowen, 1988; Minuchin & Fishman, 1981). In addition to the parental subsystem, the children also have a subsystem in which they learn to cooperate, solve problems together, and help each other. Furthermore, subsystems emerge for temporary functions that are created for specific tasks; for example, when a father and daughter work together on a school project, or a mother helps her son get ready for school. In other words, all members of the family can be members of different subsystems (Bitter, 2014; Hecker & Wetchler, 2003; Minuchin & Fishman, 1981). The family, the system in this discussion, can also be a subsystem of a larger system, for example, the extended family of grandparents or the community in which the family belongs. Each of these systems and subsystems is a unit with its own rights (for example, a newlywed couple in an extended family living with parents becomes a new system). All these units and systems are in constant interaction with other subsystems within the family and perform their tasks in a context that allows free contact between members of various subsystems (Colapinto, 1991; Sexton et al., 2003).

As discussed above, there are also subsystems with executive functions, or units in the family systems and subsystems that take on leadership roles (Haley, 1976; Minuchin & Fishman, 1981; White et al., 2015). Parents generally take on that role, but other family members may also be leaders, such as grandparents or sometimes a child among siblings. When children take on leadership or executive roles, and the obligations and responsibilities that go with it, emotional abuse is often the result, as this represents a fundamental violation of system boundaries and hierarchy. This occurs when children are compelled to care for other members of the family, for example, brothers and sisters and sometimes even parents, at a time when they are not capable of such responsibilities. These forced roles, which are frequently accompanied by feelings of guilt, can have a lasting influence on children's experiencing of others, especially of the parents they had to care for, obey, and be available for, often unconditionally.

The next important concept in structural therapy is known as system boundaries. These boundaries refer to rules and roles that guide the family and determine who is included and excluded in specific systems or subsystems, and who is engaged in regular interpersonal interactions (Colapinto, 1991; Gehart, 2016; Hecker & Wetchler, 2003). Systems and subsystems do not exist in isolation but are in constant interaction with other systems and subsystems. Metaphorically, there are invisible fences between systems, fences that divide each group individually, and fences that determine who are members of specific groups. We refer to these as transparent boundaries. They define or delimit who is in the subsystem, although they should also allow communication outside the subsystem. Put another way, boundaries need to be sufficiently strict to facilitate the unhindered functioning of the system and sufficiently open to allow contact with other members of the family, other subsystems, and external systems. All of this will determine the functionality of the family or system as an organizational unit. Boundaries are important more in terms of how a given family functions internally than the image the family projects to the outside world (Bitter, 2014; Minuchin & Fishman, 1981). In short, the transparence of family boundaries is one of the most important characteristics in the evaluation of the health and functionality of a family in the context of the structural family paradigm, both in theory and in practice (Hecker & Wetchler, 2003).

In families where boundaries are weak and ambiguous, family members are in constant fear that someone will trespass into their individual space. In such cases, there is too little autonomy: for example, marital or parental issues become the children's issues. When the executive system does not properly perform its role, we often encounter adultized children. In such situations, we observe extremely permeable boundaries where roles are intermingled and there is too little space and autonomy for individual family members. This occurs because differentiation between and among family members and other subsystems is lacking (Hecker & Wetchler, 2003). If the cooperation between members of the subsystem does not allow healthy and autonomous relationships to develop among the family members, then extreme forms of immature relationships and systems, where everyone knows everything about everyone else, are likely to develop. In such situations, difficulties emerge both in the parental and children's subsystem, and family members do not know where or to what subsystem they belong. It follows that the optimally functional family system requires parents who are able to present an executive subsystem that creates clear boundaries between members of the family (Minuchin & Fishman, 1981; White et al., 2015).

In contrast to weak or ambiguous boundaries, there are also overly strong or strict limits, referred to as rigid boundaries. These can lead to the closure of a subsystem and prevent the absorption of external information. In families with rigid boundaries, little is shared among members, neither good nor bad experiences. Such a family is closed, and contacts with the surrounding environment are absent or few. For example, the parents in such families might give their children allowance and be convinced that they are providing their children with appropriate autonomy. The parents do not instruct the children in responsible management of the money, but simply expect them to independently handle it. They have no time for their children, only strict expectations. They expect that their children will be obedient, that they will unconditionally meet their demands, and if this is not achieved, the parents inflict harsh punishments, not least taking the allowance away. (In the opposite situation, parents with unclear boundaries give their children money without demanding anything of them, literally buying them, when in truth they are not interested in them.) For rigid parents, it is not important what their children are feeling. They often do not know what their children want and all that matters to the parents is that the children fulfill parental demands, plans, and expectations even if these are opposed to the children's wishes. This can sometimes even be seen in the choice of the adult children's careers, which are expected to be in accordance with the parents' expectations. It can also be manifested in the choice of friends and marital partners, sometimes decided in advance in accordance with strict family principles and rules, or with religious, racial, and cultural standards (Bitter, 2014).

There are also cases of boundaries that exclude the outside world (Hecker & Wetchler, 2003; Minuchin & Fishman, 1981; Pinsof, 1995; Pinsof & Lebow, 2005) and any information that comes from the outside world. Family problems that emerge within the family are not shared with the outside world. In extreme situations, these families are similar to families with rigid boundaries, because they are not interested in how individual family members actually feel. They can also be similar to families with unclear boundaries, where parents often don't even know where their children are, with whom they socialize, how they are doing in school, what they are interested in, and what their plans are. Finally, there are families that externalize their inner world, in other words, that have no appropriate boundaries with the outside world, for example, families who publicly discuss their problems or publicly criticize their children.

1.1.4 System Dynamics

Connections or alliances are created when several family members join forces to perform a certain task (Colapinto, 1991; Hecker & Wetchler, 2003; Minuchin & Fishman, 1981; Pinsof, 1995; Pinsof & Lebow, 2005). In a healthy and functional family, the connections among members of the family are understood and accepted as positive. Sometimes it is necessary, for example, for two brothers to create an alliance in order to implement a project. Other family members may also participate in such an endeavor. It is also possible and even an indication of functionality that certain members of the family get along better with some members than with others. Alliances therefore are not limited to the subsystem, and new subsystems can actually emerge from them (Bitter, 2014; Hecker & Wetchler, 2003; McCormack, 2000).

Coalitions emerge when several family members unite against one or several other members of the same family. This happens, for example, when there is a conflict between two family members and a third family member allies with the weaker with the apparent goal of establishing a kind of equilibrium (Catherall, 2004; Colapinto, 1991; Pinsof, 1995; Pinsof & Lebow, 2005). In addition to the fact that such coalitions can be hostile, they are often secretive by nature and frequently emerge when family members can no longer openly discuss certain problems. The more open the coalition, the more quickly it can be dissolved. Coalitions can be very destructive, especially when several family members are arrayed against a single member, for example, two brothers against a sister or two sisters against a brother. Cross-generational alliances can be even more problematic, for example when a son allies with the mother or a daughter with the father against the rest of the family. Such situations can cause a great deal of discord that can be difficult to eliminate later.

Triangles or triangulation, the phenomenon when two family members combine forces against a third, represents a specific kind of coalition (Bitter, 2014; Catherall, 2004; Hecker & Wetchler, 2003; Minuchin & Fishman, 1981). Although such triangular alliances are usually benign and can be quickly resolved, that is not always the case, for example when two family members from different generations form an alliance against a third in an intergenerational triangle: mother and son against a father, grandparents and a child against the parents or one of the parents, mother-in-law collaborating with her son against his wife. While such a triangular coalition may seem to provide balance between the two spouses, this is only an illusion (Colapinto, 1991). Usually, a problem cannot be resolved in this manner and in fact only becomes more acute, taking up enormous time and energy with no real promise of resolution. In general, problems are best solved with open and honest conversation between the couple, rather than relying on outside intervention. A particular kind of intergenerational coalition or triangle emerges when, for example, children become third parties involved in parental conflict. By their nature, children will try to please both their mother and father, and ultimately such a triangular coalition is extremely painful to children. Children fear that they will automatically lose the affection of one or the other parent, the one not allied with. In such situations, children are forced to walk a fine line between both parents (Hecker & Wetchler, 2003; MacFarlane, 2004; Minuchin & Fishman, 1981).

A variation of this situation is conflict avoidance (Dallos & Draper, 2005; Gehart, 2016; Minuchin & Fishman, 1981; Sexton et al., 2003). For example, because of an unresolved marital conflict, parents might redirect their attention onto one of the children, who becomes a temporary scapegoat. This might occur when the conflict between the parents comes to a boiling point, or they feel they are approaching a level of tension that they will not be able to handle. At this point, the parents may not be consciously thinking about their own problems, may not even fully realize what is happening, but transfer or deflect their tension onto the child who in their view is problematic. Frequently, such a situation causes the child who must process her or his parents' marital problems to show the symptoms of a psychosomatic illness (Bitter, 2014; Gehart, 2016; Hecker & Wetchler, 2003; Minuchin & Fishman, 1981).

To paraphrase one of the fathers of systemic therapy (Minuchin & Fishman, 1981), no individual family structure is a conclusive indicator of a healthy or unhealthy family. One indication that a given family is healthy is its ability to adapt to new circumstances and to change structures when necessary, demonstrating a certain competence at dealing with the various challenges of life. Problems are a normal part of life and the ability to solve them requires the favorable organization of family members (Hecker & Wetchler, 2003; MacFarlane, 2004). For example, newlyweds face the challenge of establishing both internal and external boundaries (Dallos & Draper, 2005; Hecker & Wetchler, 2003), and they will seek in each other a regulator of difficult affects, which each individually might be unable to carry and process. They are experiencing a new beginning, one that may be completely different from their families of origin. They will have to harmonize both their individual needs and desires, and their shared needs and desires. They will have to establish new rules that they might not have known in their families of origin. Slowly, they will construct new patterns that may or may not be similar to those from their own families. It often happens in such situations that a child becomes the regulator of their parents' unresolved differences, in other words the scapegoat, or the identified patient, and thus the carrier of the painful marital or partnership problems (Cummings & Davies, 2010).

If the relational family therapist determines that it is not possible to find a solution on the systemic level, or that the system does not change and become functional—emotionally, cognitively, and behaviorally—this may indicate more serious and intractable problems. The therapist will then progressively search for solutions, first on the more superficial and then the deeper levels of the system. In short, the therapist will strive to dig down to the interpersonal level, to the arena of the couple's relationship. The therapist is intervening as an active agent of change, striving to restructure the painful and dysfunctional models of behavior.

1.2 The Interpersonal Level

Delving into the interpersonal level, the relational family therapist will first try (for instance, after any children present have gone to the waiting room) to find out what is happening in the relationship between the spouses or parents: where and how did they meet, what attracted them to each other, where do they come from, how do they communicate, what values do they live by, and especially, what made them decide for therapy? The systemic level involves finding out about the spouses' respective families of origin, how they felt growing up in them, about their fathers and mothers, what these relationships were like, with whom they lived when they were growing up, about brothers and sisters, and when they left home. Just by asking these general questions, the relational family therapist has already entered the couple's intrapsychic world, their world of internal images, the core affects that are generated between them, and the intrapsychic dynamics that play out in their relationship. The therapist must be attuned to the themes from the intrapsychic world of their relationship. This is essential; otherwise everything remains on the cognitive level. At this stage, the relational family therapist will seek to address parental themes in particular, which will demand a reorganization of their functioning. The therapist will carefully organize, combine, and weave a new tapestry of their relationship, resolve their conflicts and fears, and try to bring an end to the constant repetition of the conflicts and problems that manifest in parental functioning. The goal is to repair, heal or restructure the couple's intrapsychic structures that were created in childhood and early adulthood, and now carry over to their parental functioning. Above all, the therapist will try to demonstrate and teach the couple the mechanism of affect regulation, which is crucial for the prevention of emotional and physical suffering. The therapist, akin to an archaeologist, will empathically unveil the relationship and its systemic and interpersonal structures, and then help the couple to build new forms of relating to each other, working together, and parental functioning. Already at this stage, there is substantial overlap between interpersonal and intrapsychic dynamics, but the therapist can move forward only when the core affect—still safely camouflaged by a variety of defense mechanisms and affective psychic constructs that prevent healthy functioning—is revealed.

1.2.1 Dynamics of Longing and Attraction

The relational family therapist first attempts to answer the question of attraction and love. In other words, what is the psychological content that provided the basis of longing and attraction between the two spouses? A therapist in the relational family therapy model is interested in why certain people fall in love and find satisfaction in a love relationship with the other, and why others desperately long for love and intimate relationships but are unable to achieve it, and why still others avoid relationships all together, fearing and sometimes actively rejecting them. The relational couples paradigm centers around the notion that to love and be loved, wanted and desired is deeply engrained in our intrapsychic structure, that children raised with a healthy upbringing and the adults they become cannot help but long for experiences of love, desire, and belonging. The person on whom we focus our intrapsychic longing is not the result of conscious choice, but rather is an unconscious psychic project in which our past experiences with the most significant others from our early developmental years dictate the choice of the best partner for us. With this chosen person, we will repeat the most deeply engrained relationship affects and dynamics that we experienced with significant others in the past, this time hoping to find resolution.

Modern psychoanalysts, such as Bowlby (1982), Carlson and Sperry (2010), Cummings and Davies (2010), Pines (1999), Poulton (2013), Siegel and Solomon (2013), Solomon (2009), Stern (2010), and J.S. Scharff and D. E. Scharff (2014), posit that experiences from early childhood, which are mostly unconscious and part of our organic memory (Rothschild, 2000, 2003, 2006, 2010; Schore, 2003, 2012; Siegel, 2011), have a profound effect on our later choice of intimate partner and on the development of our relationship with that partner. The experience of attachment is determinative, and especially children's first connection with a fellow human being, usually the mother. The ability for attachment and the creation of relationships is psycho-organically inherited, but the form of attachment and relationships is dependent on the relationships that children have with their first caregivers (Schore, 2003, 2012; Siegel, 2010, 2011; Stern, 2010). Children will suffer terribly, almost irreparably, if this relationship is interrupted or lost. This trauma will be revealed later when, as adults, these individuals establish relationships with potential partners, or, in contrast, fear and avoid any attachment that leads to an intimate relationship. Certain individuals may even seek out destructive relationships since they feel familiar and for this reason attractive.

1.2.2 Internal Working Models

Bowlby, the author of attachment theory, presented a series of internal working models in which he described the way children develop feelings regarding the self and others, and that the interaction with children's primary caregivers is of essential importance (Bowlby, 1982; Clulow, 2001; Pines, 1999, 2001; Siegel, 2010, 2011; Siegel & Solomon, 2013). Interaction with the mother, and especially the core affect that marks this interaction through the projective and introjective mechanism of identification, will significantly impact future relationships. Adults will passionately, albeit unconsciously, seek out people with whom the scheme of those primary relationships can be relived, and in this way will try to compensate or correct for what was missing in their childhood experience (J. S. Scharff & Scharff, 2014).

1.2.2.1 Internal working models, constructed on the basis of early relationship experiences with others that are internalized through introjective identification, dictate adult intimate relationships (Bowlby, 1982; Pines, 1999, 2001; J. S. Scharff & Scharff, 2014; Siegel, 2011; Stern, 2010). In other words, we identify with them, internalize them, and repeat them in adulthood by seeking out similar people with whom the same internal models can be recreated. These intrapsychic mental representations of significant others are now known as object relations theory (Fairbairn, 1952; Mitchell, 1988, 1997, 2000, 2002). They provide the basic content for the construction of intrapsychic psycho-organic structures and indeed are so binding that we constantly search for them in our relations with significant others.

1.2.2.2 Internal working models create and shape our convictions about our own worth in terms of being loved, whether we can trust others, surrender to them, and in this way experience love, acceptance, support, and the feeling of belonging and being wanted (Bowlby, 1982; Siegel, 2011; Stern, 2010). This is the foundation upon which we experience ourselves as loved, wanted, desired or, alternatively, as worthless and unacceptable. In this way, we do everything we can to confirm our psychological selves (Clulow, 2005; Kohut, 1984; Mitchell, 1988, 2000, 2002; Winnicott, 1988), and repeatedly relive our early childhood relations with significant others that we choose, as it is through the transference or the projection of identification onto another that we recreate the feeling that we had during our first experience of being loved. To a great degree, our self-image is the result of our relationship with the primary caregiver or mother (J. S. Scharff & Scharff, 2014).

1.2.2.3 These internal working models strongly influence all the interactions into which we enter with others and mark our perceptions and understandings of interpersonal interactions with significant others. Object relations theory posits that these are the basic behavioral, emotional, and cognitive patterns that we repeatedly and unconsciously produce in adulthood with significant others. Interpersonal psychoanalysis posits that this repetition is performed with exceptional precision without us knowing how or why, and represents the core affect generated from the interpersonal relationship between mother and child (Mitchell, 1988, 2000; J. S. Scharff & Scharff, 2014; Siegel & Solomon, 2013; Sullivan, 1972). Core affects are extremely binding, as they recall the earliest attachments and thus represent the fundamental mental construct for attachment to the other. Ultimately, we unconsciously strive to awaken these core affects with all significant others and especially in our intimate relationships. This will happen even when the affects are painful because they signify vibrancy and vitality, the essential content of attachment. Moreover, we actively reproduce these conditions with the unconscious hope that this time the life drama that first took place in childhood will play out in adulthood in a more healthy and functional manner.

Like Bowlby and other relational analysts such as Cummings and Davies (2010), Mitchell (1988, 1993, 2000, 2002), Pines (1999, 2001), Poulton (2013),

J. S. Scharff and D. E. Scharff (2014), Siegel and Solomon (2013), Solomon (2009), Stern (2010), we believe that human beings have an innate need for attachment, which emerges from the very crux of evolutionary development. Infants at birth are already equipped with a repertoire of behaviors that have the sole goal of achieving and maintaining closeness with the mother or primary caregiver (Siegel, 2010, 2011; Stern, 1995, 1998, 2004, 2010), even if this relationship is highly dysfunctional. Preserving closeness to the mother or primary caregiver is aligned with the infant's innate capabilities as well as with the desire for close attachment to those who are present, and are willing and able to respond to the infant's needs. The experience that the infant has with the mother is internalized and becomes the mental model for relationships with the self and others. These internalized working models are later carried over to relationships with other people. Because these models are genetically imprinted in each human being and are responsible for all forms of attachment, especially romantic attraction, they can be changed or adapted to new situations only with great difficulty (Bowlby, 1982; Clulow, 2005; Siegel, 2011). Schore (2003, 2012) called the attachment models that are formed during the preverbal period psycho-organic states. Because they stem from the primary atmosphere with the mother that generated the basic content for our mental, psycho-organic structure, the impulse will always be to try to recapture or recreate that atmosphere. It follows then that precisely these models, or psycho-organic states, will have a strong influence on our love relationships in which we try to emulate the primary symbiosis with the mother (Fonagy et al., 2007; Geher & Kaufman, 2013). If this symbiosis did not occur in infancy, then we will have an unconscious fear of intimacy and will tend to enter destructive and oppressive relationships.

From the standpoint of relational family therapy, it should be noted that these internal models are not remembered verbally and therefore cannot be put into words. Because they were experienced in the first weeks and months of life, they are imprinted in the organic memory, which is formed on the basis of projective and introjective identification and therefore is not accessible through verbal or explicit memory (Rothschild, 2006, 2010; J.S. Scharff & Scharff, 2014; Schore, 2003, 2012). These organic memories become most apparent during the period of adulthood when we begin to search for contact with others, especially during the search for potential intimate partners when these memories arouse physical attraction. These feelings from organic memory are awakened during encounters with potential partners, especially strongly when an encounter triggers these organic feelings and somatic memories and also recreates them on an unconscious level (Cvetek, 2009; Repič, 2008). The more painful these feelings, if we were neglected or rejected as children, then the more painful will be the relationships that are established through the mechanism of projective and introjective identification. The other can be experienced as the primary caregiver was experienced, or can recreate the feelings that the child had with the mother (Schore, 2003, 2012). In this context, abuse generates the strongest emotions and can have a catastrophic influence on attraction itself, because the intensity of the abusive relationship, deeply etched in the organic memory, is exceptionally binding, traumatic, and tragic (Fishbane, 2013; Repič, 2008; Siegel & Solomon, 2013).

1.2.3 Psycho-Organic States

Organic memories are created in the unconscious on the basis of communicative or physical interaction between mother and child. Psycho-organic states emerge from these interactions in the earliest phase of life and unconsciously guide us through all subsequent psycho-organic development. For this reason, psychoanalysis is recognized as the science of unconscious processes that are active throughout our entire lives (Siegel, 2011; Schore, 2012). In terms of the marital paradigm, we may speak of unconscious communication and interactions between the two spouses. The unconscious sphere of our mental structure functions as a receptive organ or a mechanism, and, at the same time, as an organ or a transfer mechanism whereby specific psycho-organic content is transferred to the other. It is, in other words, an essential means of influence (Poulton, 2013; Rothschild, 2000, 2003, 2006, 2010; Schore, 2003, 2012). When we unconsciously discover in the other similar psycho-organic content, a passionate attraction is awakened that promises the beginning of something seemingly new and ecstatic. Namely, the mechanism of projective and introjective identification (Klein, 1975; J.S. Scharff & Scharff, 2014) enables the transference of mental content from one person to another. We know that the unconscious system of one person influences the unconscious system of the other, and, at the same time, mutually determines intrapsychic processes and interactions, and sometimes triggering an irresistible attraction between them. Projective and introjective identification is therefore by its nature the most fundamental means of communication between two people. It is nothing less than the transference of the psycho-organic states (Schore, 2003, 2012) and core affects (Poulton, 2013; Rothschild, 2000, 2003, 2006, 2010; Siegel, 2011) that are linked to mental representations of the other. The latter are deeply engrained in our mental structure and projected, on the basis of unconscious interpersonal interactions, onto the other, and in this way constantly recaptured and renewed (Carlson & Sperry, 2010).

The recipient of projective and introjective identification becomes the carrier of the projected material of the sender who, in this process, attempts to reduce painful or unbearable mental psychosomatic content. But the recipient cannot be just anyone, but rather is someone with a mental structure suitable for receiving the intrapsychic material of the sender (Ogden, 1994, 1997), a match that we refer to as valency (D. E. Scharff, 1992; J.S. Scharff & Scharff, 2000, 2006, 2014). To some extent, these processes explain the question of attraction, or why two people become infatuated with each other and why romantic love emerges between them. Partners are unconsciously attracted to each other precisely because of these similarities, the complementarities of their mental or psychosomatic content—their valency—and they unconsciously begin to communicate with each other through projective and introjective identification. This is the condition for growing closeness and will continue to confirm their shared interactions (Carlson & Sperry, 2010).

The partners project unacceptable emotions onto each other because that is the only way they can function. Schore (2003, 2012) clarifies that what is projected is not only cognitive and emotional but above all psycho-organic states (Rothschild, 2010; Schore, 2003, 2012). Thus we are not only referring to the earliest mental-cognitive and mental-emotional elements, but above all to organic content and memories that emerged from physical contact with the mother. Here we are referring to psycho-organic states that underlie reciprocal interaction between the mind and the body (Schore, 2003, 2012). The development of these psycho-organic states assumes that affective states are an essential part of the developmental interactions between mother and child, and organically guide the individual through life. At the same time, because they reside in the deepest core of the unconsciousness, they represent the quickest method of emotional communication between mother and child.

1.2.4 Fundamental Communication Dynamics

Recently there has been a surge in research focusing on psycho-organic affective states and neurobiological emotional processes that take place in the right hemisphere of the brain, and are therefore linked with the mechanism of projective and introjective identification (Chiron et al., 1997; Rothschild, 2006, 2010; J.S. Scharff & Scharff, 2014; Schore, 1994, 2000, 2002, 2003, 2012; Siegel, 2003, 2011). This research shows that in the first three years of a child's life, development takes place predominantly in the right hemisphere of the brain, which is responsible for the processing of emotional information. This occurs because of strong connections with the limbic system that is autonomously linked to the right hemisphere of the brain cortex. An extensive network collecting subjective information that is emotional in nature and unconsciously guides or determines our behavior is located in this part of the brain. Processes in the right hemisphere of the brain also unconsciously evaluate the positive or negative importance of emotions in connection with the social environment and receive the non-verbal emotional expressions that appear on the human face (Fishbane, 2013; Geher & Kaufman, 2013; Goleman, 2006). The right hemisphere of the cerebral cortex not only evaluates non-verbal communication, but it is also responsible for implicit learning. In particular, psycho-organic research focuses on the implicit absorption of affective information that is communicated through facial expressions (Cvetek, 2009), the strongest conductor of emotional communication. Communication that takes place from face to face is processed unconsciously and plays a role in determining our choice of intimate partner. Later, it determines the essence of our verbal communication and has a powerful influence on the development and maintenance of the intimate relationship between partners (Goleman, 2006; Johnson, 2014). Rothschild (2006, 2010) and Schore (2003, 2012) added that the transfer or subconscious communication of this information, or affect, is the primary mechanism of projective and introjective identification and determines the quality of the intimate relationship.

Research on the development of emotional communication between mother and child has also focused on psycho-organic affective processes and the essential role of the right hemisphere in emotional communication (Goleman, 2006; Schore, 1994, 2000, 2002, 2003). The right hemisphere transmits basic information about emotional safety, closeness, distance, and the fear of intimacy. This research has provided us with a deeper understanding of the affective communication that takes place between partners on the level of facial expressions during conflicts, or when they feel fear or are threatened. This communication is frequently a manifestation of the earliest interactions with the mother, carried over through projective and introjective identification into intimate adult relationships. It generally emerges from the relationship with the mother, which is repeated in adulthood in situations of passion and attraction as well as fear and threat. Adults have a difficult time admitting that early relationships with their mothers, however they might have been, could have such a strong influence on their adult relationships, but if they begin to explore their early childhood experiences, their own relationships often becomes more relaxed (Ringstrom, 2014; J.S. Scharff & Scharff, 2014). For this reason, the relational family paradigm always directs reflection back toward the earliest relationships because that is when the first seeds for all future relationships are sown. The patterns in these early relationships are very difficult to change since they represent the very essence of relationships.

Right hemisphere communication is the first connection between mother and child. Research confirms (Schore, 2003, 2012; Siegel, 2011) that the mother plays an essential role in the process of establishing the patterns of unconscious communication that characterize us throughout life, and a part of this communication will also inevitably enter the therapeutic process. In all future relationships, we seek to relive the primary affective communication with the mother that is manifested above all in facial expressions, and marks our essence to the extent that we will always look for a partner with whom we can relive that primary communication. In other words, we search for faces that provide the same information once received from the mother. The earliest relationship with the mother will become the foundation for all deep longing and attraction and, through the mechanism of projective and introjective identification, we will look for similar relationships that allow us to once again enter that deep primary relationship (Cvetek, 2009; Repič, 2008; J.S. Scharff & Scharff, 2014). We unconsciously recreate through attraction and romantic love that primary relationship with all of its positive and negative aspects. Thus we strive to evoke in the other feelings familiar from the earliest period of psycho-organic development (Poulton, 2013; Ringstrom, 2014).

Research proves that early social communication with the mother has an extraordinary influence on the child, whether positive or negative, as it is crucial to the development of the right hemisphere of the brain. The development of the right hemisphere is not only essential for the development of the affect regulation mechanism, but also for the development of other fundamental strategies used to survive, strategies that reduce stress and help us to confront the challenges of life (Goleman, 2006; Ringstrom, 2014; Rothschild, 2000, 2006, 2010; Schore, 2003, 2012) —in other words, important life functions that facilitate the healthy development and functioning of the child, and later the adult's healthy and functional connections with intimate others. In this context, we examine above all how the child developed the defense mechanisms that allowed confrontation with difficult or cruel affects, such as terror or rage, that remain present in adulthood. Interdisciplinary research (Ringstrom, 2014; Rothschild, 2006, 2010; Schore, 2000, 2002, 2003, 2012; Siegel, 2010, 2011) shows that fundamental defense mechanisms such as projective and introjective identification and dissociation are gradually established in the child's development in order to deal with stressful situations that could otherwise damage and destroy homeostatic balance. Dissociation is the most primal defense mechanism helping the child to face traumatic experiences (Ringstrom, 2014; J.S. Scharff & Scharff, 2014). At the same time, it plays an essential role in the emergence of the mechanism of projective and introjective identification.

Both early childhood experience and the defense mechanisms that emerge during that period are deeply imprinted in the developing brain. Research on early traumatic experience (Rothschild, 2000, 2003, 2006, 2010; Schore, 2012) shows that traumatized individuals make use of the mechanism of projective and introjective identification to "cleanse" themselves of the traumatic affect, ultimately with the purpose of later establishing a relationship with a narcissistically vulnerable person, who will re-experience the traumatic affect without knowing why. People who are unable to confront their own internal conflicts—anguish, anxiety, nervousness and occasionally the experience of actual terror—try to rid themselves of the unwanted affect through the mechanism of projective and introjective identification. The tragedy is that they also lose important functional parts of themselves and their intrapsychic structures that are necessary for psychological equilibrium, and this can lead to a feeling of emptiness and dependence on others. Such individuals will be attracted to people who unconsciously project their own inner distress and destructive feelings into that internal void and draw sustenance from that (J.S. Scharff & Scharff, 2014).

Individuals who unconsciously accept otherwise unacceptable feelings and affects so as not to have a sense of emptiness will constantly strive to calm anger, rage, and even terror in others. In this situation, the relational family therapist gradually becomes the essential recipient of unacceptable affects. Individuals may consciously blame themselves, but also others, for how a partner behaves. The partner will only be strong when flooded with the unacceptable feelings that have been evoked. Thus the two partners will live exploitatively from each other, while the therapist will become increasingly entangled in the relationship. The therapist will continually strive to process and regulate the negative content and return it to the partners in palatable form. The various forms of physical sensations felt by the therapist will provide crucial information in this process. This is known as therapeutic countertransference: namely, the therapist engaging in right hemisphere communication with the individual or couple. This is an unconscious process reminiscent of the fundamental right hemisphere communication between mother and child (Maroda, 2010; Ringstrom, 2014; Schore, 2003, 2012).

Therapists using the relational family paradigm will be surprised at how often they encounter the core affects of clients that are a part of their own intrapsychic structure. An affect will be evoked in the therapist that did not get processed during childhood, and consequently the therapist encounters deeply buried, unprocessed parts of their own mental content, a sort of painful residue. The therapist repeatedly faces the challenge of processing this content with the individual or couple in therapy, thus enabling collective growth. Put another way, therapy in the relational family paradigm involves the collective growth of both the therapist and the individual or couple being treated. If the therapist does not want or is incapable of meeting this challenge, then the value of the therapeutic relationship comes into question. It seems surprising that the individual or the couple unconsciously engages in right hemisphere communication that transmits to the therapist the affects that are the most familiar—for example, sadness, fear, and anger. But, in fact, the therapist becomes an instrument for affects, either those that are familiar or those that have not yet been processed, and also for affects that are in collective or dynamic opposition with those of the clients.

We often find such a dynamic in couples that have experienced extreme abuse (Poulton, 2013; Repič, 2006, 2008), namely relationships where the partners treat each other as both victim and abuser. The victim carries a sense of worthlessness, oppression, self-destruction, anger, and rage, much of which remains unconscious, the consequence, according to the theory of self-psychology (Clulow, 2005; Winnicott, 1988), of unsatisfied needs from early childhood. In such circumstances, a child develops an extremely negative self-image and is crippled by emotions that should have been directed toward the mother. But because a child cannot risk losing their mother and fears, according to object relations theory (Fairbairn, 1952; Klein, 1948; Ringstrom, 2014; J.S. Scharff & Scharff, 2014), that such emotions would destroy the mother, these feelings are directed inward and became part of the self. In adulthood, this individual will transmit these emotions to the other through projective and introjective identification and will often wind up in a relationship characterized by vengefulness, torment, and cruelty. According to interpersonal analysis (Ringstrom, 2014; Sullivan, 1972), this is how painful self-destructive relationships evolve, and in order to truly understand why this process occurs and what is the source of the destructive affects, it is necessary to experience them again and again.

The two partners in such a relationship will each sense that they can save the other for a while, but this does not last long, and the relationship flounders. Nevertheless, the partners will soon be longing for each other again with the same passion as before, which is in fact the unconscious dictate of the psycho-organic state that creates the foundation for attraction. The two partners will inevitably begin to pursue their desires again, aided by the dynamic of repetitive compulsion (Poulton, 2013). Once again they will find themselves in the uncomfortable position of feeling vulnerable, sometimes feeling the desperate need to end the painful relationship. Soon, however, the partners will again begin to feel a strong attraction for each other, and peace will be attained at least temporarily, the outbursts of anger and even rage or terror will be silenced, and so on and so forth. The negative parts of the cycle may even be accompanied by physical and sexual abuse (Repič, 2006, 2008). Each new attempt to be together will fail unless the couple confronts the destructive emotions that are at the root of the cycle. Sometimes, the couple turns to prayer, other times to professional help (Cvetek, 2009). Often partners in such relationships will try to save themselves from the vicious cycle by looking for a new partner, but until they confront their own issues and look for help, the old story will be repeated.

1.2.5 Regulation-Dysregulation Affects

The next important concept in the relational family therapy paradigm is affect regulation (Ringstrom, 2014; Rothschild, 2000, 2003, 2006, 2010; Schore, 2000, 2002, 2003, 2012). Affect plays a very important role in the mother-child relationship, in later relationships between partners, and also in therapist-individual and therapist-couple relationships. The dynamic of affect dysregulation is connected to stress and conflicts experienced by the couple and also in the therapeutic relationship, and the therapist will quickly and organically feel it. The therapist's physical sensations serve as an instrument that recognizes unacceptable affects and sensations, and also as an instrument of change. The therapist must search in the early mother-child relationship for the source of these dynamics, which extend into adulthood, being reawakened in partner relationships. According to the history and development of attachment, mechanisms of affect regulation and dysregulation evolve along with strategies developed by the child in relationship to their mother and serve the purpose of helping the child cope with stressful situations and encounters. The mother must know how to accept and then regulate the difficult feelings that the child cannot process alone. It is precisely here that the therapist searches for the psychogenesis of later relationship traumas (Ringstrom, 2014).

From the standpoint of the relational couples paradigm, it is not enough for the therapist to merely interpret affective traumas that appear in the relationship between partners. Instead the therapist must regulate them as a mother might. Partners who suffer from affect dysregulation are extremely vulnerable as a result of deep wounds experienced in childhood and need a therapist who is sensitive and active and can regulate the affects that are projected by partners onto the therapist. This can be difficult for the therapist, especially when the therapist has not processed these specific affects and they remain unregulated in her. Examples of such affects in situations of abuse are anger and fear, and, above all, shame and disgust. These sorts of therapeutic situations can be difficult for the therapist to deal with because it requires an intense effort for the therapist not to simply reject the individual or the couple with destructive affects, thus shaming them and increasing feelings of anger and sadness. Instead, the therapist must strive to recognize the problem and resolve it. This is a significant responsibility for the therapist who will often need external supervision to be guided toward collective growth with the individual or couple in therapy.

The dynamic of affect regulation and dysregulation is closely connected to the mechanism of projective and introjective identification, which is the earliest unconscious mechanism for organizing the regulation of right hemisphere communication particularly in stressful situations and affective states. Because affects are a psycho-organic phenomenon and the self is based in the organism and the body, projective and introjective identification is not only a mechanism for the transfer of verbal-linguistic behavior, but also and above all for unconscious communication between the organism and the mind (Rothschild, 2006, 2010; J.S. Scharff & Scharff, 2014; Schore, 2003, 2012; Siegel, 2010, 2011). The communicated information emerges from the development of affects based in the organism, a phenomenon that has mostly been researched in the field of neurobiology. For this reason, one of the primary principles of the relational family therapy paradigm is that therapy is not only research into and excavation of the past, but also and above all the pursuit of a strategic logic of affect regulation.

While the past that an individual or couple remembers is important, the atmosphere, or affective state, that pervaded the family(ies) of origin is much more important psycho-organic content, which the therapist must try to reveal, address, process, and regulate. The therapist will perceive psycho-organic states by engaging in the strongest unconscious communication, the mechanism of projective and introjective identification, and this can be extremely uncomfortable, harsh and dysregulating. So, for example, anger, rage, and fear can explode between the partners in a therapy session and at times be directed at the therapist. The therapist must be prepared to address these affects, process them, and offer them back to the partner or partners in palatable form; otherwise they remain dysregulated.

Projective and introjective identification represents the basic communication mechanism between partners. This mechanism assumes that a specific kind of interaction already exists between the partners (Ogden, 1997; J.S. Scharff, 2010; J.S. Scharff & Scharff, 2006, 2014): specifically, a reciprocal process that organizes communication with the significant other, that is with the partner, and also with the therapist. Thus projective and introjective identification organizes interactions with the other and determines the role of the other in interactions, while merging the functioning of the other with the affect of the individual. Each partner has unconscious expectations and uses unconscious communication to compel the other to behave according to those expectations. The partner also projects onto the other unacceptable emotions and psycho-organic states. The concept of projective and introjective identification extends from the intrapsychic dynamic to the interpersonal and systemic levels of communication (Gostečnik, 2004, 2007, 2010, 2015). The systemic dynamic of projective and introjective identification is especially important in the exploration of the unconscious attachment of the individual to the family.

In Bowlby's development model (1982), we can say that the mechanism of projective and introjective identification is especially important for the transfer of attachment styles that the partners evoke in each other as each attempts to regulate his or her own unacceptable emotions. This kind of regulation usually takes place in the arena of disagreement and conflict where the couple attempts to deal with dysregulated affects and psycho-organic states from the early phase of development in the interpersonal field by regulating deep mental states (Fosha, 2009; Schore, 2003, 2012; Siegel & Solomon, 2013). The mechanism of projective and introjective identification also represents the interpersonal mental space (Winnicott, 1988) between partners, the psycho-organic attachment between them, and the communication transference of both positive and negative symbiotic states between mother and child in the partnership relationship. This dynamic of unconscious transference of psycho-organic states not only means the separation of the negative aspects of these states in the child's, and later the adult's psycho-organic structure, and the transfer of these to the mother's and later to the partner's mental structure, but it also enables the healthy development of the child and later the adult (Poulton, 2013; Ringstrom, 2014). When the child unconsciously forces the mother to accept the negative aspects of their intrapsychic state, she is given the opportunity to recognize the child's intrapsychic distress, regulate it, and empathically respond. Later this same challenge takes place between partners, where one partner transfers negative psycho-organic states to the other, and expects that they will be regulated, that the partner will respond with understanding and empathy.

In other words, with psycho-organic regulation, the transfer of affects is an effort to enhance the positive regulated responses from the mother and later the partner, and reduce the negative responses. The creation of positive affects is the essential role of the relational family therapist, because only on the basis of the mechanism of projective and introjective identification can unregulated psycho-organic states be accepted, restructured, and returned to the partner in a changed and palatable form. Although projective and introjective identification can be viewed as a primitive defense mechanism, it is also a fundamental communication instrument of psycho-organic states and their regulation between mother and child. This communication continues throughout life and plays an essential role in the relationship between partners, as it is on the basis of projective and introjective identification that an individual creates and recreates the primary relationship between mother and child, the intimate relationship between partners, and also the relationship between the partners and the therapist. On the basis of projective and introjective identification, partners, with the help of the therapist, can establish an effective system of affect regulation.

1.3 The Intrapsychic Level

The novelty of the relational family therapy model lies in the original synthesis of relational theories: it integrates object relations theory with interpersonal psychoanalysis, and self-psychology with psycho-organic and somatic aspects, to create a relational systemic and family model that is an innovative psycho-organic paradigm. The basic assumption of the described model is that establishing and maintaining interpersonal relationships is what drives and motivates us. Because we are not simply individuals rooted in an inevitable developmental process, this demands a fundamental trust in the human experience. The relational family model also assumes that distress in the child-parent relationship has a significant impact on subsequent distress in adult relationships. However, contrary to various forms of self-theories, this is not because the childhood self is frozen and damaged. Rather, it is due to the fact that early relationships form how children (and later adults) build their intrapsychic and interpersonal worlds of relationships, perceptions and affect regulation. Aided by projective and introjective identification, all of this generates the affective psychic construct, the fundamental tenet underlying our emotions, perceptions, cognition, and behavior.

This dynamic process repeats itself from generation to generation, and, if negative, can seriously disable an individual within the system, intimate relationships between individuals in the system, and the system as a whole. In this way, an affective psychic construct can threaten an entire generation, as individuals within the system are marked by the destructive consequences of these constructs in all areas of their psychological lives without knowing why they suffer or why they are caught up in repetitive traumatic relationships. They remain in a vicious circle of constant conflict all their lives, unconsciously seeking out people with whom they can create relationships similar to the ones they've known since childhood (Cummings & Davies, 2010; Mitchell, 2002; Ringstrom, 2014; Robins, 2010; Schore, 2003). These are the relationship patterns buried deep within the interior of their psyche that promise the closest connection, and because they provide the sole model of attachment, they are cultivated and maintained. The first priority of the relational family therapist is to be attentive to the most powerful factors and dynamics that created early psycho-organic states as well as related affects (Fosha, 2009; Schore, 2003; Siegel & Solomon, 2013). The therapist should also not neglect important traumatic events in later periods that may have an impact on the individual, the couple and the system as a whole.

The relational family model works not only with conscious mechanisms or missing early experiences, but it also places at the forefront the transformation of the unconscious mechanisms of affect regulation, the processing of unconscious affective psychic constructs, affect regulation, and changes in fundamental relational structures, that is patterns of relationships in the individual's intrapsychic world and system. The relational family model therefore seeks appropriate solutions to problems of affect regulation and affective psychic constructs on the systemic level. If transformation cannot take place on this level, then the therapist must look progressively deeper, into interpersonal dynamics and the individual's intrapsychic world. Thus, relational family therapy approaches the intrapsychic world from many different angles. During this process, the therapist focuses on various factors in the relational matrix—the organization of the self, psychosomatic content, object attachments, relationship patterns, and transactions between members of the system—and tries to understand the meaning and power of past experiences in the current life of the individual, couple, or family, and particularly the interpersonal and systemic experiences that have a strong impact on the present.

The therapist will encounter the dynamic of transference-countertransference, the mechanism of projective and introjective identification, as well as right hemisphere communication, all of which are synonymous with the unconscious intrapsychic relationship that emerges between the therapist and the individual, the two partners in a couple, and the members of a family system. The therapeutic relationship is essential at all three of these intrapsychic levels, and specifically in the manifestation of core affects with which the therapist will be familiar due to their own personal history. Of particular interest are those affects that remain unprocessed in the therapist and are forcefully reawakened in the therapeutic relationship. The therapist will once again face the basic challenge of processing unresolved psychic content, without which the collective growth of the individuals in the therapeutic relationship will not take place (Maroda, 2010; Ringstrom, 2014). This is a process that offers the possibility of eliminating old forms of behavior as well as the emotional processing of painful affects that may be connected to destructive ways of perceiving the other and a skewed and negative self-image.

1.3.1 Object Relations Theory

Object relations theory researches the dynamic of configuring the intrapsychic system of objects, or the intrapsychic images of objects in the relational field of the individual (Fairbairn, 1958). In the relational field, various kinds of identification and attachments to other people serve as a network that individuals create within their own personal intrapsychic world (Mitchell, 1988, 2000, 2002; Poulton, 2013; Ringstrom, 2014). This takes place though the mechanism of projective and introjective identification and enables the internalization of images of others, thus deeply influencing individual development. The mental and organic or psycho-organic structure and system of object relations are intrapsychic in their design. Experiences flow from the intrapsychic level to the interpersonal and systemic level of relationships, where they leave an imprint on individuals as well as on the reciprocal and systemic structure of relationships, thus becoming an affect regulation mechanism of psychic experience on all three levels vis-à-vis the self and others. Of particular importance in this context are somatic memories or psycho-organic states that are created by the first touch with the mother through breastfeeding, caressing, and tenderness: namely, physical sensations together with affects. The latter become embedded in the organism since it is the earliest mental and organic content on which the individual's intrapsychic, psycho-organic structure is constructed (Fosha, 2009; Schore, 2003, 2012; Siegel & Solomon, 2013). These impressions or psycho-organic states remain connected to certain internal images, usually to images of parents or other important caregivers with whom core affects were created and continue to have an influence throughout life.

On the basis of affects or somatic psycho-organic states that others evoke in them, the individual perceives the other similarly to someone who deeply influenced their mental structure in the past. Aided by the mechanism of projective and introjective identification, the individual will transfer or project these deeply engrained intrapsychic images and the mental and organic content that goes with them, and which has been consolidated in their intrapsychic world, onto external interpersonal and systemic relationships through repetition compulsion. As a result, the individual perceives and understands relationships similarly to how they experienced important relationships, attachments, and related core affects with significant others in the past (Carlson & Sperry, 2010; Cummings & Davies, 2010; Ringstrom, 2014). The individual thus experiences fear, anger, sadness, and other deeply engrained feelings of anxiety without knowing why. Moreover, these feelings also will be provoked in significant others in such a way that they may become angry and feel unloved. They may retreat and this in turn will awaken the hurt and fear of rejection that already has been experienced in the individual's past. Thus a couple will become progressively interpersonally enmeshed, which will result in an increasingly painful relationship. Thus, intrapsychic images, along with affects and somatic memories, that is psycho-organic states that emerged from relationships with significant others, are reawakened and repeated in adult relationships.

The individual recreates and projects onto others these intrapsychic images in various ways with various people. The individual compulsively reproduces these images without knowing how or why and assigns certain characteristics to objects from the present, characteristics and affects of intrapsychic images of significant others that have been grafted onto their intrapsychic world of relationships. For example, a man and wife will experience feelings of being humiliated or ashamed with each other, feelings that they once might have each experienced with their own mother or father, and not realize that the same process is being played out on an unconscious level (Poulton, 2013; Silverstein, 2007). The affects that are manifested between them on the basis of intrapsychic images are linked to core affects, such as anger, and will stoke conflict or create an affective psychic construct that will block productive communication. These affects have been grafted onto the intrapsychic image, and, although they may be repressed or dissociated, they are repeatedly reawakened in communication with significant others from the present and bring to life other affects that are linked to objects from the past.

In the context of object relations theory, the therapist will first ask the following questions: What is the mental content of the client's early experience with others? What left the strongest mark? What are the intrapsychic images of objects, along with related affects, that are most deeply impressed onto the client's mental structure? What did the client experience consciously or unconsciously in early interactions with other people and what influence do these experiences have today (Mitchell, 1988, 2000)? What images are reawakened and what affects are grafted onto these images through repetition? At issue here are core affects that emerged from the family of origin and relationships with parents and caregivers. These affects become constitutive elements of the intrapsychic level of human experience and are present throughout the individual's life as a very specific subsystem in the wider family system. These affects are repeatedly triggered in contact with significant others, and, as a result, an affective psychic construct is created that has exceptional power in intimate relationships. They are most strongly triggered in intimate relationships, but also can be evoked in various situations with people who only vaguely remind the individual of important early experiences (Robins, 2010). They can also manifest as fear or hurt in completely different situations when they are reawakened by similar experiences or people that remind the individual of the past, arousing somatic physical memories that are carried over from past traumatic experiences (Poulton, 2013; Ringstrom, 2014; Rothschild, 2000, 2006, 2010).

Drawing on the relational family model and object relations theory, the therapist will try to discover the intrapsychic images that the individual experiences, as well as the affects and psychosomatic memories grafted onto these images that the individual experienced with significant others in childhood and are now being reawakened and recreated in adulthood. In short, the individual unconsciously creates these images anew, constantly reliving the same or similar affects or traumas. Without knowing why, the individual ascribes similar properties to significant others in the present, the same as in the earliest phase of development, behaving and responding to others in the same way as to the parents when still a child (Cummings & Davies, 2010; Ringstrom, 2014). In an effort to identify and clarify the images from early development that continue to have a strong influence in the present, the therapist will first intervene in a way that will encourage conversation. This may be achieved by discovering the core affect that is at the very heart of the affective psychic construct and pursues the individual through all mental states, thus preventing healthy functioning.

The therapist will try to introduce a fundamental change in the individual's perception of the present, which, while producing similar affects, may differ in many ways from the past. The individual may experience the present with exaggerated criticism, disproportionate to the actual challenges of the present (Mitchell, 2000, 2002). A disproportionate reaction to the experiences of the present is crucially important because it presents a clear sign to the therapist that some sort of complex is hidden within the individual's mental structure. It is also important that an individual realizes how their attribution of extraordinary emotions and thoughts to experiences, events, or people in the present actually emerges from the past. It is also essential to realize that people in the present do not have the same power or emotional charge that people had in the past, during childhood, when others had the power to mark the mental structure through the creation of intrapsychic images, which in turn created painful affects that play an ongoing and forceful role in life. The most essential element here is the therapist's effort to first accept the individual's destructive affects, process and regulate them, and then return them to the individual in palatable form.

This kind of intervention on the systemic and interpersonal level sometimes triggers excessive anxiety in the individual who becomes blocked and sometimes even physically "frozen." If this happens, the therapist must try to discover the affective psychic construct (such as fear, anger, uncontrollable sadness or shame): that is, the fundamental structure of affect regulation that was tailored on the basis of object relations in the individual's developmental period and now prevents active communication and functioning with others in the present. The mental structure of children is composed of their earliest experiences of and relationships with their parents, which in many ways determines the subsequent course of their lives. What remains in the memory of children is their affective experience of their parents, which colors how they experience themselves and the world. The therapist will seek out the primary affective experiences, the child's world in the individual, because this world holds the key to their experiencing of relationships in the present (Fosha, 2009; Ringstrom, 2014; Schore, 2003, 2012; Siegel, 2011; Siegel & Solomon, 2013).

The therapist's role is to discover the fundamental structural intrapsychic images and the corresponding affects that create the basis of primary organic memory (Rothschild, 2006, 2010; Schore, 2003, 2012). The therapist will feel this memory, which is a direct expression of the individual's experiencing of their significant others from childhood, through physical sensations and through the mechanism of projective and introjective identification as it is transferred into the therapist (J.S. Scharff & Scharff, 2014). These memories are often hidden and can be extremely painful, and for this reason they can be deeply repressed. These are implicit memories (Schore, 2003, 2012), memories of the atmosphere, experience, smells, and images that the individual unconsciously seeks out, trying to include them in the tapestry of their present-day relationships (Rothschild, 2006, 2010). The individual conceals these memories with the aid of the affective psychic construct that manifests itself in various forms of dysfunctional behavior. The individual namely senses that the emotions, sensations, and especially affects that were created in early childhood represent the relationships without which survival is virtually impossible (Mitchell, 2000, 2002). These early relationships are replete with core affects that represent a primary sense of belonging that unconsciously extends into the present.

These primary core affects are the most binding and represent in these theories the means or system of affect regulation, which is possible to discover on the basis of the five senses that are engrained in the mental content: scent, taste, touch, hearing, and sight. These senses and the sensations associated with them represent deeply buried verbal and also organic or preverbal aspects of human experiencing that determine a great deal in the individual's ongoing perceptions and experiences (Fishbane, 2013; Schore, 2003, 2012). For this reason, the therapist will try to include all of the dimensions of the individual's approach to their own reality as well as to the reality of others, and discover the core emotions, thoughts, and affects that determine the relationship to the present, regardless of whether the present and the specific people in it are different or not from the important experiences and people in their formative years. The child's world of images is a deep and emotionally rich treasure trove of the adult's psychic structure (Fonagy et al., 2007; Ringstrom, 2014).

1.3.2 Self-psychology

Self-psychology is understood and researched as a dynamic system of intrapsychic images of the self in the individual's relational configuration. Winnicott (1984, 1986, 1988) focuses on the internal fragmentation and division of experiences of the self, and the presence or absence of authenticity and reality. Kohut (1984) emphasizes the significant need of the self to preserve continuity and cohesion, and the complex intrapsychic and interpersonal process (transmuting internalization), which is built and preserved with the help of projective and introjective identification. In this way, others are at least implicitly included in the system created by the affect regulation mechanism around which the sense of self is organized and orchestrated. At the same time, the system also constitutes an affective psychic construct that can limit healthy development and functionality. This is expressed in the false self (Kohut, 1984), which is a consequence of maternal absence, a mother who doesn't understand her children, who rejects them, leaves them in danger or even abandons them. It can also be a consequence of inappropriate maternal care, a mother who uses her children (or child) for her own confirmation, to confirm her womanhood, for example, in the case of an absent partner, a situation that can leave children with extreme mental and sometimes even physical wounds (Clulow, 2005).

The theory of self-psychology (Kohut, 1984) assumes that basic unconscious human experiencing and functioning tends toward the preservation of a cohesive self. The individual will repeat old models of behavior in the therapist-client relationship as well, with the unconscious hope that desires and needs will be understood and mirrored, and will receive an empathic response in this new context (Robins, 2010; Siegel & Solomon, 2013). But what is new can also be dangerous because it emerges outside the perceptions and experiences in which the individual recognizes the self as a cohesive and integrated being. It deviates from the usual pattern, which is why it is necessary to recreate the affective psychic construct of the false self. Spouses will, for example, constantly repeat old relationship patterns, thus striving to avoid the fear they feel when faced with their own marital and systemic disintegration. If the therapist's response to old patterns is different, if they provide new insight and a deeper understanding of the relationship, if they are able to reveal the core affect and build a deeper level of affective psychic constructs, the couple also will be able to bring something new to their own intrapsychic structure and to their family, a new manner of attachment that is no longer based on the painful and difficult affects of the past (Clulow, 2005; Siegel & Solomon, 2013).

In his research, Winnicott (1971, 1984, 1986, 1988) emphasizes the function of the mother who supplies experience and thus enables a basic sense of vitalization and realization. Kohut (1984), in contrast, believes that the self is developed and stimulated when the individual searches for attachment with others. If Winnicott emphasizes the maternal ability to respond to her child and open a space, which facilitates development and expression of the self, Kohut emphasizes the capability and effort of the self as it searches for people in the environment who understand them and reveal who they are and how to exist. According to Winnicott, others (the mother) can fail to awaken or hear the self (the child). According to Kohut, others (the mother) reject the self (the child). In both cases, the basic axiom is present: namely, that the self can only develop to the extent others allow it to (Clulow, 2005; Siegel, 2011; Siegel & Solomon, 2013). Because of this, the individual develops a system of affect regulation, and a corresponding affective psychic construct, which then enables the avoidance of painful affects. These constructs are later linked to cognitive and behavioral components and can block the development or sense of self, which is then expressed in a distorted self-image.

The fundamental questions posed by self-psychology are: How does the individual experience the self now? How did the individual experience the self in early attachments to significant others? What residue was left behind by these attachments and what does this mean for the individual's personal experience of the self? What core affects are connected to the individual's self-image (Mitchell, 1988, 2000)? We could say that family and family relationships represent the foundation upon which children recognize themselves as independent entities and, at the same time, as part of a wider system. Here lies the dilemma that is often discernible in the ability to distinguish the past from the present. In the theory of self-psychology, the individual acquires a sense of the self during the earliest period of childhood, a self-image that is also linked to self-confidence and, for various reasons, can be highly distorted (Clulow, 2005; Kohut, 1984; Siegel & Solomon, 2013; Winnicott, 1984, 1988). In other words, some people develop a very low or distorted self-image, experiencing themselves as bad, of little worth or even worthless, and this awareness or definition of themselves can be carried throughout life regardless of success, maturity, and the positive reactions of others (Poulton, 2013; Schore, 2003, 2012).

In a sense, such individuals live in the past, in the time when they were most wounded, hurt, rejected, and even abandoned. Not surprisingly, such individuals can feel incompetent, unsuitable, and unworthy in relationships with others, even though there is not necessarily a reason for such feelings or thoughts in their encounters in the here and now (Maroda, 2010). Such individuals are metaphorically locked by heavy chains in a past characterized by unresolved pain that leads them time and again into new problems and traumatic relationships in which they do not dare to express their needs and desires or even expect to be understood by others; rather, they anticipate that they will feel rejected, abandoned, humiliated, and shamed as their parents made them feel in their childhood (Bruschweiler-Stern et al., 2010). In short, such people experience, behave, and think—without fully realizing it—as if time stood still in the period when they were most injured. They interpret the entire world through the prism of the past that most deeply affected them.

In couples therapy, the therapist using the relational family model will first try to encourage partners to actively communicate with each other, to describe their desires and demands and verify if they are acceptable or not. If either partner in the couple is unable to do this, the therapist will try to discover why. These interventions are aimed at revealing the partner(s)' self-image, which may be distorted, as indicated by the fact that they do not dare to express their needs, perhaps because of a sense of deep shame, possibly even disgust, a feeling that they do not deserve attention from others, and that, because of the shame and fear of rejection, or even abandonment experienced as a child, they cannot express their desires (Clulow, 2005; Fonagy et al., 2007; Schore, 2003, 2012). The therapist will strive to discover the affective psychic construct that dictates this kind of affect regulation and inevitably leads to the same sort of difficulties. The therapist will strive to discover what happened to the partner(s) when they expressed their desires in the past: were they rejected, shamed, humiliated because of it, and accused of being too needy and demanding? Were they told that their desires had nothing to do with their actual needs? Were they made to feel worthless, ugly, and unwanted (Kohut, 1984)? The therapist will show how even now, in adulthood, the individual experiences the same feelings as in childhood, and that these past experiences prevent the partner(s) from taking the risk of expressing their emotions and desires today; because if they do express them, they risk experiencing the same bad feelings as they did in the past. Thus, due to this distorted self-image, desires do not get expressed so as to avoid evoking the same affects that were experienced in childhood: namely, the feeling of not being worthy of expressing needs and desires and thus being exposed to renewed rejection and a consequent sense of shame.

According to this theory, the self develops complementarities with the character structures of significant others (Kohut, 1984). Areas of deprivation, boundaries, and intrusion caused the child to form an unconscious attachment to the emotional content experienced with parents, in other words to the intrapsychic images of objects on the basis of which a connection between the child and parents was possible (Bruschweiler-Stern et al., 2010; Siegel & Solomon, 2013). These connections become the tools for preserving emotional attachments and relationships with others, and for directing and guiding the entire marital and family system using the mechanism of projective identification. These attachment patterns are then confirmed and maintained using the mechanism of compulsive repetition, which creates a permanent affective psychic construct that will determine the individual's and the couple's mental experiences. Early attachments with the family of origin are preserved as the foundation of intrapsychic experience and existing object relations, experienced in accordance with internal objects, organic implicit memory, and structured on the basis of the ongoing reintegration of old experiences with new experiences, the latter constantly being shaped according to the unchanged old configurations (Mitchell, 2000, 2002; Ringstrom, 2014).

Therapeutic change on this level is comprised of the transformation of these internal structures and relationships with intrapsychic images of objects deeply ingrained in somatic memory (Fishbane, 2013; Fosha, 2009). The individual inevitably experiences the other—for example, the spouse, the child, and also the therapist in the therapeutic situation—as someone from the past and transforms her or him into a negative object. In the therapeutic situation, old images and objects, somatic memories are transformed through the process of interpretation (Clulow, 2005; Siegel, 2010, 2011). The internalization of the experience allows the individual, and eventually the system as a whole, to give up compulsive attachments to old relational patterns, that is attachment to negative objects; this in turn enables the dismantling of affective psychic constructs and associated defense mechanisms. In this fashion, the intrapsychic field of the individual's systemic relational matrix can be reshaped. The individual (and subsequently the whole system) no longer experiences the self only as a new and more functional personality, but they also experience the environment and people in a completely new way.

The relational family model maintains that it is precisely the therapeutic relationship between the therapist and the individual that recreates the organization of the self. The therapeutic situation enables the individual to discover, restore, and re-experience aspects of the self that had been discarded, hidden or expropriated in the family of origin, but which nevertheless influences the systemic relational configuration (Fishbane, 2013; Fosha, 2009). The relationship with the therapist must be structured according to old parameters and directed toward the discovery of archaic mental, organic content, which influences the family system, the couple system, and also the relationship with the therapist (Mitchell, 1988, 2000, 2002). In this relational paradigm, the therapist always expects anxiety and disappointment precisely where the individual experienced a destructive relationship in the early period of development (Mitchell, 2000, 2002). What is being attempted is a different way of experiencing the self, which had previously been hidden, but is newly awakened in the individual, couple, or family system. During the therapeutic process, the therapist must also be alert in observing their own unprocessed but familiar affects and physical sensations that countertransference evokes.

The therapist's contribution to change takes place within the newly co-created relationship that enables the individual to encounter, name, and evaluate the archaic aspects of experience that were hitherto obscured, but that guided and regulated couple and family interactions and transactions. This new relationship provides the basis upon which the individual can begin to build a different experience of the marriage and the family, and thus actually become different. It has the potential to change the entire system of marital and family interactions and transactions. From the standpoint of self-psychology or the subsystem of self organization, the therapist will try to help the individual to discover, merge, and fully experience the split-off aspects of the self that had been projected into their interpersonal and systemic world. The therapist explores the individual's distorted experience of the self and discovers the dysfunctional regulation of emotions and the affective psychic construct that gave rise to it, the goal being to use the therapeutic relationship to bring a new and as yet unknown relational experience into the individual's world.

The therapist must then strive to introduce the individual, couple, or system to a new way of communicating, all the while letting all members of the system know why the old systemic dynamic prevailed, and how new relational patterns experienced in the therapeutic process can be established. The therapist will therefore need to pay particular attention to the regulation of core affects that have a destructive influence on the individual's self-image. This will only be possible if the therapist remains sensitive and attuned while dismantling the affective psychic constructs that fortify the distorted self-image on the organic, emotional, cognitive, and behavioral levels.

1.3.3 Interpersonal Psychoanalysis

Relational theory essentially deals with the intrapsychic affective space between the individual and the other and is supported by interpersonal analysis (Bruschweiler-Stern et al., 2010; Cummings & Davies, 2010; Fosha, 2009; Mitchell, 2000, 2002; Poulton, 2013; Ringstrom, 2014; Schore, 2003; Sullivan, 1972). It explores specific interactions that play out on the basis of projective and introjective identification between the self and the object in the intrapsychic arena and are fortified by repetition compulsion. It is a dynamic of interplay between intrapsychic images of the self and the object, but focuses on the affective space between them. In this psychic affective space between the self and the object (which exists on the intrapsychic level but can also be manifested on the interpersonal and systemic levels), distinct affects are generated as well as models of behavior and structures of perception that characterize the individual in all dimensions of experience including marital and family systems and interpersonal relationships.

In this context, Stern and his colleagues researched the interpersonal world of the child and the results showed that the gentle and subtle interactions and mutual emotional regulation, or mutual responsiveness, between parents and child are extremely significant for children's ongoing development (Bruschweiler-Stern et al., 2010; Stern, 1985, 1995). Similar interpersonal analytics emphasize the actual transactions that take place between the individual and others on the basis of projective and introjective identification, although many theorists do not mention the mechanism specifically (Carlson & Sperry, 2010; Cummings & Davies, 2010). A concrete picture of early relationships in the individual's family, including affects and the experiencing of affects, can be drawn from what occurs between the individual and the therapist. This is the central question of transference and countertransference, the fundamental unconscious dynamic of projective and introjective identification, and the process of right hemisphere communication that develops between the individual and the therapist and characterizes the therapeutic relationship. Both the individual and the therapist contribute to this dynamic, which is colored by various affects and essentially creates the therapeutic process (Maroda, 2010; Mitchell, 2000, 2002; Ringstrom, 2014; Sullivan, 1972).

The therapeutic relationship resembles the relationship between partners (or spouses), having a similar configuration of the individual and the other and the affects that create the mental space between them (Carlson & Sperry, 2010; Fosha, 2009; Robins, 2010; Siegel, 2010, 2011; Siegel & Solomon, 2013). A similar dynamic can also be detected on the systemic level where there are many individuals and others, and the mental spaces created between them, from which a specific dynamic emerges known as the core affect. Taken all together, this constitutes the integrated family system and includes the many categories and subcategories that comprise the system. The relational family therapy or model researches and uncovers where a specific problem has its roots and at the same time strives to solve the problem on all three levels: systemic, interpersonal, and intrapsychic. In other words, the goal is to discover the core affect on all three levels along with the affective psychic construct that preserves specific relational patterns, which in turn often necessitates certain problematic behavior for its existence and maintenance.

Interpersonal psychoanalysis, which is an essential part of relational theory (Mitchell, 1988, 2000, 2002), emphasizes that the therapeutic process no longer involves a "doctor-patient" relationship, but rather a shared search for new ways of experiencing that are not possible until the therapist and the individual experience a common core affect that binds them together (Bruschweiler-Stern et al., 2010; Fishbane, 2013; Maroda, 2010; Mitchell, 2000, 2002; Sullivan, 1972). The theory of interpersonal psychoanalysis also emphasizes that the individual in relational configurations unconsciously strives to transfer the affect to the therapist, and, that if this doesn't occur, the therapeutic relationship cannot be fully realized. The therapist's role is to provide an empathic and therapeutic atmosphere in which the emotions and affects that pervaded the individual's early interpersonal relationships can be safely explored and resolved, especially when complications have emerged from them (Bruschweiler-Stern et al., 2010; Maroda, 2010; Poulton, 2013; Sullivan, 1972).

The interpersonal therapist must ask the following questions: What is the client actually doing? What is happening between the client and their significant others? What is happening here and now? What is being repeated in the present situation that has deep roots in the client's past (Levenson, 1983; Maroda, 2010; Mitchell, 1988, 2000)? According to the relational family paradigm, core affects are carried over through the mechanism of projective and introjective identification to interpersonal relationships in the family, and are anchored in the individual's mental structure through repetition compulsion. Affects are the constitutive mental material in human development, but they can also provide the fundamental structure for the dysfunction that the therapist must discover and resolve. In this process, the individual unconsciously strives to recreate similar conditions in which the fundamental elements of certain affects from the past will be awakened and relived (Carlson & Sperry, 2010; Cummings & Davies, 2010; Poulton, 2013).

The relational family therapy model considers the affective space between the individual and the other one of the most important mental and organic structures in the system, which, when placed within the wider system of integrated family affects, creates and guides the entire family atmosphere. Therefore, affects of anger, fear, sadness, etc., tend to characterize the entire family and influence individual relationships within it. The relational family therapist will focus on the strongest core affect that permeates and regulates relations between children and important others, and which are often suppressed and split off. The therapist will first focus on the systemic arena of the individual's experience with others in the here and now. If it is not possible to establish a suitable level of communication, the therapist will focus on the individual's history and try to discover the core affects, such as fear, shame, sadness, and disgust, that are repeated in various relationships in the present (Bruschweiler-Stern et al., 2010; Carlson & Sperry, 2010; Cummings & Davies, 2010; Fosha, 2009; Stern, 1995).

The therapist will need to be aware that the client will try to suppress, deny, or split off the destructive affects that are too upsetting. The mechanism of projective and introjective identification will be triggered and it will be necessary to try and rediscover and encourage these affects in relationship with others (Fosha, 2009; J.S. Scharff & Scharff, 2006, 2014). During this process, the individual, couple, and family will develop certain affective psychic constructs that will allow them to avoid these destructive core affects. Families and individuals will, for example, constantly be overwhelmed with agitation and fear; partners will create conflicts; children will act out painful behavioral responses. All of this prevents healthy functioning. The therapist will strive to discover the core affect or affects that disable healthy functioning and communication with others in the present. In general, this will be deeply suppressed content that has become the primary generator of the affective psychic construct that prevents development and functionality.

The therapist will strive to discover which affect or affects—evoked through projective and introjective identification, or transference and countertransference, and then restructured through repetitive compulsion—prevent the healthy functioning of the individual, couple, or family. The therapist will find it helpful to be sensitive to physical sensations that are picked up from the individual, because affects tend to be somatically based (Rothschild, 2006, 2010; Schore, 2003, 2012), and the sensitive and attuned therapist can virtually always detect them this way. The intrapsychic relational structure will continue to influence interpersonal and systemic configurations; that is, it makes a strong impact on the interpersonal and systemic levels. The therapist will search these levels for the residue of somatic, implicit memories imprinted on the spouses. Children are especially sensitive to oppressive family dynamics that include somatic content. These intrapsychic structures of perception and emotion have a specific organic response, being repeatedly renewed or projected onto the interpersonal and systemic arenas, and they become a constant part of the experiencing of the relational system within the family as a whole. This, for example, is usually what is occurring in families where children suffer from psychosomatic illnesses (Catherall, 2004; MacFarlane, 2004; J.S. Scharff & Scharff, 2014; Siegel & Solomon, 2013).

Relational family therapy represents a synthesis of relational systems that include the integration of interpersonal psychoanalysis with interpersonal couple dynamics and fundamental systemic concepts. The pioneers behind these models based their theories on the assumption that the establishment and maintenance of human relationships derive from core affects in early development that are part of the constitutive organic maturation process in human experience (Bruschweiler-Stern et al., 2010; Maroda, 2010; Robins, 2010). The therapist's task is to discover the block or the affective psychic construct that is preventing healthy development. The relational family paradigm also assumes that disorders in early relationships with parents can seriously influence all later relationships in life, not in the sense of freezing infantile needs from a certain period onwards, but rather in the sense of creating a complex process of emerging affective psychic constructs on the basis of which the growing child perceives the interpersonal world.

On the basis of these affective psychic constructs, the individual will later in life continually try to recreate the old systemic relational models that essentially influenced affect regulation methods, and this is repeated in each developmental period in its own way and with its own configuration. Relational family therapy gives meaning to the expansion of the consciousness and the effort to discover missing early experiences (Clulow, 2005; Kohut, 1984; Mitchell, 2000, 2002; Winnicott, 1988), and yet the model places change in the basic structure of the individual's systemic relational and affective world and the system itself at the center of the therapeutic work. This is why the main goal is the discovery of core affects and the affective psychic construct that are maintained and fortified through the mechanism of projective and introjective identification. It must be emphasized that this is not merely a corrective experience—that is a correction of old and unfinished processes of development—but also a new understanding of and change in fundamental relational patterns. It provides a space for varied therapeutic interventions that stimulate change, with an emphasis on different aspects of systemic relational matrices such as the organization of the self, object attachments, transaction models, and system structures and transactions (Catherall, 2004; Fishbane, 2013; Kim, Fonagy, Allen, & Strathearn, 2014; MacFarlane, 2004; Mitchell, 2000, 2002).

Change in therapy is founded on the recognition of fundamental patterns of behavior, core affects, and the affective psychic construct that create the individual's relational world. Relational change occurs on the basis of a deeper understanding of the answers to the following questions: Why is my world the way it is? What are the fundamental assumptions of this world that perhaps do not apply anymore? In short, interpersonal psychoanalysis is directed toward helping the individual, the couple, or the whole system to live in the here and now (Carlson & Sperry, 2010). The relational family model focuses on the way the therapeutic process causes change in the individual's transactional models, and at the same time in the transaction processes of the entire system. The therapist attempts to dismantle ritual actions that are compulsively repeated and thus determine the experience of the self in contact with others (Bruschweiler-Stern et al., 2010; Siegel, 2011; Sullivan, 1972). By articulating and explaining these models, the therapist helps the individual to risk having a new response, to place the self in a different interpersonal situation, and allow change in the systemic structures thus enabling a richer experience of the self and others.

These changes must become part of the transactional models in systemic interactions. They occur as a result of the therapeutic situation in which the therapist enters a relationship with the individual, couple, or entire family, and sensitively observes the stereotypical models and how they are compulsively played out (Cummings & Davies, 2010; Fishbane, 2013). The essence of relational family therapy is that the therapist and the individual together look for a way to be different with others outside the usual models that have become the foundation for interactions with others. This offers a decisive interruption of the repetitive compulsion of old models, and of the individual's unconscious search for familiar and interpersonal control and mastery of the world (Bruschweiler-Stern et al., 2010). The latter represents deeply engrained affective psychic constructs that are extremely difficult to dislodge. Individuals in a family system unconsciously fear confronting new forms of relationships because they feel threatened by them and fear insecurity and loneliness. Instead, they stick to tried and true models that were mediated to them through their parents and signify interpersonal relationships to them, even if those particular methods of interpersonal relationships are painful, traumatic, and problematic (Schore, 2012; Siegel & Solomon, 2013).

Viewed from this perspective, relational family therapy provides an essential and innovative contribution to therapeutic practice, since it proposes that the therapist and individual establish an interpersonal, potentially sacred space, a space of creativity, a space in which the therapist and the individual collaborate using transference and countertransference, and projective and introjective identification. This interpersonal sacred space becomes a safe, empathic, and sensitive environment in which a corrective and curative dynamic can develop that enables the individual to acquire new and corrective experiences and thus embark on a new beginning. The therapist's contribution is constitutive since their role—on the basis of their own feelings of countertransference, right hemisphere communication and physical sensations—is to continually discover different levels of core affects, regulate them, and enable the individual to live fully in the here and now. This process demands that the therapist must continually confront the countertransferential content that is evoked in the therapeutic process, and must always know that this content is instrumental to interpersonal communication and growth.

Relational family therapy defines the individual that carries and maintains symptomatic patterns of relationships in the family as the identified patient. The identified patient is therefore the consequence of the systemic formation of projective identification and repetition compulsion. The system finds its own balance that allows it to regulate affects and needs the constant reproduction of the identified patient, or the carrier of the most complex somatic content and related affects in the system. Based on this definition, the therapist introduces compromise into the family content, complexes, conflicts, and even painful unprocessed affects from previous generations, and seeks a new balance or homeostasis that promises a more functional and integrated family system.

1.4 The Fundamental Premises of Relational Family Therapy

The following chapter will provide detailed definitions of the five fundamental concepts that form the basis of relational family therapy: core affect and the corresponding affective psychic construct, and the mechanisms affect regulation, projective and introjective identification, and repetition compulsion, the latter two being unconscious forces that enable the individual, couple and entire system to transfer mental content—or core affects—onto each other, and thus establish behavioral, emotional, and cognitive patterns. These patterns are then consolidated through repetition compulsion. At the same time, the process also necessitates affect regulation, which internally regulates and guides the mechanisms of projective and introjective identification and repetition compulsion, and then creates the affective psychic construct, which serves as a basic defense mechanism against confrontation with painful affects and their content.

1.4.1 Core Affect

Core affects, or organic emotions, are comprised of deep-rooted unconscious psychosomatic content, the nature of which is clarified by the reference to somatic, organic or implicit memory (Rothschild, 2006, 2010). Core affects are integral to psycho-organic states (Schore, 2003, 2012) that, along with systems of memory, deeply characterize each of us. For this reason, discovering core affects is the focus of relational family therapy. Core affects represent the basic dynamic that both creates and maintains functionality as well as the pathology in virtually all relationships. Physical sensations, primarily created in the authentic bodily connection between mother and child, are the source of such psychosomatic content and its corresponding affects or psycho-organic states. There are six core affects: disgust, shame, anger, fear, sadness, and joy (Fosha, 2009; Rothschild, 2006; Schore, 2003, 2012).

One of these affects is constitutive to each individual, couple, or family structure, is generally located deep in the unconscious level of mental experiencing, and thus can be difficult to detect (Rothschild, 2006, 2010). The core affect is more discernible in the complex and variegated relationships in which we engage, and it is thus easier to detect the affect in interpersonal relationships where it tends to manifest more obviously, regulating and orienting cognitive and behavioral patterns, and also creating the main affective dynamics in a system. These dynamics continuously play out, while the individual, couple, or family system often do not know how or why, and thus frequently find themselves in similar distressful situations. In such cases, the establishment of a therapeutic relationship is essential. The therapeutic relationship reawakens the core affect and corresponding psycho-organic states in a safe and secure therapeutic environment; here, these affects can be recognized and processed in a more functional and constructive way because the therapist and client will co-create a different kind of psychic space in which it is possible to form a new psychic structure.

The core affect is usually expressed in the systemic or interpersonal area as a disproportionate response to a specific behavior in the present moment.

For instance, the behavior of a partner, child, or entire family system might reflect an exaggerated attempt to draw attention. This might lead the therapist to keep searching until the integral components are revealed. An individual's personal history and intrapsychic world, both of which carry the basic characteristics of the affective world, is truly significant. The primary elements of the core affect are organically imprinted already in early childhood through the mother-child connection. In adulthood, the core affect acquires the cognitive, behavioral, and emotional components of experiencing (Schore, 2003, 2012). This mental content unconsciously promises the individual connection, a relationship and also a sense of belonging, without which survival is not possible. Relational family therapy focuses on these themes in an effort to locate the central problem and its potential resolution.

The core affect is present at all three levels: systemic, interpersonal, and intrapsychic. For instance, the affective content of fear, anger, sadness, etc., will be dispersed across all three levels and the therapist's primary concern is to discover the origins of the core affect (Bruschweiler-Stern et al., 2010; Schore, 2003, 2012). The core affect drives the basic organizational dynamic. This is particularly important in the transgenerational transference of core affects, such as sadness, shame and other emotions, all of which have the capacity to organize and determine behavior in the present (Fosha, 2009; Ringstrom, 2014; Siegel, 2010, 2011; Siegel & Solomon, 2013).

1.4.2 The Affective Psychic Construct

The affective psychic construct safeguards the individual and the system from mental, organic content that could otherwise endanger the intrapsychic structure. Affective psychic constructs are defense mechanisms composed of cognitive, behavioral, and emotional configurations as well as organic components. All of these components emerge from the core affect in a sort of mental compromise that brings forth emotional, affective, organic, and cognitive symptoms that are manifested on all three levels: systemic, interpersonal, and intrapsychic. If an individual experiences something intensely traumatic, such as abuse, during the life cycle, and especially in early childhood, the trauma will continue to play out in an array of relationships, thus being reinforced in the mental structure and eventually becoming an inherent part of it (Cvetek, 2009; Repič, 2008). Trauma victims will continue to seek out destructive relationships in which they will experience themselves as shamed, guilty, or disgusting. The affective psychic construct represents the deepest type of connectedness with primary relationships, which in some cases means with physical, sexual, cognitive, emotional, and mental abuse (Cvetek, 2009; Repič, 2008; Schore, 2012; Siegel, 2010, 2011; Siegel & Solomon, 2013).

The affective psychic construct is comprised of cognitive, behavioral, and emotional elements as well as an organic component. Among these elements are obsessive and neurotic behaviors, irrational thinking, and psychosomatic diseases, all of which prevent the individual from confronting painful affects stemming from feelings of rejection, displacement, and neglect as well as actual abuse. The individual regenerates the patterns marked by core affects as they promise connection with and attachment to others, even though the process means the repetition of pathological and traumatic relational patterns and the preservation of the affective psychic construct. Here lies the deep-rooted connection to primary relationships, and especially physical, sexual, cognitive, emotional, and mental abuse. The affective psychic construct is a complex defense mechanism that forms a wall around the basic mental structure of the self, the object and the affect together with the organic components. In this way, it protects the individual from being wounded again and having to confront the affect that created the mutuality. If the affect were to be confronted and re-experienced, then the false attachment would vanish and emotions of loneliness, uncertainty, rejection, shame, abuse, and humiliation would enter into the former "safe" space. This would create new foundations for the relationship, which would also carry risk, or at least the illusion of the risk of absolute rejection by the other (Repič, 2008; Ringstrom, 2014; Siegel, 2010, 2011; Siegel & Solomon, 2013).

This defense mechanism enables the individual and system to repress, deny, and disassociate from painful and traumatic mental and organic content, thus invoking protection from further intrusions of distressful emotions such as sadness, hurt, loneliness, abuse, rejection, neglect, fear, etc. It temporarily quiets these painful emotions. The affective psychic construct is made up of all the defense mechanisms—disassociation, denial, and rationalization—that enable the individual to avoid direct confrontation with their own mental block or trauma. In relationships with new people, this makes it possible for them to find their affective psychic construct, as it is precisely what prevents healthy and functional communication in their current relationships (Cvetek, 2009; Rothschild, 2006, 2010; Schore, 2003, 2012).

The affective psychic construct is the deepest driving force behind every dysfunctional relationship and often compromises the survival of the individual, couple, and family system. It is the integral part of affect regulation that guides the individual in relationships. Thus the affective system and all of its ramifications are recreated in each new relationship. The individual denies and disassociates from the distressing parts of the self and transfers them onto the other. In a new relationship, the individual will initially feel freshness and novelty. However, it soon becomes clear how similar the new relationship is to the primary affective relationship that was present in early development when the psyche was evolving. In some cases, this is the result of trauma, which makes the deepest imprint on the psyche in terms of affect and the promise of attachment and belonging. The same or similar affects are expressed uniquely with each new relationship and with each new significant other in the system. Intergenerational affective complications along with biological or organic pathological elements can significantly contribute to the dysfunction of both the individual and the entire system (Repič, 2008; Rothschild, 2006, 2010; Schore, 2003, 2012). Seeking out the affective psychic construct that inhibits healthy functionality is therefore grounded in the affect itself, and the therapist senses it in the clinical setting and tries to trace its roots through the layers of the individual's mental experiencing.

1.4.3 Projective and Introjective Identification

The mechanism of projective and introjective identification (Carlson & Sperry, 2010; Klein, 1940, 1975; D. E. Scharff, 1992; J. S. Scharff, 1989, 2010; J. S. Scharff & Scharff, 2000, 2006, 2014) links the mental and biological structures of individual, couple, and systemic perceptions and experiencing, while at the same time creating a mutual interaction between the body and the mind. This mechanism is a psycho-organic strategy that works on the basis of homeostasis and enables affect and biodynamic regulation (Schore, 2003, 2012). The concepts of transference and countertransference (Maroda, 2010) are also relevant here, as well as right hemisphere communication (Fosha, 2009; Siegel & Solomon, 2013), both of which are likewise derived from the mechanism of projective and introjective identification. In addition, the mechanism of projective and introjective identification emerges from the dynamic processes of the biological sympathetic and parasympathetic nervous systems (Rothschild, 2006, 2010; Schore, 2003, 2012) as well as the mechanism of systemic feedback. In short, all of these mechanisms facilitate, maintain, and repeatedly reinforce the affect regulation system on both the psychic and organic levels.

The mechanism of projective and introjective identification is an intrapsychic, interpersonal, and systemic psycho-organic process whereby the mother, father, child, or partner are the senders, and projects upon the other—the recipient—denied and dissociated internal aspects of the self, internalized forms of the other (J.S. Scharff, 2010; J.S. Scharff & Scharff, 2014), or even the entire system of relationships with others. Through repetition compulsion, senders force recipients to identify with these aspects. This process involves projecting intrapsychic and somatic content and aspects of the self and object so that they can play out on the intrapsychic, interpersonal, and systemic levels. In addition to projective identification, there is a second essential component—introjective identification—that continues the psychological process as certain aspects of the other are internalized and become part of the recipients' self, a process which is then fortified through the mechanism of repetition compulsion (J.S. Scharff, 2010; J.S. Scharff & Scharff, 2006, 2014). The primary recipient or family scapegoat always emerges from a sort of compromise within the entire family. Most often, one family member, usually a parent, carries a deeply rooted (parental) marital conflict that was never addressed or dealt with. Instead the parental couple transfers the intolerable and distressing content to the scapegoat who becomes the carrier of the unresolved mental content. This reestablishes balance in the system, which is being threatened by the marital conflict. Each family has a scapegoat or identifying patient on whom the relational family therapist will generally focus the most attention.

Projective and introjective identification creates an intrapsychic, interpersonal, and systemic dynamic. When recipients ascribe disowned intrapsychic parts of the self to the other, they must identify with these aspects or parts (Fosha, 2009; Siegel & Solomon, 2013). If recipients fail to identify with the projected mental and somatic content, then the psychological process remains at the level of projection and doesn't truly impact the recipients. The main point of this process is that senders project—via behaviors or persistent invitations to recipients—and recipients can choose to respond to the invitation and thus become "the dumping ground" for senders' projections or not. If senders have a strongly distorted self-image, then they deny the role and begin to take interest in the image of the other, leading to further distortions in the perception of the self and the other. If recipients have a secure self-image, then they will not be likely to identify with the senders' projections; rather recipients will sense that something is distorted about the sender's self-image (J.S. Scharff, 2010; J.S. Scharff & Scharff, 2014). In this context, it becomes immediately understandable how sensitive and vulnerable children are when their self-images are still developing. J.S.

In cases where the recipients' have an uncertain self-image, they will be vulnerable to the projections of senders, having the mental fragility upon which the distorted self-image of senders can grow. Consequently, recipients will feel uneasy, experiencing an increasingly unattractive self-image and rising anxiety levels. Senders then witness the discomfort of the recipients, identify with the anxiety, and can even learn how to deal with their own feelings of unattractiveness. This interpersonal and intrapsychic process is most acute therefore when both senders and recipients are insecure about their self-image (Fosha, 2009; Siegel & Solomon, 2013). Senders will try to defuse anxiety by denying and disowning these feelings and projecting them onto someone else whom they can control. In this mutual process, recipients will accept the projections or emotions that coincide with the perception of the self and a generally negative self-image.

Returning to the central concept of the identified patient in systemic theory, relational family therapy understands this mental and/or organic construct as a product of systemic projective identification. In the case of the system, the dynamics and process are the same as those on the intrapsychic or interpersonal level, only that it is the family that projects and consequently induces or forces the scapegoat to identify with certain mental and somatic content that the family cannot carry or confront. In conclusion, positive and negative feedback, sympathetic and consequently parasympathetic nervous systems, transference and countertransference processes in the therapeutic relationship are mechanisms that emerge from projective and introjective identification. The core affect is what provides these mechanisms with content, and is at the same time the primary motivational and developmental force, demanding constant regulation, which in turn continuously creates new compromises and the affective psychic construct.

1.4.4 Repetition Compulsion

The mechanism of projective and introjective identification provides the foundations or the psycho-organic content that was originally part of the sender's psycho-organic system, which is then reinforced through the process of repetition compulsion (Bruschweiler-Stern et al., 2010; Caspar, Rothenfluh, & Segal, 1992; Fonagy et al., 2007; Fosha, 2009; J.S. Scharff, 2010; J.S. Scharff & Scharff, 2006, 2014; van der Kolk, 1996). The body remembers everything, even experiences that belong to the systemic organism or family system. This means, for instance, that traumatic content not only transfers from parents to children but also to subsequent generations (Dutton, 2007; Poulton, 2013) where it thrives. This mechanism creates a dynamic in which the individual, couple, and even the entire family compulsively repeat primary patterns of interpersonal interactions and communications, reawakening early forms of organic memory or somatic content (Rothschild, 2006, 2010), and triggering core affects (Fosha, 2009; J.S. Scharff, 2010; J.S. Scharff & Scharff, 2014; Schore, 2003, 2012). What occurs is that conflicts, affects, unconscious somatic content and trauma and corresponding behavioral and relational models are recreated and repeated at all levels of being: personal, interactive, interpersonal, systemic, behavioral, cognitive, and emotional.

These dynamics also provide the infrastructure for the relational family therapy model. Only relational processes of projective and introjective identification and repetition compulsion can explain and interpret individual, couple, and family dynamics. These two processes enable the transference of core affects and unconscious psychosomatic content and psycho-organic states (Schore, 2003, 2012) to the partner or entire family, or to the identified patient, who specifically justifies—with each individual, couple or family unit—the dynamics of both healthy and functional, and pathological relationships (MacFarlane, 2004). The mechanisms of projective and introjective identification and repetition compulsion shed light on how partners in a relationship, or how the mother and child in a mother-child relationship, can become the "dumping ground" for split-off aspects or emotions of the other. At the same time, they clarify why two partners who are very different can nevertheless be strongly attracted to each other on the basis of valency.

Considered at a systemic level, why then do parents unconsciously strive to keep a child dysfunctional? Why not just let the child grow up? Why do the parents always blame the child for their own unresolved emotions, thus preserving their own split-off, repressed and denied psychosomatic content? It is precisely the mechanisms of projective and introjective identification and repetition compulsion, which play on the dynamics of core affects and their affective psychic construct, and thus facilitate and encourage this process. Relational family therapy pays close attention to the principal mechanisms that play a key role in establishing and then resolving distressing psychic and organic content (J.S. Scharff, 2010; J.S. Scharff & Scharff, 2014; Schore, 2003, 2012). These mechanisms are also central to the development of separation, individuation, and differentiation in every healthy relationship. When senders and recipients remain relatively undifferentiated, distorted perceptions and recognition of others naturally occurs. For instance, partners intuitively recognize the responsiveness or valency of the other and the suitability of the projections elicited from one another. This harmony with the other is defined on the conscious level as love or the feeling of mutual fulfillment. In this process, deeply rooted affective psychic constructs are formed and later reinforced through repetition compulsion.

The affective psychic construct places us in the world armed with defense mechanisms used to protect us from the pain and despair of internal collapse, distress, fear of rejection, actual rejection, and abuse—emotions so deeply anchored in our psyche that they change the basic psycho-organic structure (Carlson & Sperry, 2010). The affective psychic construct is reactivated in adulthood on the basis of a similar affect or deeply rooted somatic memories

(Fosha, 2009; Rothschild, 2006, 2010; Schore, 2003, 2012), and this prevents us from behaving functionally in new circumstances or new relationships. The unconscious memory, which reawakens in similar relationships and situations, ensnares the individual who then responds in the manner that was deeply engrained and reinforced during the original trauma—also known as the mental barrier—despite the fact that the new relationship is not the same, sometimes not even similar, to the archaic experience. The sympathetic-parasympathetic mechanism is triggered, and the individual responds with defense mechanisms that were formed during the early painful experiences and distressing psychosomatic trauma of childhood.

In short, these mechanisms are triggered in the same way as they were during the original trauma when the complex defense mechanism was created and then reinforced on the basis of repetition compulsion. They become a defensive wall surrounding the basic mental and organic structures of the self, the object, and the affect together with organic components, protecting the individual from further sensations of vulnerability. These defense mechanisms enable the individual, or the entire system, to repress, deny, and disassociate from specific painful and traumatic mental content (Rothschild, 2000, 2006, 2010; Schore, 2003, 2012). Thus the individual is able to protect the entire system, and all members in it, from further intrusions of disquieting emotions such as sadness, hurt, isolation, abuse, negation, rejection, fear, etc. These painful emotions are at least temporarily silenced and repressed. However, the affective psychic construct also keeps them alive as defense mechanisms (e.g. dissociation, denial, rationalization) that prevent the individual from directly confronting psychological problems or traumas, and, via the mechanisms of projective and introjective identification, problems and traumas are transferred to the other where they are reinforced through repetition compulsion. They are repeated in new relationships or similar situations with the unconscious hope of ultimately achieving an alternative resolution to the psychosomatic drama (Beilock, 2015).

1.4.5 Affect Regulation

The essential goal of the relational family therapist is to regulate the core affect and psychosomatic content that permeates the relationships of the individual, couple, or family in their dysfunctionality and pathological psychological dimensions, on the systemic, interpersonal and intrapsychic levels of psychological experiencing. These relationship patterns were usually established in very early childhood, or at least anchored in the psyche through traumatic relationships only to be reawakened in adulthood via the mechanisms of projective and introjective identification (J.S. Scharff, 2010; J.S. Scharff & Scharff, 2014; Schore, 2003, 2012). The relational paradigm maintains that new relationships will provide the arena for these complexes to be resolved in a primary relationship with a new significant other, which, no matter how painful and traumatic, always carries the promise of new hope. Relational family therapy will first reawaken the affects from early relationships and make them known. The therapist then uses the new relationship established with the individual (or couple or family) to regulate intense and painful affects, and instigate change in the manner of interpersonal relating. In other words, the therapist strives to change the basic system of affect regulation that directs and preserves the relationships within the system in order to promote more functional ways of relating that will facilitate the resolution of painful and complex affects rather than transferring them to the children in the system.

The problematic behavior of children is almost always the result of affect regulation in relational complications where parents can no longer control or are not prepared to confront their emotions. The entire system of affect regulation is triggered, including organic components and their subsystems—the hormonal system, the system for regulating organic tension, relaxation, and initiative, cortical and subcortical connections between the limbic system, and cortical cognitive functions. In addition to affect regulation, this process easily switches between physical and cognitive processes, as well as between the parasympathetic and sympathetic nervous systems. This marks the fundamental reciprocity between affect regulation and problematic behavior, as the two processes trigger, encourage, and maintain each other. The core affect, formed during the primary and constitutive relationship with the mother and father in early childhood, unconsciously seeks out other individuals and circumstances with a similar affect. The core affect can then redevelop and fully manifest with the unconscious hope that this time—with new people and circumstances—it will attain a functional level of regulation (Poulton, 2013; Schore, 2003, 2012; Siegel & Solomon, 2013).

Abuse, in this regard, presents a true paradox. Abuse harshly transforms the individual's psychological structure, establishing a powerful affective connection between the abuser and the victim. The victim, on the basis of precisely the relationship that proved to be such a cruel intrusion, unconsciously seeks out similar abuse in new relationships and circumstances, the unconscious goal being that this time the tragic outcome will resolve in a healthy and functional manner. Relational family therapy promotes an innovative approach to the victim by focusing on and understanding the emotional dynamics at the core, and ultimately discovering a new resolution. In abusive situations, the affects are shame, disgust, and anger, along with the corresponding affective psychic construct of guilt and the sense of being sullied. These constructs maintain the entire dysfunctional system of abuse while at the same time regulating the painful affects of abuse through dissociation (Rothschild, 2006, 2010; J.S. Scharff, 2010; J.S. Scharff & Scharff, 2014; Schore, 2003, 2012).

It is noteworthy that affect regulation is essential for the survival of all systems. The affective psychic construct regulates emotions and provides the deepest motivational force for dysfunctional relationships, and thus is crucial for the individual, couple, and family's survival. It is an essential component in affect regulation, guiding the individual in relationships in which the affective system is reenacted. The individual denies and disassociates from the painful parts of the psychological structure, only to later transfer them to a significant other through the mechanism of projective and introjective identification. At least initially, the individual feels and thinks that the relationship is novel and different, but soon it becomes evident that the affective relationship is similar to the primary one experienced during early childhood. This can also be the consequence of trauma, which graphically promises a new relationship and a sense of belonging on the basis of the affect that made the deepest impact on the psyche. The same or similar affects can express themselves differently in each individual and relationship within the psycho-organic system.

Transgenerational affective complexes and organic pathological elements are also noteworthy. They make a significant contribution to dysfunction and to how affects are regulated in the individual and the entire family. Tracking the affective psychic construct, which thwarts healthy functioning, is done through the core affect: the therapist senses the core affect in the clinical process and attempts to trace it at the systemic, interpersonal, and especially intrapsychic level. This is possible because of the fundamental reciprocity between affect regulation and problematic behavior, the two precipitating each other, establishing and then preserving balance. This reciprocity can be found in all types of abuse. The chemical and hormonal systems also play powerful roles in abuse, bringing two individuals together to establish a relationship, regardless of how painful and traumatic the experience is.

The abused individual will lean towards such relationships as the dynamic of the abusive relationship is deeply rooted in the psychological core and is the most powerful motivating force, promising euphoria and excitement, both of which are addictive despite the trauma and distress. This is why the traumatized individual finds it so difficult to leave the traumatic relationship, because despite its terrors, it promises a sense of belonging as well as the kind of relationship that was imprinted on the mental structure in early childhood (Rothschild, 2006; Schore, 2003). Such an individual feels calm only when re-experiencing the shame and disgust that was experienced while regulating the traumatic experience of the original abuse. As has become evident in clinical practice, traumatized individuals unconsciously seek shame and disgust, because that facilitates regulation, albeit on the basis of the unsuitable intrapsychic boundaries that were destroyed by the original abuse, leaving the victim vulnerable to new forms of abuse. The bodies of abuse victims are unable to differentiate and evaluate what is safe and what is not, what is healthy and functional and what will only lead to more shame and disgust (Repič, 2008; Rothschild, 2006, 2010; Siegel & Solomon, 2013).

Regulating the core affect, psycho-organic states that produce the affective psychic construct, maintains the entire family system in its dysfunctional condition. This occurs at the systemic level, where the affective psychic construct is imprinted. The therapist attempts to trace the affective psychic construct or constructs at the outset of therapy. These constructs manifest in a variety of symptoms, all of which are compromises aimed at hiding the distressing affects. These compromises are discernible in the core affects of anger, shame, fear, and sadness that typically characterize relationships within the system, although their roots can be found elsewhere, sometimes even brought to the new relationship from external sources and circumstances. The relational family therapist first endeavors to find the resolution to the problems that created the affective psychic construct that regulates the painful affects at the level of the family system. If resolution cannot be found at this level, or if the system fails to calm down and become functional at emotional, cognitive, behavioral, and organic levels, then the relational family therapist realizes that the affective psychic construct has a deeper source and must look for the core affect at a deeper level. The deeper the core affect is anchored in the nonverbal and unconscious mental structures, the more inaccessible it is.

The therapist traces the core affect, seeks resolution to the problem on the deeper levels of the system, and attempts to reach the affect at the interpersonal level, while at the same time directing insight toward the intrapsychic arena of family members' experiencing and perception. The therapist continuously searches for how regulatory systems tend toward compromise for painful psychological structures. The goal is to understand the complex dynamics that condition the transfer of psychological and somatic content to individual members of the family, a process in which each member plays a specific role. As discussed above, this process is the direct result of projective and introjective identification, repetition compulsion, and the specific needs of the family as a system. Systemically, it is clear why children from the same family will often cultivate such different relationships with and responses to their parents as well as their brothers, sisters, and the wider environment. After all, each child carries specific affects, identifies with them, internalizes them, and acts in accordance with them.

Four dimensions regulate the individual: the self, the relational field, and the affect that develops in the psycho-organic space between the self and object, and finally the systemic family environment. The sum of these four dimensions composes the systemic whole, which is the focus of relational family therapy. All of these dynamics mutually condition each other and create systemic harmony. The dialectics between the definition of the self and the connection with others, as well as with the entire organic system of the family, is complex and mysterious. It's as if one or another dimension alternately gains the advantage. Self-regulation, regulating relational fields, and regulating affect and the organic system are all processes that at times fortify each other, while at other times they remain in opposition to each other and thus generate conflict. Intrapsychic, interpersonal, and systemic components are constantly overlapping with each other, each with their own set of processes and mechanisms, and wide range of aspects (Mitchell, 1988, 1993, 2000; Schore, 2003, 2012; Siegel & Solomon, 2013).

The three relational models—interpersonal psychoanalysis, object relations theory, and self-psychology—are at their best in the systemic configuration presented by the relational family paradigm. The system adds up to much more than an integration of relational models; it is also a synthesis in which each of the relational models acts independently and jointly, creating a fuller and more integrated whole on the basis of the projective and introjective identification mechanism, which is the facilitator for the regulation of core affects. Viewed in this way, the relational family paradigm is not only a combination and integration of relational and organic, biological models, but it also posits a novel and more integrated system that transcends the relational configurations of various interpersonal parts. The family system in particular forms a new and very specific psycho-organic dynamic as it incorporates somatic and relational configurations, that is, interpersonal dynamics, giving them new and different meaning in this new synthesis and especially a different approach to interpersonal relationships.

The family system has its own set of rules, demands, and needs, and thus creates its own fundamental and organically conditioned affects that permeate all relationships, influencing the entire system. The system confirms organic, biological, and relational configurations while at the same time creating its own framework in which each somatic and relational configuration—with all of its affects, complications, and conflicts—fully attains its place, meaning, and power. Relational family therapy makes room for and integrates all three relational models, each of which focuses on a particular subsystem, along with its corresponding theory. Guided by interpersonal psychoanalysis, relational family therapy explores core affects and psycho-organic states in the system as well as how affects are regulated and how they are transferred to other individuals during interpersonal interactions. It attempts to break down the projective and introjective defense mechanism that maintains the affective psychic construct, which creates blocks in communication. The latter are the primary source of dysfunction and preserve the pathology of the individual, couple, or entire system of relationships.

Relational family therapy similarly incorporates object relations theory, which taps into the impact of early objects, psychosomatic content, and memories created by parents or significant others. These intrapsychic images are created in early relationships and subsequently recur in a variety of affective and often entirely organic and sensorially triggered connections with others. These new connections recall early intrapsychic images and organic implicit memories and provide the "go-to method" for affect regulation as well as the foundation for the affective psychic construct of past "failed relationships" that were cultivated through the mechanism of projective and introjective identification (J.S. Scharff & Scharff, 2014). The relational family therapist attempts to understand and evaluate these elements as defense mechanisms against painful feelings of rejection and not being wanted, and to build a new system of relationships. Relational family therapy turns to self-psychology to focus on the development of the self and the intrapsychic images that emerged from the primary relationships experienced in the family of origin. It is on the basis of these affective relationships and on the self-image that guides and maintains the relationships with the self and others, which are sometimes very distorted, that the individual is created.

Affect regulation also orients the perception of the self and others, and through the mechanism of projective and introjective identification it preserves certain primary affective tones of self-awareness. When these are destructive, they need to be reshaped. The three relational models observe an intrapsychic subsystem and a reciprocally linked interpersonal system in the framework of the systemic dynamic that reflects the experience of the individual within a family system. This dynamic predisposes the individual, couple, and family to recreate early organic, emotional, behavioral, and cognitive models that may prove to be destructive in the new situation. At the same time, it makes these models more binding as it conceals the core affect that inevitably seeks connection with others. The more distressing and pernicious the affect, the deeper it is imprinted in the psychic and somatic structure. Only the most powerful affects continue to promise a sense of belonging and a relationship through the course of life. Paradoxically, relationships that emerge from such an affect seem exceptionally safe only because they are familiar. They produce no sense of rejection and abandonment, despite the fact that rejection marks their essence. Rejection, in such cases, is the core affect and, despite its grim unpredictability, it comes across as being predictable and safe. Its certainty is what makes it irresistible. The individual carrying such a core affect will seek out an atmosphere of rejection and abandonment, identify with it by feeling safe and certain in it, and feeling the promise of a relationship and a sense of belonging. The paradox is affectively powerful and drives all the pathways, psychological and organic, of affect regulation.

All three relational models perceive an intrapsychic system that is governed by systemic principles. The subsystems of the self and object, connected by affect, make up the intrapsychic systemic unit. Boundaries and hierarchy are highly significant in their role of providing the foundations for all subsequent intimate relationships. The deepest unconscious relationships between the self and object are formed in this intrapsychic, somatic world, and they are connected through affect and relations in the interpersonal world as well as through family relationships. As such, the self and object create systemic intrapsychic balance. When one or the other dominates, or when affect floods them both, this is referred to as intrapsychic systemic imbalance. Similarly, systemic intrapsychic diffusion occurs when boundaries are blurred, and that results in a distorted perception of the self and others.

The relational dynamic is comparable to an orchestra in which each instrument has its own specific and independent place. All the instruments are different and yet connected. It is the divided harmony they produce that ultimately gives off their true meaning and content. To take the metaphor further, string, brass, and percussion instruments each represent their own system or subsystem. When all are connected in a system of reciprocal coordination and interaction, they create harmony. Likewise, each family subsystem carries its own melody and harmony that is created when all the subsystems are interacting. Tempo is also important to harmony. Each melody has its own rhythm, color, and tone, just as each subsystem in the family has its own emotions, thoughts, affects, and relationship style. And yet harmony cannot be achieved if all the melodies play at a different tempo. In such a situation, the family collapses. Finally, each instrument needs to be in tune, just as each part of the system needs to be internally in tune (as regards the self) and externally in tune (as regards the family system). Otherwise, harmony is unattainable. A dysfunctional system results in disharmony. Each individual part of the system lets it be known—by its being out of tune—that something is happening in the system that prevents harmony.

The following is a clinical example of relational family therapy. A young couple—Mark (M) and Vita (V)—sought therapy because they were experiencing difficulty with their son who did not want to go to school. It becomes clear as early as the second session—a transcript of which is presented below—that the problem of the son and his school is in fact only a symptom of the couple's marital conflict, which is deeply ingrained in their interpersonal and intrapsychic world. During the first session, the therapist (T) tried to shed light on the problem from the systemic viewpoint. During the second session, the couple's interpersonal and especially intrapsychic worlds come into full view. The couple looks deep into their own psychic structures in an effort to discern what is preventing their functional communication and what is the core affect that they are unconsciously regulating through their son's behavior. The therapist first focuses on the affective psychic construct that keeps the couple from confronting their distressing and now repetitive childhood affects, while at the same time preventing their functional adaptation to new situations.

T (*feeling a slight uneasiness and tightness in the throat*): How do you feel today? There was certainly a lot of tension during the last session. We were talking about your son and about how he somehow can't manage to get to school and stay there the whole day.

V (*anxious, feeling slight numbness*): Yes, he just doesn't want to. He can't. He says he doesn't want to go to school. You know, he's a sensitive sort.

T (*nodding, and feeling her throat relax*): Yes, and how do you feel about this?

V (*emanating a sense of tension*): I feel afraid.

T (*feeling sadness*): You're afraid? Of what?

V (*feeling fear mixed with sadness and numbness*): Well, you know, they're very strict at school and he's not used to it. He's an only child and we've always taken care of him, and now all of a sudden there are 20 kids in his class. It's not an easy transition for him to make.

The projective and introjective identification mechanism manifests right away. In the early stages, the mother denies the fear that she is experiencing, disassociates from it, and her son expresses it instead of her. The therapist and the child feel the fear through countertransference. Once the therapist recognizes this, she then better understands the small and unprotected child, and even the mother, who, it turns out, is experiencing loneliness as well. Using right hemisphere communication, the therapist unconsciously and safely connects with Vita and Mark. This creates an increased sense of openness and vulnerability in the therapeutic process. It is imperative here that the therapist is aware of her role, or else there might be a strong negative impact on the process. The therapeutic process quickly revealed that Vita's fear is the core affect that is preventing her son's healthy functioning. In reality, Vita feels expendable and she unconsciously fears the debilitating emotions that recognizing this might trigger. The son unconsciously internalizes her emotions and now fears going to school. He also feels the need to stay home so he can emotionally take care of his parents. This, in turn, enables Vita and Mark to project the fears of their own expendability on to him. This underlying dynamic results in conflict between the couple and also conveniently conceals their feelings of expendability as they focus on tending to their son and "his" problems instead. This is how the child in the system takes on the role of acting out the parents' unconscious feeling of expendability, which prevents them from healthy functioning. This is also how interpersonal conflict transfers to the systemic level.

T (*still feeling sadness and thus speaking with great compassion*): Who takes him to school?

The therapist asks this question in an attempt to return the conflict to the interpersonal level and to explore what is truly causing it, what is the emotional source.

V (*clearly upset*): Well, what can I say? We certainly didn't come here to lie.
M (*agitated*): Go on and tell it like it is then.
V (*angrily*): That you're never home and that I have to do everything.
M (*having difficulty curbing his anger*): I have to go to work in the morning.
V (*resentful*): We both do! Only I have to do everything else as well ......
M (*staring in front of him*): Yes, and who do you think has a more stressful job?
V (*incensed*): You stop right there! A comparison of stressful jobs is not part of this discussion!
T (*feeling tension building in her chest*): Okay. We arrived at a similar emotional atmosphere in our last session. There's so much anger, fear, and distress, and it's all so familiar to both of you. This feeling, without you wanting it, keeps emerging from within you and between you.
M (*calming down*): Yes. We talked like this last week too. But she's obviously focused only on me, always blaming me, as if I have to make all the changes, as if it's all my fault.
T (*still feeling pressure in her chest*): And how does that make you feel?
M (*hurt*): Well, it's really unfair ......
T (*the pressure in her chest beginning to subside*): Unfair? Could you say a little more about that so that I can understand you better?
M (*still visibly hurt*): It's as if she doesn't even hear me or see that I have an enormous amount of work to do. I have a lot of responsibility at my job. I don't know why, but she only sees herself. She just doesn't understand me.
V (*clearly offended and angry*): And I'm supposed to listen to all this! I'm sick of it!
T (*trying to calm both of them down*): Hold on, Vita. This is how your husband experiences you. (*addressing them both*): I can see that you are both hurt and neither of you feels understood.
M and V (*simultaneously*): Yes.
T (*feeling her legs and arms trembling*): You are obviously both hurt and wounded and misunderstood, and this makes you feel upset and

angry. But it's impossible to know only from our immediate emotions what is really happening. Let's try and narrow our focus a little, to see what's happening between the two of you. Vita, let's take a closer look at you first. If I understand correctly, with the birth of your son, you began to feel that your marriage changed and now with the beginning of school come a whole new set of worries. You feel completely misunderstood.

The therapist tries to understand the conflict at the interpersonal level and carefully monitors the couple's and her own bodily sensations. The therapist indicates to the couple the desire that she wants to hear about what happened when their child was born, what changes occurred in the system, how their relationship should have changed and been adapted but was not, what roles they found themselves in, and what prevented the two from coming together to face the new circumstances. Furthermore, the therapist wants to know how her clients respond to their conflicts, what is concealed under the surface, imprinted in their relational configurations. She observes what their body postures express, the consequence of somatic memories, what distorts their perceptions of each other, and which emotions mark their affective regulatory system.

V (*threatened*): Yes, of course. I have do everything all by myself.

T (*again feels her legs trembling*): Can you tell me a bit more?

V (*uncertain, with a note of anger and sadness*): I don't know if it's worth it. I've gone over this so many times already. You know you get tired of it.

T (*senses tears*): You're in despair, aren't you?

V (*despairingly, she leans back and crosses her arms*): Yes.

T (*feeling fear, and knowing it also comes from a part of herself*): What if you just try to be with your despair a little longer. I'd like to know what's behind it.

V (*her legs jiggling*): Oh I'm desperate all the time. (*acts as if she is threatened*) What else can I do if I have to do everything on my own? I wake him up in the morning and it takes him a half hour to even wake up.

T (*still senses tears and a vague fear*): And your child?

V (*crosses her legs and leans back*): Yes, of course. My husband sleeps (*turns angrily towards her husband, her voice becoming sarcastic*), my loving husband has to sleep because he worked on his computer until 2 in the morning. And let's not forget that I always have to prepare his clothes, check his school bag. I have no time for myself. There's all sorts of things that I need to get done in the house before I go to work, and then I have to take him to school. While my husband . . . (*She turns angrily towards Mark.*)

T (*feeling anger also from the husband*): Mark, how do you feel about all of this?

M (*resentful, he leans back*): She doesn't let me get involved. She isn't satisfied with anything I do. Everything I do is wrong.

V (*gesturing angrily*): What do you do? I have to beg you to do anything, remind you constantly, and all you do is get angry and then withdraw and sulk. I'm sick of it. I've had enough.

The therapist observes that the couple cannot come to an agreement and adapt to their new circumstances, first the arrival of their son and now his starting school. The therapist now tries to go deeper into their interpersonal relationship. It is clear that the problems with their son and his schooling are expressions of the affective psychic construct that prevents the couple from facing their own painful affects. The therapist also senses that anger is not the core affect, rather that there is something more distressing behind the anger. It is becoming increasingly clear to the therapist that the affective regulatory system is not driven by anger, but by something more primal. The therapist strives to uncover what is concealed beneath the anger: that is, the core affect that the couple camouflages with anger. However, first it is necessary to address the couple's communication style and to try and regulate their relationship at a purely cognitive level.

T (*concerned*): Vita, we'll get to that too, but first it would be important to know what has happened between the two of you. Can you describe to me what changed when your son was born?
V (*with disappointment*): Everything.
T (*feels her disappointment*): If I understand correctly, initially you two were a fairly happy couple?
V (*resentfully*): I thought we were, but I guess I was wrong.
T (*feeling concern and at the same time Vita's anger*): And then you had a child. What changed in your life then?
V (*angrily, making the therapist feel tension in her shoulders*): Well, I got this sweet little package in my arms (*She turns angrily to her husband.*) and I lost my partner. I got the child I wanted, but it's a burden, you know, having a child isn't a piece of cake. There are all sorts of things you have to do and all the worries fall on my shoulders. This has nothing to do with how much I love my son. Only I know that.
T (*confronted by the wife's anger, she also feels sadness and uneasiness, but above all is flooded with anger*): All of a sudden, you found yourself alone with this terrible burden on you.
V (*angrily*): Yes.
T (*concerned, and still feeling tension in her shoulders*): Plus you have this baby. You love your child dearly, but how did he change your life? More than just making you lose your partner, as you said?
V (*angrily; the therapist feels the tension in her shoulders, head, and legs increase*): Yes, that's what changed.
T: How did it change?
V (*even angrier now*): He's gone all the time except for occasional day trips on Sunday. Sometimes he cooks Sunday lunch. But I could

go to my mother's for that and at least there I'd get to rest. But, of course, he doesn't want to go to my mother's.

T (*feels the tension increasing*): And these difficulties keep you two stuck in the same situation. (*turning towards Mark who is slouched in his chair*) When you listen to this, what do you feel?

M (*agitated*): Well, I feel angry when I listen to her. Because I don't see what changed when our child was born. Okay, we have more problems, yes, and she changed completely while she was on maternity leave. She changed even before our son was born and she had to stay at home. I still had to go to work and then, when he was born, I guess I felt that it was hard for her to stay home. She was focused on the child, while I, well, I guess I was able to go out and to work and she stayed home. That's when I feel the problems started.

T (*senses that the wife's anger and distress is rising*): Vita, what do you feel? How do you experience this?

V (*barely able to contain her rage*): It's not true. It's just not true. But what can I do if he doesn't want to be involved?

The therapist feels the anger, distress, and tension in Mark and Vita's bodies rising, and realizes that the couple cannot hear each other anymore. They have lost their internal boundaries in the flood of the affect of anger. To prevent them from hurting each other anymore, the therapist attempts to provide structure and calm. The goal is to allow them to hear each other, to calmly explore the deeper layers of their misunderstanding, and to tap into the horror and fear that they conceal with anger. The goal is also to find the core affect with which the therapist will be able to more effectively access the interpersonal level. This core affect feeds the affective psychic construct that prevents the meeting of the couple's intimate worlds. The therapist begins to actively address this core affect at the interpersonal level. She tries to discover who in their lives and childhoods was unable or unwilling to include them and which intrapsychic images were imprinted on them, because those are the foundations that determine how the two experience each other and themselves. The therapist must be mindful of her own history and careful not to insert her own emotions and views into the process.

T (*empathically, but assertively*): Okay, let's make an agreement. Vita, this is your experience and how you feel. It's your reality. If I understand you correctly, you suddenly felt all alone when your son was born. That is how you experienced it and your solitude is very a painful place. (*turns towards Mark*) Mark, that does not mean that you left her alone. You probably experienced something similar, that you lost your wife. (*to both of them*) You have both been deeply hurt and feel very angry about it.

M and V (*both visibly calmer, nodding*) Yes.

T (*the tension in her head, shoulders, and legs begins to decrease*): Each of you experiences the sense of being on your own and that an injustice is being done to you, and that is very painful. What is even sadder is that you are both so alone with these problems that it is difficult to uncover the emotion that you actually fear; you're rather be closed off and alone. Ultimately, we need to address the feared emotion. It feels like a catastrophe is looming over you. You are experiencing true solitude and isolation, anger, sadness, and hurt. What we don't know yet is what is it that each of you fears so much that you cannot face it or connect with each other, and would rather blame each other for the loneliness and misunderstanding. I think there's enough space here to explore this. I want to create an atmosphere of safety where the two of you will be able to connect again. You are both so exhausted from your many attempts that you're in despair. Neither of you believe you will ever get better, that it's possible to feel alive with each other again. What would you need or want to change, but do not dare to ask for?

M (*sounding worried*): Only what would help her?

T (*still feeling the husband's covert anger*): Okay.

V (*in a bind, also seeming to feel covert anger*): That it would cross his mind once in a while to be with his son. You know how it is when you love someone, when you . . . Basically I'm just disappointed because I know that he should be there but he's not.

T (*tension growing again in her shoulders*): Vita, hang in there, we'll get to that in a minute. But first tell me what broke down? How did Mark contribute to the breakage? Let's first try to find out what would help you, because then it will be easier to figure out what you need. Let's first evaluate your maternal emotions and needs.

V (*with agitation*): He should help me more.

T (*still feeling tension in the shoulders*): That he should help? How, in what way? What is it that you're feeling?

V (*still agitated*): He should just be there!

T (*the tension begins to decrease again*): More present.

V (*assertively*): Yes.

T (*feeling her anger, taking an empathic risk in hope that Vita will be able to speak about what hurts her so deeply*): And what exactly should he do?

V (*hardly able to conceal her disappointment and anger*): What exactly? He should just know what to do. Why did I have to say what he should do? If he's any kind of a husband at all, he'll figure it out.

T (*concerned, since their anger is increasing again*): Okay. Those are your expectations, but I'm not so sure that Mark knows what to do, how to approach you.

M (*calmer, but also hopelessly*): I really don't.

V (*flustered and visibly angry at the therapist*): Well, then you tell him!

T (*feels her anger*): I understand your anger, and it's legitimate. I'm guessing that you feel more and more alone in this room right now, expecting and hoping for help . . . . . .

The therapist assesses that the risk is still too great for the wife, that her expectations are catastrophically high. Nonetheless, the therapist presses on for two reasons: she wants to establish if the primary roots of the conflict are at the couple's interpersonal level, meaning that it will be resolvable at that level, and she wants to confront the couple with their core affect as well as their affective psychic construct. This is the path the therapist will pursue in order to uncover the deeper layers of the Mark and Vita's wounded psyches if the conflict cannot be resolved at the interpersonal level. The feeling is of rejection and it is present in both Mark and Vita. The affect is a fear of abandonment, which calls for further exploration, as it has become the foundation of the couple's affective regulatory system. This affect is likely to be rooted far back in Mark and Vita's histories with early primary figures that today remain in their intrapsychic images along with very painful affects. This makes it hard for them to risk connection with each other as these images would be reawakened along with the related affects, and neither is psychologically prepared for that. The therapist's bodily sensations, such as tension in her shoulders, increased heart rate, and shallow breathing are crucial to her awareness of the couple's situation.

V (*calmer, but still angry*): I just think it's ridiculous to be asking that. He should know. As if I should do everything for him! Come on!

T (*feels her heart rate go up and her breathing becoming shallow*): I understand how hard it is to take a risk and bridge this impasse. Because essentially, if I feel you correctly, you've been disappointed so many times that it is simply too risky to try again.

V (*visibly calmer, but still disappointed*): What if he says he can't? I already know that's what he'll say.

T (*feels her dilemma, as well as increasing tension in her own chest*): Do you fear being rejected? Is that the emotion you cannot risk experiencing again?

V (*long exhale*): Yes.

M (*disconcerted, interrupting in anger*): She doesn't know that.

T (*feels his anger and turns towards Mark*): Hang in there.

V (*visibly unnerved*): Well then he should ask me . . .

T (*feeling tension in her chest and her shoulders beginning to tremble*): It's too dangerous to ask him, so you would rather risk waiting for him to ask first. (*Once she sees that Vita has indicated the slightest wish for connection, she turns to Mark.*) How do you feel when you understand that your wife cannot risk communicating her basic needs and desires to you?

M (*cynically*): I think she doesn't even know what she wants.

T (*feeling the tension rising in the husband*): She doesn't know what exactly?

M (*angrily*): She doesn't know what she wants; she actually doesn't know.

T (*empathically, but assertively*): That's how you experience it and it frustrates you . . .

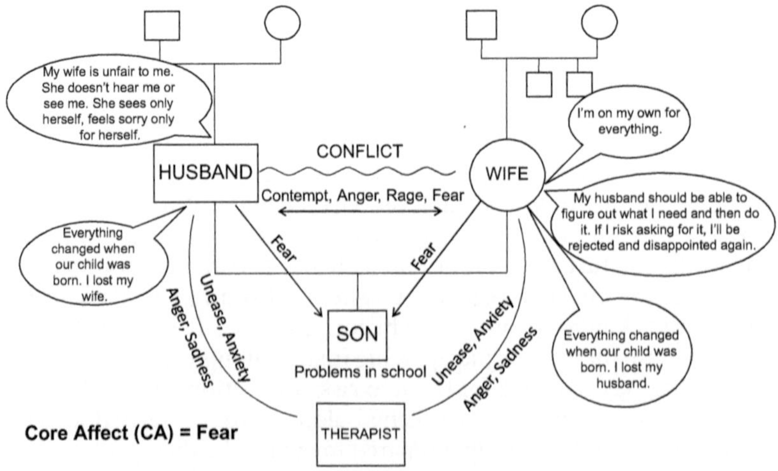

Figure 1.1 Interpersonal level (husband – wife)

Figure by Tanja Repič Slavič and Janko Slavič

M (*calm at first, but then increasingly angry*): Yes, that's how I experience it. That she doesn't know what to say. In fact, I am at home a lot. Yes, I do sometimes go out but not very often. She says I'm not at home enough and that she wants me to be, but she does everything she can to drive me away.

The therapist realizes that the conflict is much deeper than the interpersonal level, and that the core affect, an integral component of the affective psychic construct, is expressed through anger rooted in the intrapsychic level. This leads the therapist to orient intervention towards this level of their experiencing. Her own emotions and bodily sensations play a significant role in the therapeutic process. The key mechanism at work is projective and introjective identification whereby the couple transfers emotions and somatic content from the intrapsychic to the interpersonal level, the level that the therapist also feels. This content also gets reflected at the systemic level. The therapist continuously probes into the core affect, which is being unconsciously transferred because it is too painful for the couple to confront directly while their intrapsychic images are reawakening. The therapist also explores how and what the husband and wife are experiencing in the face of the affects that are transferred to each other.

The therapist soon senses that Mark and Vita reciprocally and unconsciously protect each other at this level and that they have a "psychological pact to not attack" that enables them to survive (and to have survived in the past) terrible wounds of rejection. Consequently, they have unconsciously decided not to address these themes. Their affect of anger is conducive to supporting this endeavor and it becomes an exceptionally efficient regulator of their non-transferable content of fear and sadness.

T (*feels through the tension in her hands and head and her increased heart rate that Vita and Mark's anger is on the rise again*): I'd like to turn things around at this point. Mark, I'd like you to bear with us while Vita tries to tell you what she feels and which emotions you trigger in her, emotions that are deeply rooted and are now reawakening in your relationship.

M (*slightly sullen, withholding his anger*): All right.

T (*empathically*): So, Vita, what was it like for you while you were growing up? What were the circumstances? Describe your family.

V (*a little confused*): When do you mean?

T (*continues to be empathic*): Think as far back as you can remember. Have you felt this way before? Perhaps as a child you were alone and had no one to turn to, no one to rely on, and there was no point speaking about things that bothered you because you wouldn't be heard anyway? Perhaps that's where this feeling comes from, that the people around you would know what you needed them to know if they really loved you, but they don't.

The therapist tries to arouse as many emotions as possible in Vita with the aim of her being able to connect with them. Gradually Vita will get in touch with the core affect that orients her interpersonal relationships on the unconscious level. The therapist also continues to maintain a connection with Mark so that Vita can understand that he is merely reawakening these emotions in her that are already familiar; that is, these emotions are precipitated by him but they belong to the world of intrapsychic images from her past. After all, her responses seem disproportionate to the emotions generated by Mark. Vita has catastrophic expectations; she expects that a catastrophe looms, that she will be rejected and abandoned, and this is her greatest fear. The therapist, on the basis of her own emotions or countertransference, understands Vita; so, while these emotions facilitate a deeper connection with Vita, the therapist also needs to be mindful that she does not transfer her own feelings to Vita—for example, by jumping to conclusions.

V (*surprised, slightly resistant*): Why bother? What connection does any of that have to my relationship with my husband?

T (*persists*): Well, let's take a closer look. You feel that you are on your own for everything, that no one is there to help, you're afraid . . .

V (*a little confused*): Well, I guess, with my family at home, I don't know, there was always some sort of conflict and resentment.

T (*empathically*): What images arise, what emotions come to the surface, when you think about that?

V (*calmer*): I don't know. Now that you ask me, I guess it seems I really was alone most of the time. My mom had to go to work and I had two younger brothers. I had to take care of them all by myself.

T (*empathically*): How old were you then?

V (*thoughtfully*): I was in the seventh grade.

T (*sensitively*): And you had to take care of them all by yourself . . .

V (*reminiscing*): Yes, for my two younger brothers. They expected me to do everything. I know that my mom got a lot of things ready, but I had to finish everything and make sure that my brothers were home and that they did their homework, everything really. And then there was always something that had to be checked. It was really demanding, too demanding. It was a lot for me.

T (*feeling her fear*): What was it like feeling so alone? You were in the seventh grade, no one understood you, you had enormous responsibilities, and no one to rely on. Could you talk about your feelings to anyone?

V (*sadly*): No.

T (*trying to understand*): What would you have risked by telling someone how you felt?

V (*slightly surprised and disconcerted*): Well, it was expected, it was taken for granted that I would take care of everything.

T (*persists because she feels the release of tension*): And if you had dared to say something to someone? What were you afraid would happen?

V (*visibly anxious*): Well, that they would say I was incompetent. Just like Mark probably would—I was the one who wanted a child and now I can't take care of him. So it's better that I just stay quiet and deal with it by myself.

T: And what if it turned out that you were incompetent? What would happen then?

V: Well, they would reject me. I would be unwanted because I was incompetent, not good enough to take care of things.

T (*turns to Mark who is visibly nervous*): We'll be with you soon, Mark. Thank you for waiting. I can see that you must be feeling angry, though perhaps a little less now. But right from the start, when Vita began to speak of her feelings of being unwanted and incompetent, these emotions were thrown your way. Maybe you feel emotions similar to your wife's only we haven't uncovered them yet. We will. (*She turns back to Vita.*) Vita, you didn't have anyone to turn to who would understand and support you. You were truly caught in a vicious circle: feeling incompetent if you risked talking about how hard it was for you and that you didn't feel you could manage it all, how alone you felt. Today, you're all grown up and there is someone here, your husband, who wants to understand you, and yet he doesn't know how.

V (*upset*): I'm not sure he wants to understand!

T: Perhaps you might take a risk now. We only need to establish if he's ready to listen to you.

V (*anxiously, she turns towards her husband*): Do you understand me at all?

M (*tentatively*): Well, yes, I see that you're angry and dissatisfied. But when you said . . . when I asked you what you want, you didn't know how to answer.

V (*calmer*): It's not that I don't know how to say what I want. I'm ashamed to talk about it. And you should already know what I want.
M (*shifting in his chair uncomfortably*): I get the feeling that you, well, that you're just angry, and maybe you don't even know what you want.

The therapist realizes that the two are not yet connected enough and that they are still afraid to really hear and understand each other. This, of course, further hinders their connection, although it also protects them from deeper distress. Anger is an exceptionally strong affective psychic construct and at the same time acts as a regulator that manages the intense fear of rejection. The couple is willing to do almost anything to prevent the painful affect of fear from entering their conscious minds and their lives, so the husband randomly interrupts his wife's story and tries to provoke her. His wife obliges and unconsciously allows him to remain angry, cynical, and even sarcastic with her, although on some level he is also caring and attentive. The therapist persists, trying to change the flow of their unconscious processes. She carefully attempts to reveal and explore the experience in Vita's intrapsychic world that prevents her from telling Mark what she wants and what distresses her. The goal of the therapist is to encourage Vita to risk talking about her needs. This would lead toward the resolution of the couple's most painful issues and allow them to empathically care for and cooperate with each other.

T (*turning to the couple*): Let's try and get a better grasp of this. (*addresses Vita*) The seventh grade girl you were could not talk about how she felt because then she would become really conscious of her situation and feel the fear and horror of it. This would have paralyzed her and she wouldn't have been able to function at all anymore. She would have been completely useless, and then what would have happened?
V (*sadly*): Then it would have been better for mom not to go to work. And then I'd not only be useless but unneeded, because I wouldn't even be capable of . . .
T (*empathically*): So your mother needed to be protected and if you didn't do it, then you would have been expendable and unneeded. Were you afraid of being abandoned?
V (*decisively*): Yes!
T (*feels her distress, and at the same time knows that the source is deeper*): Protect your mother or else you're incompetent, expendable, rejected. And now who do you need to protect?
V (*angry and decisive*): Well, my son!
T (*very empathically*): What about your husband?
V (*apathetically*): He knows how to take care of himself. But it's not our son's fault that we had him.
T (*persisting, because she senses that she is approaching the root of the problem*): So you protect your son and also your husband in a way.
V (*disgruntled*): Well, I don't want to be difficult.

T (*Mark shifts uneasily in his seat. The therapist feels the tension again in her shoulders.*): Okay, we'll come back to this in a moment. (*She turns to the husband.*) Mark, how do you feel about all of this? How does it make you feel when Vita says that she needs to protect you, in addition to your son, because you can't otherwise . . .

M (*confused*): Well, I don't really know or understand what's going on. If I try to understand, I don't even know where to begin or how to make things better. Believe me, I've tried.

T (*caringly*): She knows many things . . .

M (*calmly*): Yes.

T (*turning back to Vita*): But your husband still doesn't understand some things. Vita, what doesn't he understand that you wish he could?

V (*pouting slightly*): Well, that I need him.

T (*empathically, sensing that this is a very vulnerable theme*): That you need him . . .

V (*still hurt and pouting*): Yes, I keep having to say it, that I need him, and that it's only natural that he is there for me, with me. (*She turns towards Mark.*) And I'm not the only one who needs you. We're both his parents. I need you for the both of us.

T (*feels her distress*): That was a big risk for you to say that.

V (*full of yearning*): If only he could understand!

T (*trying to draw closer to Mark while also protecting Vita*): Mark, when I watch you and listen to your wife, I feel as if it puts you somewhere . . . a place where you have to understand . . . or that, if you're a man, if you're a father, it's taken for granted that you will be present and available, that you will understand and accept . . .

M (*upset*): But I am there. I'm there. She just doesn't . . .

T (*feels his fear and predicament*): I do believe you're there, but she doesn't feel you.

M (*agitated*): I think she just feels sorry for herself.

T (*feeling Vita's anger rise again*): Vita, will you please try to bear with Mark right now. I know it hurts, but this is his experience. This is how he feels it.

The therapist senses how this is also a very distressing theme for Mark and that these painful feelings of incompetence trigger cruel and destructive, hitherto repressed, affects of rejection and fear of abandonment in him as well. These emotions are awakened in the couple and exchanged between them. They adeptly transfer them to each other, constantly attacking each other in anger and despondency. This manifestation is a shared and well-established affective psychic construct. Each sometimes feels extremely sad and hurt because these emotions, the fear of abandonment in particular, are the core affects that form the affective psychic construct and the entire conglomerate of defense mechanisms of repression and dissociation. It is what regulates their psychological world of experiencing as well as their relationship. These emotions are repressed by both Mark and Vita, and due to the corresponding intrapsychic images that are connected to the painful affects, they each repeatedly reawaken them and also react to them in the other. This causes them to blame each other, resulting in constant conflicts that ultimately serve to repress the core affect that is the fear of rejection. At the same time, these emotions also profoundly connect them to each other because being similar in this way is what attracted them to each other in the first place. Furthermore, these are the emotions that promise a sense of attachment and relationship. Because they are internalized in their psychological spheres, Mark and Vita will have difficulty dealing with them on their own.

T (*taking a risk, with great empathy*): Okay, so, what is felt and believed by each of you reveals that you are both experiencing similar emotions of anger, sadness, misunderstanding, and especially the fear of rejection and abandonment. You each transfer these emotions to the other with exquisite precision, and then without really wanting to or knowing why, you blame each other for the resulting situation. You both want to be understood and you both feel that an injustice is being done to you and that it is too large of a load for you to carry. At the same time, neither of you knows how to just be there, to simply be present for the other. And in the end, no matter what either of you does, it's never good enough. It always could be better. It's a vicious circle and neither of you sees the way out. This is how I imagine each of you sees the situation and it feels pretty desperate to you.

M (*relieved*): Yes, that's exactly how I feel.

T (*carefully, empathically, and decisively, not wanting to expose Mark*): Mark, where does it come from, this feeling that you never quite understand things completely and that what you do is never enough?

M (*sadly*): Well, I sure had enough of that at home growing up. I always had to take care of people at home, and I could never do enough. I feel the exact same way now.

T (*feeling concealed fear from both sides, pushes forward very gently*): So basically each of you had to take care of others. Vita, you had to take care of and protect someone as a child and it was horrible for you. It frightened you and you had no one to talk to about it because you would have been labeled incompetent. (*turns towards Mark*) How was it for you?

M (*more relaxed*): Well, I had to take care of myself. First for myself, and then for others, (*cynically*) but I don't feel sorry for myself.

The therapist feels the husband's cynicism but chooses not to address it. She senses that this is also an affective psychic construct—"feeling sorry for oneself"—another product of projective and introjective identification. Specifically, the husband now experiences his wife the way he used to experience a significant other in his life. Thus exceptionally strong intrapsychic images are repeatedly evoked and lay the foundations for new and similar relationships. Core affects seek resolution in current relationships, but actually belong to early psychic development.

Nonetheless, they are powerful regulators of emotions and of the self and the other experienced in the present moment.

T (*feeling Mark's frozenness*): Well, I understand this must be difficult. And you also didn't have anyone to talk to. Where were your parents?
M (*sadly*): My dad died when I was very young.
T (*feeling Mark's numbness, his frozenness as if it were also a part of her own experience, the therapist pushes forward with greater empathy*): And how was that for you, when your dad was gone?
M (*sadly*): Everything changed.
T (*the therapist meets him in sadness at a very deep level*): Was there no one who you could talk to about it, who could help you process it? Who was it that felt sorry only for themselves?
M (*growing angry*): My mother.
T (*proceeding carefully as she could also feel Vita's agitation*): And this feeling then shifted over to your wife . . .
V (*indignantly*): How exactly do I feel sorry for myself?
T (*turns towards Vita*): Bear with us just a little longer. We'll get back to you. This is how your husband experiences it. (*turns towards Mark*) And how do you feel now in relation to your wife?
M (*beginning to smile*): It's very much like I felt with my mother.
T (*feels a release in tension*): A smile came across your face as you responded. What does that mean?
M (*serious again*): Well, that's exactly how I feel.
T (*empathically and attentively*): And yet we don't know if your wife really does feel sorry for herself.
M (*concern rising*): That's how I experience it, that I have to take care of her and I don't quite know how.
T (*carefully and concerned, she feels his tears rising along with a slight feeling of contempt*): So you feel that you have to take care of Vita, and you're not quite sure how. In what way did you have to take care of your mother?
M (*thoughtfully*): Practically for everything. She went to work, but everything else . . .
T (*empathically, but quite decisively in the face of the husband's confusion*): Was it ever made clear to you where and how she needed to be helped, how you had to be present with her?
M (*concerned*): No, I always had to guess. I mean I saw that she wasn't satisfied, that she was unhappy, and I felt like I had to do something to make her feel better.
T (*still feeling slight contempt from him*): Something like how you feel now with your wife?
M (*nodding*): Yes!
T (*feeling both the husband and wife freezing up*): You both had to take care of your mothers and you were both often confused about how to do it. You also both knew what might happen if you didn't succeed in taking care of them.

M and V (*simultaneously nodding*): Yes!

T (*feeling that both have relaxed a little, that the deep freeze that was flooding them has released its grip*): The burden was too large for either of you, but it also marks where the two of you meet, precisely in this shared burden. How was it to have to care for your mother instead of her caring for you?

M (*very seriously*): Well, at the time it felt like it was just taken for granted.

T (*feeling his predicament*): If you didn't take care of her what would have happened? What would you have been risking?

M (*sadly*): That I'd lose her too and then I'd be completely alone.

T (*feels his suppressed fear*): Are you also afraid that you might lose your wife?

M (*fearfully*): Sometimes, yes. She's angry all the time and that frightens me.

T (*feels slight contempt in addition to fear*): She's angry all the time. Was your mother also angry all the time?

M (*confused*): Maybe she was more sad than angry. I was the angry one.

T (*feels tension in her chest*): And now your wife is the angry one and you the sad one. Were you ever able to talk with anyone about how all of this made you feel?

M (*sadly*): No.

T (*feels her voice is failing*): And now it's the same. You have no one to talk to about how awful you feel. Thank you, Mark, we'll get back to this shortly. (*turns to Vita*) Vita, what were you able to hear when Mark was speaking? Which emotion touched you?

V (*serious, looking angrily at husband*): I don't think it's fair that you say I feel sorry for myself . . . that I also feel sorry for myself . . .

The feeling of pity, or that the wife feels sorry for herself, is a direct transfer of emotions through projective and introjective identification. The husband's mother felt sorry for herself and the husband couldn't bear it as a child. The loathing and contempt he felt for his mother were deeply imprinted in his intrapsychic world. After losing his father, he was left alone, abandoned and sad. He had to repress his own emotions in order to take care of his mother, and here lie the roots of his own catastrophic expectations—that if he failed to take care of his mother or she too would abandon him. In a way, he felt abandoned by his father when he died and these deep-seated emotions, which he had to repress as a child, are repeatedly evoked in relation to his wife. After all, this relationship is reminiscent of the primary mother-child relationship. During this session, the therapist also had to face her own catastrophic emotions evoked as she recalled the loss of her own parents. Although this was conducive to feeling increased empathy, especially for the husband, she also had to be careful not to insert her own emotional processes into the sphere of the couple's relationship.

T (*turns to the wife who is now highly agitated*): I understand that Mark's statement hurt you, and that it seemed unfair to you . . .
M (*interrupting*): It's just how I experience you sometimes.
T (*doesn't want to lose the opportunity, so chooses to push empathically forward*): We'll return to the theme of pity later. But, tell me Vita, how does your husband's story resonate with you?
V (*sadly*): Well, it was pretty much the same in our house. My dad was a truck driver and he was away for six months at a time.
T (*empathically, feeling the wife's uneasiness*): And how was it without a father?
V (*almost angry*): I had to take care of my mother and help her all the time. I was the oldest child.
M (*interrupting his wife, restless*): I had to take care of my mother and help her too.
T (*feeling agitation from both*): Help her? That must have been difficult. I mean, who was there to see and hear you? To feel you? To care for you when you were just children? Because this pity—or more accurately compassion—that you are talking about, should have been there for you as well, you who both grew up without fathers while you had to take care of your mothers, brothers, and sisters . . .
M (*sad and with a shade of contempt*): There was no other option.
V (*still agitated*): I didn't have any other choice either.

This session reveals that both Mark and Vita were "parentalized" as children, becoming emotional partners for their mothers, either when the father was away or when he died prematurely. Both had been neglected in many ways and had felt frightened. Neither dared to express their desires and needs as this would mean risking something each feared most—to be misunderstood and labeled incompetent, unable to fulfill their mother's demands. Each experienced a deep fear of abandonment. Their self-images, created on the basis of self-object relations with their parents, were extremely fragile. Their style of affect regulation was built on this feeling of a fragile self, including an overwhelming fear of isolation and rejection. Consequently, their affective psychic construct prevents the two from being able to risk real connection as they feel too worthless and incompetent to express their own needs and desires. This dynamic leaves them feeling exposed and vulnerable, a feeling they cannot handle due to their fragile self-esteem. The vicious circle continues and they become increasingly isolated and misunderstood. Here lies the paradox: just as they once were unable to risk exposure, they cannot risk it today, and it is precisely this no-risk strategy that makes them open to rejection. Each lives in their own world, challenging and provoking each other, and thus making it all but certain that they will face another rejection. In fact, they each unconsciously do everything possible to be rejected by the other.

T (*feeling Vita's fear*): It seems that for the first time in your lives each of you is taking a risk by expressing to each other how you really feel, how you felt before, and what consequences this had on you. Each of you is crying out for empathy and understanding. You both seem so lonely. If you two could try to share your feelings, because both of you know exactly what loneliness is like and how painful it is, then you would know what you need to give to your son—whatever wasn't given to you as a little boy and girl. Because you're both religious, perhaps you would benefit by trying to meet in prayer. Prayer will widen your horizons and it will be easier for you to experience each other from this broader perspective. You need your vulnerability to be felt. You need to give each other compassion.

M and V (*both nodding*): Yes.

T (*empathically and decisively*): There's still a lot of work to do on your relationship. Your child, with his presence, only evoked the old emotions that each of you repressed so long ago. Whatever you were not allowed to experience, your child is now, loudly and clearly, demanding of you, and you will be entirely capable of giving it to him if you let yourself feel him. But first, you'll have to feel your own self as well as each other's.

V (*curiously*): How are we going to do that?

T (*aware of Vita's fear*): It seems that you both were deprived of a lot in your childhood. So much was not allowed. It would have been a risk to ask for anything. Neither of you knew empathy, only fear, the fear of being expendable, the fear of rejection. So maybe this is the first time that you have risked something this scary. Does that sound right to you?

V (*pensively*): It would be good to connect with each other again. Otherwise we'll have another week like the last one . . .

T (*empathically*): And you two are good at that, aren't you?

V (*curious*): At fighting?

T (*feeling her trembling*): Yes. I know it's hard to self-regulate, to allow yourselves to be vulnerable and ask for compassion. How would it be for you, Mark?

M (*pensively*): I guess what we were doing before wasn't really a solution. Maybe it's time to find a new way.

T (*feeling both of them gradually letting go and relaxing*): If I understand correctly, you just want to be accepted, and you'll do anything for that. But if you just tried, you would be accepted.

M (*anxious*): Yes, if I only knew what to do.

T (*feeling his confusion*): You've spent your whole life guessing and that's always a risk: either you guess right, or you guess wrong and lose. If you have the information, it's okay, but if you don't have the information . . .

M (*more relaxed*): Then you usually guess wrong.

T (*feels Mark's concealed fear*): And you can't solve the riddle because the answer doesn't add up . . . (*turns to Vita*) You actually have a lot of the information that is missing in order to solve the riddle. What if you offered it to him?

V (*relaxed, she faces her husband*): Look, I can do it all. I know how to manage by myself; I'm good at that. I just need you to be there and to ask how I am.

M (*slightly nervous*): But if you're in a bad mood, then I'll do it all wrong again.

V (*assertively*): But you shouldn't be afraid of me!

T (*turns to the Mark*): Oh! That sounds strange, doesn't it?

M (*pensively*): Well, because I immediately think it's my fault if she's in a bad mood. That I didn't solve the riddle.

T (*feels Mark's unease*): Yes, because you didn't figure things out, just like with your mother, and then you might feel expendable, even rejected. (*to Vita*) And for you it's horrible to have to say what you need, because if you do, then you're the one who is incompetent. And if you are incompetent, then you might not be needed. (*to Mark*) You can feel angry and you can go into rages as you did as a child, but nothing changes. This is exactly where the two of you meet and lock horns. Now you have the opportunity to resolve this, but it is painful and it feels risky. You two are grown up now. The feelings that connect you are part of your past, and yet they connect you very deeply. The emotions are cruel, simply because it's unbearable to feel rejected and unneeded and incompetent. As a child, it's a matter of survival. But now you are adults and what you are feeling has been evoked by the son you have together. The situation today is entirely different even though the same feelings are triggered. It seems that you have each found someone with whom it will be possible to find resolution at last. (*to Vita*) Your goal is to let yourself be vulnerable so you can talk about your needs and desires, and risk letting your husband hear them. You know, as an adult, that it is bearable and that you will survive and that you're not risking abandonment. (*to Mark*) And when you take a risk and actually ask Vita for information—so that you can solve the riddle—that will be a new day for you. Just look at your child, he's a riddle too. And when you feel him, you will know what needs to be done. I think we took many risks today. How do you both feel?

M (*positively*): We, or rather I, feel better understood. I just don't feel certain yet about stepping into a new day.

T (*feels Mark's anxiety*): Well, if you'd like, we'll take a few more steps together! (*feels that some pressure has been released*) Vita, how about you? How do you feel?

V (*nodding*): Much better than when we began.

T (*feels that the way forward has opened*): So we'll meet again next week. Thank you both.

Mark and Vita discovered something new during this session: how much they are under the influence of their intrapsychic worlds, and how early relational configurations that became constitutive parts of

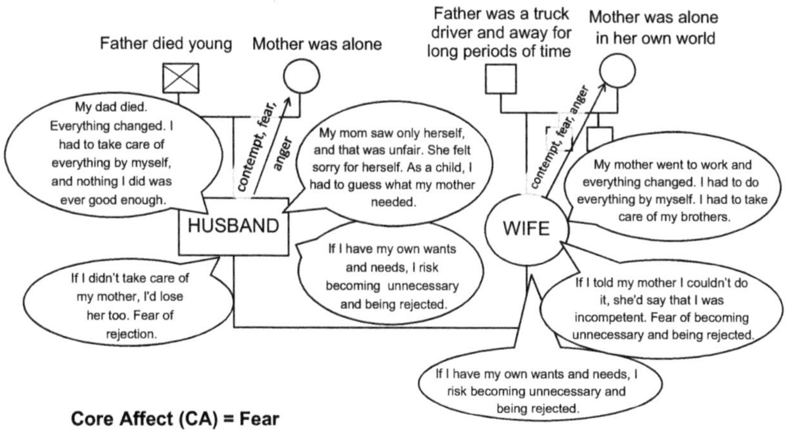

Figure 1.2 Intrapsychic level (childhood)

Figure created by Tanja Repič Slavič and Janko Slavič

their psychological lives have been reawakened in their current relationship. Furthermore, because they feel familiar, old emotions are evoked, like a nightmare or some horrifying paralysis or numbness, the purpose being to find a new resolution to old problems. The therapist needs to carefully dig deep from one psychological layer to the next, moving back and forth between these layers, linking and trying to uncover the origins of the psychological trauma or affective psychic construct that prevents healthy functioning. Once the core affect is discovered, such as the fear of abandonment, then the couple will be able to relax and take more risks.

In the coming sessions, the relational family therapist will continue to move back and forth between the three systems—systemic, interpersonal and intrapsychic—trying to locate feelings of misunderstanding, expendability, and fear of rejection as these prevent the couple from actively responding to new situations as they unfold. The therapist will strive to connect the three systems. She will persistently seek to understand why the couple cannot respond and adjust to circumstances in the present but instead insist on reliving patterns from the past. She will look for the motives in the intrapsychic structure of both Mark and Vita that drive the projective and introjective identification mechanism to transfer the deepest affects to the interpersonal and systemic levels. The therapist will search, take risks, and test new approaches for Mark and Vita to respond and find new ways of regulating intense affects, especially the fear of abandonment. She will persist until she discovers the path to resolution for the most binding affective psychic constructs, their constitutive affect, and the affective regulatory system that preserves the core affect, which, without intervention, will always find new ways and new situations in which to manifest itself.

2 Relational Dynamics in Systems Theory

In this chapter we will be taking a closer look at the basic relational dynamics that influence deep affective models within a family. These relational dynamics dictate specific family dynamics and mechanisms that maintain relationships between subsystems and individuals within the system. Unconscious affective dynamics constitute the entire family dynamic, bringing together a deep-rooted economy of the psyche. We will be discussing the basic principles of family systems, and introducing two essential relational mechanisms: the mechanism of projective and introjective identification and the mechanism of repetition compulsion. Both mechanisms characterize all interactional dynamics within a psycho-organic family system. They enable psychosomatic or psycho-organic content, which shapes the core affect, to be transferred from an individual's intrapsychic sphere and psycho-organic structure to the interpersonal and systemic level. While systems theory does not explicitly refer to the two mechanisms, it is implied; after all, these two mechanisms clarify the process of transference and transplantation of basic emotions from one system to another. They also explain the formation of symptoms and symptomatic behavior as a compromise between the system and the individual. According to relational family therapy, the concept of the identified patient is thus a result of systemic family dynamics.

This chapter will focus on concepts of relational family therapy, including core affect, affective psychic construct, and affect regulation. These are basic components of every family system. Each system needs to create, regulate, reinforce, and maintain these components in order to function. The entirety of family dynamics is comprehensible through the relational dynamics of projective and introjective identification, repetition compulsion, core affect, affective psychic construct, and affect regulation. These terms help clarify and grasp the interpersonal and intrapsychic components of a family system that are assumed by systems theory, even though not directly employed.

2.1 Systemic Wholeness

The primary stance of the systemic approach, and fundamental principle of any system, is systemic wholeness. This essentially means that the system as a whole is always greater than its individual components and subsystems. Moreover, each system forms an organic whole integrating the complexity of any living organism as well as its systematic organization (Bowen, 1978;

Gehart, 2016; White et al., 2015). This is especially evident within a family system where the members are organically related by blood. Together they form a primal organic cell or human family, characterized by organic language or right-right hemisphere communication (Cummings & Davies, 2010; Fosha, 2009; Schore, 2003, 2012). Viewed this way, the system of a family comprises an organic-social-affective system of mutually dependent interactive elements or relationships. These interactions are heavily tinted with affect and create the crux of an affective regulatory system. Each family is based on different core affects that maintain its existence and protect its system from excessive exposure. However, the affects also awaken affective psychic constructs or fundamental boundaries, which prevent the system from evolving in a healthy manner. These interactions and interpersonal connections between family elements establish the system in its totality.

A family system works as a unit of mutually interactive elements that can act uniformly in a particular setting. The system as a whole is much greater than an arbitrary assembly of components, and is therefore more powerful than its independent elements (Bitter, 2014; Bradshaw, 1996; Carlson & Sperry, 2010). It creates a very specific dynamic and affect, which in turn substantiate and regulate the system itself. Essentially, the system is a reflection of all possible relationship combinations between its parts. These relationships generate the system's atmosphere—its core affect. This interactional atmosphere pervades a system to its very core and in an exceptionally unique way. It is a product of mutual relationships and connects all the particles into a specific unit. This unit is a live, dynamic system, powered by a constant internal and external communicative exchange.

Active exchange refers to the context in which life is organized, how it develops and transpires (Catherall, 2004; Gehart, 2016; Umbarger, 1983). It is rooted in the dynamic process of projective and introjective identification and repetition compulsion—the mechanisms that drive and preserve its structure. They provide the organizational communication force, which triggers primary right hemisphere communication between individuals (Schore, 2003, 2012). It also organizes all subsystems into a larger system of core affects. Each individual is a unique manifestation of the system itself. The intrapsychic imagery of an individual's relationship to his or her father and mother, as well as the relationship between the parents, forms an individual's mental structure or the self. The individual internalizes the imagery and continuously recreates it in a distinctive way, thus becoming the sculptor of their own organic intrapsychic structure from materials acquired from the parents, and the relationship between the two, via mechanisms of projective and introjective identification, repetition compulsion and affect regulation. Of course, personal characteristics and individual creativity, including perceptive, cognitive, organizational, and affective capacities, are applied during this process. These are the foundations for forming models of relationships and behaviors, emotions, thoughts, and perceptions. Eventually these elements will direct the style of affect regulation within a family, and create the affective psychic construct, which enables and maintains systemic homeostasis (Carlson & Sperry, 2010; Catherall, 2004; MacFarlane, 2004; J.S. Scharff, 2010; J.S. Scharff & Scharff, 2014; Sperry, 2004).

The entire process dictates a strong economy when it comes to intrapsychic and interpersonal systems, which gain purpose through systemic organization. The relationship between the parents, and their relationship with their child(ren), plays a very important role in the children's creative power and how they form their own internal image. They also define what elements are most important within this formulation, both consciously and unconsciously. People are always consciously and unconsciously co-creators of the system they are part of, whether actively or passively (Bitter, 2014; Catherall, 2004). This is all a part of systemic coherence, the driving force underlying all interpersonal relationships within a family. All human life is organized into a hierarchy of living organic systems. While the lowest form of this organization of life is a simple organic cell, the highest is human society (MacFarlane, 2004; Pinsof, 1995; Pinsof & Lebow, 2005). The social system of a family therefore belongs to an undefined space, organically characterized with a wide range of sensations. All individuals have their own psycho-organic relational space and subsystem within the larger system, which is defined by the sense of organic belonging and family ties (Pinsof, 1995; Pinsof & Lebow, 2005).

2.2 Subsystems-Hierarchy-Boundaries

Each organic system is comprised of mutually dependent parts. Each organism is divided into subsystems organized in a hierarchal manner. They are always a part of a whole that is also organized in a hierarchical manner (Catherall, 2004; Cummings & Davies, 2010; MacFarlane, 2004; Umbarger, 1983; White et al., 2015). In other words, each system is organically constituted, and any change in any part of the system ultimately affects the system as a whole (Cummings & Davies, 2010). Each system is in a process of constant movement, continuously evolving and transforming. In order to survive, it has to transform in each stage of the process, both internally and externally. For example, when a child is born, the very core of the marital system must readjust. Similarly, it readjusts when a child grows up and leaves home. Additionally, the child must adjust to new surroundings outside of the home. For example, if a father loses his job, the entire family system has to undergo a process of adaptation. This process happens within the marital subsystem and the psycho-organic system of each family member (Pinsof, 1995; Pinsof & Lebow, 2005).

Another defining characteristic of the family system are the psycho-organic internal systemic boundaries (Catherall, 2004; Gehart, 2016), which occur on both interpersonal and systemic levels. Family members experience boundaries as the rules that regulate how emotions, thoughts, forms of behavior, and values transfer from one individual to another. These transfers establish themselves through relationships between family members within a certain time span (Umbarger, 1983). They also undergo the process of repetition compulsion, which reinforces them. The unconscious transference of vulnerable emotional and mental information unfolds through the process of projective identification (J.S. Scharff, 2010; J.S. Scharff & Scharff, 2014). This mechanism is a fundamental instrument of transference, implied by systems theory, even if not defined with the same term. Without projective identification, the dynamic of these transfers would be quite difficult to explain. Boundaries are an instrument, helping to attain, define, and establish borders between subsystems. On an intrapsychic level, boundaries enable us to differentiate between what we are feeling and what feelings we are receiving from outside. Similarly, boundaries are the core of any healthy, functional interpersonal relationship.

The affect regulation system plays an important role in organizing intrapsychic and interpersonal systemic psycho-organic relationships (Schore, 2003, 2012). It creates the affective psychic construct, which continuously strengthens boundaries in our relationships. From a practical systemic perspective, we can hope that boundaries prevent marital complications and disagreements from affecting the child's subsystem. Unfortunately, this is unlikely, because the information will still be transferred on an unconscious or unspoken level. This is why it is crucial for partners to work through their marital issues regularly. In fact, an unresolved conflict has the same effect as openly expressing it. If parents do not work on resolving their conflicts, the children will feel as though they have to intervene in order to preserve their parents' partnership. Children unconsciously feel that conflict separates them to a point of detachment and that their parents' subsystem is not strong enough to withhold such pressure. Hence, children will take on different roles to help ensure the marital system doesn't dissolve. When parents include their children in relationship conflicts or cover them up, the children become conflict carriers—suddenly they hold the burden of their parents' unresolved, destructive, emotional, and mental content or information.

All of these actions occur on an unconscious level through projective identification, which—in line with repetition compulsion—continuously instills destructive emotions within a child. In fact, children learn to take their parents' conflicts on themselves in order to relieve and protect them. Doing otherwise would be too frightening. Children, in fact, encourage the transfer of destructive emotions to themselves through certain behaviors, and hope to see their parents connect and stay together. Consequently, parents might punish their children for their inappropriate behavior. All boundaries then break down and feelings may flow from one subsystem to another, both consciously and unconsciously. In short, boundaries within a family can change based on whether or not family members achieve their basic goal of connecting on an interpersonal level, as well as with the outside world. Families gain certain knowledge about their own surroundings by collecting information on various elements: basic forms of behavior and communication, ways of perceiving and sensing things within their environment, and types of judgment, analyses, and understanding. Children learn basic critical thought this way, as well as how to respond to hardships caused by others and their surroundings (Bitter, 2014; Catherall, 2004; Gehart, 2016; White et al., 2015).

The strongest indication of family boundaries is the dynamic between open or expressive relationships and closed or inexpressive relationships. The interaction between these dynamics either enables or prevents specific information about a family, and its individual members, from being passed on to the next generation (Bradshaw, 1996; Poulton, 2013). For example, parents might routinely withhold certain marital information and events. These are often dark areas of a couple's past; perhaps they have to do with something prior to their marriage, or secrets that have been withheld through generations and are therefore taboo (Cummings & Davies, 2010). This censored information creates strong boundaries around the marital subsystem. However, as a result of projective and introjective identification, these feelings will gradually spread throughout the whole psycho-organic system, no matter how hard the couple tries to suppress certain information—especially if they are unable to work through it themselves. The core affect, created through this dynamic will be continuously passed on to all members of the family. For example, children may feel something oppressive, frightening, or sad has taken over the family. They will then internalize these feelings and re-establish them in future relationships. They will compulsively build relationships upon these foundations with the intention of resolving them sometime in the future. They will hope to meet someone who will understand them and relieve them of these negative feelings.

On the other hand, a couple might be very open and share information freely with others, inviting them to be part of the family. However, all families should have an intimate space to share delicate subjects. It is impossible for people outside the family to fully grasp and assess certain things about a family. This intimate psycho-organic space is not meant to feign or disguise—that would be unhealthy and false. Rather, it should offer a place to protect family intimacies and shelter family members from having to experience shame. In fact, certain subjects are meant to be private, such as the intimacy of the human body. If there are no boundaries, many crucial family processes are unable to develop, including progressive separation, and the definition of family roles for each individual. For instance, intrapsychic structures will lack the chance to develop in a healthy way, and then the individual will be deprived of feeling as though they belong to a specific subsystem (Bradshaw, 1996; Fishbane, 2013; Poulton, 2013). Instead, individuals will carry and personify the psycho-organic destructive elements, such as those of a marital subsystem, and this will avert healthy growth.

Without systemic boundaries, individuals are unable to develop and maintain plasticity or adjust to their surroundings. In such cases, the system experiences trouble and its specific parts will express a variety of symptoms (Bradshaw, 1996; Cummings & Davies, 2010; Siegel & Solomon, 2013). Boundaries regulate the flow of information, and the energy of core affects. They ensure living systems can maintain harmony with the context of their surroundings (Bitter, 2014; Bradshaw, 1996; Catherall, 2004). Boundaries secure a free pathway for specific information to flow throughout the psycho-organic family system, while preventing external information from entering. By doing so, boundaries define the manner in which the system regulates affects. This is also the foundation of the affective psychic construct and its structure. The information traveling throughout the system is not only that of a family's past or specific memories and incidents, but rather a family's core principles, either accepted or rejected. These principles include values, worldviews, and decisions made by the individual, as well as the marital system and the family itself (Carlson & Sperry, 2010; Poulton, 2013).

Parents may encourage specific views of the world, and reject opposing opinions, perspectives, positions, or views. They may even completely avoid these views and beliefs. For example, they may only promote certain career paths and devalue others. This deeply affects children, especially when it comes to concrete information like the family's history. If children do not learn basic information about their parents, they will feel as though something unforgivable or shameful might have happened (Poulton, 2013). For this reason it is important that they learn about their origins and relatives, as well as their family members' occupation and the relationships relatives have with colleagues and friends. If parents withhold those details, children may feel as though they are not worthy of receiving the information. In this case, they will internalize deep feelings of guilt and shame, which will color their connections in future relationships and surroundings. These emotions, or core affects, may also become a part of their personality. They will form the basis for their intrapsychic structure (Cummings & Davies, 2010; Siegel & Solomon, 2013). This will cause children to feel as though they are unworthy or that their past is somehow corrupt.

It is important to stress that information can affect the structure's expressed and unexpressed emotional, mental, and behavioral content, which characterizes a family psycho-organic system and all its members (Bitter, 2014; Cummings & Davies, 2010). It is the emotional energy or core affect, however, that triggers the transfer process. Information can accumulate for some time before a core affect, such as anxiety, causes change. For example, if a parent suddenly fears that their child is becoming a drug addict, this will ignite the process. Each new piece of information will then be seen through the eyes of that fear. Only by processing this fear will the family be able to function and understand the subject matter in an objective and flexible way (Catherall, 2004; Cummings & Davies, 2010). Information and energy are significant terms in systems theory because they help explain family processes. They vividly describe the core affect of a family psycho-organic system, which is compulsively repeated. In this manner, information and energy create daily activities and emotions within a family. Information relates to expressed and unexpressed signals. These reveal the extent to which parts of the system align with its ideal goals and intentions. This includes deep emotional information pervading the family system, such as whether or not it is acceptable to speak about uncomfortable subjects or to feel happy, sad, disappointed, angry, and frustrated (Catherall, 2004; White et al., 2015).

This foundation enables the affective psychic construct to develop. The construct prevents tension from getting released. Affects, essential to the affective psychic construct, define and indicate relationships. In cases where anxiety is the core affect, all members of the system will experience and internalize it; anxiety will become a part of their intrapsychic structures, and will regulate daily activity within the family structure. Furthermore, it will characterize interpersonal relationships (Catherall, 2004; Poulton, 2013). The same thing happens if a child or parent experiences or expresses destructive feelings of anger, rage, and anxiety. These emotions create a very specific piece of information the family system will have to accommodate. With the power of its affect, this information begins to control the whole system through projective identification, as the fundamental mechanism of emotional transference. All types of addictions and the emotional distress triggered by them are typical examples of this process. The energy or core affect here corresponds to the force and type of transfer observed or experienced through the exchange of informational signals (Catherall, 2004; MacFarlane, 2004; Poulton, 2013; J.S. Scharff & Scharff, 2014; Umbarger, 1983).

2.3 Systemic Mutual or Circular Causality

While the main concepts that led to radical and revolutionary change in psychological paradigms stem from a biological or organic, cybernetic, and informational theoretical background, psychological behavioral science, by studying interpersonal relationships, soon discovered that relationships are governed by a mutually interactive circular causality rather than a linear one (MacFarlane, 2004; Pinsof, 1995; Pinsof & Lebow, 2005; Umbarger, 1983; White et al., 2015). Systemic and psycho-organic paradigms focused on the idea of cause and effect being a mutual or circular process, which soon proved to be the influential factor on the relationship between individuals and their relational contexts (Pinsof, 1995; Pinsof & Lebow, 2005; Umbarger, 1983). The mechanism of projective and introjective identification enables family members to define and influence each other, and to mutually induce and create certain mental, emotional, and behavioral interpersonal relationships. These relationships shape the way affect is regulated within a family. In sum, it is not only an individual family member who causes others to have a specific reaction—it is also the other family members who influence the individual's behavior, emotions, and actions in a unique way (McCormack, 2000, 2004; J.S. Scharff & Scharff, 2014).

Different subsystems cause a variety of reactions. However, they are not all equally impactful. For example, parents who abuse their children are accountable for their inappropriate actions because they have all the power in the relationship. Even if children behave in a way that seems to "deserve" being disciplined, parents should never act in an abusive manner. Parents will always be fully accountable for abusive behavior. The parents' task is to find an appropriate way to raise and discipline their children, no matter how they behave. This type of mutual influence materializes in three different levels of mental action: the intrapsychic, interpersonal, and systemic level. Each of these levels is simultaneously its own system with its numerous subsystems. Each and every subsystem affects other subsystems, as well as the larger system—which consequently affects the subsystem in return. This creates a very complex interpersonal dynamic of interaction (Pinsof, 1995; Pinsof & Lebow, 2005). As a result, each system is rooted in mutually dependent relationship patterns that repeat compulsively throughout the subsystems. This mutual entanglement of relationships creates the psycho-organic system as a whole, as well as the affective psychic construct. It would be impossible to speak of a system in its entirety without looking into the dynamic of relational patterns that maintain and repeat themselves, linking systems to each other (Bradshaw, 1996; Catherall, 2004; Poulton, 2013).

All members within a system have certain systemic, intrapsychic, and interpersonal characteristics. All bear the mark of the system as a whole: each member is a representative of their own family, while at the same time each of them materializes as a unique and autonomous personality. Family members shape and determine who they are based on projective and introjective identification. They mutually regulate each other's cognitions, emotions, and behavior (Bitter, 2014; Catherall, 2004; MacFarlane, 2004). It follows that we, as individuals, carry the psycho-organic reality of our own families of origin. The unconscious level of the self uniquely relates to the unconscious content of other family members through projective and introjective identification, and this in turn enables each member of the system to develop their own reality. Systems theory and projective and introjective identification give us an insight into the sphere of organic connection between blood relations, and their deepest realms of unconsciousness. Organic-social-affective dynamics are what establish this connection, making it far deeper and stronger than any friendship (Cummings & Davies, 2010; J.S. Scharff & Scharff, 2014).

2.4 Rules and Roles Within the System

According to research (Lebow, 2003; Minuchin & Fishman, 1981; White et al., 2015), each family has its own rules that guide and organize the family system. These rules and roles maintain balance and systemic homeostasis within a family and are constantly changing (Nelson, 2003). In other words, the rules and roles create and preserve affect regulation in the psycho-organic system, and constitute the affective psychic construct that is reinforced by repetition compulsion. Rules include a number of things, such as house rules, the social life of the family, celebrations, privacy and boundaries, finances, education, career paths, values, principles, parental guidelines, etc. (Bradshaw, 1996; Catherall, 2004; Pinsof, 1995; Pinsof & Lebow, 2005). In additional, there are unconscious rules that define and determine the family system even more powerfully. An example of an unconscious rule would be expressing or not expressing emotions: knowing which emotions are allowed to be shown, as well as knowing how, when, and to what extent conflict is encouraged or allowed to be expressed. Unconscious rules define to what extent internal tension can be tolerated. They also determine the acceptable levels of intimacy, closeness, and vulnerability (Feldman & Pinsof, 1982; McCormack, 2004; Pinsof, 1995; Pinsof & Lebow, 2005). These levels are defined by intrapsychic and interpersonal levels as well as by the psycho-organic system as a whole.

The parents' role is to create a safe environment and make their children feel accepted, loved, and wanted. Their role is also to portray roles of masculinity and femininity, fatherhood and motherhood. In this way, they model ways for children to develop as a person, as well as teaching them how to express feelings, desires, and demands. Parents also need to model how to regulate conflicts and intense emotions (Cummings & Davies, 2010; McCormack, 2004). The child's role is to be curious, obey, learn, follow, and imitate the behaviors, thought processes, and emotional reactions that adults model for them (Bradshaw, 1996). Thus the interpersonal dynamic in the marital relationship between the parents is essential for the self, partner, and entire family. It is the dominant force in the family's relational system. A functional relationship between parents is conducive to children developing mature, independent, and integrated personalities. To the contrary, a dysfunctional marriage will result in the children having to adjust by taking on unhealthy roles. They will repeat these roles compulsively in order to ensure the balance within their family system and thus secure their own survival (Bradshaw, 1996; Cummings & Davies, 2010). The mechanisms of projective and introjective identification and repetition compulsion provide clear insight into the complex system of relations within a family psycho-organic system. These mechanisms organize and manage the system through intrapsychic, unconscious needs and processes. They are relational concepts that help to explain, define, and analyze how the system, including all of its organizational factors and especially affect regulation, maintains its existence (Cummings & Davies, 2010).

Children will always be entrapped in certain systemic rules and roles. Through them, they indicate and activate hurtful and traumatic psycho-organic family factors, which affect the entire system. This happens on both the intrapsychic and interpersonal level. Focusing specifically on systemic roles, we are able to observe the following: roles are deeper and more dramatic, the more forceful and destructive the marital conflict (Cummings & Davies, 2010). In a destructive setting, the roles are systemically structured through projective and introjective identification and reinforced with repetition compulsion. They create and maintain the affective psychic construct. Usually the sequence in which the children were born will determine their roles (Bradshaw, 1996; J.S. Scharff & Scharff, 2014). At birth, children will take on roles that will meet the most important unfulfilled needs within the psycho-organic system at that point. By taking on roles, children will represent a specific dynamic in response to an unresolved marital conflict. For example, if the parents were forced to marry because they had a child, this child may grow up feeling unwanted. In this dysfunctional setting, the child may act out by taking on the role of a rebel who the parents physically discipline. To the contrary, children who feel unwanted may grow into perfectly behaved children who never disappoint their parents. Regardless, the parents in a dysfunctional marriage will find reasons to criticize, underestimate, or neglect their children because of their own unresolved emotional issues (Catherall, 2004; Cummings & Davies, 2010; MacFarlane, 2004).

In the example above, the child fulfills the system's unfulfilled need for acceptance, appropriateness, and feeling needed and loved. If the parents had to get married, then neither knows whether or not their partner actually wants them, neither is sure that the other fully chose to be in the relationship. They will both feel a lingering uncertainty about whether their partner desires, loves, wants, and accepts them. Children will resolve these unanswered questions and feelings of anger, fear of rejection, and a foreboding sense of being abandoned simply by existing and becoming the parents' excuse for being together. Such parents may keep telling each other that they are only together because of their child, or that they are unhappy because the child is so difficult or they may console each other by seeing the child as perfect, well-behaved, and exceptional. In this case, the child will feel as though he or she must behave well in order to gain the parents' affection. Roles can change over the course of time, depending on the marital subsystem's needs and specific dynamics (Cummings & Davies, 2010; McCormack, 2004).

In the following paragraphs we will discuss some of the more stereotypical roles children play that research suggests is indicative of a fundamental circular dynamic of emotions. The mechanism of projective and introjective identification creates the dynamic, and repetition compulsion maintains it. By enacting systemic roles, children either cause a disturbance within the system or reestablish psycho-organic systemic stability (Cummings & Davies, 2010; McCormack, 2004). In either case, children end up feeling guilty, useless, devalued, or shamed. If a marriage acquires further traumatic dimensions or ends in divorce, children feel deeply hurt, especially if they have made sacrifices that did not hold the marriage together (Carlson & Sperry, 2010). All roles are a result of systemic and interpersonal dynamics, or intrapsychic projective and introjective identification. Emotional patterns in relationships are passed on and create the core dynamic of these roles. The patterns tend to create an identified patient within a psycho-organic family system. The rules that organize family systems are determined by the way in which the roles manifest. Individual family experiences and specific family members' personal characteristics further influence the family system. Other influential elements include ethics, culture, and religion (Bradshaw, 1996; Catherall, 2004; J.S. Scharff & Scharff, 2014).

While the roles are stereotypes and organically conditioned, their manifestation depends on the actual needs of the marital system. There is little need for the roles to be manifested if the system is well-structured and orderly. The more the system suffers, the more prominent the roles. The connection between parents and children is strong and organic. Together, they continuously yet unconsciously aspire to preserve harmony and balance within the system. Usually, family members are not aware that they are performing roles, and they don't realize how much they are willing to do to achieve a balanced system. The main purpose for the unconscious role a child will manifest, no matter how pathological it may be, is to calm and support the family system. Children's inappropriate behavior is a reflection of their parents' unresolved psycho-organic content (Bradshaw, 1996; Cummings & Davies, 2010; Poulton, 2013). The following pages provide a breakdown and analysis of various stereotypical roles.

2.4.1 The Responsible Firstborn Child

Firstborn children bear an unconscious responsibility for returning pride and dignity to the family, if it was lost, and to replace a father's absence. In many ways, these are the father's children; they carry their father's unconscious internal world, especially elements that the father may have suppressed or was unable to realize. They may have been too painful or perhaps unattainable, even shameful and non-transferrable (Bradshaw, 1996; Cummings & Davies, 2010). In this context, the transfer represents the unconscious communication that occurs between fathers and their first children. It is a highly right hemisphere-based communication, generated by projective and introjective identification. First children often represent and fulfill the role of the family hero, the child that brings pride to the family. Sometimes they take care of the family's emotional safety and functionality. By doing so they nurture their parents' dysfunctionality. For example, in a family with an alcoholic father, first children reinforce their father's addiction by taking on his responsibilities:

working and taking care of the younger children, etc. Alternatively, first children may struggle with their father to make him more responsible. They may try to protect their mother from their father's destructiveness. By taking on their father's roles and functions first children replace the father in the eyes of their siblings (Bradshaw, 1996). In essence, first children have a strong emotional connection with their father, although they do not really understand or know what to make of it. They carry their father's deepest emotions, especially those their father may have denied. These children will reenact these emotions throughout their life. By doing so, they nourish a deep internal connection with their father (Catherall, 2004; Poulton, 2013).

Stories of firstborn children are remarkable, especially in cases where the father was surreptitiously unfaithful to his partner. When they grow up, these children may marry into relationships in which their partner is unfaithful or they may be unfaithful themselves (McCormack, 2004). In this context, children reenact their father's suppressed or denied emotions through their own behavior. They feel angry and envious without knowing why, yet they deny their own emotions (MacFarlane, 2004). As adults, they may direct that anger toward their partner or recreate a condition in which they hate, scorn, and underestimate themselves, similar to how they felt in relation to their father, especially when it is difficult for them to blame their own father for his unreliability. Thus, firstborn children may begin to perceive themselves as unworthy of their father's love. The foundation for this emotion is their rage, envy, and jealousy. They are able to hold onto their father through this unworthiness, experiencing him as alive and functional. It is easier to live worthless besides a worthy father than to not have a father at all. When the firstborn child is a daughter, she often marries a man whom she continuously waits for, or allows him to do the unacceptable, just as she once did with her father. The type of man her father is provides the only model of masculinity she knows. Often, she will stick by her husband, despite all of her disappointments, because that is the only version of femininity she knows. Her relationship with her chosen man will be a reflection of her mother's relationship and feelings towards her father. And yet responsible firstborn children tend to defend their father. They have a deeper empathy for him that may be incomprehensible to the other children (Catherall, 2004; Poulton, 2013). For example, while the others may condemn their father, firstborn children tend to protect and defend him. This dynamic can lead to catastrophic events without the children knowing what happened or why.

Firstborn children often take on the role of the emotional father (or mother). For example, they will be there for their alcoholic father when he has no one else to talk to or rely on. They will try to help their neglected and emotionally unsatisfied mother (Cummings & Davies, 2010; McCormack, 2004). By doing so, first children play the role of defenders or saviors, unconsciously encouraging their father's alcoholic habit and protecting their mother from having to face a failed marriage. Consequently, the parental couple sidesteps confronting their own conflict and the problem of alcohol dependency (Bradshaw, 1996; Carlson & Sperry, 2010; McCormack, 2004). Instead, the child attempts to raise the dignity of the family by protecting them, organizing the family psycho-organic system, and eliminating catastrophic expectations and anxieties—all in an effort to keep the parents together. Responsible firstborn children usually attempt to make their siblings feel loved and cared for, and to protect them from their parents' frightening marital conflicts. In a way, the firstborn children become the father or mother figure for an emotionally distraught family, as well as the father and/or mother's emotional partner. This happens on an unconscious level in an effort to hold the family together.

The tragedy with responsible first children is that their sacrifices are often never acknowledged. No one in the system fully comprehends that they have sacrificed their childhood to keep their family together. This dynamic deeply characterizes these children's personalities. It is reflected in their future relationships, especially as regards their choice of life partner (Carlson & Sperry, 2010; Cummings & Davies, 2010; Steinberg, 2014). Perhaps this is the reason they seek out similar atmospheres as those experienced by an alcoholic father or mother in their marital and family relationships: the atmosphere feels familiar to the one mastered in childhood and so promises a sense of security.

2.4.2 The Rebellious Second-born Child

Rebel children, or the scapegoats, are usually the second-born children. In contrast to the firstborns, rebel children are much more spontaneous, emotional, creative, and capable of taking on risks. They are considered the mother's children, as they often have a unique relationship with her. They carry their mother's hidden and suppressed emotional content and hold onto her painful or non-transferable emotions, thus having the deepest understanding of her feelings. The relationship they have with their mother represents a deep and organic connection (Kim et al., 2014). They are able to feel her in subtlest organic ways (Schore, 2003, 2012). Consequently, they usually have a well-developed grasp of sympathy and gentleness, regardless of their gender. They can be attentive in unique ways and capable of stronger sensitivity towards the needs and pains of others. In extreme cases they enact their mother's aggressive elements, and the aggressive elements of the entire psycho-organic family system. They may continuously act out rebelliously, behave irresponsibly or aggressively, abuse drugs and alcohol, or become problematic at school. The spectrum and intensity of their problems depend on how traumatic the parents' marital conflict is. They also depend on how serious the pathology and aggression are. The parents often have suppressed aggressive feelings, especially the mother (Bradshaw, 1996; McCormack, 2004). By playing out the rebellious role, these children are able to maintain a certain balance within the family. In fact, the parents are then able to avoid dealing with the aggressive, anxious, catastrophic, and destructive elements in their own intrapsychic and interpersonal experience. After all, their "problematic" second-born child often keeps the parents occupied as they work together to correct their rebellious child's inappropriate behavior (Bradshaw, 1996; Cummings & Davies, 2010; Kim et al., 2014; Steinberg, 2014).

Rebellious children respond to the family system's emotional needs in a peculiar way. They try to meet everyone's needs and feel especially responsible for their mother's emotional state. The internal connection shared with their mother is unique and organically emotional. They are able to feel each other without having to openly discuss their emotional state. Second-born children will repeat their mother's behavioral patterns most accurately, even reestablishing her defense mechanisms. Later in life, they will grapple with internal problems, traumas, and conflicts the same way their mother used to. Furthermore, they are able to feel the mother's unconscious world, although they are usually unaware of it (Feinstein, 2013; McCormack, 2004). They will use these same patterns later on in life in relationships with partners or close friends. This may transpire in patterns of depression, alcoholism, or addiction to prescription drugs, and they may respond to events in an angry manner and feel constantly threatened. Or they will tend to feel as though their friend or partner is unfaithful. Envy or jealousy may erupt even when there seems to be little cause for suspicion. In sum, rebellious children will perceive others as they once did their mother. Their actions will ensure the story repeats itself as they relive their mother's unresolved emotional conflicts (Catherall, 2004; Steinberg, 2014).

Second-born children can be extremely sensitive, even when it comes to matters rarely discussed in the family. They often best voice symbolic communication. They do not handle secrets, denial, or hypocrisy very well. They want to ensure family relationships will crystallize and that family members will be able to talk openly. However, if and when they do not succeed, rebellious children use inappropriate behavior to spark painful and suppressed emotions in their father or mother. They become their parents'—especially the mother's—medium for anger, harshness, and rage and will reenact these emotions through their behavior. Furthermore, they take on other family members' feelings. Second children often have trouble differentiating between other people's emotions and their own, especially when it comes to their own intimate relationship in later life (Bradshaw, 1996; Cummings & Davies, 2010; Feinstein, 2013). They may run away from home, sending a message that it is unbearable to live in such a family. They may react angrily to the smallest provocation—and by doing so, relay the message that their family is suppressing extreme amounts of anger.

2.4.3 The Third-born Child

Third-born children are the emotional children, the offspring of the marriage itself. They are sensitive to minute emotional disturbances within a marriage. In their own specific way, they ensure peace and help their parents (as well as other family members) to find compromises. Third-born children will know how to find the right time and way to absorb marital and family conflicts. Similarly to second-born children, they may become their mother's emotional partner, especially if she lost her husband to his work, alcohol, or drug addiction (Bradshaw, 1996; Cummings & Davies, 2010; Feinstein, 2013). Their fundamental role is to reenact marital conflict. Similarly to how firstborn children carry their father's unconscious feelings and second-born children carry their mother's, third-born children represent the marital relationship. In other words, they are the mirrored reflection of the marriage itself. Their behavioral patterns indicate whether the marriage is calm and harmonious or filled with unpredictable fear and terror. They reveal whether the parents' relationship is cold or filled with frustrations. Third-born children feel the need to take care of both their parents: they acutely observe emotional dynamics in each of their parents and try their best to encourage consensus. They often suffer if their attempt at salvaging their parents' marital conflict fails (Feinstein, 2013; Poulton, 2013; J.S. Scharff & Scharff, 2014; Steinberg, 2014).

These children go out of their way to make sacrifices in order to save the parental relationship. For example, they may direct attention towards themselves if one of the parents is experiencing strong aggressive feelings. They try to absorb the parents' internal disorder and anxiety and point towards themselves in order to distract them. They may try to conceal their deeply felt emotions, although theses emotions will eventually influence their behavior (Cummings & Davies, 2010; Steinberg, 2014). Third-born children also can become scapegoats. Their parents often find a way to see them as the actual problem, without realizing that they are, in fact, only the carriers of their parents' unresolved emotions. The way these children act out in school or at home may signal painful and suppressed marital content. They will activate this content by behaving inappropriately, which is a reflection of their parents' relationship. If their cry for their parents' attention does not suffice, these children may give up or become apathetic. In many cases, their psychosomatic disorders lead to physical illness, their bodies signaling the fear, terror, anger, shame, and even disgust pervading the family. These powerful affects are difficult to resolve—for parents and especially for their children (Beilock, 2015; Feinstein, 2013).

In many cases, the emotional or marital children, like the rebellious and responsible children, have a diminished chance of developing in a healthy way. Immersed in their parents' relationship, the roles they play have absorbed them to a point where it is difficult for them find the energy and motivation to develop their own identity. Nevertheless, their main concern will always be their parents: they may be frightened to live without them and end up remaining at home. Finishing school, starting a career, and moving out may be especially difficult. They may feel lost and defeated by the world around them and this only encourages them to return or stay at home. The roles within a system, especially the marital system, reflect the powerful and organic economy of the psyche (Bradshaw, 1996; Cummings & Davies, 2010). The futures of these children are determined by their childhood experiences and their family's relational dynamics. As adults, they will choose relationships—especially intimate ones—that are similar to those they perceived while growing up in their psycho-organic family of origin. In doing so, they continuously relive the most complicated aspects of the family drama (Carlson & Sperry, 2010; Cummings & Davies, 2010; Robins, 2010; Steinberg, 2014).

2.4.4 The Fourth-born Child

Fourth-born children are family children, whose main concern will always be their family. As with most children, fourth-born ones are willing to do anything to keep their family together. Fourth children are often perceived as the family's clown, bringing happiness, levity, and laughter to the family (Bradshaw, 1996; Cummings & Davies, 2010). Fourth children try to minimize tension, distress, sadness, and anxiety in the marital and family psycho-organic system as a whole. They try to take care of the entire family in order to maintain its unity. They feel as though bringing harmony and peace to the family is their job (Feinstein, 2013). Furthermore, they feel as though they have failed whenever the family experiences disorder, pain, or discord. In order to maintain balance, their goal will always be to bring positive spirit to a disrupted family. They try to deter the family from catastrophic expectations and fantasies that may cause anxiety. Families are often grateful for how fourth-born children bring new, fresh, and playful elements into a conflicted family system (Bradshaw, 1996; Cummings & Davies, 2010). Although these children may not directly experience uneasiness or disorder, they will convey it in their future relationships, particularly intimate ones (Robins, 2010; Steinberg, 2014).

If a family has fewer than four children, these children (or child) will take on a larger role. In such cases, children will unconsciously aspire to preserve the family, no matter how pathological it is. All children directly carry and often maintain their parents' unresolved affects and psycho-organic content. Children absorb this content by means of projective and introjective identification and right hemisphere communication. From a strictly systemic point of view, one could argue that children may contribute to creating negative feedback. By approaching a certain level of behavioral deviation they, in fact, receive positive feedback that encourages them to overstep the boundaries of acceptable behavior. Children often use different ways to bring peace and balance to the family. They might try to provoke negative feedback in order to redefine boundaries of acceptable deviation. In this respect, children take on a heroic role. They might actively interfere while their parents are arguing and try to convince each parent to make peace with the other. It is also very common for children in these cases to misbehave, despite negative consequences. They may also develop health issues or psychosomatic symptoms (Bradshaw, 1996; Catherall, 2004; Cummings & Davies, 2010; Feinstein, 2013; MacFarlane, 2004).

2.4.5 The Fifth-born Child

Fifth-born children are similar to firstborn children in many ways. The role of the firstborn is repeated with the fifth. Similar to a firstborn child, the fifth child ends up taking care of the father. If the fifth child is a girl, she becomes the princess of the family, her father's emotional partner. In this case, the daughter becomes her father's emotional wife. (However, this is not always the case. If the child is a firstborn and only child, he or she becomes the "family miracle," especially if the parents have wanted a child for a long time.) Fifth-born children are often freed of having to assume heavy emotional roles. They may take on their father's unresolved feelings after the other children have become preoccupied with other roles to maintain the system. This occurs especially if the mother is emotionally cold, unapproachable, or depressed, filled with tension and anxiety, or harbors a catastrophic fear of intimacy that may also mark the father as well, and causes the couple to avoid each other (Bradshaw, 1988; Catherall, 2004; Feinstein, 2013; McCormack, 2004). In these cases, fifth-born daughters receive special attention from their fathers who make them feel extremely important up until their adolescent years. The father must withdraw at this point in order to avoid feeling any sexual attraction to his own daughter (Cummings & Davies, 2010; McCormack, 2004), who then suffers her own type of catastrophe: she suddenly feels rejected and abandoned by her own father. These feelings have the power to deeply affect her and will likely manifest in the type of partner she chooses in the future. Often it will be a man who takes advantage of her or abandons her (Poulton, 2013).

Children from conflicted families and marital systems suffer negative consequences because of the roles they have assumed. When a child takes on the "princess" role, she will be prone to feelings of abandonment and their repetition in later relationships. Men may see great emotional potential in her and feel extremely comfortable around her. However, they will likely fear intimacy and close attachment, and will repeatedly back away, leaving her alone and deeply hurt. This will close the circle and return her to her loving relationship with her father, who ultimately made her feeling abandoned (Bradshaw, 1996; Catherall, 2004; Cummings & Davies, 2010; MacFarlane, 2004; McCormack, 2004). The "princess" role can be adopted by any of the children, although it is usually the fifth child. Even though the second-born child has a deeper connection with the mother, the fifth-born can become the "princess," especially if her father feels his role is unnecessary. Often in these cases, the father is struggling with feeling uncomfortable or incapable of emotionally unifying his family. His daughter then becomes his emotional partner with whom he forms a special, loving relationship that could significantly affect later her choice of a future partner (Feinstein, 2013; Poulton).

2.4.6 The Sixth-born Child

Sixth-born children are considered the loved ones and often the lost ones. They usually cause very little trouble; they are loving, sensitive, and accommodating. They are often the mother's children, as are second-born children. Their close connection with their mother drives them to comfort and console her after all the older children have left home. Sixth-born children are often favored by the entire family system for providing comfort to their parents in need, sickness, and other troubles in their old age. The connection that forms between sixth born children and their mothers is deep-rooted and earnest, as the mother may be much more available than she was for her older children. Furthermore, a mother may be more attentive and loving towards her sixth-born child's children—she may give in and spoil these grandchildren in a special way. In a healthy family, older siblings will appreciate the care sixth-born children offer their mother. However, this special relationship may cause older children to feel angry or envious in a family without a healthy balance. Their anger will cause an upheaval of family conflict, especially if both parents, due to their own unresolved problems, expressing a deeper attachment towards the sixth-born child (Berman, 2014; Bradshaw, 1996; Catherall, 2004).

Sixth-born children can easily become lost, especially when they carry deep and hurtful projections of unresolved parental conflicts. These may often directly relate to the specific child—perhaps the child was unplanned, or from an unfaithful marriage, or even from a newly made promise to stay faithful (Berman, 2014; Bradshaw, 1996; McCormack, 2004). These children may be emotionally neglected and feel unloved, unworthy, unvalued, and inwardly depleted. They may become addicted to food or other substances as a substitute for feeling loved, desired, wanted, and that they belong. As adults, these children may develop partnerships in which they will feel neglected or they may neglect their partners. By doing so, they will express the deepest emotions that have been cultivated since childhood but never resolved. They will continuously enact these issues through their behavior, emotions, and cognitive processes in later life (Feinstein, 2013; Poulton, 2013; Steinberg, 2014).

2.4.7 The Youngest Child

In most cases, youngest children are the spoiled ones. They receive the most love and compassion from all family members. Naturally, children adopt multiple family roles if they are an only child in the family. The specific roles they take on will depend on what the family needs to become stable and balanced. Otherwise, youngest children will hold a special spot in their family in which others satisfy their needs. They will find the same position in social situations (Bradshaw, 1996; Cummings & Davies, 2010; Feinstein, 2013). Their life goals and choices in intimate partners will align with it as well. Parents can become very attached to their youngest children, and may have trouble letting go. In contrast, they will have encouraged older children to leave home sooner. Youngest children frequently become prisoners of their parents' unresolved affective content, although other children can take on portions of that burden as well. Youngest children are often their parents' last chance to hold onto this affective content, so it can prove especially difficult for the parents to let go. The urge to spoil and protect last children in a dysfunctional way is powerful, for if they leave, their parents usually unconsciously fear they will lose an exceptional regulator for their unresolved affects (Berman, 2014).

In sum, multiple researchers (Beilock, 2015; Bradshaw, 1996; Catherall, 2004; Cummings & Davies, 2010; Feinstein, 2013; Kim et al., 2014; MacFarlane, 2004; McCormack, 2004; Robins, 2010; Schore, 2003, 2012; Steinberg, 2014) have concluded that children intuitively understand their parents' affective-organic struggles and conflicts. This occurs especially in closed families, and families with undefined boundaries, as well as in those with unresolved conflict and negative consequences, including catastrophic expectations and anxiety. Children are well aware of frightening or threatening elements in their family system, and will do anything to preserve the balance (Bradshaw, 1996). They will take unresolved content upon themselves, incorporating it into their mental and organic structures, and it will make an impact upon them and reflect in their future friendships and intimate relationships (Bruschweiler-Stern et al., 2010; Carlson & Sperry, 2010; Fosha, 2009; Maroda, 2010). Children are quick to learn where their place lies within a family and what they must do to keep the system from falling apart. The mechanism of projective and introjective identification causes them to unconsciously engage in reciprocal feedback with the family system. The feedback conveys information on how important it is to adapt or accept certain modes of behavior. It also introduces children to various rules and roles they may have to assume in order to prevent the family psycho-organic system from dissolving.

Children innately feel that preserving the family psycho-organic system is a matter of survival. Using projective and introjective identification and repetition compulsion, they internalize the family scenario, including its conflicts and traumas. They try to minimize anxieties and negative powers within the family and block catastrophic expectations. By enacting certain roles, children maintain the balance within the family scenario, and it becomes their reference for relational experience, influencing the way they perceive and behave in future relationships. When presented with a similar experience in the future, they will always turn to what they learned through the scenarios in their family of origin. They will react and behave in ways similar to their early childhood roles. Thus they will reenact the core affects experienced in their original family setting. These core experiences characterize children's development, including their lifestyle, and how they will form their own families. In sum, children will always follow the guidelines they learned early in their past. These guidelines will manifest in their awareness, emotions, mindset, and behaviors (Feinstein, 2013; Steinberg, 2014).

2.5 The Deviation Level of a Family System

All family psycho-organic systems are able to change to a certain degree. These changes occur based on feedback (Catherall, 2004; Pinsof, 1995; Pinsof & Lebow, 2005). Feedback encompasses communication paths within a family system, enabling emotions to move around and transfer between subsystems. They can regulate the degree to which change occurs within the system. Emotions cross boundaries and give signals to individual members within specific subsystems. They measure the level of deviation, differences, and ability to adapt—all based on the goals and intentions of the system as a whole (Bitter, 2014; Gehart, 2016; MacFarlane, 2004; Umbarger, 1983). Communication paths enable affects to travel from the intrapsychic to the interpersonal level of experience, and then to the systemic level. Ultimately, affects make their way back to the intrapsychic level. They form the essential emotional dynamic of the system as a whole. Systems are constantly adapting their systemic needs to their surroundings (Catherall, 2004). The essential outline of the psycho-organic system refers to its goals (and the way it adapts to its surroundings), its core affects, and the style of continuous transference between the system and its surroundings. The entire family psycho-organic system strives to become balanced and achieve systemic homeostasis. This creates the pathways for how affect is regulated and how it guides the family system through its psycho-organic content (Schore, 2003, 2012; Siegel & Solomon, 2013).

These specifics must become a part of the system as a whole, including the subsystems that process information and respond to it in a certain way regardless of its adaptation to any given context (MacFarlane, 2004; Pinsof, 1995; Umbarger, 1983; White et al., 2015). Information and affects are constantly passing through the boundaries between different yet interdependent subsystems. We are only able to fully understand this complex dynamic through the relational concepts of projective and introjective identification and repetition compulsion. They establish the affective psychic construct and continuously work towards maintaining it. For example, when a couple is planning to have a child, they prepare in advance—and so does the family system as a whole. It undergoes continuous adaptation, including when children leave for school, and as they grow up to leave their family. Certain events may take place and change the family dynamic even more drastically. For example, if the parents separate, the entire family must adapt to the new circumstances: living without one of the parents, or in a completely new environment. All members must adjust to losing the safety they had previously known. Family members might need to become accustomed to a new member as one or both parents join with new partners. If one of the parents or children dies, the family has to adjust to an irreversible loss. Another example that demands adaptation is when one of the parents loses a job or falls ill. Changes like these will always turn the rhythm and relationships in a family upside down. Not only does the family need to adapt to changes, but they must also reestablish systemic balance and homeostasis (J.S. Scharff & Scharff, 2014).

The flow of information and energy within a system is organized through two essential feedback loops: one loop encourages and maintains stability and homeostasis within the psycho-organic system or affective psychic construct, and the other loop accelerates and encourages growth and change within the system (and consequently the dismantling of an established mental construct). The concept of positive and negative feedback is the foundation for the structure of systemic rules. It represents the essential mechanism of systemic organization, guidelines, and function (Catherall, 2004; Pinsof, 1995; Pinsof & Lebow, 2005; Umbarger, 1983). However, we have yet to define the systemic force that encourages and organizes how positive and negative feedback operate. In other words: what is the fundamental operating mechanism that enables positive and negative feedback to take effect? The answer lies in an unconscious affective dynamic and can be understood by applying the relational mechanism of projective and introjective identification (J.S. Scharff & Scharff, 2014). The systemic mechanism of projective and introjective identification is a new model and concept, applicable to the family psycho-organic system and its unique dynamics.

The family system and the "systemic self" both function as projective and introjective mechanisms. They organize systemic organic structure and the relationships in the system through positive and negative feedback. They arrange complex communications and interactions in the intrapsychic, interpersonal, and systemic spheres. The family system is more than just a unit of interpersonal and multi-personal relationships. It is a model of systemic integrity, in which these relationships form a specific systemic structure. The complex interaction that takes place during right hemisphere communications is what regulates this structure. Dynamic processes, including projection, coercion, introjective identification, and transforming the other, play an important role in the family and create roles for identified patients. These processes repeat compulsively, thus reinforcing systemic homeostasis. They establish affect regulation and the affective psychic construct. The main difference between the two is in the system's dynamics: the sender is the system itself, while the recipients are family members.

The dynamic of systemic balance is the main factor encouraging and organizing interpersonal relationships. Systemic balance is, in fact, the fundamental systemic principle and condition, while projective and introjective identification maintains and coordinates it. Positive and negative feedback function as warning instruments: they define whether the system is durable and homeostatic, and they secure stability and the affective psychic construct, and consequently also systemic balance. Each individual relationship is shaped by a core affect and dynamics determined by systemic coherence. In this respect, the system is determined by more than just interpersonal or multi-personal projective and introjective identification. Mechanisms of feedback and projective and introjective identification interact and determine each other's existence. They create and nurture the system's structure, based on the relational mechanism of repetition compulsion.

Compulsively repeating roles and rules within the system substantiates positive and negative feedback and determines the extent to which the system is able to adapt to its surroundings. Information and energy travel in a way that enables a relatively balanced functionality. This balance is defined as homeostasis or repetition compulsion of specific affects, such as ways of thinking and functioning, which creates the affective psychic construct. The compulsive reiteration of certain patterns keeps the system intact. This steadiness is necessary for the system to function efficiently, and minimizes unnecessary stress within its component parts (McCormack, 2004; Pinsof, 1995; Pinsof & Lebow, 2005; Umbarger, 1983). Feedback loops are also known as reinforcing and balancing loops, and they encourage balance through systemic projective and introjective identification. The function of feedback is therefore to preserve consistency and a relative state of equilibrium on intrapsychic, interpersonal, and systemic levels. A formal term for this process is negative feedback, which bespeaks loops that oppose deviation (Bitter, 2014; Feldman & Pinsof, 1982; Gehart, 2016; Pinsof, 1995; Pinsof & Lebow, 2005). Its main function is to maintain stability within the family psycho-organic system.

When the level of behavioral deviation within a system becomes apparent, it causes a chain of reactions: the operational mechanism of projective and introjective identification returns the behavior pattern to its original state, which is more acceptable within the family psycho-organic system in question, being in line with the predominant systemic outline (Feldman & Pinsof, 1982; Pinsof, 1995; Pinsof & Lebow, 2005; White et al., 2015). For example, if adolescents overstep the acceptable boundaries with inappropriate behavior, their parents set restrictions. The limits of what is considered acceptable are different for each family system; some parents may ground their children, others may demand different behavior or obedience, or implement more rigorous expectations. This plays into the principles of homeostasis and the repetition compulsion of established patterns of acceptable mindsets, emotions, and behavior. It determines the affective psychic construct and affect regulation system. Nonetheless, every living system is in a constant state of dynamic tension, as it continuously grows and evolves.

What is at issue here is the tension between stability and growth, which can bring either relief or pain (Bitter, 2014; Catherall, 2004; MacFarlane, 2004; Pinsof, 1995; Umbarger, 1983). This dynamic tension transpires on the intrapsychic, interpersonal, and systemic levels. Each family system, including all interpersonal relationships and intrapsychic circles within it, has the ability and capacity to grow. Projective and introjective identification enables the system to redesign its foundation by redefining and adapting to the specific needs of individual members. While these needs are not intended to threaten the system's equilibrium, they do force the system to adapt to the pressure of change in the environment. Positive feedback enhancing growth and change feeds a reinforcing feedback loop. It propels the development of deviation and difference, creating new modes of behavior. The formal term for this is positive feedback or positive loop gain deviation (Feldman & Pinsof, 1982; Pinsof, 1995; Pinsof & Lebow, 2005).

When a new type or sequence of behavior, emotional reaction, or mindset occurs—both on an interpersonal and intrapsychic level—other members of the system react in ways that ensure the existence of these changes. The enabling mechanism is systemic introjective identification. A living system must continuously grow and evolve, albeit in a way that enables it to remain relatively the same. Therefore, changes will occur gradually in different stages, thus giving the family the reassuring sense that the system remains the same. A healthy family presents itself as comfortably conservative and constant, while promoting appropriate growth and development in its subsystems (Catherall, 2004; Gehart, 2016; MacFarlane, 2004; McCormack, 2004; Umbarger, 1983). After all, the family is a dynamic, organic, and social-emotive system. It functions based on interpersonal relationships and their codependence. Positive and negative feedback coordinate family relationships and roles through systemic projective and introjective identification. Both positive and negative feedback preserve emotional equilibrium in the family and function as the emotional thermostat. They maintain family stability and functionality. Both types of feedback are rooted in specific family rules, roles, and values. These can change to a certain degree until change becomes a threat to the system's stability. On an unconscious level, the deviation of these rules, roles, and values is very strictly defined (Pinsof, 1995; Pinsof & Lebow, 2005; White et al., 2015).

Families either openly express their principles or try to conceal them—often for unknown reasons or without a rational explanation. Either way, family principles are an important unconscious factor in balancing the system. The dynamics organizing family systems, such as rules and feedback, and the maintenance of systemic psycho-organic equilibrium, are often referred to as relational responses or compromises that determine and limit the behavior of family members (Catherall, 2004; Pinsof, 1995; Pinsof & Lebow, 2005). They are largely unconscious. When they become a conscious factor, they are a measure of family systemic behavior. They define the quality, quantity, type, and level of acceptable behavior, which then undergoes the process of repetition compulsion. Once a group or individual family member's behavior oversteps the acceptable level of deviation, it triggers the mechanism of negative feedback to direct the family system back towards its permissive deviational limit and stability. The capacity of family systems to preserve themselves within the structure of their own rules makes them homeostatic (Bradshaw, 1996; MacFarlane, 2004; Pinsof, 1995; Pinsof & Lebow, 2005).

To conclude, it is through compulsive repetition of accustomed states that psycho-organic family systems are able to maintain homeostasis. In other words, they are self-organizing systems. Negative feedback is the instrument that helps family systems maintain homeostasis (Feldman & Pinsof, 1982; Pinsof, 1995; Pinsof & Lebow, 2005). It helps preserve specifically determined specters or deviational levels of change, which are established through the organic right hemisphere communication between family members. In contrast, positive feedback activates constructive deviation. It leads towards growth, development, and adaptation to change. However, when the deviation is destructive, positive feedback can escalate to the point where the system collapses completely or ends up in a state of systemic flight (Feldman & Pinsof, 1982; Pinsof, 1995; Pinsof & Lebow, 2005). This can occur in many situations, including when parents separate or one of the children runs away. More examples include dysfunctional behaviors, such as emotional, physical, or sexual abuse. Both positive and negative feedback play an important role in maintaining the family's affective psychic construct and managing problematic behaviors. Problems and conflicts occur when a family's negative feedback models are blocked or maladjusted—especially since negative feedback is what creates homeostasis through projective and introjective identification (J.S. Scharff & Scharff, 2014) or right hemisphere communication. Family members fear, whether on a conscious or unconscious level, destructive elements of positive feedback, which can lead to systemic flight.

2.6 The Cybernetic Model

According to the cybernetic model, problematic and symptomatic behavior is considered an alteration of natural deviations. It defines deviations on the generally accepted "rules of balanced homeostasis" (Catherall, 2004; Feldman & Pinsof, 1982; Pinsof, 1995; Pinsof & Lebow, 2005), which refer to individuals' intrapsychic or interpersonal deviations that manifest through their parents' unresolved and painful content (McCormack, 2004; Poulton, 2013). Once a problematic behavior has been identified, the mutually caused spiral of positive feedback amplifies in strength and frequency. The spiral materializes through the unconscious relational mechanism of projective and introjective identification. Once it crosses the boundaries of a family's homeostasis, it triggers the system to try and repair internal problematic behaviors (Catherall, 2004; Pinsof, 1995; Pinsof & Lebow, 2005). In time, the problematic behavior will decrease. For example, a hardworking father may choose to start coming home earlier to help his wife take care of their problematic children. However, problematic behavior will reoccur once the behavior oversteps the boundaries of the system's homeostasis. This may be the onset of a vicious cycle. In time, the father may begin to feel stifled and start increasing his workload, coming home late once again. This can re-trigger the child's problematic behavior. The wife may then threaten her husband with a divorce, which will force him to stay at home more often.

The cybernetic model helps us understand why the following three patterns occur within the family system (Pinsof, 1995; Pinsof & Lebow, 2005):

2.6.1. Children develop an ongoing and increasing display of symptomatic behavior on the intrapsychic and interpersonal level when their parents' conflict rises to a tipping point (Pinsof, 1995; Pinsof & Lebow, 2005).

Children then internalize their parents' conflict through the relational mechanism of projective and introjective identification and begin to behave inappropriately. The parents have to join forces to focus on helping their children, hence being deterred from their own conflict (Carlson & Sperry, 2010).

2.6.2. When the less symptomatic of two partners begins responding with symptomatic behavior or conflict, the children's symptomatic behavior reactivates and increases (Cummings & Davies, 2010; Pinsof, 1995; Pinsof & Lebow, 2005). The child might calm down temporarily, but this will cause the parental conflict to flare up once again. In other words, conflict will pass from an intrapsychic to interpersonal level by means of projective and introjective identification. In some cases, this behavior will move on to the next child.

2.6.3. Family and marital conflict regenerates and escalates when the intimacy between partners deepens (Cummings & Davies, 2010; Feldman & Pinsof, 1982; Pinsof, 1995; Pinsof & Lebow, 2005). For example, parents will become more open and then begin to fear this closeness if they are vulnerable from previous conflicts. If intimacy frightens them, they must tread lightly. This leads to disagreements on how to raise their child(ren) or to new marital conflicts, all in response to the fear of becoming too close and vulnerable on the interpersonal level. At this point, children will have interfered in the relationship as saviors or scapegoats. Once again, they begin to act out. This process transpires through projective and introjective identification, which continuously transmits unresolved or painful mental content from one system to another, hence regulating systemic equilibrium.

The principle of mutual reciprocity is particularly noteworthy. It hypothesizes that family members influence others through projective and introjective identification and are, in return, influenced upon by others. This is especially evident in a marital conflict where both parties manage and guide each other and their mutual interests (Cummings & Davies, 2010; Gehart, 2016; Pinsof, 1995; Pinsof & Lebow, 2005). A similar situation occurs in a psycho-organic family with a symptomatic child. The mutual and unconscious goal is to maintain a homeostatic level of behavior, which through repetition compulsion reestablishes equilibrium in the marital and family system. Family rules guide and direct the behavior within a psycho-organic family system and define the level of homeostasis. The most important family rules organize the quality and quantity of constructive and symptomatic behavior of any given family member. The quality and extent of conflict and intimacy in the family as a system, or in one subsystem, are also of significance (Feldman & Pinsof, 1982; Pinsof, 1995; Pinsof & Lebow, 2005). Every family system allows only a certain level of intimacy or closeness between individual members, and this determines how affect gets regulated. As core affects mark our mental structures during childhood, projective and introjective identification will facilitate conflict when family members get too close (J.S. Scharff & Scharff, 2014).

Emotions spill over and spread among members of the family psycho-organic system, who split them off and maintain them at a safe and tolerable distance. This distance corresponds to the level of internal tension or anxiety within an interpersonal or intrapsychic subsystem, and it marks the generation of a binding affective psychic construct. The construct comprises affective, cognitive, behavioral, and organic components, which jointly interact in a powerful and complex way. The dynamic of yearning for closeness and intimacy plays a similar role. It brings family members closer and connects them. However, this only happens to a certain degree in accordance with the existing fear of vulnerability (Cummings & Davies, 2010; Robins, 2010). At a certain point, the affective psychic construct must reestablish itself, and this may cause pathologic relationships. The family psycho-organic system will try its best to maintain these, in order to keep its balance and preserve relationships, however painful or destructive they may be.

The dynamic of catastrophic expectations and anxiety plays an important role on both intrapsychic and interpersonal levels within the psycho-organic family system (MacFarlane, 2004; Pinsof, 1995; Pinsof & Lebow, 2005). Catastrophic expectations are visions of frightening thoughts, feelings, or behaviors, and their catastrophic consequences. They can be a product of individuals or even entire groups (Feldman & Pinsof, 1982; Pinsof, 1995; Pinsof & Lebow, 2005). Such expectations can be both conscious and unconscious, and can affect everyone in the system or just one individual. For example, a child may think along these lines: "If my mother and father get in a fight, they may hurt each other, and possibly divorce. Or one of them may leave." Two more examples are the following trains of thought: "If one of my family members becomes too frustrated, confused, or depressed, they may neglect or leave us, or end up in treatment." Or: "If we grow too close to each other, we might lose our sense of self and have to leave." These kinds of expectations arise from how we interpret our family systems and especially from our childhood experiences. These experiences are passed on through mechanisms of repetition compulsion and projective and introjective identification, which also generate the affective psychic construct. In fact, anxiety and catastrophic expectations are the foundation of the affective psychic construct and establish how affect gets regulated. This type of regulation then further influences interpersonal and systemic relations (Pinsof, 1995; Pinsof & Lebow, 2005; Poulton, 2013).

The emotional and physiological reaction to catastrophic expectation manifests through anxiety, internal distress, extreme fear, and tension. People will unconsciously re-experience danger, which serves as a warning, signaling a forthcoming collapse or catastrophe (Feldman & Pinsof, 1982; Pinsof, 1995; Pinsof & Lebow, 2005). Anxiety will trigger psychobiologic defense mechanisms, sympathetic, and parasympathetic systems, and dissociation connected to projective and introjective identification. Defense mechanisms can thus protect a psycho-organic family system from painful affects. For example, they can shield a parent from having to deal with hurtful content. However, this content will be transferred to another family member through projective and introjective identification, thus activating feelings of anxiety. The problematic behavior displayed by one of the family members is a defense reaction to the catastrophic expectations and anxiety of others (Cummings & Davies, 2010; Pinsof, 1995; Pinsof & Lebow, 2005; Schore, 1994, 2012).

Problematic behavior will prompt a range of reactions from other family members, whether they are symptomatic or not. Intrapsychic disorders of one individual will always trigger a response on the interpersonal and systemic levels. On one hand, this lessens the impact of catastrophic expectations and anxiety, provoked by constructive behavior. On the other hand, the same behavior may prompt a new level of anxiety and catastrophic behavior in other family members through projective and introjective identification, and this causes the others to react defensively. An increasing spiral of anxiety and defense mechanisms begins to form. This is also known as the spiral of positive feedback (Cummings & Davies, 2010; Feldman & Pinsof, 1982; Pinsof, 1995; Pinsof & Lebow, 2005). In time, the level of symptomatic behavior will transgress the system's acceptable or tolerable levels of deviation. Anxiety will then settle upon all family members. These internal reactions will directly or indirectly encourage constructive behavior, which serves as negative feedback. It helps reestablish systemic balance. The individual will try to solve the system's complications by behaving in a non-problematic manner. This process will repeat until symptomatic behavior once again oversteps the acceptable deviational levels. Hence the new cycle begins to unravel.

Both types of interpersonal feedback are encouraged by and conducted through systemic projective and introjective identification, and both are based on intrapsychic reactions to catastrophic expectations and anxiety. The intrapsychic, interpersonal, and systemic dynamics of family relations all play important roles. They determine the acceptable deviational levels of change. The sympathetic and parasympathetic organic-neurological systems translate catastrophic expectations and anxiety into bodily affliction. In other words, the process of homeostasis unfolds together with the psychological, which is also psycho-organic mechanism of projective and introjective identification, which transfers dissociated content to other family members (Schore, 2003, 2012). By doing so, it secures relational patterns and enables them to create systemic structure. This structure is actually the affective psychic construct, which forms relatively stable relationships within subsystems. The models and connections between family members, which create structure, become the essential regulator that conducts the daily flow of information and emotional energy of the family (Cummings & Davies, 2010; Pinsof, 1995; Pinsof & Lebow, 2005; Umbarger, 1983). Thus, structure does not refer to static interpersonal exchange; rather, it is a metaphor for how behavior is repetitively exchanged. According to Minuchin (Minuchin & Fishman, 1981), structure also can refer to an invisible set of functional demands that organizes relational patterns between family members.

2.7 Systemic Needs

All social systems, including the system of a family, have certain needs that dictate whether it is open or closed. These are the deep intrapsychic organic needs of each individual system. All families have specific priorities and values. In order to maintain balance, lessen anxiety, eliminate catastrophic expectations, and create the affective psychic construct, family psycho-organic systems establish rules and roles through right hemisphere communication and projective and introjective identification. In line with its interpersonal, intrapsychic, and systemic structure, each family expresses the need for safety, self-value, productivity, intimacy, relationships, connection, belonging, challenge, acceptance, and spirituality (Blatt & Layton, 2009; Bradshaw, 1996). A functional family also requires a hierarchy and appropriate boundaries between its subsystems. Coalitions and triangles—and also identified patients protecting their family—will emerge whenever families lack distinctive hierarchy and boundaries. Functional families are relatively open and flexible systems, infused with spontaneity, creativity, and healthy vitality. They are continuously moving entities and have flexible rules and roles. The boundaries between subsystems—such as marital and children's subsystems—are structured based on functionality. The boundaries in open systems are permeable, operational, and functional (Cummings & Davies, 2010; Minuchin & Fishman, 1981). The flow of content between intrapsychic, interpersonal, and systemic levels is unimpeded and relaxed.

In dysfunctional systems the family's needs are very different. These types of systems are generally more closed, inflexible, and rigid. Their rules and roles are fixed. The boundaries between their subsystems and surroundings are strictly predetermined. In such systems, family members do not share their emotions, beliefs, or mindsets. The flow of emotions between the intrapsychic and interpersonal levels is hindered, although it may occur more efficiently on the unconscious level. Sometimes these boundaries are only systemic and there are no boundaries between subsystems. In such systems, everything is in flux. All members know everything about the others, but none of this information crosses the system boundaries into the outside world (Cummings & Davies, 2010; Pinsof, 1995; Pinsof & Lebow, 2005; Umbarger, 1983). Negative feedback is what prevents closed systems from changing, keeping them ossified through projective and introjective identification. Affects in a closed system propel repetition compulsion within its subsystems through projective and introjective identification, creating the affective psychic construct, and providing a way to explain the complexity of family dynamics (J.S. Scharff & Scharff, 2014). The tension, conflict, and disturbance within a family is transferred onto the children's intrapsychic world, rendering these children carriers of their family's conflict and trauma (Catherall, 2004; Schore, 2010).

Each family needs a healthy relationship between the father and mother in order to function well. If their relationship is not healthy or fully functional, systemic needs will be transferred onto their children through projective and introjective identification, thus forcing the children to act out certain roles to keep the family intact (J.S. Scharff & Scharff, 2014). They may assume roles as emotional fathers or mothers to their dependent siblings, or as emotional partners to one of their parents. Either way, their purpose will be to nurture love, protection, and safety in their family by adjusting their behavioral model to fit their family's needs, and taking over functions of the marital subsystem. Children learn quickly what they are allowed to say, think, feel, and want, as well as what they must keep to themselves. They learn what behavioral models are acceptable, and what roles need to be fulfilled in order to maintain equilibrium in the psycho-organic family system (Bradshaw, 1996; Cummings & Davies, 2010; McCormack, 2004; Pinsof, 1995; Pinsof & Lebow, 2005).

Based on projective and introjective identification, children develop specific mechanisms of perceiving, feeling, thinking, explaining, judging, functioning, and understanding. These shape how they view their world, organize it, and find meaning within it. Their mechanisms mold the way they react to challenges and look for them—all in accordance with their family's views (J.S. Scharff & Scharff, 2014). Children take on more roles in families struggling with marital conflicts or alcohol and drug addiction, brutality, rage, envy, depression, and other emotional and mental disorders (Bradshaw, 1996; MacFarlane, 2004; Poulton, 2013). The mechanism of projective and introjective identification facilitates the formation of roles, pushing children to carry family disturbances in order to generate family balance and security, When the affective psychic construct in marital or parental subsystems is unbalanced, families become dysfunctional. In order to restore equilibrium, marital subsystems unconsciously incorporate children's subsystems, which are intrapsychic organic systems forced to absorb unresolved, painful mental content from parental subsystems. They learn to adjust for the sake of survival. After all, the need to maintain a relationship with your parents is, in fact, stronger and more compelling than an individual's personal growth (Bitter, 2014; Bradshaw, 1996; Catherall, 2004; Cummings & Davies, 2010; Pinsof, 1995; Pinsof & Lebow, 2005).

The most traumatic human dynamics take place on the intrapsychic, interpersonal, and systemic levels in the psycho-organic family system. They materialize through positive and negative feedback, projective and introjective identification, and right hemisphere communication. These are the psycho-organic family dynamics that establish affect regulation. Because families are the most important factor in human development, family crises become crises of individual development as well. Families can reach points of crisis because traumatic and depressive patterns of thought and emotions repeat and pass onto children through generations (Bradshaw, 1996; Cummings & Davies, 2010). This is a characteristic of dysfunctional families. It manifests through marital or parental subsystems that disregard conflict or those that express it outwardly to an excessive degree. The atmosphere of conflict and anxiety will always be transferred to the children, whether directly or indirectly, through projective and introjective identification. It is, in fact, the parents who create and determine the rules and roles in the family through their own unresolved trauma, conflicts, disappointments, and misunderstandings. The children unconsciously become carriers of their parents' conflicts (Catherall, 2004; Cummings & Davies, 2010; MacFarlane, 2004).

The following changes occur in the way dysfunctional families perceive and portray ideas (Bitter, 2014; Bradshaw, 1996; Gehart, 2016):

a) "See and hear whatever you see and hear" becomes "see and hear what you are supposed to see and hear";
b) "Think whatever you think" becomes "think what you are supposed to think";
c) "Feel whatever you feel" becomes "feel what you are supposed to pretend to feel";

d) "Want and desire whatever you want and desire" becomes "want and desire what you are supposed to want and desire";
e) "Imagine, explain, and realize who you are" becomes "Imagine, explain, and realize what other people want you to be" (Bradshaw, 1996).

These modified phrases can have catastrophic consequences in children's lives: they will grow up not realizing that these modifications have created a deep emotional divide in them. They will never know what they truly want, feel, or think. They may lose their fundamental connection to the self, which can cause complete emotional absence or "emotional death." In this respect, parents can be considered the "assassins" of their children's souls, as children become the property of their parents' unresolved conflict (Cummings & Davies, 2010).

In the final part of the chapter, we will take a closer look at family therapy and the paradigms of relational family theory, using a therapeutic example that illustrates how a therapist approaches the issue of drug abuse. According to the relational family therapy model, drug abuse is a cry for help in resolving painful relationships. It is a symptom of dysfunctional and complex relationships in the family. We present the second therapeutic session with a family of four: the father Peter (P), the mother Martha (M), the 16-year-old daughter Natalie (N), and her 15-year-old brother Alex (A). Both children are in high school where they are exposed to alcohol and drugs. When the mother called to schedule a therapy session, she stated that both children had been caught smoking marijuana, although the school failed to provide any proof. She then discovered some marijuana at home and chose to seek therapeutic help.

During the first session, the group agreed that it would be important for the father to spend more time at home to help ensure that there were no more drugs in their house and the children would no longer be abusing them. In addition, it was decided that he would communicate with the school on a regular basis to make sure the kids were clean, and attending school and extracurricular activities as required. The two children had admitted to skipping class so they could go outside and smoke marijuana in a park. They had both assured their parents this had only happened once or twice in the past six months. During the session it was agreed that their father would regularly verify the children's grades, observe their behavior, who they socialized with after school, and when they left and returned home. The group decided that this regime should continue until both parents felt they could completely trust their children.

Natalie and Alex were forced to accept these new regulations, albeit with much anger and disapproval; both believed that smoking marijuana was not that big of a deal. The therapist addressed this issue in their first session and began working with them to resolve it. The adults gave the children full responsibility for their own actions and the consequences that followed. The parents agreed that the father would be the one in control until they were able to prove themselves responsible. Until that point, the father had rarely participated in raising his children. The therapist informed the parents that drug abuse is often a consequence of a father's absence and that he should become more engaged. The father was unable to fully understand how the two were connected, but he accepted his new role, agreeing to become more involved so they could resolve the problem.

T *(feeling pressure in her throat)*: Hello. How was this past week? How did you do?

M *(uneasily):* Well, I think something has started to change, although I'm not sure what. We were all on edge as though there was something threatening in the air. We checked on the kids a lot this week even though they resisted it.

T *(feeling the transfer of anxiety)*: Can you tell me more about this?

M *(more calmly)*: I'm not quite sure what to call it. I care, and I'm not sure what to do to make it better. I'm not sure if they smoked this week.

T *(still feeling pressure in her throat)*: What are you feeling?

M *(sadly)*: Well, I feel horrible and powerless, and afraid because I have no power in all of this.

T *(feeling the distress coming from the husband)*: Peter, what about you? What are you thinking?

P *(nervously)*: I don't know if that would help . . .

T *(feeling tension in her shoulders)*: But what do you feel?

P *(uneasily)*: Well, it's like Martha said. Of course, I care too. They haven't smoked any marijuana. I know because I didn't even give them any opportunity and if I suspected something, I would have become even more controlling and imposed an even stronger regime.

T *(feeling the father's anger)*: If I understand correctly, you've all tried your best. What do you feel now? What sort of feelings do you have when you think about your children and their problem with drugs?

P *(angrily)*: What does emotion have to do with any of this? We're not here to talk about what everyone is feeling—I want to know whether you can help us with the drug problem. I don't understand why you're interested in anything else. Emotions, emotions! What about the drug problem that we should be dealing with?

T *(feeling the anger and knowing that a large part of it belongs to the father, resumes with more sensitivity)*: I seem to have upset you. I see you are angry. You came to get help, and here I am, asking about emotions.

P *(more calmly)*: Well, yes, I really don't see how that has anything to do with drugs.

T *(feeling the anger dispersing)*: What if we took a look at the connection between the anger I just caused in you and the drug issue itself?

The therapist persists in approaching the issue of anger, as it is evident that it plays a very important role. The therapist tries to evaluate the anger, even though she realizes that it is not the core affect or the essence of the affective psychic construct in the family system's constellation.

However, anger is an affect that needs to be taken seriously in their family dynamic. In fact, in this case anger provides a means for the therapist to gain trust from the family at the beginning of the therapy session, demonstrating sincere interest in the family's situation and the affect that is concealed behind the anger. Here, the therapist must first contain and reprocess the anger, especially since the father feels the same affect. The therapist's job at this stage is to discover the primary forces holding the family in their orbit on the systemic level.

P *(calmly)*: I'm angry because no one seems to understand how upsetting it is that I cannot do anything about this.
T *(sensing anger from the two children, she turns to them)*: Are the two of you also angry?

The therapist's purpose is to give everyone enough time and space to feel accepted and give each of them a chance to speak about their thoughts and emotions. The therapist then needs to evaluate these thoughts and emotions, because all feelings are legitimate and everyone must realize that they are allowed to think and feel anything. This approach will lead to the true cause of their critical behavior. The therapist understands that the family system is currently revolving around the drug issue, but that the core of the issue lies much deeper and that everyone will have to participate if they are to resolve the issue. This is the only way for them to discover their core affect and the role the drugs play in the situation—at this point they are playing the part of affective psychic construct and preventing the system from being functional.

N *(distressed)*: Our parents are constantly giving us a hard time and no one seems to care how we feel! *(She turns to her brother.)* We don't even count in this family.
T *(feeling the anger and sadness that the two siblings share)*: You have the feeling that the only important thing is what your parents say and that you are not important at all.
N *(nodding in agreement)*: Yeah, something like that.
T *(notices how much stronger the sadness is than the anger)*: And how does that make you feel?
N *(sadly)*: Well, I feel like they don't care at all what's happening to us, as if it's all about that stupid weed, which we only tried for fun. We never even touched it at home. It's unfair and it makes me mad.
T *(picking up on the connection between the siblings and addressing them both)*: It seems like the two of you are very close. You're speaking for both of you together.
P *(angrily)*: Yeah, they're in this together all right, instead of . . .
T *(turns to the father to regulate his anger)*: Excuse me, Peter, let's give them a chance to express what they're feeling and thinking. *(turns towards the son)* Alex, what do you feel about what's going on?
A *(holding back)*: I don't know. They just keep bugging and nagging us. . .

M *(interrupting him, seemingly outraged)*: Why all the negative terms?

T *(turning towards the mother, feeling her anger, and especially her disappointment)*: Martha, I understand this bothers you, but let's just wait a moment. *(turns to the son)* Please, finish what you were saying.

A *(angrily)*: It's just like at home, they keep annoying us, nagging, going on and on...

T *(feeling his disappointment)*: And how does that make you feel?

A *(upset)*: As if it's not at all important what I think! They don't care how I'm doing! All they care about is the weed, like it's the most important thing in the world.

T *(feeling pressure in her chest)*: So, if I understand correctly, you feel angry as well. You feel as though they don't care about you unless you do something wrong?

A *(nodding in agreement)*: Yes, all they care about is the weed.

T *(feeing the disappointment, and anger as a sensation of pressure in her head, she turns to face all four)*: So, let's see if we're all on the same page. Last time we agreed that all drug use has to stop. At the same time, we spoke about how drug abuse is a consequence of the painful relationships between you. You are experiencing distress, anger, and fear because the situation seems impossible to understand. You all share some bigger emotion, that is stronger than you and controls you, but we're not sure what it is yet. In order to discover the real problem, we are going to have to work together. We'll have to look for the feelings that are driving you, and discover the anguish and pain that the two of you *(looking at the two children)* were trying to express but were unable to, letting the drugs speak instead of you. I'm curious to see what you think about this.

M *(disappointed tone)*: I think the problem may be a consequence of our absence. When my husband and I were building our house, the kids had to stay with their grandparents. Then we had to pay off a large loan so my husband started working a lot. I understood that my husband had to work all the time in order to make enough money to pay back our loans. But the kids, I guess they missed him a lot. He spent some time at home, whenever he was able to...

T *(feeling a tingling sensation in her legs)*: So, the three of you were alone together quite a lot. Martha, you must have done the best you could. How was it being alone with the kids?

M *(thoughtful)*: Well, I missed my husband very much, but I understood. I didn't want to bother him with the kids' problems when he came home in the evening.

P *(upset)*: I had no idea that anything was wrong. Anyway, they just have school, and I'm pretty sure they can do that on their own. It's their responsibility.

T *(sensing the father's fear, although it is concealed by anger)*: Of course. But you must also understand that everyone missed you very much. You had to take care of the finances and you were forced to work a lot more to provide for your family. This is also why it was hard to spend time at home.

P (*more relaxed*): Exactly. And I should be working more now as well. I really don't understand why we can't fix this whole problem and get on with it.

One of the fundamental hypotheses of relational family therapy is that parents' suppressed mental content is reactivated in their children through projective and introjective identification and right hemisphere communication. The children react to this content in an organic and symptomatic way. This occurs when the family system as a whole begins to sense that something catastrophic is going to happen. This triggers positive feedback, which causes symptomatic behavior—in this case, drug use. The symptomatic reaction is a reflection of the affective psychic construct, created through mental content, which serves as a shield from the parents' painful affect. However, this affect slowly infiltrates the entire system and everyone has to absorb a part of it. These feelings soon become the main method of regulating affect. In this example, drugs are what take on the function of the symptomatic reaction. Hence, the therapist will try to carefully unravel all levels of their experience, starting at the systemic level. The therapist's intention is to reveal the core affect that is blocking functional behavior, emotion, and activity. The core affect is also what will help the therapist discover the deeper aspects of each individual's mental structure, as well as that of the family system as a whole.

This process can be very complicated. In this example, the parents are not willing to confront painful affects that are completely unconscious. Doing so would mean they would risk feeling exposed and vulnerable. It is thus crucial that the therapist carefully observes all levels of what they are experiencing, from bodily sensations to emotions, and how they are thinking, as well as their reactions to countertransference. This will be very helpful to the therapist and she must not allow her own personal mental content to get in the way. The therapist is able to discover a lot of important content through right hemisphere communication and bodily sensation, which can help to locate the core affect and essential psycho-organic content.

T (*experiencing pressure in her throat*): I would like to help resolve this as soon as possible so your family could function normally once again. However, we're talking about feelings that are very deeply buried and are impossible to resolve quickly since they are rooted in your unconscious.

M (*musing*): I should have been more decisive, demanded more, but I had no idea any of this was going on.

T (*picking up on the mother's sadness*): We are not looking for a culprit to blame for this situation; instead we can learn something from it. We can discover the deeper feelings behind the problem; feelings that affect your family. We do not even know what they are at this point. This is why I'd like to find out what your children are feeling. *(turning towards them)* What do you feel? What feelings do you think the drugs might be covering up?

N *(angrily)*: Argghh! Nobody understands me!
T *(experiencing tension in her chest)*: Who do you want to understand you? And what needs to be understood?
N *(still angrily)*: This is pointless. Dad is never home, and even when he is, he is either fighting with one of us, or he's too tired to do anything but fall asleep in front of the television set.
T *(experiencing throat and chest pressure)*: I sense a lot of fear behind your anger. Can you tell me what you are afraid of?

At this point, the therapist approaches the concept of catastrophic experience, as it seems that there is dread hiding behind Natalie's anger, dread of something unspeakable, something that might happen. Natalie feels completely misunderstood, but the therapist senses that deeper emotions hide behind the children's anger and resentment. The therapist tries to find a way to go beyond the surface and into their internal mental world and their most frightening emotions.

N *(worried)*: I'm afraid of mom and dad getting a divorce.
T *(feeling her legs go numb)*: I'm guessing that this fear floods over you occasionally and makes you feel powerless. I wonder if the marijuana helps to obliterate that fear, at least for a while, makes you forget to feel the dread.
N *(in a more relaxed tone)*: Yeah, maybe. When I smoke, I don't think about anything that's going on around me.
T *(empathically)*: Do you think you could say that to your father?
N *(shyly and a little bit afraid)*: Dad, you're never home, and when you are, you're always in a bad mood. It's impossible to talk to you; it's as if you're not even here.
T *(turns towards the father)*: How do you respond to that?
P *(reluctantly)*: I think she's exaggerating.
T *(sensing his fear)*: But this is how she experiences you. She's afraid you and your wife might get divorced.
P *(cynically)*: Well, I don't know where she gets those strange ideas.
T *(sensing the father's fear, which has actually become his daughter's)*: Peter, she's just afraid. It seems she wants to know that you will always be her father, and she your daughter, no matter what happens.

At this point in the therapeutic process, it has become clear that the parents' hidden conflict has become the reality of their children's experience. The therapist carefully tries to probe these intense emotions but treads lightly in order to maintain systemic and interpersonal boundaries.

P *(facing his children)*: Of course I'll always be your father and take care of you no matter what. But look, your mother and I do fight once in a while. . .
T *(interrupting him, as he seems to be directing anger at his wife)*: Excuse me, Peter, I believe we need to stick to talking about your relationship

with your kids for now, not your wife. The two of you will have plenty of time later. First I want to hear what your children have to say.

P *(calmly)*: All right, I'll do my best.

T *(facing the daughter)*: Natalie, would you tell your father what's worrying you and what you want from him?

N *(fearfully)*: I'm just afraid that you just won't show up one day. I'm afraid that one day you'll just pack your bags and leave *(starts crying)*, and then we would be... *(sobbing)* left all alone!

T *(facing the father)*: Why don't you comfort your daughter?

P *(taken aback)*: I had no idea you felt this way!

T *(feeling a deep sadness)*: And how does this make you feel? How are you comprehending this?

P *(moved)*: Well, I understand why you're so angry with me. I understand that my long workdays upset you. I understand that not knowing where I am and what I'm doing makes you feel scared, that something might happen.

N *(crying)*: I'm terrified, and no one understands me.

T *(experiencing sadness as pressure in her throat)*: Your daughter is yearning for you to give her some kind of reassurance: that you will try your best to repair your relationship. Perhaps by being willing to hear her out and by working on your marital issues...

Here the therapist must be very careful. It is important that the parents do not involve their children in their marital conflict. They also should not make promises they cannot keep. For example, it would be unrealistic for the couple to promise that they can easily resolve their marital conflict. The therapist must also be mindful of the family hierarchy and boundaries, emphasizing how important it is for the parents to assure their children they will try to resolve their marital issues and also improve their relationship with the children. This is especially difficult in families where one of the parents has been unfaithful; in such cases the parents may feel as if there is no hope and this will be clear to their children. Therapists must always try to guide couples through a healing process, even in the most painful of relationships. However, the marital problems should be addressed in couple's therapy, that is, in a setting removed from the children.

P *(more confidently)*: Natalie, from now on I will try my best to find more time to talk to you, and your mother and I will try to resolve our conflicts through therapy.

T *(empathically, yet firmly)*: What do you propose doing, so Natalie can feel you are more present?

P *(turning towards his daughter)*: Natalie, how about we find half an hour every day, perhaps after the evening news when I will be completely available to you and you can decide whether you'd like to talk or not. If it happens that I can't find the time, I will let you know and we'll find another time to talk.

T *(noticing Natalie's face becoming more relaxed)*: Natalie, would you like that?
N *(calmly)*: Yeah, that would be great. But you have to stick to your agreement!
P *(firmly)*: I will!

This conversation revealed that Natalie is carrying the burden of her father's suppressed and unconscious fears, sadness, and other affects. She yearns to be in contact with her father, almost as if she wants to protect him from something. However, the marital issues will be addressed in a couple's session. The therapist knows the children are experiencing a core affect, deeply rooted in the fear that one of the parents may leave; perhaps the parents share this fear. The children unconsciously, and successfully, hide their fear behind the affective psychic construct, expressing this affect openly by accusing their father and mother of not caring about them. Consequently, the children try even harder to get their parents' attention—in this case through the use of drugs.

T *(sensing Alex's increasing distress, she turns toward him)*: Alex, what would you like to say to your father?
A *(staring in front of him)*: Well, I liked hearing what dad said to Natalie.
T *(sensing fear and sadness as pressure in her throat)*: So, you were also afraid your father might leave?
A *(deep in thought)*: Yeah, but I didn't really want to think about it. I feel better now.
T *(empathically, yet firmly)*: What would you like your father to do? How could the two of you become closer?
A *(decisively)*: I want him to find time for me too!
P: How do you suggest we find time for just the two of us?
A *(looking at his father)*: Well, whenever you're home, we seem to connect through sports. I don't know. . .
P *(inquisitively)*: What would mean the most to you?
A *(decisively)*: Well, I'd like you to take time for basketball, maybe on Saturdays, after lunch.
P *(contentedly)*: Not at all a problem. I'd like that too. It's a deal!
T *(sensing they have both relaxed)*: Okay! So the two will do that! *(They both nod in agreement.)*

After the children have relaxed around their father, the therapist turns to the mother. The therapist could have led this conversation by alternating and including the mother earlier, but it seemed that the children needed to talk to the father first in order to get a sense of security before speaking to their mother who although she is physically present, seems mentally distant. During their conversation, the mother seemed lost in her thoughts, distancing herself, and then suddenly coming back to the situation and shifting restlessly in her chair. The therapist now plans on giving the mother more time and space, as well as giving the children a chance to speak openly about how they feel in her presence. The therapist has to be careful to avoid catastrophic emotions. The therapist has a chance to better understand these emotions through right hemisphere communication. However, it is important to maintain distance between personal feelings and those that belong to the family, which has now become part of the therapist's affective sphere.

T *(turning to the mother, sensing her restlessness)*: Thank you for holding on, Martha. It must have been quite difficult for you at times.
M *(reflecting)*: No, it wasn't easy, especially when Natalie cried.
T *(feeling tears welling up)*: What did that mean to you?
M *(sadly)*: I hadn't imagined that what was going on with my husband was so painful for the kids. My husband can be very cruel.
T *(stops her as she senses the boundaries are being compromised)*: Martha, I understand there are many things you are going through in your marriage, but we will have to get to that later. I don't want to involve your children in your marital relationship. I want to focus on your children right now. Could you find a way to meet your daughter halfway?
M *(distressed)*: I know it's not all right. *(facing her daughter)* Natalie, I understand you sense my irritation, and I am sorry about that.
N *(staring ahead)*: Are you really sorry? *(angrily)* Do you even understand me? Do you even care what's going on with me? All you do is nag and give me a hard time! You're always trying to control me. You never give me any freedom.
T *(stopping her)*: Natalie, I know you're very upset and angry. Could you tell your mother that?
N *(more calmly)*: I am extremely angry with you. It's impossible to agree on anything with you. You're always right. You never listen to me.
M *(interrupting her angrily)*: What do you expect? You keep closing up, running away from me. You never want to talk to me!
T *(trying to calm her)*: Martha, I sense your distress. This is not easy for you. So many feelings are coursing through you. Could you hold onto them for just a moment and try putting yourself in your daughter's shoes? It seems as though she has to carry a lot of your emotions.
M *(calming down)*: Okay, I'll try.
T *(sensing their sadness and fear)*: Martha, could you look at your daughter calmly and ask her how she is feeling? It seems she is carrying so many hurtful emotions and I am sure you understand that. All you need to do is listen to her. She's such a strong part of you and your feelings.
M *(uncomfortably)*: Natalie, I understand it's not easy for you. I'm trying to understand. But why drugs? Can you tell me that?
N *(mistrustfully)*: You know everything's all wrong. We're just kidding ourselves. *(Emotions erupt rapidly from her):* I'm angry with you because you don't do anything to fix it! You backed away and now

you say it's all *my fault!* I don't clean up, I don't dress the way you'd like, my grades aren't good enough, and now, on top of everything else, you're upset about the weed. It's completely ridiculous!

M *(with more understanding)*: Natalie, I'm sorry. I didn't know that you were experiencing it this way. It's true, I didn't dedicate enough time to you, I wasn't the way I wanted to be. I should have done that. Can you tell me what would help you?

This conversation reveals that Natalie is the identified patient: her mother criticizes her constantly and blames her for everything. She is unable to step in her daughter's shoes and feel her emotions. Meanwhile, Natalie is completely lost, does not know how to react, is acting out rebelliously, and letting her emotions out through outbursts of rage. Both mother and daughter keep getting trapped in a vicious circle of fights and battling affective psychic constructs. Their fights cause destructive emotions and actually function as a means to avoid the real issues that in fact belong to the parents and not their children. The marital conflict is too painful for the mother to address and so she transfers it onto the mother-daughter relationship through projective and introjective identification. In this respect, Natalie is taking on the role of the mother's emotional partner because her true partner is absent. The mother's criticism, anger, and rage are directed at the daughter, although they belong in her own marital relationship.

N *(carefully)*: Well, I want you to stop blaming, accusing, and criticizing me! I want to be able to talk to you calmly. I want you to trust me!

M *(very attentively)*: Natalie, I only now feel I understand what's going on between us. And how unfair it is, especially to you...

T *(slightly worried, sensing a numbness all over the body, and having trouble breathing)*: Natalie, are the drugs a means of escaping from all of this?

N *(nodding)*: Well, that's not that, I guess, I mean, at least I can unplug for a bit, and forget...

M *(gently and seemingly worried)*: Oh, Natalie... I will take the time to talk to you; we can talk as long as we need, so we can figure things out the way we need to.

T *(sensing she has relaxed)*: Is that okay with you, Natalie?

N *(contentedly)*: Yes, it is.

In the past few minutes, the therapist senses increased tension coming from Alex. While his father followed the conversation between his wife and daughter, Alex seemed restless in his chair, almost bored, yet also giving off a sense of anger and distress as though he were afraid of being excluded from the family. It is evident he is holding in his anger. Every now and then it seemed as though he were about to say something but held back. He would look down at his shoes, distracted, and then would look up at one of the participating family members. His restlessness seemed like a cry for help, understanding, and empathy. All the members of the family seemed to be flooded by a strange type of fear—evidently the core affect in the family's constellation. This core affect creates the family's affective psychic construct and is maintained by affect regulation that is mainly reflected in Alex.

T *(empathically, sensing Alex's fear)*: Alex, thank you for waiting and holding back. I sense so much distress coming from you. What is it you are afraid?

A *(responding without taking time to think)*: That mom is going to leave!

T *(feeling her heart racing and taking shallow breaths)*: Could you say that to your mother?

A *(with difficulty)*: Well, I don't know. It's pointless. Everything is pointless. Everyone just keeps on nagging. Everyone keeps on criticizing.

T *(sensing his anguish and fear)*: There seems to be a lot of anguish behind your words.

A *(more relaxed)*: Yeah, when Mom and Dad get into a fight, he goes quiet and my mom keeps going at him: It's horrible. She often says that no one even wants her around anyway, that she's just going to leave.

T *(turning to the mother)*: Martha, it seems that your son experiences terrible feelings during your fights although he may not ever express it. How do you respond to him?

M *(facing her son)*: I don't know, Alex. What am I doing that makes you feel that way?

A *(mistrusting, looking at each of his family members)*: I don't know, Mom. But when you lose it, you become so annoying, constantly picking on everyone. And then you go silent. I don't know. It all seems so pointless.

T *(experiencing pressure in her chest)*: Alex, you seem so uncertain. What's this all about? You seem to feel very upset and afraid.

A *(suddenly relaxing)*: Yeah, maybe I do.

T *(experiencing increased agitation, sadness, and shame from the mother)*: Martha, I'm guessing you feel upset and afraid as well. If you try to step into your son's shoes, do you find a lot of your own distress and fear in him?

M *(having trouble staying calm, then experiencing sadness, and finally relaxing)*: Alex, you know it's normal to fight sometimes. We've fought so many times and nothing's happened! But I suppose. . . Well, Alex, I can only assure you that I'll try to approach things differently from now on. What's important is that your father and I work through things privately. We won't involve you in our conflicts anymore.

A *(uneasily)*: Yeah, but what about when you freak out again and threaten to leave?

M *(calmly)*: I cannot promise I won't ever get angry, but I can promise I will talk to your father directly about things first.

A *(exploding)*: And if you two can't work through it out, then what? You'll just disappear!

T *(feeling tension in her head and legs)*: Martha, your son is afraid that you will give up one day and he will be left alone.

A *(angrily towards his mother)*: You don't get it at all! You don't even know how much you nag us all and make stuff up.

M *(taken aback, ashamed, and then responding calmly)*: Well, no. I wasn't aware of that. I must really seem impossible to you. But, Alex, now that I'm hearing you, hearing all of you, it's becoming clear that we're going to need to make a lot of changes in this family. But I can promise you this: I will never leave you, no matter what. I will always be your mother and you can always come to me.

A *(apprehensively)*: I know you're my mother. But what are you going to do with Dad?

M *(with more certainty)*: Your dad and I will work through our issues in therapy. And, once again, I promise you we will discuss things differently. Now I understand your distress, your anger, and your fear. You really can tell me anything from now on.

A *(slightly more relaxed)*: Fine.

At this point, it seemed as though everyone had calmed down and regained hope. It seemed that they had discovered the true problem: that the parents will have to approach their issues more seriously. All four family members were able to speak to each other with more certainty and trust. They were able to calm each other down by committing to work harder on creating a friendlier family atmosphere, one filled with understanding and empathy. The parents realized that their marital

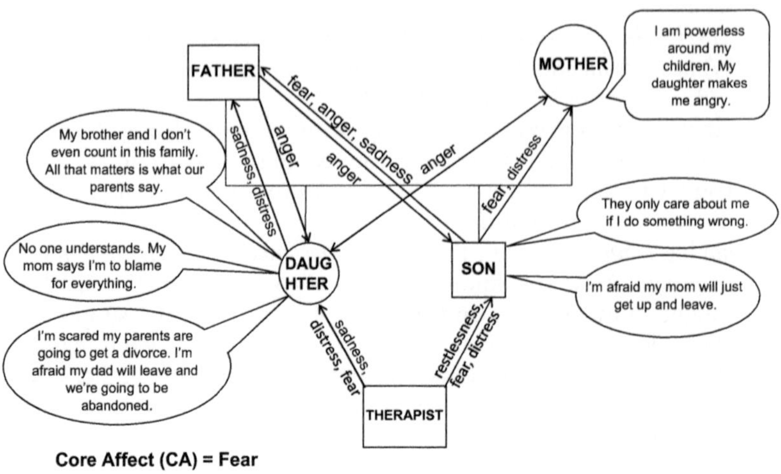

Figure 2.1 Systemic level (father, mother, daughter, son)

Figure created by Tanja Repič Slavič and Janko Slavič

conflicts, including the shame and fear they had been covering up, had been transferred to their children. Their children's reaction to their conflict resulted in drug use, which represented a symptom of their parents' painful relationship. The drugs became the family's "disease" and the positive feedback of their family system, hence throwing their family off balance. A completely new family issue—drug use—served to cover up the affective psychic construct, that is, the dread of a possible divorce. The surface problem of drug use caused the family to exceed the acceptable levels of deviation and led the family to seek therapeutic help.

At the next session, the therapist asks how their week has gone, what had evolved with the drug use, whether or not it was under control. The therapist pointed out that if the drug problem progressed to addiction and abuse, it needed to be addressed first with professional help. Fortunately, this particular case was more of a "cry for help" and additional therapy specifically for the drug problem was not required. Once that was established, the therapist asked the father to let the children leave the therapy room temporarily in order to work with the couple on their personal issues. They understood their conflict is a separate area from which the children need to be protected. In other words, the couple needs to set appropriate boundaries. This is the most important functional strategy of change within their family system. It takes the burden off of the children's subsystem and gives them a functional environment in which to grow and develop healthy personalities.

T *(sensing everyone is more relaxed)*: It looks like you made progress this week.

P (*nodding in agreement with everyone else*): Yes, we did. Martha and I started talking more, my son and I spent Saturday afternoon outside on the field, and my daughter and I also talk regularly.

T (*facing the mother*): How do you feel? What are you thinking?

M (*happily*): Well, I think our family can count on turning a new page soon.

T (*looking at the daughter*): And how did this week go for you?

N (*with a slight playful tone*): They didn't nag us as much, that's true. I liked talking with my dad a lot. And my mom and I worked through some things as well.

T (*turning towards the son*): And how did it go for you?

A (*seeming more relaxed*): Yeah, they didn't bug us as much. I was happy my mom and I talked more. I'm glad she said I can always come to her with any questions, and she promised she'd always answer truthfully. And I always got along with Dad anyway. . .

T (*sensing they have all relaxed*): From what you are saying, I feel that you are happier with the relationships you're building. I think it's time we look further into the parental relationship. (*turning to the father)* Peter, how about you tell your children they can wait outside while we talk more with you and your wife.

P *(slightly uncomfortable)*: All right. Natalie and Alex, would you step outside while your mom and I talk for a bit?
N *(getting upset)*: But, what are you two going to . . .
T *(feeling a lump in her throat)*: Your daughter is worried. Can you reassure her?
P *(surprised)*: Natalie, it's okay! There are a couple of things we need to talk about, and I think it's better that we're alone.
N *(turning to her mother nervously)*: Is that okay with you?
M *(surprised)*: Of course it is! We have quite a bit to talk about and the therapist is going to help us!
T *(facing Natalie)*: Is that all right?
N *(calmer)*: Yes, it's all right.
T *(looking at the father)*: Would you let your son know that he can leave as well?
P *(facing his son)*: Alex, I'd like you and Natalie to step outside.
A *(at first unfazed and then with nervous)*: Yeah, okay. *(looking at his mother)* Are you okay?
M *(surprised once again)*: Of course I am, Alex! You've said yourself that my nagging and bugging is something that I need to work on alone, and with your father.
A *(still not sure)*: But will you work it out? What if. . .
M *(moved)*: Yes, we're going to do everything we can, and the therapist is going to help us. Everything will be fine.

The children leave the room calmly. The therapist could have intervened by speaking directly to the children if the parents were unable to do so. It is, however, much better if the parents do this themselves. It gives the children a greater sense of certainty.

T *(after the children have left)*: So: how does it feel in here without the kids?
M *(uncertainly)*: Well, kind of strange, actually. I didn't realize they filled up the space so much.
T *(sensing her agitation)*: What do you mean?
M *(sadly, starts crying)*: Well, I had no idea they were so worried about us.
T *(feels her sadness)*: What do your tears mean? Can you give them a name?
M *(wiping away the tears)*: Uh, I have no idea. Despair, anger, distress, sadness.
T *(feeling numb)*: Which of the emotions seems strongest?
M *(still wiping her tears)*: I think despair. Because I really *have* given up. I am terrified that I will actually drop everything and leave one day. I can't take it anymore!
T *(feeling a lump in her throat)*: It seems really hard for you: in your relationship, maybe even in the family. Can you tell me about it?
M *(calming down, still weeping)*: I feel I'm no longer myself, almost as if I've disappeared, died in a way. I feel as though I'm using what's

left of my energy to stay in this family. I don't blame anyone for this. That's just how I feel.

T *(sensing an even deeper sadness)*: You must be so tired from all of this, feeling like there is no way out of this dread, despair, and sadness. You've exhausted yourself. You must feel as if you're completely alone.

M *(starting to cry again)*: At first I thought that it would work itself out. I tried really hard. I hate these feelings. I really can't go on anymore.

T *(sensing that the husband has emotionally removed himself)*: Thank you, Martha. We will get back to you in a moment. *(turning towards the husband)* What do you feel? What do you think about when your wife opens up like this, expressing her pain and distress?

P *(seeming very upset)*: Well, I don't know. Am I supposed to feel guilty? We agreed on everything.

T *(sensing his frustration)*: I understand you two agreed on certain things. However, you didn't check in with each other and see how you were feeling. You were both left alone, without support.

P *(slightly calmer)*: Yeah, something like that. It's horrible for me too! I feel like I'm alone in everything as well. I feel like I no longer have anyone to talk to, that all we do is argue. And on top of everything else, there are the kids and their problems! I don't know where to turn anymore.

T *(empathically)*: It seems you both understand that your children have become the carriers of your painful emotions, emotions that you never even wanted to admit you had.

M, P *(both nodding in agreement)*: We didn't know.

T *(sensing that the time has come to elaborate)*: Peter, your daughter is carrying your deepest and most painful emotion: fear, fear that you will be so disappointed that you might just leave and never come back home. These are really deep emotions and you have been unwilling to accept them. And Martha, your son carries your feelings of fear and dread. He is afraid you might just disappear one day, as he told you earlier. How does this make you both feel?

M *(slowly calming down)*: I feel terrible for not being able to understand my children better, and that I don't know how to be closer with them anymore.

P *(lost in thought)*: Yes, it's bad. I feel guilty for not noticing it sooner.

T *(empathically, yet firmly)*: It's terribly hard for you. You both feel like you've mishandled certain things and lost an opportunity to change them. You feel as though you should have approached matters differently. However, we need to take a deeper look to discover where the roots of these problems are. Let's look at your childhood. What can we find there? Who was there, taking care of you? What was your childhood like? Who would like to go first?

At this point, the therapist's task is to uncover the deepest parental and marital affects that create their relationship. These affects establish, guide, and maintain the family's homeostasis through projective and introjective identification. They also generate the family's affective psychic construct and the way in which each family member regulates it. By digging deeper, the therapist is able to discover the multiple layers of the family members' psyches. This is done empathically and with tact, as the layers conceal very deep affects that were involuntarily evoked in the couples' children who became symptomatic identified patients carrying their parents' unresolved mental content. The couple had successfully concealed this content until it erupted in this therapy session. The therapist will approach this by letting each of the parents work through their own upbringing, and then helping them through their relational strife.

If the family has trouble discovering their core affect, the therapist will help them by exploring two mental layers: first, the relationship between the parents, and then each of their intrapsychic positions. The therapist will have to pay attentive to her own physical sensations. The therapist will be mindful of these feelings of countertransference because they enhance empathy, which each of them seems to be have lacked and yearned for during their childhoods. As a result, both parents feel as if they live past each other.

M *(adamantly)*: I'll start. My father worked a lot and drank too much. He always came home late from work. My older sister and I always waited for him, terrified about what would happen when he came back.

T *(feeling slightly dizzy)*: If I understand correctly, those hours of waiting were the worst of times. You felt powerless.

M *(sadly)*: Yes, those hours felt like they went on and on forever. That was almost the scariest part.

T *(empathically)*: What feeling has stayed with you the most?

M *(crying)*: Dread. And despair. Feeling like nothing would ever change.

T *(experiencing numbness in her chest and head)*: Fear, dread, and despair. What was the most frightening of all these feelings?

M *(sobbing)*: That my mother would get fed up and leave.

T *(still experiencing numbness)*: All of your mother's fear and dread seems to have flowed directly into you. Her feelings of powerlessness and despair flooded you as well. Worse still, your mother wasn't able to comfort you. She was suffering too much to be able to see your pain as well.

M *(sobbing louder)*: She didn't even notice us! That's how I experienced it. She just kept crying and saying she couldn't go on, and how horrible everything was. How she had lost all hope, was fed up. She said the only reason she was still trying was for my sister and me.

T *(feeling a deep sadness but maintaining a calm body)*: And how did that make you feel?

M *(still crying)*: I was terrified. I lived in constant fear that I would be left alone.

T *(empathically)*: That's similar to what your son is experiencing now and your daughter as also.

M *(calming down slightly)*: Yes, I didn't know that until now. I never wanted my children to experience something like that. But what can I do? I feel so powerless.

The therapist tries to find connections between the mother's childhood experience and the experiences of her own children. It is becoming more apparent that her children have taken on experiences that belong mostly to her. The therapist's intention is to help the mother address these experiences and take responsibility for her emotions in order to liberate her children from holding feelings that do not rightfully belong in their mental structures.

T *(empathically, yet firmly)*: I think you'll know what to do. You know now that your children are carrying your suppressed emotions. All you have to do is give your children exactly what you would have wanted your mother to give you. By doing that, you will finally be able to unburden yourself and your children of these terrifying and harmful emotions. What would you have wanted your mother to do for you that she never did?

Relational family therapy hypothesizes that parents can release their children from carrying feelings that don't belong to them. By doing so, parents also liberate themselves. They can resolve their organic and psychobiologic experiences from adolescence. In this way, parents can take care of their children and give them whatever they most yearned for but never received as children. This stops the flow of projective processes and dissolves the affective psychic construct. In this case, the construct contains feelings of dread, despair, fear, and abandonment. This construct was created during the mother's childhood and still manifests in her family today, creating a blockage in communication between her and her children. This construct emotionally entraps the children. They both continuously experience the feeling that everything will fall apart, their parents will divorce, and they will be left alone.

M *(anxious)*: I wish my mother had resolved her relationship with my father on her own, without burdening my sister or me. I wish she had known how to show me that she loves me, and I wish we could have talked more. If only she had known how to tell me she was always going to be my mother, and that she would always be there for me, no matter what happened.

T *(knowing they are on the right path)*: Would you be able to tell and show your children the same thing you wanted as a child?

M *(adamantly)*: Yes, I will try!

T *(turning to face the father)*: Peter, how was it for you growing up?

P *(lost in thought)*: It was similar. My father drank a lot. He would often disappear, sometimes for days and nights together. We wouldn't know where he was.

T *(sensing sadness fear)*: This affect, this fear of abandonment, is in fact what brought you and your wife together. That is where you two understand each other so perfectly. We can elaborate on that later. But first tell me how you felt when your father disappeared?

According to relational and family systems theory, partners are attracted to each other based on similar core affects. In this example, the two partners share the affect of dread and fear of abandonment. They both had a father who often left and a mother who suffered. The children internalized the fear, dread, stress, and pain of the family. The core affect, which later becomes the affect regulation system, drives people to seek partners with similar mental content and unconsciously gives them hope to resolve it in a new relationship. Any other type of affect seems unfamiliar and dangerous. In this case, where both fathers suffered from alcohol dependency, the two children did not repeat the same pattern. They did, however, maintain the mental structure of an alcoholic: uncertainty, low self-esteem, and a fragile self-image.

The therapist should not need explicitly present all of this information. Rather, it is necessary that both parents confront their own family issues, as well as the mental content preventing them from displaying empathy as parents. What the therapist is focusing on is discovering the couples' core affect and affective psychic construct, which is a mirror image of their own parents' structure. It includes everything their parents projected onto them and that they are now projecting onto their children: dread and fear of divorce and abandonment. On one hand, this fear paralyzes both partners. On the other hand, the fear unconsciously inclines them to act in a way that they re-experience solitude, despair, and distress. This, of course, could also lead to divorce.

P *(deep in thought)*: I felt as if I was completely alone in the world and that no one understood me. Worse still, I felt guilty.

T *(displaying empathy in reaction to the construct of guilt)*: Guilty?

P *(relaxing slightly)*: Yes, guilty. For my father's drinking. He would often tell us how impossible we were and that's why he left home so often.

M *(adding her voice to the conversation)*: I used to feel guilty too.

T *(displaying understanding and certainty)*: You both know that it cannot be the child's fault. Sometimes, however, guilt becomes the only connecting element: if you feel guilty you know there's still a chance of changing something. But neither of you were able to change anything. The guilt, unfortunately, remained; it was ingrained in you, probably from your father's side. *(turning towards Peter)* How much of that guilt do you think your children are carrying?

P *(perplexed)*: I don't know. I didn't even think of that.

T *(adamantly)*: Do you think you would be able to release your children from these deeply ingrained feelings?
P *(still perplexed)*: I'm not sure I understand. Could you. . .?
T *(empathically)*: Well, what did you experience when you were growing up besides the guilt? What were you afraid of most?
P *(adamantly)*: That my father would leave. That he would leave us alone with our mother, and I would be the one that would have to take all the blame. My little brother was still too young.
T *(feeling tension in her chest and head)*: I could sense guilt when I spoke with your children earlier, especially in your daughter. She seemed terrified that you would leave. She is willing to do anything to show how much your family needs you. That's part of why she enjoys the times you two spend talking.
P *(doubtful)*: I'm not following anymore.
T *(sensing fear hiding behind his doubt)*: Well, can you understand that your daughter is frightened that you might leave? She feels guilty and is willing to do anything to make you feel needed, welcomed, and accepted in your home. That's what she wants to achieve by spending time talking to you. In fact, she's doing you a great favor this way.
P *(staring ahead)*: I never really thought of it that way.
T *(sensing his distress and shame)*: What if you were to show your daughter—this little girl who is yearning for her father's affection, his love, his embrace—show her that. . . She is so afraid her father will leave without saying goodbye.
P *(still staring into space)*: That's exactly how I felt with my father and with my mother. I thought my mother would just decide one day that she'd had enough.
T *(sensing his shame, and even more a deep sadness)*: How was that for you?
P *(sadly)*: It wasn't easy.
T *(sensing more than just sadness)*: Can you tell me more about that?
P *(sadly looking at the therapist)*: It was terrible. I was afraid I'd be left alone with a sad mother, lamenting and talking badly about my father, instead of comforting me.
T *(empathically)*: What would have comforted you? What could your father have done? And your mother?
P *(more adamantly)*: My dad could have stopped leaving us all the time and drinking. He did stop drinking later on, but it was too late for me. My mother should have been firmer; she should have looked into treatment for him sooner, not waited until my brother started doing drugs. That changed everything.
T *(sensing fear and experiencing numbness in her legs and pressure in her head)*: It seems as though drugs were a kind of warning, something like what is happening in your family now.
P *(lost in thought)*: I suppose. I never connected the two. But I guess I was leaving home a lot at that point.

T *(sensing sadness and disappointment)*: What did you yearn for the most before that? Aside from your father being home more, drinking less, and your mother being stronger?

P *(embarrassed)*: I wish they had cared more about me, spent more time with me. My father could have shown more interest. He could have praised me once in a while, played games with me. My mother could have protected me from my father's cruelty. He always said it was all my fault. She could have talked to him like she did later about my brother's drug problem. She could have at least told me it wasn't my fault, that she'd be there for me.

T *(sensing they have found a real connection)*: That is very much like what your children need from you now. Do you think you can give it to them? Could you praise your son, teach him how to play tennis, tell him that none of this is his fault, that you will always be his father? Could you tell your daughter that this isn't her fault either? Tell her she is yours, that you'll never leave, that she will always have a father. Tell her that you love her.

P *(after a long pause)*: I had no idea it was the same thing. I will try my best. It might be hard, you know, I never really got any of that myself.

T *(empathically, facing both parents)*: It is never easy giving to others what you never received yourself. You two both know what it is that you didn't receive—so now you must try giving that to your children.

P, M *(both nodding in agreement)*: Yes.

T *(sensing it is time for the children to come back)*: It's time to call the kids back. Would you talk to them when they come in, Peter? And then you, Martha?

P *(worried)*: What should I say?

T *(sensing fear and awkwardness)*: Whatever you feel needs to be said. Whatever you think is important that they hear so they can feel safe and accepted, so they can feel things are changing.

P *(adamantly)*: Yes. I can tell them that we've talked about this and that things are going to be better for us at home, and that none of it is their fault.

M *(seeming lightly worried)*: And that we won't leave them or let them feel abandoned. We will try harder to get along, and by understanding each other more, we will be able to understand them more!

T *(sensing they have completely understood each other)*: Wonderful!

P *(after calling the Natalie and Alex inside)*: Your mother and I want to thank you for waiting outside. We talked a lot about ourselves, about our childhoods and we will continue to do so. *(looking toward the therapist)* We think *(then looking at his wife who is nodding in agreement)* that we will all be able to turn a new page at home. We also talked about how unfair it was for the two of you to have to feel so afraid and worried about us. This will all work out. And we'll try to talk about it as much as we can.

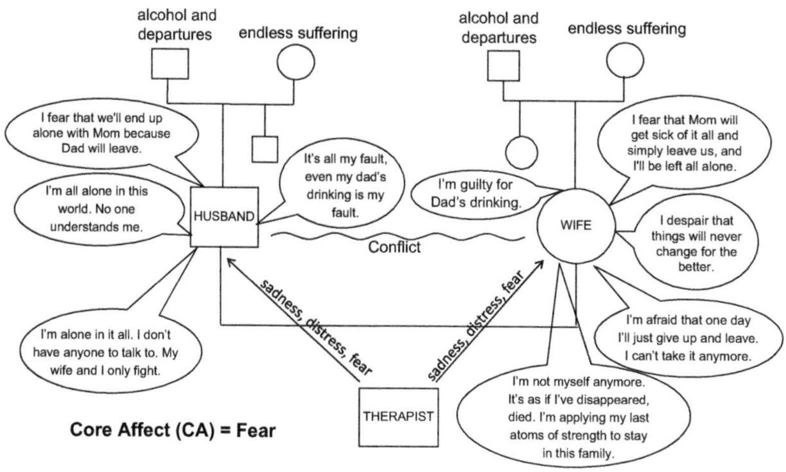

Figure 2.2 Interpersonal level (husband – wife) and intrapsychic level (childhood)

Figure created by Tanja Repič Slavič and Janko Slavič

M *(turning gently to face her children)*: I also want to tell you that both that your father and I will try our best to talk more. We will do anything it takes so that neither of you will feel like one of us is going to leave or abandon you. That's exactly what we *don't* want to happen.

T *(with understanding)*: To close, let's say perhaps a word or two about prayer. I think it would be good for you to try connecting as a family through prayer, Pray for more openness, understanding, and empathy. Prayer can help you develop a sense of availability for each other. All right, enough for today. I will see you next week. Thank you!

In the next few therapy sessions, the therapist worked on making sure that the parents stuck to their decisions in mediating the children's subsystem. They would make sure the children would be supervised in terms of their drug use and possession, and that they would take more responsibility for their behavior. The therapist would encourage them to be given more independence based on how responsibly they behaved. The family agreed to keep each other in check. If there were any slips, such as continued drug use, they would carefully assess the situation and seek help, primarily within the family system's boundaries, but if need be, with professional help, especially if the drug use developed into addiction.

In the ongoing therapeutic process, the group would focus mainly on the parental and marital system. The therapist would begin to uncover what drives the family into old dysfunctional patterns of behaviors, emotions, and ways of thinking. They would delve deeper into the parental subsystem and its intrapsychic structures, as well as into the marital system, analyzing both partners separately. In this way, relational family therapists are able to address a family's affective psychic construct at its deepest level. In this family's case, the construct was rooted in the core affect of fear and despair, which originated in loneliness causing a feeling of abandonment. The therapist would then show the couple how to take a closer look at the way they regulate their affects as partners, as well as a family, and help them realize how their family's restrictive structure had hindered the system's functionality.

In the following chapters, we will focus on the dynamic of core affect transference, including how it is transferred to others and to the entire family system. We will discuss the unconscious mechanisms that shape the way people experience themselves, others, and the world around them. We will be looking at these matters through systemic and relational approaches, referring to the many authors who have elaborated on the subject of transference, as well as behavioral and emotional repetition. Despite the vastness and variety of mental experiences, the work of these authors forms a certain set of definitions and perspectives.

3 Relational Family Therapy and Clinical Practice

This chapter will focus on the basic integrating systemic concepts of relational family therapy and present an innovative therapeutic view of the individual. On the basis of the mechanisms of projective and introjective identification, repetition compulsion, core affect, affective psychic constructs and affect regulation, we will detail the principles of intrapsychic, interpersonal and systemic dynamics and processes. We will clarify how and why the relational ties bind together the psycho-organic family system, what establishes and maintains them, as well as how they are then continuously repeated and reinforced.

3.1 Projective and Introjective Identification

Melanie Klein (1940, 1946, 1962) was the first analyst to introduce the concept of projective and introjective identification into the science of psychoanalysis; she also applied this mechanism to the internal mental experiencing of a child. Thomas Ogden (1979, 1982, 1986) later discovered in his research and clinical studies that this mechanism is the basis for the transfer of emotions and intense affects in interpersonal interactions and transactions. Cashdan (1988) continued this work on the basis of Racker's studies (1968). Over several decades, Cashdan researched the concept of countertransference and established two types of introjective identification, concordant and complementary, which became two of the most significant concepts in clinical practice. The two forms of countertransference differentiate into concordant and complementary countertransference. In the relational "dialogical twin" mechanism of projective and introjective identification, projective identification represents the beginning of the dynamic process and introjective identification mutually follows. This relational mechanism, presupposed by these latter two processes in mutual functioning, composes the complex dynamic of transference that regulates and drives the core affect. Projective and introjective identification and the corresponding core affect also form the affective psychic construct, which prevents the healthy functioning of the individual, couple, or entire family system. In terms of projective and introjective identification, it always begins with withdrawal, denial, suppression, and dissociation from painful, traumatic, or intolerable mental content that the individual, couple, or entire psycho-organic system projects on the basis of valency onto specific individuals (Fosha, 2009; J.S. Scharff, 2010; J.S. Scharff & Scharff, 2014; Schore, 2003, 2010, 2012).

These individuals become the recipients or carriers of this unresolved and intolerable psychological, and often organic, content. Systems theory refers to these individuals as identified patients as they act out this content in a variety of ways. Recipients, identified patients, or carriers of this psychological and organic content basically provide a compromise for the painful trauma and conflicts that have become part of both the individual's intrapsychic structure and interpersonal and systemic dynamics. The process of concordant introjective identification begins with the experiencing of a certain affect that another person is internally experiencing: for instance, when a wife is describing to her friend how her husband abuses her and the friend begins to feel anger towards the husband, or when a therapist begins to feel bored during a session, experiencing concordant responses to the patient's internal emotional boredom. Concordant introjective identification thus lays the foundations for empathy. In other words, it is countertransference that is based on the clients' experiencing of their own selves and is transferred to the therapist who identifies with the projected part of the clients' selves (J.S. Scharff, 2010; J.S. Scharff & Scharff, 2006, 2014; Schore, 2003, 2012).

Complementary introjective identification refers to when the recipient's feelings are affects connected to the parents or other significant persons from the sender's early childhood. Therapists during sessions will feel that clients are equating them with their internalized object representations. They may behave, feel, and react similarly to the way the client's parents used to (Cashdan, 1988; J.S. Scharff, 2010; J.S. Scharff & Scharff, 2006, 2014). The therapist's own psychological and/or psycho-organic content, which is similar to the client's early experience of responses to his challenges, will be triggered on the basis of the client's projections in the form of countertransference.

In relational therapy, the process of introjective identification and the corresponding countertransference is not limited to therapy with individuals, but also transpires with couples and family therapy and the psycho-organic family system. For instance, a couple or even an entire family can evoke the same psychological and psycho-organic content in the therapist as is in their own psychological structures; this is referred to as concordant introjective identification. This content may be part of the therapist's intrapsychic structure that has already been established in connection with significant others. The therapist may experience this content at a cognitive, emotional, organic, or even behavioral level: for instance, the sudden fear of how a client will physically react to a certain challenge. The therapist may have the inclination to react similarly. Likewise, it is typical for the therapist to experience similar bodily sensations when processing a client's physical or sexual abuse. For instance, the therapist might feel pain in the legs, back, shoulders, stomach, throat, head, etc. These pains will subside only when the particular abuse that the client experienced is addressed. Similarly, a partner or family member can experience physical sensations that correspond to emotions connected with abuse, especially when abuse has been suppressed and never spoken of (J. S. Scharff & Scharff, 2014; Schore, 2003, 2010, 2012; Siegel & Solomon, 2013).

Differentiation is important for correctly understanding the mechanism of projective and introjective identification, especially as concerns the strongest affects, fears, and attachments, and the manner in which the sender adjusts them. For instance, the sender can take on a parental role and try to control the other in the same way that the other's parents used to do, or act out and experience the same role and addiction that was experienced in relation to the parents in childhood. This phenomenon can vividly manifest in the safe environment of a therapeutic office where clients may experience themselves in the presence of the therapist as a hostile other from the past. There are many possible affective reactions with which the therapist can respond, and this marks the fundamental challenge in the therapeutic relationship (Cooper, 2000; Donavan, 2003; Johnson & Whiffen, 2003; Maroda, 1994, 2010; J.S. Scharff, 2010; J.S. Scharff & Scharff, 2006, 2014; Shur, 1994; Solomon, 2009; Solomon & Siegel, 2013; Solomon & Siegel, 1997).

The mechanism of introjective identification answers the following key questions: Why do people allow themselves to become the target of the projective identification process? Why do recipients expose themselves to manipulations that always end in the process of introjective identification and the absorption of emotions such as anger, frustration, depression, etc.? Why do people persist in relationships that mark them with projective and introjective identification, and repetition compulsion, despite the fact that it causes them chronic anxiety, frustration, and dissatisfaction? Generally, recipients are vulnerable and lacking suitable internal boundaries. Each external influence can prove catastrophic for them. They are highly susceptible to the external world and the people around them, both of which can impact their psychological balance and render them "easy prey" to all sorts of abuse. Consequently, the abuse they suffer becomes deeply imprinted in their psyche and ultimately results in the constant seeking out of similar affects that promise a relationship.

The premise is that each projective identification carries a powerful prohibition, promise, or threat that the recipient preserves in the relationship, facing rejection and isolation if they do not accept the sender's content. Through introjective identification, recipients accept, sometimes unconsciously, forceful content and threats upon which they become dependent in order to ensure survival. This emotional communication conveys the following message: if you are not what I need, if you do not fulfill my wishes, then you no longer exist for me (J.S. Scharff & Scharff, 2006, 2014). This interactional pattern relies on nonverbal messages and subtle physical cueing, all projected in such a way so as to force others to remain in a relationship. Cashdan (1988) refers to this covert communication as "metacommunication," best revealed in pathological relationships. Contemporary literature terms it right hemisphere communication (Bruschweiler-Stern et al., 2010; Fosha, 2009; Schore, 2003, 2010, 2012).

3.1.1 *Substitution of the Psychoanalytic Paradigm*

Cashdan (1988) later pursued his research in accordance with the radical change in the psychoanalytic paradigm introduced by Mitchell (1988, 2000, 2002), whose methodology and research led to the definition of four types of projective and introjective identification: dependence, power, sexuality, and ingratiation (self-denial). All four types are developed and maintained due to powerful behavioral inductions and the unique response of recipients.

3.1.1.1 In the case of dependence projective identification, recipients learn that they cannot survive on their own and so seek out someone else to offer help and support. Their powerlessness is paradoxically often their strength, as they manage to compel others to be always available to them in their helplessness. A typical example is an adult child who doesn't leave home even when sufficiently old and psychophysically mature. Believing their role is key to maintaining balance in the family and marital system, such adults will remain at home, feeling powerless, thus enabling the psycho-organic system to remain within the limits of the permitted deviational level (Cashdan, 1988; Catherall, 2004; J.S. Scharff & Scharff, 2014).

A variety of psychosomatic conditions and phobic symptoms may emerge when such individuals experience anxiety attacks just at the thought of leaving home. Unconsciously, they are risking rejection, loneliness, and isolation, as well as the feeling of their own disloyalty. Not surprisingly, such individuals choose to stay home, often without really knowing why. Sometimes they develop social phobias, a feeling that they cannot survive on their own, a fear of the unfamiliar social environments and novelties such as entering university. This kind of behavior serves to preserve the family and couple system. The parents then complain and criticize their child for not leaving home and may even occasionally try to force him or her leave, but, through the mechanisms of projective and introjective identification, they keep their child home. The affect is fear, triggering a feeling of powerlessness and the dread of loneliness. The affect, in fact, comes from the parents but has been subtly transferred to the child who cannot leave home (McCormack, 2000; Siegel & Solomon, 2013).

3.1.1.2 In the case of overly powerful individuals, the recipient must take control in order to survive. A wide range of dynamics occurs here as well. The clinical indications in such cases demonstrate the paradox of how strong, controlling, and outwardly arrogant people are, in fact, terribly frightened in their psychological core and often have a fragile self-image, being full of anxieties and the fear of being taken advantage of (Cashdan, 1988; MacFarlane, 2004). Consequently, they will do anything to always maintain control so that they will never be taken by surprise. Their psychological structures are often steeped in fear. This affect is then transferred through the mechanisms of projective and introjective identification onto someone else, who becomes powerless and fearful, relinquishing all power to the controlling individual who takes advantage of them. In this instance, neither is aware of the core dynamic that so forcefully connects them (J.S. Scharff & Scharff, 2014).

Many of these individuals come from families where they were pushed into the role of parentalized children. They had to play nurturing roles for their parents and siblings and establish a sense of security, and also of pride, in the family; otherwise they would feel guilty for not having done enough, regardless of whether it was in their power to do so or not. These children learn in their family of origin that they must always maintain control or face dire consequences. They learn that no one is there to nurture them and feel that that is their own fault. They come to hope that someday someone will take care of them in exchange for their nurturing of others. And here is the paradox: they will have difficulty trusting anyone or being subservient to or dependent upon anyone, they will not dare let themselves be vulnerable as this would be taking the risk that others will not take care of them, that they will once again be exposed just as they were when they saved themselves by taking control and caring for others. These individuals face great difficulties trying to "step down from their pedestals" regardless of how lonely they feel and how often they are taken advantage of. It is always the feeling of guilt that draws them back into relationships where they once again take care of the other (Bradshaw, 1996; McCormack, 2000; Rothschild, 2006, 2010).

3.1.1.3 As regards sexuality, such individuals learn to establish an interpersonal relationship through eroticism. This is characteristic of those who approach others, attract attention, and secure basic care through eroticized connections. These are people who repeatedly enter relationships led by eroticism, in which they are again refused and perhaps even rejected without quite knowing why, failing to recognize how others repeatedly take advantage of them on the basis of their sexual availability. This often happens to so-called "Daddy's girls," the daughters who become their father's emotional partner because their relationship with their father is colored by the emotional and physical absence of his wife (Cashdan, 1988; MacFarlane, 2004; McCormack, 2000). This is especially true if the father-daughter relationship is in any way erotically tinged and the father dismissed or even rejected the daughter as she entered puberty due to her developing sexuality (Steinberg, 2014).

This characteristic can be even more pronounced among those who were sexually abused, because abuse destroys the intrapsychic structure. Due to the damaged intrapsychic boundaries, victims of sexual abuse no longer know how to differentiate between an authentic relationship and one that is false and exclusively sexual. Victims of sexual abuse may be exceptionally sensitive but lack the capacity to gauge what will lead them into an authentic relationship and what will lead them into new abuse. The trauma of abuse destroys their ability to regulate affect, so they seek out similar abusive circumstances that generate a similar affect precisely because it promises a relationship. At the same time, such a relationship fulfills the organic-hormonal-chemical addiction that drives victims into abusive relations.

There are also victims of sexual abuse who tend to decline all relationships for fear of further abuse (Fosha, 2009; Schore, 2003, 2010, 2012). These tend to become emotionally and organically blocked, inapproachable, and incapable of intimate connection. They reject all emotional closeness due to their unconscious fear of relationships. It is difficult for them to fall in love because their organic-hormonal-chemical system is blocked (Beilock, 2015).

3.1.1.4 In cases of ingratiation through self-sacrifice, the individual secures relationships by turning others into their debtors. These are people who repeatedly trigger feelings of guilt in others; this is the core affect that binds others to them (Bradshaw, 1996; Cashdan, 1988; Catherall, 2004). Those with an ingratiating manner will continuously prompt others to feel they are never quite grateful enough for what was being done for them. Often these individuals are suffering, but they are able to make others feel that gratitude is insufficient for the sacrifice. This may be achieved so subtly that, although it is always felt, it may not be discerned directly. A typical example is when a mother makes constant and demonstrative sacrifices for her children, showering them with attention and overwhelming them with her favors and services, and thus basically tethering them to her. If this proves unsuccessful, then she attempts to evoke a sense of guilt in her children for their insufficient appreciation of the sacrifices she has made. Such a mother will never be truly satisfied with the gratitude and acknowledgement received in response to her sacrifices. It will always fall short in terms of amount or expression. Such a mother unconsciously binds her children to herself, rendering them incapable of emotional independence (Kim et al., 2014).

It is a challenge to directly address relationships that take place on the level of nonverbal and unconscious metacommunication. It can be difficult to recognize how these types of relational strategies are actually about seeking, creating, and maintaining relationships with others (McCormack, 2000; Rothschild, 2006, 2010). In such cases, it is necessary to detect the unconscious mechanism of projective and introjective identification and its core affects that serve as the basis for both the affective psychic construct and the affective regulation system.

The four examples mentioned above present a unique view into how projective and introjective identification mechanism is imprinted in the dynamic between the sender and recipient, facilitating relationships and self-preservation while simultaneously maintaining homeostasis, emotional cognitive disorders, and their corresponding pathologies. All of this effort goes towards creating and maintaining a relationship. These patterns are deeply engrained and repetitive, sometimes even in new circumstances and with new people (J.S. Scharff, 2010; J.S. Scharff & Scharff, 2006, 2014; Schore, 2003, 2010, 2012). These are patterns that become integral to the individual's intrapsychic and interpersonal worlds and constitutive parts of all of their relationships.

3.1.2 Slipp's Typology of Right Hemisphere Communication

Samuel Slipp (1988, 1996, 1993) never specifically, theoretically, or formally defined the concept of projective and introjective identification. Nevertheless, his unique and independent application of this concept represents a significant advance in our understanding and integration of the intrapsychic dynamic with interpersonal and systemic relational configurations, as well as our understanding of the formation of the identified patient. Virtually all of Slipp's theories, clinical classifications, and definitions of schizophrenia, depression, hysteria, and delinquency refer to it (Slipp, 1996). Projective and introjective identification is an eloquent demonstration of right hemisphere communication (Rothschild, 2006, 2010; Schore, 2003, 2010, 2012) in the family system, a dynamic that is an unconscious force, exerting pressure upon the identified patient to accept a certain role, identify with it, and become the carrier of a parent's or partner's unresolved distressing content. Slipp (1996) defines projective and introjective identification is an intrapsychic and interpersonal defense mechanism. The individual emits good and bad self or other images and affects upon the recipient who serves as a container for these projections. The recipient is unwittingly forced, either through verbal or nonverbal communication, to assume a certain role and way of thinking, feeling, and acting in accordance with the sender's projection.

According to Slipp's theories, the process serves to induce split-off and unwanted object images and aspects of the self in another person in an attempt to create a sense of increased control over and psychological distance from these unwanted affects. The recipient's response, processed and in altered form, is then re-internalized by the sender on the basis of introjective identification. Thus the process is essentially a kind of negative feedback, confirming the sender's internal world of images and affects (Slipp, 1993, 1996). Although Slipp does not specifically define the systemic mechanism of projective identification on the basis of which he would have then been able to clarify the formation of the identified patient both clinically and theoretically, he explicitly draws on the conceptualization of systemic cybernetics. Thus, Slipp's formulation of projective and introjective identification (J.S. Scharff & Scharff, 2014) remains conceptually congruent with the fields of intrapsychic, interpersonal, and multipersonal dynamics, although it's clinical application does not reach the systemic level. The identified patient is the consequence of interpersonal and multipersonal projective and introjective identification, all of which maintains systemic homeostasis (Schore, 2003, 2010, 2012). Relational family therapy adds to this the affective psychic construct founded on the above-mentioned dynamic and affect regulation.

Slipp (1996) states that we project intrapsychic content or elements into the interpersonal sphere where they remain active and constitute transpersonal defense mechanisms that may be manipulative. Thus, the sender manipulates the other and lives parasitically off the relationship, preserving his or her own self-confidence and identity. Poorly defined boundaries between the self and other, denial of separateness, differentiation, and a lack of awareness regarding the needs and motivations of the other serves to enable this process (Feinstein, 2013). Rather than real intimacy and giving, the lack of differentiation and taking advantage of the other satisfy the needs of the sender in fulfillment of the self. In this regard, children are exceptional containers or embodiments of their parents' projections, activating both positive and negative feedback (J.S. Scharff, 2010; J.S. Scharff & Scharff, 2006, 2014; Slipp, 1996). The following section defines the forms this takes.

3.1.2.1 In families with a schizophrenic child (Slipp, 1996), the parents fear that open expression of aggression would destroy the marital relationship, so the partners idealize each other and their roles as mother and father. Aggression towards the partner is denied, split off, and projected onto the child who is perceived by the parents as demanding and a poor maternal object. The child is forced into the role the family scapegoat. The child internalizes this introjection, carries the affect, and develops a negative self-identity. This mechanism is founded on the shared family fantasy that aggression is destructive, which only further increases the child's omnipotent and destructive fantasies, thus blocking the development of the self and object constancy (Scharff, 2010; J.S. Scharff & Scharff, 2006, 2014). The child feels unworthy, is incapable of self-defense, and fears that his or her own aggression will destroy the approaching object and self (Slipp, 1996). Another form of this type of interaction, whereby the child is not pushed into the role of scapegoat, entails the neglect of the child who becomes narcissistically wounded as a result.

This interaction is a *folie à deux* dynamic in which both parents, despite the mental disorder of one of them, function as a good maternal object for the other. They share, create, and realize each other's unsatisfied, childhood developmental needs and neglect those of their own child (Slipp, 1996). They ascribe the affect and the insufficient object to their child who as a result feels worthless and a burden, the same way the parents felt when they were growing up. Ultimately, the child, through the mechanism of projective and introjective identification, experiences the self as adverse and demanding, responsible for the parents' emotional rejection. This destructive feeling is only augmented by the operative psycho-organic family belief or myth that the child's demanding behavior is the cause of physical and emotional wounds, and sometimes even the cause of the death, of one of the parents (J.S. Scharff & Scharff, 2014; Steinberg, 2014). Such circumstances cause the child to feel responsible for the neglect or rejection, and also guilty that the anger and rage felt regarding his or her own rejection wounded the parents (J.S. Scharff, 2010; J.S. Scharff & Scharff, 2006, 2014; Slipp, 1996).

3.1.2.2 In families with a hysterical adolescent or a child with a borderline personality structure (Slipp, 1996), one of the parents is not collaborating in mutual supervision and there is an exploitative marital relationship. This is often the case in families that have a schizophrenic member and a marital relationship that needs constant confirmation. Both parents function as a good maternal object for the other (Feinstein, 2013). The partner who does not collaborate has a satisfying autonomy and cannot be exploited for the fulfillment of the other's needs. In response, the neglected partner uses the defense mechanism of talking, overt resistance, and risking rejection, yet is not strong enough to satisfy their own needs or to leave the marital relationship. So this partner will be emotionally distance himself or herself from the other, often turning to the child in the family (Slipp, 1996). If the identified patient is female, the husband degrades the wife as a poor maternal object and idealizes the female child. The father, in such a case, uses the defense mechanism of denial and disassociation as well as projective and introjective identification. Because the mother is emotionally unavailable to her husband, the husband turns to the daughter to satisfy his emotional needs (J.S. Scharff, 2010; J.S. Scharff & Scharff, 2006, 2014; Slipp, 1996).

The child becomes an emotional partner, thus keeping the conflicted parental relationship alive (Slipp, 1996). The daughter unconsciously serves her father as a good maternal object, satiating his narcissistic needs (J.S. Scharff, 2010; J.S. Scharff & Scharff, 2006, 2014). The seductive elements of such a relationship may lead the daughter to eroticize relationships in adulthood, and to use her sexuality to satisfy the narcissistic needs of others, much in the same manner as her father emotionally exploited her. This will become the way she builds and maintains relationships with others. The borderline personality can be differentiated from the hysterical personality in that the former is first seduced and then emotionally rejected, while the latter is simply rejected, remaining identified with the seductive father or mother (McCormack, 2000; Slipp, 1996). Such cases often are the result of emotional or sexual abuse in which the child was first exploited and then rejected. This sequence often leads to the grown child seeking similar abusive relationships in adulthood

(Catherall, 2004; MacFarlane, 2004; McCormack, 2000; J. S. Scharff & Scharff, 2014; Slipp, 1996).

3.1.2.3 In families with a depressed child (Slipp, 1996), one of the partners is experienced as unsuccessful or a failure. The dominant partner humiliates the unsuccessful partner as a bad self. The good self is projected upon the child who is overtly pressured to succeed. The dominant partner can thus identify with and live parasitically on the child's success. The child feels the need to always succeed and serve as the family savior, in other words as the antidepressant factor that preserves the self-confidence of the dominant partner (Bradshaw, 1996; McCormack, 2000; Slipp, 1996). Children in such circumstances equate failure with rejection. At the same time, they do not enjoy their own success, develop self-confidence, or separate and differentiate as their dominant father or mother impedes their very essence. The parents' unconscious envy and need to control prevents them from recognizing or reflecting the successful child who is experienced as the source of the parents' narcissism (J.S. Scharff & Scharff, 2014). Such parents often praise their child in front of others. By boasting of their child's successes, they gratify themselves and quench their own thirst for importance but fail to give their child validation. Success is taken for granted, while the child is never considered quite good enough, any success being attributed to circumstance and luck. The overt message is that positive results are demanded; the covert message being is the child must remain weak and dependent. The situation is a double bind: a dual message regarding success where the child cannot and must not succeed despite being socially successful (McCormack, 2000; Slipp, 1996).

3.1.2.4 In families with a delinquent youth (Slipp, 1996), one of the parents projects their own bad self, together with the core affect, upon the child, thus pressuring him or her to act out the parent's anger and aggression. This child will function as the family "avenger." The pressure to collaborate and adapt is less pronounced in examples with depressed or delinquent children than those with schizophrenic or borderline personality structures as the social environment encourages or limits such behavior (Catherall, 2004; Feinstein, 2013; Slipp, 1996). Children and youth who are forced to act out these dangerous games are generally unaware of their circumstances and why they behave so inappropriately. Usually these children cannot control their behavior, They cannot regulate their intense emotions such as anger, rage, internal disquiet, and distress. They are incapable of controlling their own responses to the victims of their acting out, which pushes them into new uncontrollable situations. The tragedy for such children is that there is no one to calm them, set boundaries for them, and help them process their unacceptable emotions. Occasionally, the parents actually need such a child to remain delinquent as they play the significant role of carrying the anger, rage, and vengeful emotions in the family (Feinstein, 2013; McCormack, 2000; Steinberg, 2014).

Slipp (1988, 1993, 1996) also discovered that various combinations of these typologies can be projected on to a single child. For instance, some individuals demonstrate schizoid and depressive characteristics and alternately act as the family scapegoat and family savior. In other families, the dynamic of scapegoat and avenger are acted out, and the children demonstrate both schizoid and psychopathic characteristics. In other families, these roles are distributed across several children—one becoming the family savior, another becoming the family scapegoat. Sometimes in response to changing environments or extraordinary events in the psycho-organic family system, these roles can be established anew or reversed. In cases where the identified patient is no longer symptomatic, another child can take on the role through the mechanism of projective and introjective identification (J.S. Scharff, 2010; J.S. Scharff & Scharff, 2006, 2014). These processes represent powerful right hemisphere communication, with unconscious rules and roles that maintain the systemic homeostasis.

Slipp's research theorizes that the senders' goal is to manipulate external reality through projective and introjective identification in order to make it match their internal fantasies. The senders are trying to repeat their drama, causing recipients to act out a drama similar to the one acted out in the family of origin. As a result, external reality becomes parallel to internal reality. The responses triggered in recipients are internalized; they prompt negative feedback, which fortifies the internalized world of object relations, thus maintaining the family homeostasis. The relational family model also develops the concept of the affective psychic construct and corresponding affect regulation, both of which fortify certain typologies. This process is similar to what takes place in early childhood, creating the foundation, with the help of fantasies, of the internal world. These omnipotent fantasies enable the individual to enter into the object, exploiting, manipulating, and controlling him (Catherall, 2004; J.S. Scharff & Scharff, 2014). Whenever the relationships among family members are created on the basis of projective and introjective identification, the entire system becomes one of relationships colored by mutual control and coercion, a symbiotic form of survival.

Viewed from the perspective of the relational family model, processes of projective and introjective identification develop into an affective interaction between husband and wife even before the birth of any children. Later, different aspects of this prototype are unconsciously distributed among the children; this is how children preserve systemic equilibrium and the affective psychic construct. Each child contributes their own character to the unconscious communication of the projective and introjective identification processes taking place between parents and children. Each child develops a specific relationship to one aspect of the parental connection. These are the foundations for so-called family roles. On the basis of projective and introjective identification, each child's personality adapts to the characteristics of each of the parents individually as well as to the characteristics of their marriage (J.S. Scharff, 1992, 2010; D.E. Scharff & Scharff, 1987; J.S. Scharff & Scharff, 1994, 2006, 2014). The symptomatic family member demonstrates a compromise between his or her own independence and family belonging. At the same time, symptomatic families also represent the compromise between family goals and goals that were valid in previous generations. Symptoms form as a signal of anxiety, as a sign that an anxious system is seeking a new balance that will be in agreement with ongoing development, or as a sign of resistance to too much change.

In theory, the relational family paradigm understands the individual or family symptom as a crystallization of the experience in family relations. It represents the variety of microscopic projective and introjective identifications that are distributed among family members in a specific systemic family model. It is the result of several combinations of intrapsychic, interpersonal, and systemic relationships in the psycho-organic family system that form the affective psychic construct that continually reinforces how affect is regulated. The model implicitly draws on systemic theory when it describes the phenomenon of the identified patient. Jill and David Scharff (1992, 1994, 2000, 2006, 2010, 2014), for instance, expressly affirm this, and their theory presupposes and applies both systemic theory and the cybernetic system. However, they do not define or develop the mechanism of projective and introjective identification on the systemic level. To the contrary, it is clearly defined in the relational family paradigm, which posits that the identified patient carries and maintains symptomatic family models, facilitates compromise between family goals and the goals of previous generations, and seeks out new psycho-organic family homeostasis.

The relational family model basically considers the identified patient a product of the systemic formation of projective and introjective identification. The systemic projective and introjective identification dynamic can also be explained on the basis of the model presented by Slipp and the Scharffs, even though these authors do not explicitly mention it. The main processes—such as projection, induction, introjective identification, and object transformation—are all observable at the systemic level. The main difference lies in the dynamic of the system, which sends out its own projections with the family members acting as recipients.

Also noteworthy are the dynamics of positive and negative feedback, which maintain systemic balance and generate the affective psychic construct. These two systems determine the functions, needs, roles, rules, and structure of the family system, which allows them to establish the core affect of the family system, which in turn provides the foundation for the affective regulation system. For its part, the core affect defines the tone of the entire family dynamic and marks all systemic relationships and the corresponding systemic structure.

The core affect influences all elements in the system while maintaining balance on the basis of intrapsychic images of the self, objects, and affects. The only way to remain connected with the family is merging with this family affect, adapting to it, and continuing to generate, internalize, and reinforce the intrapsychic images of the self and object. This represents an exceptionally complex dynamic of relationships, which only attains true meaning within the context of the entire system. The relational family model is what enables our full comprehension of this dynamic. Any change in the system (or within any of its subsystems—marital, parental, child, and the intrapsychic systems of self images, objects, and affects) will impact the entire system, which is always changing in its effort to maintain systemic balance. The mechanisms of projective and introjective identification, the fundamental communication elements of positive and negative feedback, and right-hemisphere communication is what keeps the system running. All of these processes together create the affective psychic construct.

The following example demonstrates right hemisphere communication and the process of projective and introjective identification, both concordant and complementary. During the therapy sessions, it becomes clear how the internal images of the self, object, and affect between the self and object repeatedly carry over from the interpersonal and systemic levels, causing old issues, which had already been reinforced in the intrapsychic spheres of the parents' psychic structure ages ago, to flare up. The excerpt below is from a family therapy session with the following family members: the father Frank (F), the mother Maria (M), and their 17-year-old daughter Sarah (S). The family sought therapy because Sarah had gotten herself involved in bad company. The males among her group of friends were coarse and rough, treating her with her contempt. This was especially true of her boyfriend who had already physically abused her. Nonetheless, Sarah just couldn't get herself to leave him. Sarah turned a deaf ear to her parents' pleas, threats, and efforts at persuasion. Ultimately, her mother chose to seek professional help. The father presented considerable resistance, believing it was entirely unnecessary for him to be present at the therapy sessions. The therapist had to invest extraordinary effort during the first session simply to persuade the father that there was much he could contribute and change—in himself as well—that might prove crucial to bringing functionality to the entire family.

After getting through the first bumps that are inevitable during the onset of therapy, the family began to relax a little more. Furthermore, once the father witnessed the change in the family atmosphere, and that Sarah was able to resist meeting her boyfriend and his friends for several consecutive days, his hope and faith in the therapeutic process increased. The following excerpt is from the third therapy session with all three family members present. It was already palpable in the waiting room that something distressful was transpiring among them. The parents blamed it on the Sarah's most recent "escape" to her group of friends, including her old boyfriend. However, the therapist (T) also senses that there was more to their distress, anxiety, despair, and deep hurt mingled with emotions of sadness and disappointment. The transcription that follows includes all of the therapist's feelings and sensations—forms of countertransference—as well as all feelings and transfers from the family members—physical sensations and transference of affects and other emotions. This method of transcription aims to give validation to these emotions, which is essential in all therapeutic sessions.

T *(feeling a sense distress and pressure in her head)*: I feel a sense of deep distress among all of you, something that's blocked you all (*looking around*). Can any of you tell me about it?

F *(fidgeting angrily)*: Sarah got back together with that group of hers. I'm sure that her old boyfriend was there too.

M *(also angry)*: I don't know if this will ever end. We're in such agony.

S *(angry, scowling)*: Do you really have to start nagging all over again? I am so sick and tired of it all. Nobody understands me anyway. It's all pointless.

The therapeutic approach is still targeted at the systemic level: Sarah is the scapegoat, or the identified patient, and carries within her symptoms of unresolved and painful family and marital emotions. The therapist's interventions are focused on the systemic level of their experiencing, which is also doubtless a reflection of much deeper interpersonal and intrapsychic dynamics. It becomes clear that the core affect, and consequently the affective psychic construct and its defense mechanisms, is more deeply rooted. However, the therapist must uncover this during the early stages of the therapeutic session by trying to trace and examine the core affect at the systemic level.

T *(feeling fear from the daughter, as well as the disappointment and anger of the father and mother)*: Frank and Martha, you seem to feel increasingly angry, disappointed, and hopeless in the face of your daughter's distress which simply doesn't seem to come to an end. And Sarah, you're increasingly agitated. It's as if you're afraid of their angry responses, and yet, like them, you're also powerless. It's as if some hidden force is drawing you into that group of friends, and you feel increasingly alone, isolated, hopeless, and sad. I sense that this it really hurting you and yet that you can't seem to help yourself. I imagine that's how you're feeling. In order to get some relief from these feelings, to quiet and control them, you return to your social group. That gives you a sense of at least some temporary relief.

F *(disappointed and angry)*: We've told her time and again to stop hanging out with them, with these young guys who just take advantage of her, but it's like she's addicted to them. No matter how badly they treat her, she runs back for more the moment they call. And then she cries and everything is in complete shambles for days afterwards. But then she goes back to them again, or I'm guessing, to him. We were hoping that with your help something would change, but . . .

T *(feeling the father's anger as tension in the chest)*: You're so disappointed that not even I can help.

F *(calmer)*: I'm not blaming you. I was just hoping that things would be better by now. Is there any hope of solving this problem?

The therapist senses in this initial exchange that the father is transferring through projective and introjective identification his anger and disappointment, denied components of his intrapsychic structure—first to his daughter and her boyfriend and other friends, and then to the therapist and wife. Frank glances contemptuously at his wife every so often. Nevertheless, the therapist senses that Frank is really angry with himself for being powerless in the face of his daughter's poor choices. Maria is also angry with herself but even more so with her husband.

She also looks upon her husband with contempt because he can't do anything but spew anger and disgust upon his daughter and his wife. Maria is also splitting off certain emotions and experiencing them in her daughter and sometimes in her husband. This realization brings clarity to the goals of the therapeutic intervention at this stage. The first goal is to uncover the core affect in the family, which the daughter currently carries and acts out by continuing to self-destructively return to the group of friends who take advantage of her, leaving her feeling empty, disappointed, and worthless. The therapist must follow the indications of the interpersonal and intrapsychic dynamics and trace the core affect in order to resolve the affective psychic construct that is preventing the parents from intervening in their daughter's life more appropriately, and is also obstructing Sarah from her own affective and cognitive capacity to make better judgments and choices that correspond with her emotional needs.

T (*feeling her heart beating faster*): Frank, what would happen if you could really feel your daughter in her own distress, really feel what is compelling her to repeatedly go back to that group?

F *(suspicious)*: Are you implying that I don't do enough? It's my wife who's let her get away with things all these years. She's the one who's spoiled her, and now I'm . . .

M *(barely containing her anger)*: So now it's all my fault!

T (*feeling a lump in her throat and sensing that a wound has been reopened*): Maria, please hang in there just a little longer. Frank, we're not looking for who to blame here. And even if we find the culprit, we still haven't resolved anything. I believe it's more likely that what's happening here is that your daughter is calling out to her father, that she wants to include you in her world. She misses you!

F *(angry)*: Then she should behave better!

T *(still feeling a lump in her throat and sensing that the father feels attacked and guilty)*: Frank, I do understand it, how difficult this must be for you right now. And I don't know what old wound we have uncovered. Maybe it's also your daughter's pain and she is simply seeking resolution, while only bringing on more grief and disappointment.

F *(attentive)*: Well, I really don't understand any of that!

The therapist senses in her own bodily sensations that the father is angry. She also senses that the father feels deeply disappointed and powerless. He comes across as both helpless and hopeless. However, through active listening, the therapist discerns that he's also hurt, triggering more disappointment. The mechanisms of denial, disassociation, and transference to others ease the intensity, but hurt and vulnerability continue to accumulate nonetheless. This analysis points to Frank's intrapsychic sphere of experience where he was probably wounded at some previous point in his life. Now his own daughter, also increasingly wounded by the responses she's receiving in her surroundings, is hurting him. By doubting the therapist's capacity to help, the father hints at his feelings of being misunderstood, powerless, and unsuccessful, at his inability to receive from others, and his failure of empathy. His disappointment, hurt, despair, and anger—clearly exaggerated in the current circumstances—seem increasingly transparent, as Frank seems unable to control his responses at the systemic and interpersonal levels. The core affect is thus anchored at a deeper level and is preventing functional communication between father and daughter in the present. This core affect in his relationship with the daughter is growing stronger and fortifying the affective psychic construct, a constitutive element in the affects of fear and anger, which are manifested also in vulnerability, woundedness, and powerlessness. The affects of anger and despair appear to be guiding Frank's perceptive capacity as well as his style of affect regulation.

T *(feeling sadness)*: What would happen if you tried to understand?

F *(resisting)*: I don't know what would happen. Would something have to happen? I'm not sure I understand you.

T *(still feeling sadness)*: I don't know what you would feel if you tried to understand your daughter and her pain.

F *(sadly)*: I guess I'd feel sad.

T *(feeling her own sadness subsiding as if it is moving into the father)*: You probably would.

F *(sad and anxious)*: Probably. You know, I do care how my daughter feels. Although I don't understand why she does everything she can to get herself hurt. And in doing that, she also hurts me and my wife.

T *(feeling that the sadness has been fully transferred to the father yet still feeling a lump in her throat)*: So the sadness and hurt, the disappointment and despair: it just moves among you?

F *(uneasily)*: I guess so.

T *(feeling fear and a sense of numbness)*: Are you afraid to actually address these emotions?

F *(uneasily)*: I don't know what to say.

T *(feeling numbness in her hands, decides to take a risk)*: Are you afraid to talk about this with your daughter?

F *(resisting)*: What's there to be afraid of? She should just get herself together and then there won't be anything to feel bad about anymore.

At this point the therapist becomes aware through her bodily sensations—the lump in her throat and the numbness—that the father really is afraid of even talking about the painful emotions his daughter is experiencing. This confirms that the affective psychic construct is obstructing the path along which she might trace the core affect to a deeper, intrapsychic level. The therapist feels that the father's intrapsychic structure is marked by images of objects, the self, and affects that are acutely threatening. If Frank were to address them, he would become extremely vulnerable. This is the source of his sadness, hurt, anger, and despair. He must have developed an affective psychic construct in his youth in order to defend himself from further vulnerability, perhaps even rejection. Now these emotions, albeit in a different context, have been reawakened and this has further reinforced the affective psychic construct that now obstructs communication between father and daughter.

Avoidance of feeling the pain of being exposed, hurt, and dejected is an unconscious choice that Frank already accepted in his early childhood as these emotions were terribly threatening to his still developing mental structure and self. Thus, he developed a defensive wall around himself—an affective mental structure—to prevent the intrusion of such intense emotions into his internal being. These emotions were only reawakened by his daughter's troubles, triggering his automatic response to block them that now he has developed as an adult. This history lies embedded in the unconscious world. The communicative block is stronger because he doesn't know how to address it. In the following conversation, the therapist will address these blocks and the corresponding mental content.

T *(caringly, feeling pressure in her head and chest)*: What if we were to do switch focus a little bit and try to discover where all of this is coming from. Have you ever felt like in your life as your daughter might feel now?

F *(hurt)*: I've always felt that way. Those are the feelings I always tried most to avoid. I felt very hurt growing up.

T *(feeling tension and fear reflected in her shallow breathing)*: What happened when you were growing up?

F *(still visibly hurt)*: Nobody understood me. Nobody took any interest in me. I was all on my own. It was really so upsetting when my parents divorced.

T *(feeling pressure in her head)*: How did you feel then?

F *(distressed)*: I was just so disappointed and I felt like a failure because I couldn't keep them together no matter how hard I tried. It made me feel so powerless.

T *(feeling fear and a numbness in her legs)*: And fear, thinking and worrying about who would take care of you?

F *(introspectively, fearfully)*: Yes, I was really scared. That's why I tried so hard to keep them together. And then when I couldn't, I just started hanging out more and more with my friends. I went through all sorts of things back then, until I met Maria, and here we are now. I just don't want Sarah to have to go through all of that.

T *(still feeling fear)*: Do you think that your daughter is afraid that you two might split up?

F *(thoughtfully)*: I don't think she had any reason to be.

M *(exploding)*: She has no reason to worry about that at all! All our fights are just normal fights!

T *(feeling fear and uncertainty)*: Okay, Maria. Please hang in there a little longer. We'll get to you in a minute. (*turning back to Frank*) Why don't you ask her?

F *(turning to Sarah thoughtfully)*: Are you afraid of something like that?

S *(fearfully)*: Yes! I'm totally scared that you'll get a divorce! You know what it's like . . .

F and M *(simultaneously, surprised)*: What do you mean?

S *(distressed)*: You know . . . Dad, you stay out late and you (*to her mother*) threaten, and get angry, and cry . . .

T *(carefully, feeling a lump in her throat and a sense of sadness)*: So if we all pay attention to Sarah's group of friends, to this boyfriend, then we don't have to pay attention to these fears? They're displaced somewhere else.

M *(surprised)*: You mean you think that it's because the three of us are afraid that one of us will leave?

T *(circumspectly, feeling distress and sadness)*: That's the feeling I'm getting here. What about you, Maria?

M *(sadly)*: Well, I have been deeply hurt by my husband, too often. But it never hurt as much as it does now, that Sarah can't seem to get away from this crowd.

The therapist tries to dismantle projective and introjective identification—the mechanism that transfers the affects of anger, fear, and sadness, and which manifests in hurt, dejection, and vulnerability. These fears camouflage the even greater fear that old emotions might be brought to the surface. Paradoxically, they continue to be repeated as the core affect is time and again overlooked, thus becoming a constitutive element of the affective psychic construct and preventing the family members from disclosing their fears and pain as they dread any new distress. Ultimately, it is their reticence to openly address these emotions that facilitates their repeated activation. These affects continue to seek resolution, always leading the family members to new dead ends without knowing why. The therapist thus begins to explore with the mother the affective psychic construct preventing her from addressing her own painful emotions.

T *(feeling fear and sadness, sensing that these affects are being triggered in both herself and the mother)*: Maria, what is the source of this pain? Let's take a big risk—of course, if you feel up to it. (*Maria nods.*) What was it like for you growing up in your childhood home? Is this fear and pain familiar to you?

M *(sad)*: Yes. My parents didn't divorce, although in all honesty I often quietly wished for it because things were so bad between them. My dad drank, he'd often beat up my mom, and she just put up with it.

T *(feeling the horror in her accelerated heartbeat and shallow breathing)*: How horrible that must have been for you. What do you remember feeling?

M *(visibly unsettled and distressed)*: I think horrible is too soft a word for it. It was constant terror. (*emotions erupting from her*) We were all tortured by it: my mom, my sister, my brother, and me. We were always waiting for the worst. We couldn't help each other. We were utterly powerless, always in pain, constantly wounded, disappointed, horrified. We just waited in dread for Dad to go so far as to kill her. He was savage when he was drunk!

T *(still feeling the horror and an increasing sense of sadness)*: And through all of it you learned that you had to put up with it and survive, that you have to suffer through it, and wait for the day when it might get better.

M *(crying)*: It's true. But I did decide that I would never suffer like that with my own husband.

T *(feeling immense sadness and tears of disappointment coming into her eyes)*: And you succeeded on some levels. But now you look at your daughter who's involved in an intimate relationship with a callous and aggressive man. How does that make you feel?

M *(appalled)*: Oh, it's so awful! She really doesn't have to put up with it!

T *(feeling her anger and sadness)*: Maria, you know exactly how horrifying it is, and you know exactly what the final result is. How could you help your daughter? She's just as powerless as you once were. The difference between your situations is really only that you were alone in it, while she has a mother who can fight for her.

Relational family therapy recognizes that parental traumas often get transferred to their children, who end up choosing partners on the basis of the core affect from the primary family, and sometimes even to subsequent generations if these traumas remain unprocessed. The mother in the present case successfully avoided repeating these painful traumas in her marriage while her daughter became the victim of the transference, entering into a relationship where she suffers ongoing terror. This situation reawakens all the emotions that the parents, and especially the mother, suppressed long ago. The mechanism of projective and introjective identification facilitates these emotions being triggered again.

M *(sad and also angry)*: I really can't imagine how this could happen. I just so wanted . . . I mean I tried so hard . . . I don't know if anyone can possibly understand how terrible I feel that this is the end result of all my efforts. And Sarah has a choice.

T *(sensing fear, anger, and disappointment)*: Maria, I believe that you feel awful. I also know that you are the only one who really understands your daughter. After all, her loyalty and willingness to put up with her boyfriend and friends who treat her so abusively are based on an emotion you know—a lot like what you experienced when your own mother continued to put up with your father who treated her so badly.

M *(concerned)*: But what can I do? What can we do as a family? How can we help?

T *(feeling a sense of fear and sadness)*: Well, you two were obviously taken by surprise with Sarah's call for help. You both feel horrified, angry, and disappointed. And now you're afraid because she can't seem to extract herself from the situation. And, of course, she is suffering too. First we'll address her loyalty to these harsh emotions that are manifested everywhere—in her social group, with her boyfriend—and find their roots. How and where in your life have you felt like this before?

M *(concerned)*: You think this will help?

T *(feeling her concern and sadness)*: Yes. First we'll try to free you two from the emotions that continue to live within you. I'll ask you each to talk with Sarah about all this, and to talk with her about her own pain and fear, which both of you are familiar with simply because they are a part of you and of what you each experienced while growing up. The difference is that you had these experiences because of your parents and Sarah experiences them vis-à-vis her group of friends and her boyfriend. But the emotions are certainly related. What you really need to do is feel her and be with her, and then you'll know how to help.

S *(as if suddenly wakening up)*: What about me? You know, I just want to have a normal boyfriend and it doesn't seem possible.

T *(feeling anger and sadness)*: Sarah, thank you for your voice. You know, these emotions have all become so deeply engrained within you, such a strong part of who you are, that you can't imagine being without a boyfriend. As soon as you sense him being nice, an unknown force compels you to go back to him and his group of friends.

S *(thoughtfully)*: That's true. I can't seem to stop myself even though I want to.

T *(feeling fear and concern)*: We'll be discussing all of this in much greater depth, but for today, let's just acknowledge that we seem to have dug down to some depths that we weren't aware of as of yet. I'm sorry, but we need to finish for today. I'd like to suggest that each of you say a daily prayer for the resolution of these relationships, perhaps a prayer you used to say together years ago. These are very deep wounds and they need spiritual healing as well. Okay then. We'll meet again next week. Thank you!

F, M, and S *(a little lost in their thoughts)*: Thank you!

The parents have once again begun to feel their old split-off, denied, and buried horrors and fears, and they have also begun to understand that these emotions are now embodied in their daughter. While they are still not able to fully comprehend or feel it all, they are nonetheless beginning to reach back and sift through their own distressed memories and emotions.

The parents come to the fourth session alone.

T *(feeling distress as lump in her throat)*: Hello. So you've come alone today.

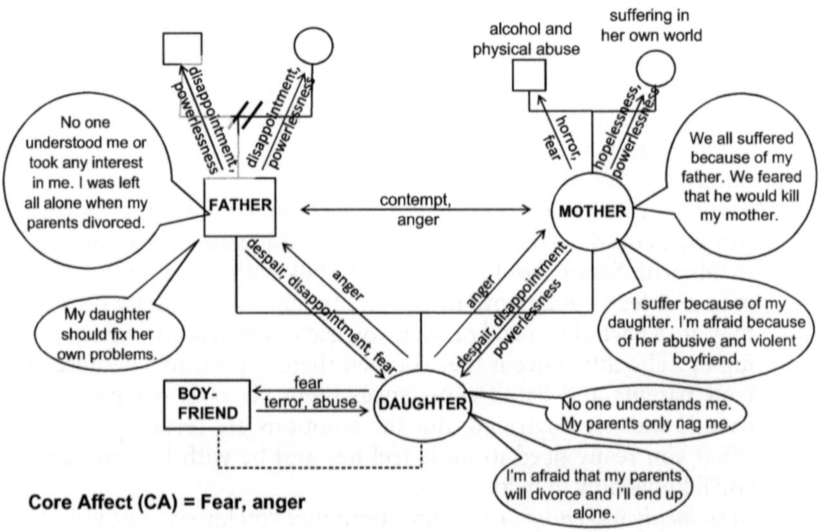

Figure 3.1 Systemic level (father, mother, daughter) and intrapsychic level (parental childhoods)

Figure created by Tanja Repič Slavič and Janko Slavič

M *(anxious)*: Yes. Sarah's sick. Lately, she's been getting strep throat. Today, she has a high temperature, and we decided it would be best that she stay home.

T *(still feeling distress)*: How do you feel about that?

M *(hiding her anxiety)*: I don't know. I guess nothing in particular. *(She looks around.)* Of course, it won't be the same as our past few sessions. It's as if something's missing.

T *(feeling anxiety and distress as tension in her chest and stomach)*: Yes, it isn't quite the same. A sort of distress and anxiety has arisen.

M *(carefully)*: We were used to being together at these sessions. You know how people are creatures of habit, and so when someone's with you, you care.

T *(feeling the husband's anger)*: What about you, Frank?

F *(anxiously)*: I think these sore throats of hers don't get her anywhere. She's constantly sick, and then when she finally gets better, she goes straight back to that group of hers, back to that same terrible boyfriend.

T *(persisting)*: But how do you feel about being here today without her?

F *(angry)*: I care too! We just started working on things and she's already missing. Otherwise (*turning to Maria*), you're the one who decided to let her stay home. I would have made her come.

T *(still feeling discomfort)*: This is a very different kind of experience for the two of you. You both miss her. Is it a similar experience at home when she goes out, and she's no longer with you, and you don't know where she went?

F *(angry)*: I don't let her go out. She and her mother make those arrangements and then . . . well, I think Maria should be more decisive, more strict.
M *(angry)*: You're not home, and she doesn't pay attention to what I say anyway. She just disappears before I get home.
F *(still angry)*: What about last Saturday? Who let her go out then?
M *(glaring furiously at Frank)*: You can't just keep her locked up at home. Or maybe you would if you could!

The therapist senses that anger and rage, mixed with fear and horror, are a strong component in the relationship between Frank and Maria, and that Sarah is largely just a carrier of their split-off, nontransferable emotions. The therapist thus decides to focus on the systemic and interpersonal levels of their experiencing, the goal being to uncover the core affect that manifests through anger, rage, fear, and occasionally even terror. The therapist increasingly senses that these emotions are generating the affective psychic construct. Anxiety and fear of the unknown are even more palpable now that the couple has come to the therapy session alone for the first time. Neither of them knows what might transpire, which makes them anxious and prompts them to miss Sarah very much, although neither is fully aware of it or knows how to express it. This confirms the fact that their daughter is the identified patient, dutifully serving as the compromise in the marital conflict located in their intrapsychic structures.

T *(feeling anger and true rage coming from both Maria and Frank)*: You both feel very angry that Sarah's not here. Do you experience the same emotions when she's not at home?
F *(still angry)*: I am in a pretty foul mood if I come home and she's not there . . .
M *(upset)*: We can't just keep her home all the time. (*turns to face her husband*) Don't you understand that she's almost 18?
T *(persisting, sensing all the anger directed at Maria)*: Maria, what would happen if you tried to stop her from leaving?
M *(angry at the therapist)*: So you also don't understand either that she's almost 18?
T *(feeling her anger)*: I'm trying to understand your anger. And I'm guessing that no one really understands it yet. But it must be terrible for you. I feel real distress. Not even I understand it yet, even though I imagine you expect that I should . . .

In the countertransference, the therapist senses that the anger is coming from an entirely different emotional world—Maria's intrapsychic world—and that the source of the emotions resides in her history. The therapist senses that Maria used to feel this way towards her mother, who tolerated the abusive father and accepted his addictions despite the fact that both mother and children repeatedly experienced true terror.

The therapist thus focuses on these emotional patterns and behaviors, which paradoxically promise a relationship.

M *(calmer)*: Well, it's true, no one really does understand me . . .
T *(feeling horror and sadness)*: Maria, who didn't understand you while you were growing up, someone who you thought should understand you?
M *(starts sobbing)*: Both of my parents. But especially my mother! My father was in a league of his own, but my mother should have been able to understand.
T *(feeling horror as a pain in her stomach)*: What didn't she understand that she should have?
M *(trembling slightly)*: She didn't understand that we were utterly terrified of our father. He terrorized us and she didn't protect us from him! She didn't protect herself. She just let it happen.
T *(feeling anger and her heart rate going up)*: You were constantly terrified by your father, feeling that there was no one there who understood you. Did that make you angry with your mother?
M *(still trembling)*: Yes, though I only realize that now. But I still can't understand why she put up with it. That was her fault.
T *(feeling the terror of the situation)*: And you somehow managed to get used to all this horror. It became your daily bread . . .
M *(beginning to gasp)*: Yes . . . it was our daily bread . . .
T *(feeling deep sadness, proceeding with care and tact)*: Try and stay fully with yourself right now. Just let yourself become aware of your emotions. When your daughter leaves to go and join that destructive group of hers, how does that make you feel?
M *(surprised, tears running down her face)*: Oh, it's just so awful, such a nightmare! Are you saying that I'm like my own mother, that I let her go into similar circumstances? Into a realm of terror?
T *(feeling her deep sadness and disappointment)*: What emotions are evoked in you as you deal with this? What are you experiencing in your body?
M *(increasingly astonished, wiping her tears away)*: I simply can't believe that there's any connection. Oh, how awful! I had no idea. I feel so guilty. I feel numb just like I did back then. My heart is pounding and I can't breathe, and then the guilt again!
T *(feeling her guilt)*: I know exactly what you mean. But guilt is not the ultimate answer—you certainly didn't do any of this on purpose. It's simply terror. Terror is the emotion that connects you so profoundly. And terror is also the emotion where you and your daughter can meet. It's the emotion where the strongest relationship can be built between you, because it was so very fundamental to you.
M *(still wiping away tears)*: Yes, we are in it together, in all the horror and fear. It's really torture.
T *(feeling the terror as the stomach cramps, tears welling up in her eyes)*: I believe that you feel that you're in a nightmare, as if it's happening

all over again, as if you're again finding yourself at home with a father who comes home drunk, everything unraveling again. And all those suppressed emotions are bursting out of you and you have no control over them. But you're an adult now and you can deal with the events happening now and change them. But if you don't, you might end up feeling even more guilty and ashamed.

M *(calming down)*: I think you've given me something significant to think about, something very powerful. But I'll need some time.

The therapist realizes that the deeply anchored core affect of fear, true terror even, has been disassociated, denied, and suppressed, thus becoming the foundation for Maria's affective psychic construct. This core affect unconsciously seeks expression and "home" rights in all the layers of Maria's experiencing and her most significant relationships. It even becomes the strongest component connecting her to her daughter. It was addressed openly for the first time in this therapy session, but this doesn't mean that it was also resolved. First it will be necessary to establish how Maria's husband contributes to the dynamic and in what way they, as husband and wife, entangle their daughter in it and allow her to connect them by acting out the terror. At the same time, thanks to the emotion that their daughter evokes in them, they avoid dealing with their own marital issues and intrapsychic issues. Their daughter always manages to draw all the attention and focus upon herself. Sarah serves as a catalyst for their interpersonal and intrapsychic conflicts, but then they end up dealing with her instead of their own relationship. In a way, their daughter represents an intense affective psychic construct, which they could resolve but it would mean having to confront their own parenting first, and inevitably their own selves. As the session continues, the therapist first addresses the husband.

T *(feeling Frank's disquiet)*: Frank, thank you for waiting. I know it isn't easy. However, it is essential that you are able to understand Maria. It will make it possible to understand your own painful emotions. What are you experiencing while you listen to this?

F *(introspective)*: Well, I can hardly believe all the connections. I was thinking . . . oh I don't know, it's not even important!

T *(feeling his distress)*: What most surprised you?

F *(still introspective)*: Well, that our daughter has actually become our victim!

T *(feeling pressure in her chest and tightness in her stomach)*: This must be so hard for you!

F *(nodding and staring forward, expressionless)*: Yes. I really don't know what to make of it.

T *(feeling Frank's distress)*: Right now you're in a lot of distress. But I believe this distress is familiar to you, and that it deeply connects the three of you. Maybe you experienced something similar when you were growing up?

F *(calming down slowly)*: I find it really hard to accept. It's hard for me to listen to this. Maybe because it goes so deep for me. I don't know what to do with it all.

T *(empathically, feeling fear and sadness)*: This distress that you're experiencing is extremely painful for you. It's as if you want to wake up from a nightmare and have everything be okay again. Maybe that's what you yearned for in childhood and it never happened.

F *(agitated)*: Yes, that's what it was like at home. We'd wait for hours and hours for Mom and Dad to calm down. I can't even describe it. It was unbearable. I'm not sure I want to relive it again.

T *(feeling the tightness in her stomach again)*: It was too painful. Of course, you don't want to remember it, much less speak of it.

F *(introspectively)*: I don't understand what it was all for, and what the connection to all that awfulness could possibly have to do with what's happening now.

T *(feeling fear and numbness in her legs)*: If I understand correctly, you're now able to make the cognitive links, but emotionally, it's still too painful. What if you tried? What if you took that risk?

At this juncture, the therapist decides to take a risk and trust that Frank feels safe enough to speak about the painful emotions he experienced in childhood. By doing so, he would risk feeling again what he felt in his childhood but had suppressed because it was too painful. Frank had created a very strong affective psychic construct in his internal psychic structure precisely for this reason. His survival strategy was to unconsciously suppress and disassociate from these painful emotions and thus to avoid inevitable distress. However, these very same emotions are constantly reemerging in the present, only this time through the daughter, and probably also his wife, a situation that the therapist will address as the session continues. As the only one with direct access to these emotions, Frank needs to confront, process, and learn to regulate them. The transference of these emotions to others cannot resolve the pain, but instead only recreates them and reengages Frank in old relational patterns.

F *(doubtful)*: Sure, I could tell stories. But what would I achieve by that? Isn't it better to just let bygones be bygones. Let go of the past and begin anew. You can't build relationships in the present when you're stuck in the past.

T *(feeling Frank's resistance and fear)*: And what if the past is too powerful? If it tethers you to it? Is it still possible to build new relationships? What do you think?

F *(resistant)*: I think we really need to deal with Sarah and her problems, how to help her, and especially how to get rid of that boyfriend of hers!

T *(feeling Frank's resistance and now also his anger)*: I understand that you feel angry, especially with me urging you to deal with something that you don't even consider a problem. But how about if you were to try and understand your daughter Sarah? What do you think she's feeling? What motivates her to keep going back to that crowd?

F *(relaxes a little)*: I think she's restless or anxious. She's so rebellious. She's also angry, she's really, really angry.

T *(still feeling his anger)*: So if I understand you correctly, she wants to demonstrate by all means possible that she can resolve her own troubled relationship, that she can be with her boyfriend, and that she's very angry that you don't trust her.

F *(angry)*: Who's going to trust her when we all know that he's not going to change!

T *(assertively)*: So your old story is just repeating itself.

F *(bewildered)*: What story?

T *(persuasively)*: Just as it was once up to you to keep your mother and father together. You did everything, you tried to prove to them that they could do it, to make them understand. But despite all your efforts, they didn't stay together, and that made you really angry, really disappointed. You probably still believe they would have stayed together if only they had tried a little bit harder.

F *(deep in thought)*: That's right. And that's what I'm trying to do here too, and it just isn't working.

T *(feeling anxious)*: What's more: your daughter is also trying to prove that she can calm her boyfriend, that if she only tries harder, some day she'll get there! It looks like you're both guided by the same belief. Only yours is old, it reaches far back into your history, and yet it still has a strong hold on you!

F *(anxious)*: So what should I do?

T *(still feeling his anxiety and anger)*: What do you feel?

F *(curious)*: I've tried everything already. Or at least I thought I did. What do I feel? I guess I feel that I'm going to have to talk to her more.

T *(feeling Frank's powerlessness)*: I know it must be extremely hard for you. And I believe that you really have done everything in your power. But let's flip things around a little at this point. Tell me, what do you think? What do you feel? When your mom and dad were fighting and fighting and finally went their own ways and divorced, what would have helped you then? What would have helped you not to feel so guilty and responsible?

F *(sadly)*: If they stayed together . . . *(smiling to himself)* . . . or at least if one of them had known how to approach me and talk with me, understand me. That was the worst, that's what I was most afraid of, ending up alone . . .

T *(feeling his sadness)*: And so you turned your attention outwards and sought comfort outside, in your social life.

F *(tears welling up)*: What else was I to do? I was lucky to have met Maria. She brought sense to me. I would have lost my mind otherwise . . .

T *(sensing Frank's total sadness, tears well up in her eyes)*: So much sadness has accumulated in you, because you feel as if you failed, as if you ended up all alone. And yet at the end, maybe it was a blessing in disguise. You met your wife.

F *(trying to stop the tears)*: I was very lucky indeed.

T *(still feeling Frank's sadness and now anxiety)*: So if we pause for a moment here and think of your daughter. . . *(Frank nods.)* She also wants only one thing. She wants you to stand by her side, encourage her, and trust her. This would mean not talking about her boyfriend anymore but focusing instead on her distress, just as you once wanted your parents to talk to you about your disappointment and hurt. You wanted them to stop blaming each other, because that only hurt you more, just as it now hurts your daughter when you speak badly about her boyfriend. You only insult her that way and she ends up being loyal to him. What are you feeling when I talk about it this way?

F *(thoughtfully)*: I never thought of it that way . . .

T *(feeling his confusion still mixed with sadness)*: Let's take a closer look at Sarah's emotional landscape and see what we find there.

F *(calming down)*: I guess I have been unfair to Sarah, even though I meant well. I really don't think she can take much more . . .

T *(feeling Frank's anxiety increasing again)*: You worked yourself to the bone, trying the best you could, getting angry, despairing, going round in circles very much like you did with your parents. And ultimately you ended up alone, afraid, defeated, and hopeless. Your daughter feels the same way! And she feels that way not only with you, but with her boyfriend. She wants to prove to both that something essential can change. But in the end, she feels alone again, disappointed, and defeated.

F *(thoughtful)*: Enough. She's had enough. I guess it really is time to try something new.

T *(with certainty)*: I am certain that you will succeed. All you have to do is feel your daughter in her distress, in her efforts, and especially in her fears.

F and M *(both nodding)*

T *(feeling a sense of release in the room)*: I believe we have addressed some essential aspects of the situation today. There's still more to get to, your marital relationship for instance, how you two experience each other and yourselves as partners and how these childhood emotions influence your marriage. That will be for next week. We'll focus on Sarah at the beginning of the session so that the three of you can connect, and then we'll dedicate the rest of the session to the two of you and your specific issues if that feels right. It might make sense to have an individual session with Sarah if we cannot resolve her issues during our family sessions. It depends on how deeply her emotions are embedded with this social group and her boyfriend. All right? Thank you for today!

The therapist will focus on the couple's personal and marital issues during the next session. It seems that their daughter is regulating their most complicated obstacles by remaining socially involved with an inappropriate social group and boyfriend. Their deep-rooted affective psychic construct conceals the core affects (fear, horror, terror, disappointment, distress, defeat, isolation, and sadness) that define the significant elements of their interpersonal relationship. These emotions are deeply repressed, and yet they repeatedly generate systemic and interpersonal interactions by being successfully transferred to the daughter through the mechanism of projective and introjective identification and thus attaining new dimensions. Furthermore, these affects have a powerful influence on the affect regulation style, which maintains a grip on the emotional atmosphere throughout the entire family system, and which ultimately impacts the intrapsychic structure of the individual family members. It is evident that these dynamics operate at all three levels—systemic, interpersonal, and intrapsychic—feeding off of and influencing each other. All of these themes will need to be addressed in depth in order to facilitate the change necessary for the family and its members to generate a healthy and functional operation.

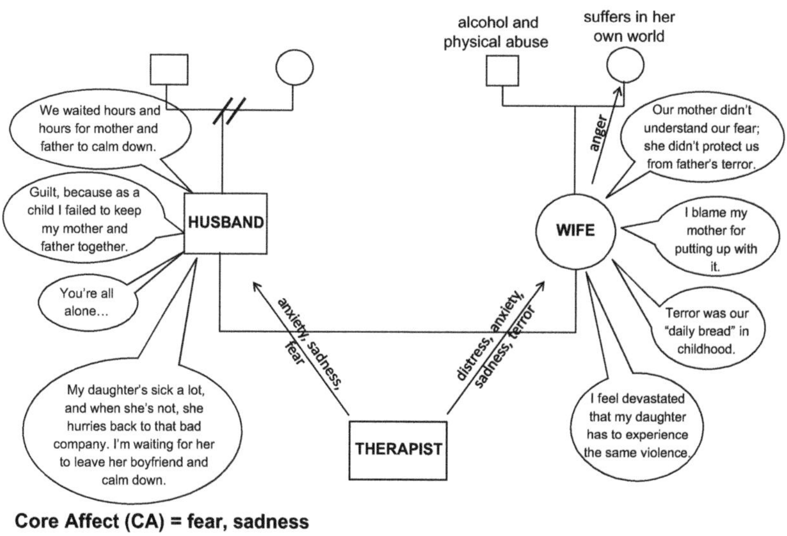

Figure 3.2 Intrapsychic level (childhood)

Figure created by Tanja Repič Slavič and Janko Slavič

In the next section, we will address the concept of repetition compulsion, an essential component in relational family theory and therapy. This concept clarifies why certain mental content and themes, along with their corresponding emotional, cognitive, and behavioral patterns and organic responses, repeat themselves. It also clarifies how the affective psychic construct and corresponding mechanism of affect regulation create, reinforce, and maintain each other.

3.2 Repetition Compulsion

The extremely complex mechanism of repetition compulsion is defined as an involuntary mechanism that repeats fundamental models of intrapsychic, interpersonal, and systemic interactions and their disassociated and suppressed affects (Poulton, 2013). It involves the repetition and recreation of conflicts, traumas, and behavioral models in human personal, interactive, and interpersonal behavior, reflection, and emotion. It is a generally accepted philosophical-psychological-anthropological concept that deals with the processes of perception and the interpretation of affects and organic responses with which human beings establish connections or parallels between past and present situations and/or experiences and recreate them in completely new situations with new people (Poulton, 2013; Ringstrom, 2014; J.S. Scharff & Scharff, 2014; Siegel & Solomon, 2013).

3.2.1 *Repetition of the Past—An Anthropological Phenomenon*

The phenomenon under discussion involves present situations that recall the past and are thus interpreted in light of the past: that is, present situations that are endowed with meaning arrived at in the past regardless of the fact that the present situations involve different people in a new context and may well carry an entirely different meaning (Caspar et al., 1992; J.S. Scharff & Scharff, 2014; Schore, 2003, 2010, 2012; van der Kolk, 1996). Past experiences that are most typical in repetition compulsion are unique traumatic experiences and relationships, internalized patterns of repetitive relationships, and permanent traumatic experiences that are deeply engrained in the psyche or organic implicit memory (Caspar et al., 1992; Poulton, 2013; van der Kolk, 1996). The individual in the present moment perceives a situation and experiences it in such a way that it matches past experiences or intrapsychic images and affects. Repetitive actions are generally similar to primary responses to past difficulties that have been disassociated, suppressed, or split off. What is most surprising here is that there is an effort to actively create situations that are similar to past situations so that affects can be dramatically replayed.

The dynamic of repetition compulsion takes place in therapy and outside of it. In therapy, the mechanism of involuntary repetition is most remarkable when the client tries to force the therapist into a specific role that belongs to an external past reality (Chu, 1991; Schore, 2003, 2010, 2012; van der Kolk, 1996). If the present experience is similar to the past, the mechanism of repetition compulsion is activated (Caspar et al., 1992). The palette of repetition ranges from the obvious in a short-term period (for example, involuntary rituals) to more complex and sometimes long-term actions (such as the unconscious choice of a spouse who is similar to an individual's mother or father, the assignment of certain roles to children who are similar to an individual's mother or father). In the latter case, the children will embody the mother or father's image from the parent's own childhood. In this way, children become the carriers of parents' suppressed and unresolved conflicts, and will repeat experiences that the parents desired but were not realized either because they were unable to or not allowed to (Poulton, 2013; Rothschild, 2003, 2006, 2010; J.S. Scharff & Scharff, 2014).

A number of authors—Franz Caspar (1995), Fred Pine (1990), Poulton (2013), Schore (2003, 2010, 2012), Siegel, Solomon (2013), J.S. Scharff and Scharff (2014), van der Kolk (1996) and others—claim that repetition compulsion is not only a psychological, pathological disorder but also a universal anthropological phenomenon that is present in various degrees in all human beings (Rothschild, 2003, 2006, 2010; Schore, 2003, 2010, 2012). In the expert literature, the concept of repetition compulsion is defined as an event that was accompanied by pain and suffering, which the individual experiences an irresistible need to reenact. The act itself usually resides in the unconscious, as does the effort to control it. What we do not find in the scientific literature is an integrated discussion of the entire mechanism with which it would be possible to explain and describe the dynamics of repetition compulsion, how this process is maintained, when it is triggered, and how it functions. For this reason, we will use relational family therapy as a way of showing the mechanism of projective and introjective identification (J.S. Scharff & Scharff, 2014) as the underlying operative mechanism that will reveal to us how the process of repetition compulsion works as well as the forces that trigger and maintain it. Namely, in this process, the individual experiences an irresistible need to project emotional or rational content onto others, identifying with others, and internalizing them through introjective identification.

It is also possible to explain how certain emotions and thoughts are suppressed as organic responses in the unconscious mind where they create the affective psychic construct in disassociated form. The reference here is to an entire conglomerate of defense mechanisms that defend against the intrusion of destructive affects in the mental structure. Only those that are deeply imprinted in the unconscious mind can seriously threaten or even destroy a fragile mental and organic structure or fragile self (McCormack, 2000; Schore, 2003, 2010, 2012). Nevertheless, the forbidden emotions are carried over to the interpersonal and systemic levels through the mechanism of projective and introjective identification. Aided by the dynamic of repetition compulsion, the affective psychic construct is continually reinforced, expressing itself in the intrapsychic, interpersonal, and systemic arenas, because these affects and organic responses both promise connection, that is a relationship, and at the same time call out for resolution (Poulton, 2013; Siegel & Solomon, 2013).

3.2.2 Contemporary Psychoanalytical Premises

Theories of object relations, self-psychology, and interpersonal psychoanalysis implicitly describe the process of projective and introjective identification as the principle formative interactive dynamic that forces the recipient to accept and respond to the projections of others (Ringstrom, 2014; J.S. Scharff & Scharff,

2014). Fundamental mental constructs are created in the process of introjective identification. Children embody their experiences with their parents as well as the personal traits of their parents and later identify with them. Projective identification plays a role in the basic apparatus of transferring these relationships or affects (Ogden, 1986; J.S. Scharff & Scharff, 2006, 2014). The nature of projection captures early internalized meaning and affective organic experience. Because of it, the self is capable of repeatedly experiencing itself in relationship to bad, approving, and loving objects and/or taking on the role of internalized objects and affects in relationship to desirable or undesirable, acceptable or unacceptable, loved or rejected aspects of the self (J.S. Scharff, 2010; J.S. Scharff & Scharff, 2006, 2014). In all of these examples, there is either an externalization and repetitive playing out of past natural efforts to experience a different self in relationship to the object, or the same experience of the self in relationship to an object if it was pleasant. Natural efforts can also transform a passive stance into an active one or the repetitive creation or completion of unfinished tasks with repeating conflicts and traumas (Mitchell, 2000, 2002; Mitchell & Black, 1995; Poulton, 2013; Schore, 2003, 2010, 2012; Siegel & Solomon, 2013).

In sum, this is a mechanism whereby repeating the past promises a relationship in the present. We will always search for the kind of relationship that we had with our parents, regardless of the character of that relationship. It may have been permeated with emotions such as fear, pain, anger, rage, depression, etc., and yet, as object relations theory posits, this emotional atmosphere, however negative, promises future relationships, and we unconsciously strive to create a similar atmosphere where we will be able to repeat or recreate the old relationship patterns. In cases where a patient is trying to establish a different kind of relationship or risk something new, relational family therapy often finds that catastrophic expectations emerge that have their basis on the interpersonal, and especially the intrapsychic, level of early experience. Everything that is new and different is dangerous and anxiety-provoking because it does not in and of itself promise a relationship; rather it offers a completely different emotional atmosphere, affect, and way of behaving (Ringstrom, 2014).

From the standpoint of relational family therapy, which adds a new level of meaning and understanding to the concept of repetition compulsion, the projection of intrapsychic states or conflicts to another person is a universal psychological and anthropological phenomenon, the role of which is to reinforce and preserve a certain level of intrapsychic, intersubjective, and psycho-organic systemic functioning. The individual allows changes and shifts only within certain boundaries where acceptable levels of anxiety and permitted deviation are not exceeded. Balance is thus maintained in the marital or family psycho-organic system, whether this means a permanent state of happiness and satisfaction or one of rage, sadness, and troubled relationships. Spouses, for example, can pay excessive attention to their child and thus avoid the internal or mutual conflicts that they otherwise would have to confront. And yet this strategy places the blame for their conflict on the child: "If you were better, everything in our family would be different!" In truth, the symptomatic child and related inappropriate behavior only captures the marital conflict and reflects it back, thus continually confirming the affective psychic construct that has emerged in the marital subsystem to prevent the marriage from collapse.

Children are always the mirrors of what is happening between the parents (Lewis, 1997; McCormack, 2000; Siegel & Solomon, 2013).

When we reach the boundary, the mental or psycho-organic system returns to its original state of equilibrium, and anxiety is projected onto the intrapsychic or interpersonal area of the system. These vacillations create a repetitive cycle, again based on the internal models of the object relations of the entire system from the past and continually responding to them. Also the responses of others may be internalized, probably because receiving these messages confirms a previously defined series of expectations. Once again this internalization only reinforces a dangerously threatened internal world (J.S. Scharff, 2010; J.S. Scharff & Scharff, 2014). When spouses or parents feel that they can again safely approach each other, their exaggerated attention on the child will cease, or they will correct the child's behavior when the boundaries of permissible behavior are transgressed. A clear picture of this process is revealed in therapy when parents bring in a symptomatic child with the desire that the therapist will cure him or her. The therapist who is oriented toward the relational family model will immediately direct attention toward the marital conflict and that will quickly solve the problem of the symptomatic child: the parents, or couple, will have to take responsibility for their own problems and their child will no longer need to take on the role of identified patient once the affective psychic construct is dismantled.

The relational family model suggests that the mostly unconscious process of projecting unresolved conflicts onto others becomes the driving force, a sort of predefined structure with which we later characterize our experiences. Roles in the childhood subsystem often correspond with the early experiences of parents in their families of origin. Here we are referring to specific forms of behavior and role-playing that allow the children to unconsciously connect with their parents and with which a relational systemic plan is created that will dictate later relationships. In the same way, children must play certain well-established roles for their parents. Internalized experiences of connection and affects from early childhood become the foundation for the earliest representations of connection and define and determine models of future relationships, while at the same time establishing the affective psychic construct. We internalize what is outside, for example parent-child interactions along with affects that are created; only in this way can they be engrained into a strong internal structure, model, or construct, as presupposed by relational family therapy. These models are reawakened in all future relationships. When we project them onto new relationships, repeated disappointment and frustration will occur along with the desire for connection. These experiences of connection that we repeatedly internalize and consolidate reinforce previously created judgments about experiences with others and thus create a foundation for the future repetition of relational style (Ringstrom, 2014; Rothschild, 2003, 2010; Schore, 2003, 2012; Siegel & Solomon, 2013).

From this, it clearly follows that repetition compulsion is a vicious circle derived from projective and introjective identification. Namely, the sender projects unacceptable emotional and/or psycho-organic responses to the recipient who responds to the involuntary instruction and whose behavior offers confirmation in return. This reinforces the sender's primary expectations, which emerged from early experiences projected onto the recipient. The vicious circle turns and turns again, taking on various motivational roles: it can, for example, enable the organizational cohesion that holds the self together, preserve previous connections with significant others, repeatedly awaken the primary core affect, minimize anxiety, and generally repeat and compare new experiences with old ones. It can help in introjected relationship constructs, patterns of perception, understanding, and the establishment of object relations (McCormack, 2000; Ringstrom, 2014; J.S. Scharff & Scharff, 2014; Slipp, 1996). In this way, children and the future spouses they will become transfer to each other original experiences from their childhoods. They attribute specific forms of behavior to one another and interpret them in light of experiences from childhood, even when the spouse's behavior is entirely different. So, for example, the departure of one spouse on a business trip will signify to the other the rejection and abandonment experienced when the father in the family of origin left unexpectedly or suspiciously. If the parents in the psycho-organic family of origin later divorced, this departure will be perceived by the spouse who remains at home as even more traumatic. The fear will always exist that the partner is departing on a suspicious trip and that the departures are precursors to a permanent departure.

3.2.3 The Sender-Recipient Dynamic

Both the sender and the recipient actively collaborate in the repetition of the vicious cycle. Usually, their unconscious goals and activities are completely in sync. They are awakened in each other's psycho-organic components through metacommunication, inviting precisely those affects and patterns that are the best match with their original mental structure, that is, with internalized structures from their early experience. We could call these existential determinants or a universal effort to achieve something new, since one and the same model is compulsively repeated enough times for a new kind of behavior to be accepted on the basis of projective and introjective identification, one that will hopefully be more functional (J.S. Scharff & Scharff, 2014).

So, for example, the spouse in the above example will continue to create emotional scenes when the partner departs, to be suspicious, to want to know every single move. The partner who leaves will feel the lack of trust, will feel unworthy of trust, and for this reason will begin to describe the departures in increasingly more schematic and less clear terms (J.S. Scharff, 2010; J.S. Scharff & Scharff, 2014). This may recall episodes in childhood when parents also showed a similar lack of trust. These emotions cause the partners to begin to be distant from each other, and the likelihood grows that they will start to look elsewhere for emotional satisfaction.

There are many possible examples illustrative of the mechanism of projective and introjective identification, which creates the core affect on the basis of the affective psychic construct and also determines the mechanism of affect regulation. For example, individuals who feel inferior or subordinate will use the mechanism of projective and introjective identification to locate partners to whom they can adapt. Usually, these individuals have a deeply engrained conviction or construct that awakens in others the need to constantly care for others, all in the hope that others will notice them and their needs (Fosha, 2009; Siegel & Solomon, 2013). This can also be a defense against the fear of abandonment, because not caring for others means a rejection of the archaic relationship with parents. In later life, these individuals will always provoke the response of a caretaker on the basis of powerful mechanisms of metacommunication, right hemisphere communication, or projective and introjective identification. It is as if they carried a sign written on their forehead: "I need you and cannot survive without you" (McCormack, 2000; Ringstrom, 2014).

In this situation, one of the partners will always choose someone who will be obedient, attentive to every need, who will try and respond and discover all possible desires, and show an exaggerated sense of servitude, all in the hope that they will be noticed, that their partner will be attentive and caring to them. This can create a form of exploitation that neither of the partners recognizes. A stereotypical example is the servile mother who is always available to her children in the hope that they will notice her and place her at the center of attention (Cummings & Davies, 2010). The reverse dynamic appears in the relational style of power and exploitation, where children grow up too quickly, always feeling they have to be perfect and under control. This elicits in others a need for dependence in order to play the role of replacement parents (J.S. Scharff, 2010). Both partners will repeat the relational behavioral cycle because it is crucially important for both to adhere to an old unconscious introjected construct that is the original model or the *condition sine qua non* of the relationship with the parents. The partner who is always deciding for the other, always caring for the other, representing safety for the other will, in a spousal relationship or family, try in a similar manner to turn a partner or a child into someone who needs guidance, leadership, and help solving problems that they are not able to solve on their own (Porges, 2009; Poulton, 2013).

However various psychoanalytical schools describe motivational factors, the *raison d'être,* of repetition compulsion is coordination with the internal mental structure through the mechanism of projective and introjective identification that repeatedly plays out old original experiences in a new way. Projective and introjective identification is defined as the operative mechanism of all repetitions: preverbal, psycho-organic, affective, and primal as well as verbal and symbolic. It serves as the fundamental mechanism that triggers and preserves repetition compulsion as well as transference and countertransference. In this way, projective and introjective identification always establishes and renews the most archaic primal affects and symbolic introjections that are then shifted into the new environment through projections, transference, and countertransference (J.S. Scharff, 2010; J.S. Scharff & Scharff, 2006, 2014; Schore, 2003, 2010, 2012).

Extreme traumas from early childhood or later life are most observable in the mechanism of projective and introjective identification, as the blockade of the affective psychic construct is built on the basis of the core affect present in all future relationships: for example, in repeatedly playing the role of the victim. An individual will project outward painful experiences, affects, and also organic responses that have been introjected, such as traumatic experiences, and the primary victim will thus repeatedly be re-victimized, playing out the same action through introjective identification again and again. In the case of self-destructive behavior (Flannery, 1992; Rothschild, 2003, 2006, 2010; Schore, 2003, 2010, 2012), victims will always re-identify with the traumatic introjection and will perform acts that others did to them. At the time of a repeated victimization, victims will respond, in accordance with introjection, with the same behavior as they did in the original situation. This is an extraordinary dynamic that can only be understood on the basis of projective and applicable introjective identification. It is possible to precisely define and clinically evaluate these processes. Together they create an extremely strong affective psychic construct that is difficult to dismantle. Thus, we see the pattern of women who were physically abused as children marrying men who physically abuse them.

This represents a true vicious circle that seems inescapable to the sufferer. The daughter of an alcoholic father will end up marrying a husband who is an alcoholic, unpredictable, or emotionally remote just as her father was. And if the image of her husband does not match the image of her father, either her behavior or emotional responses will create situations that remind her of her childhood. Similarly, men will also search for women that remind them of early emotional experience with their mothers. They will unconsciously create conditions in which old images, for example of an emotionally cold mother, are repeated in the wife. This involves repetitive identification with old introjected affects, fantasies, anxiety, and images from early traumas (Rothschild, 2003, 2010; van der Kolk, 1994) that were so strong that the victim cannot avoid them in the present. Nature's task or the role of the psychological-anthropological and psycho-organic mechanism is to finish what is unfinished, to resolve unresolved traumas and get control over them. The cast-off self or suppressed mental content that is too painful and awakens extreme anxiety is submerged until projective and introjective identification triggers it and it is brought to the surface again (Siegel & Solomon, 2013).

3.2.4 *Psycho-Organic Foundations*

Modern neurological trauma research has opened new insights into repetition compulsion and with it the mechanism of projective and introjective identification. The components of withdrawal into the self, powerlessness, despair, or depression are similar to the effects of opium triggering repeated identification with trauma and causing certain neurotransmitters to relax, which the victim experiences as renewed biochemical traumatization (Flannery, 1992; Porges, 2009; Poulton, 2013; Rothschild, 2003, 2006, 2010; Schore, 2003, 2012). Involuntary memories, flashbacks, and nightmares are also signs of re-identification with traumatic introjections. Using the mechanism of introjective identification, the victim repeatedly tries to experience old traumas in a new way and thus trigger the biochemical process. The same thing occurs in cases of increased levels of hyperarousal. Characteristic stimuli that the victim remembers about the trauma can trigger repeated identification with the painful traumatic introjection and the onset of biochemical processes. Because of the force of the mechanism of projective and introjective identification and the repeated biochemical processes, it is as if the trauma victim again becomes the victim of past traumatic experiences (Rothschild, 2006, 2010; Schore, 2003, 2010), and this only reinforces the affective psychic construct.

Projective and introjective identification also plays a key role in the repetition of cognitive emotional and organic experiences, which are essential components of the affective psychic construct. At the same time, the child internalizes positive and pleasant experiences of social interactions from early life via the mechanism of introjective identification, which is part of the projective sequence of the mother who cares for the child. The same projective and introjective sequence that is linked with the neuroactive system works as a functional response to stress, arousal, and happiness. Repeated identification with the original sensation, affect, or projection of a positive affect triggers in the recipient the same neuropsychological response, which is thus renewed (Panksepp, 2009; Schore, 2003, 2012). We find a very similar dynamic in the development of the pathological psychic construct that creates the affective psychic construct. This process ceaselessly repeats itself in the marital partnership and essentially changes the way the self accepts the object, or actually arouses a response in the object. Here we refer to the interpersonal projective and introjective system; family members, especially parents who awaken in each other old unresolved conflicts, repeatedly retraumatize each other (Schore, 2003, 2010, 2012), and thus replay old emotional complexes that are part of the affective psychic construct based on the core affect.

Members of the family create in their conflicted relational psycho-organic space a myriad of interpersonal interactions, a true emotional dance or systems interaction that is organically determined, defined, and in turn determines the method of reaction and response to each other. An exciting game is repeated during this emotional dance in which, using projective and introjective identification, one of the family members elicits a characteristic response from another, for example, a mother and father who have experienced a formative traumatic response with their own parents (Pines, 1999; Poulton, 2013; Rothschild, 2003, 2010).

There is a certain valency in this situation, a specific characteristic that allows, for example, one child to accept the traumatic experiences of the parents. This is an extremely specific and unconscious interaction by which the parents' experiences from their own childhoods are carried over to the next generation. These characteristic interactions are precisely repeated or rather replayed on the basis of projective and introjective identification. The reference here is to panic attacks, fear, and terror that are the reflection of traumatic experiences of war, physical abuse, etc. (Pines, 1999; Rothschild, 2000, 2006, 2010). We also refer here to secondary traumatization, the actual repetitive activation of sympathetic and parasympathetic systems that carry in them the residue of trauma that is automatically triggered in the present in new situations with other people (Fosha, 2009; Porges, 2009; Rothschild, 2000, 2006, 2010; Schore, 2003, 2010, 2012).

These dramas are reenacted with the help of the operative mechanism of projective and introjective identification until the parents or indeed the whole family consciously decides to change this frightening emotional dance (Pines, 1999; Rothschild, 2000, 2006, 2010). It is a universal psychological and anthropological process with the help of which nature on the basis of relationships resolves archaic complexes, conflicts, and traumas and thus enables ongoing human development. This process forcefully influences the development of children in the family, as it has as much to do with parenthood as with the systemic projection of unresolved mental content onto the children with which they identify. Projective and introjective identification leads to lasting changes in the mental structure of the children as recipients. An example of this is the influence of family interactions on the development of the personalities of children. On the basis of identification, children internalize their parents' images and projections and above all somatic content and memories, which then determine the way they function. Projection of some aspects of parental personality traits strongly influences children's identities that are in close relationship with the parents' identities. Also, things children learn from their parents may be actively forced with the help of defensive projections, and are thus repeated in the children (Fosha, 2009; Rothschild, 2000, 2006, 2010; Schore, 2003, 2010, 2012).

3.2.5 Continued Research

Research (Bruschweiler-Stern et al., 2010; Fosha, 2009; Kim et al., 2014; Pines, 1999; Rothschild, 2000, 2006, 2010; Schore, 2003, 2012) has consistently confirmed the finding that the repetitive projections that parents communicate to their children have a strong impact on children's development, becoming the reincarnations of the unresolved painful conflicts of their parents. These projections, patterns of behavior, emotions, and reflections received from parents shape and reconfirm children's basic psycho-organic content. Children internalize, identify, and then repeat them. Children also identify with the distorted images that their parents have about them. Their own experience of the self is deeply marked by the dynamics with which the parents strive to reduce their own parental and marital distress and anxiety, and is created on the basis of a newly activated affective psychic construct. These repeated projections of images strongly influence children's representations about themselves and subsequent intimate relationships with others when these projections are renewed with the unconscious intention of resolving them. In this way, a vicious circle of unresolved mental-organic content is repeated and consolidated through entire generations (Kim et al., 2014; Panksepp, 2009; Rothschild, 2000, 2006, 2010; Schore, 2003, 2010, 2012).

In other words, parents' relationship to their children is a function of their relationships with their own parents. Researchers (Beilock, 2015; Bruschweiler-Stern et al., 2010; Slipp, 1996) have found that parental projection of elements and content that were internalized in their previous families of origin not only have a defensive function, but also a restorative function (Maroda, 2010), that parents revive certain elements of their own experience depending on the show that parents in their new families repeatedly play out the early experience of object relations that were present in their own childhoods, and thus their children become carriers of roles that the parents internalized in their past. Parents thus perceive their children as a new form of their own history and ascribe to them what they experienced and internalized as children and project these attributes onto them. At the same time, parents often experience their children as an extension of their own projections with which children can identify. Thus, a child in the same family can be both infantilized and parentalized; both cases have to do with projective and introjective identification, that is, with a process in which children take on the role of the parent from the parent's youth and the role of the parent from their own lives. Thus, children become the carriers of their parents' early object relations models and affects, which, through projective and introjective identification, are embodied in children with amazing precision (Feinstein, 2013; J. S. Scharff & Scharff, 2014; Steinberg, 2014).

We therefore conclude that the dynamic of projective and introjective identification is a systemic operative mechanism as much in healthy and functional families as in emotionally distressed families. The development of pathology in children is a consequence of absorbing the mental elements that are projected onto them, the intensity of the parents' defensive needs, and the inability of the parents to distinguish themselves from their children, thus preserving systemic balance in the family. Given the nature of the interaction between these elements, projective and introjective identification in the family can create relationships with empathic qualities or, through the projection of conflict attributes, create a mental structure in children that is the result of the parents' defensive mental economy (Beilock, 2015; Catherall, 2004; MacFarlane, 2004; McCormack, 2000; Steinberg, 2014).

The characteristics of projective and introjective identification are manifested in projections of and challenges to the parents' unacceptable aspects, elements, and contents of themselves in their children. These are intrapsychic, interpersonal, and systemic defense mechanisms that force the children to embody the parents' internalized images of the selves and the objects as demonstrated in Slipp's research (Slipp, 1988, 1996). These dynamics play an exceptionally important role in the developmental period of separation and individuation when parents, dependent on their own experience of themselves, unconsciously experience their children's desire for independence and related actions as hostile rejection. At the same time, the parents may perceive their children's need for affection, guidance, and safety as exaggerated. The intensity of these interrelated systems of separation and projective and introjective identification contributes to weak or damaged personality formation. Because the children fear losing the love of their parents, they are unable to tolerate either their parents' or their own distress and are mentally forced to adapt their subjective experiences to their parents' projections, which are compulsively repeated (Beilock, 2015; Catherall, 2004; MacFarlane, 2004; McCormack, 2000; J. S. Scharff & Scharff, 2014).

In this situation, the family finds itself in a true vicious cycle that prevents any separation of the children from the family. Instead of the process of separation and individuation taking place, the mechanism of projective and introjective identification causes an even stronger merging of mental content, which in turn causes even greater ambiguity in terms of boundaries and the repetition of old models. The parents and other children project their emotions onto the symptomatic child, or identified patient, who is trying to liberate himself or herself and shake off the feelings of emotional devaluation that are denied by the family (Catherall, 2004; MacFarlane, 2004; McCormack, 2000; Siegel &

Solomon, 2013). With the help of their children, parents can freely experience the parasitic satisfaction of their impulses and punish their children for having the same impulses. This situation can be repeated over generations. Symptomatic behavior in children and adolescents is thus the product of a process in the family and at the same time of the whole family system, which maintains equilibrium because of the children's symptoms. In this process, the children have the task of activating unconscious aspects that are distributed among all family members each playing a precisely defined role. The impulsive symptomatic child represents the main actor, but the role is deeply rooted in the parents' experience in their own families of origin.

Parents therefore enmesh children with powerful unconscious manipulation and at the same time force them to take on specific roles that are relevant in the parents' own internal dramas, enacting the parents' early object relations and core affects. A powerful instrument in systemic relations, projective and introjective identification is used to reshape internal conflicts on the outside. In this process, the individual or the family unconsciously disassociates from a part of the self and projects this part onto another person (J.S. Scharff & Scharff, 2006, 2014). In the terminology of relational family therapy, this means that the system uses right hemisphere communication or positive and negative feedback to project dysfunctional roles and affects or symptoms onto family members in order to maintain homeostasis and with it the affective psychic construct and other methods of affect regulation. The family system triggers symptoms in family members using projective and introjective identification. All of this is based on the psychological-anthropological mechanism of repetition compulsion, which is one of the anthropological mechanisms for solving problems in the human psyche and for preserving homeostasis through growth, change, and development.

In conclusion, the metapsychological and psycho-organic phenomenon of projective and introjective identification and repetition compulsion, both anthropological concepts, describe a universal, existential, psychological, and anthropological phenomenon that connects elements of human experience on the intrapsychic, interpersonal, and systemic levels. These concepts characterize the key mechanisms with which we understand and explain the systemic relational matrix of human behavior. The two concepts are mutually related in such a way that projective and introjective identification can be triggered only with the help of repetition compulsion, which, in turn, cannot be triggered without the mechanism of projective and introjective identification.

The therapeutic example that we will present here is characterized by deep conflict between the parents, the father Eric (E) and the mother Sonya (S), who very successfully "play" their son Brian (B). Brian is 13 years old, attends the seventh grade of primary school, and has recently been creating unacceptable scenes both at home and at school. He also has begun to skip school, engage in violence, and not do his homework. He is extremely disruptive in the classroom and even verbally attacked his teacher, who reported the incident to the school psychologist. The latter suggested that the boy urgently needed professional therapy because she was unable to reach him any longer. At home, Brian is extremely rebellious, constantly quarrelling with his mother, leaving home without permission and returning late at night, leaving his parents not knowing with whom or where he was. Brian's father recently changed jobs and is not home very much. His mother can only look on helplessly at how her son is changing. In great anxiety, she finally called the Family Therapy Institute and asked for help.

During the first session, it was decided that the father would become more involved with Brian's schooling, as it seemed clear that the boy's inappropriate behavior was a cry for his father's attention. The father accepted this arrangement reluctantly, and the mother expressed her doubts that the father and son would be able to get along. The mother later agreed to leave the two alone because she had in any case despaired of her son responding to her requests for change. Brian listened to all of this with a faint smile on his face. He appeared to be feeling some anxiety and discomfort but was unable to express it.

The therapist's interventions at the first session were entirely dictated by the fundamental tenets of systems theory. First of all, she wanted to liberate the identified patient or scapegoat, Brian, from the shackles of his parent's conflicts and dismantle the transference mechanism of projective and introjective identification that transferred the marital conflicts onto the son. By including the father in Brian's upbringing and enabling Brian to bring the father back home, the conflict would be transferred back into the parental system where it belonged. Even in this early phase, the mother's resistance was felt, because she sensed that if Brian actually changed, she would have to confront the conflict with her husband that had hitherto remained hidden, dissociated, and transferred to the son. The father who would be home more often would also have to deal with the conflict and that would increase the anxiety between his wife and himself. That is the reason he also resisted the proposed solution. In the end, however, the parents both consented because their distress in connection with their son's behavior was so great that it threatened the system's equilibrium. From the standpoint of system dynamics, the positive feedback of the new exceeded the deviation level of permitted behavior, including the negative feedback on the basis of which it would be possible for the whole system to be rebalanced. The negative feedback in this case is the decision to go to therapy.

Presented below is the second therapy session, which was characterized by conflict between the father and son, who has continued to skip classes. The therapist explicitly addresses this problem and tries to discover why the agreed upon arrangement did not work out.

T *(feeling a high level of anxiety in the room)*: Hello, how did the week go? *(looks around and then continues after a short pause)* I can see that you're having a hard time today. There's a strange emotion moving around between you.

E *(reproachful and angry)*: Yeah, it's no wonder. Nothing has really changed. Brian's homeroom teacher called again to say that he was skipping school. As if I don't have enough of my own work to do, and now I have to deal with this kid who has nothing to do but make trouble.

T *(feeling his anger)*: This really irritates you, doesn't it? You seem really angry. Can you tell me more about how you feel?

E *(sarcastically)*: Yeah, like that will help. He'll still skip school. Your methods don't work. I honestly don't think I can go on like this. There are too many other serious things I have to do.

S *(can no longer hold back)*: Well, at least now you know that you were wrong when you said that it was all because I spoiled him.

E *(angrily)*: You completely spoiled him, and now I'm supposed to come to the rescue. I keep coming to these sessions even though they obviously don't help. Brian will just have to. . . Well, I don't know what he's going to do.

B *(stands up from his chair and yells angrily)*: It's always me, isn't it? You two just bitch and moan about me constantly!

The therapist feels their distress that is expressed in anger and the ongoing search to find someone to blame. The response of the parents to Brian's behavior is limited to anger, which only creates deeper wounds. All three of them are wracked with anxiety so acute that they are having trouble dealing with the therapist at the moment. The core affects include anger, fear, horror, rage, and vulnerability. The therapist will have to address each of these emotions individually, because it is these core affects that provide the constitutive foundation of the affective psychic construct that disables the flow of information through the whole system and at the same time breaks down intrapsychic, interpersonal, and systemic boundaries. It could be said that the entire family system is being guided by anxiety, which is the consequence of excessive deviational levels of permitted emotions and behavior: namely, the hidden trauma and distress that Brian, as the scapegoat, expresses in such a drastic manner. It is precisely Brian who represents the compromise for his parents' unresolved intrapsychic problems that they do not dare address themselves. The therapist must first try to calm the whole system and establish boundaries between the subsystems, as this is the only way that all members of the family can express their fears, needs, and desires, and ultimately live together more functionally.

T *(feeling their deep distress that is expressed in rage and disappointment)*: Just a moment, please. We've come together at a point that is very sensitive for all of you, one that triggers a lot of anger and fear. Now I ask that we all try and control ourselves a little bit and give each other the time and space to express our emotions, to accept that each of us has our own emotions, and sometimes a different way of experiencing the same situation. Until we are able to listen to each individual and his or her experience, we won't have a complete picture. Each of you feels differently and we need to respect and hear that. *(She turns to the husband.)* Eric, you are very disappointed with your son, and with your wife, and also with me. You're angry that you have to be here, and you feel that Brian should simply take responsibility for his actions and then everything would be different.

E *(calmer now, although still angry)*: Yes, he really should be able to take responsibility, but *(He turns to his wife.)* you are the one who spoiled him and now I have to. . .

S *(even angrier now)*: You! You're never at home. You don't even care what's happening!

B *(getting up from his chair angrily)*: Now you're just bitching again. *(Then he says an even more vulgar swear word.)*

E *(flaring up in anger again)*: Can't you ever stop, you little brat!

S *(yells)*: Brian, be quiet! That's a disgusting way to talk!

It is becoming increasingly clear that Brian, the identified patient, is using his inappropriate behavior to express the distress of the marital subsystem. Moreover, he actively rescues his parents, as he always intervenes before a larger conflict erupts between them. When the parents accuse each other of being guilty for their son's behavior, Brian once again intervenes and unites them in their inability to deal with him. At these moments, they once again enter a coalition against him. Essentially, the systemic family structure emerges to prevent overwhelming marital distress. Therefore, the therapist must first strive to establish boundaries and break down the transference mechanism of projective and introjective identification, and only then begin to discover the core affect and, with it, the affective psychic construct that prevents functional communication.

T *(feeling the growing anger)*: Just a moment, please. I still feel distress and anger moving among you. It first settles in you *(indicating Eric)*, and then it travels into Sonya, and then to Brian, who takes it all in and brings the two of you together again. His swearing is an expression of the atmosphere and emotions he is absorbing and reflects his distress and anxiety. Maybe you could try to talk calmly with Brian about what is happening.

S *(cynically)*: You see they can't talk.

T *(turns toward Sonya, feeling anger toward her that is the same as the anger Sonya feels in reaction to Eric)*: I know you're angry and anxious, Sonya, but I don't know at whom that anger is really directed. We're all on the verge of a new moment. Now it could happen that your husband and your son join forces and attack you, or we could wait and find out what happens between them.

E *(sarcastically)*: And whether this kind of cheap help accomplishes anything. *(He looks at his wife.)*

B *(crossing his arms mockingly)*: Oh, here they go again. (*He swears again.*)

T *(feeling the renewed agitation and anger, speaks in a soothing voice)*: I know that all three of you are experiencing a great deal of anxiety right now and that you feel extremely vulnerable and that precisely the dynamic we described a few minutes ago keeps repeating itself. Let's try again. What if we try and figure out what is the distress that keeps pushing you over the edge? Let's first try and control ourselves. When someone is speaking, we shouldn't interrupt, all right? *(All three nod. The therapist turns toward the father.)* Eric, what if you try to speak to Brian again and ask him what is making him so unhappy?

At this phase in the therapy, the therapist must persist. This is the only way to give the family the possibility of finally communicating with each other, as well as a mechanism for how to do it, and hope that it is actually possible. However negative the emotions become, the therapist must persist, always in a calm and understanding tone. In this way, the therapist demonstrates that they will survive these destructive emotions. They have already experienced deep anxiety, agitation, and desperation as well as sadness and disappointment. All of these emotions are probably the expression of even deeper emotions, of the core affect that creates the affective psychic construct deflecting the mutual affect that is too threatening to address but which nevertheless is present in all of their interactions. It is probably an exceptionally strong fear of rejection, as they are constantly rejecting one another in their interactions and thus revealing the deep mental content of rejection, which is very dangerous for them.

E *(speaks with great difficulty)*: Brian, can you try and tell me what is bothering you so much?

B *(looking away, speaking with slight cynicism)*: Oh, well, now that you're suddenly taking an interest...

T *(feeling Eric's distress)*: I'm sure this is not easy for either of you because it is so new, but I believe you can do it. Just try to feel what Brian is trying to say with his behavior.

E *(thoughtfully)*: Brian, you know that it bothers me when you skip school.

B *(angrily, shifting nervously)*: Yeah, I know. That's the only thing that interests you. As if school is the biggest problem.

E *(angrily)*: Yeah, well that's why we're here, isn't it?

S *(hisses toward her husband)*: And because of your...

T *(turning toward Sonya in anger, but also understanding that because of countertransference what is being felt is Sonya's anger toward her husband)*: I know this is hard for you, Sonya, but please wait. *(turns again to Eric)* What your son is trying to tell you, if I understand him correctly, is that he would like you to be interested in him.

B *(at first angry and then sad)*: Yeah, I don't know if you're really interested.

E *(angry again)*: First school and then. . .

T *(now feeling toward Eric anger, which feels paralyzing, so she tries to regulate that anger)*: I understand your anger, Eric, but your son is trying to tell you something important by skipping school. Look at him.

E *(calming down)*: Brian, I look at you now and you seem so mad at me.

B *(also calming down)*: I'm mad because you're never at home and, when you are, you just give me a hard time. That's the way it always is. We're always fighting, always yelling, always being so hard on each other.

E *(looking thoughtful)*: I don't know what you are saying with all those words.

T *(feeling pain in her stomach, pressure in her chest, and deep distress)*: Brian is using those words to say that something is bothering him, that there is so much anger and anxiety and unhappiness at home, and also that you're hardly ever there.

E *(as if he were waking up)*: Brian, I do understand that things at home trouble you. Your mother and I really should handle things differently.

B *(staring at him)*: Yeah, you should. Do you even realize what you're doing, how you're always bugging me?

E *(looking directly at Brian for the first time)*: I probably don't really know how you feel when we. . .

B *(agitated, stamping his feet)*: Yeah, you're constantly nagging me and I just don't want to be around. Especially now when you come home late and if I just look at you, you start hassling me so much that it makes me. . .

E *(worried)*: I know that I haven't been very understanding lately. I have a new job and stress related to that, although I know that's not your problem. I should behave better with you.

T *(feeling Brian's fear when his father comes home)*: Eric, do you think you could do something differently so Brian would feel more understood, calmer, so he wouldn't feel afraid of you coming home from work?

E *(surprised)*: I really am sorry. I didn't know you felt afraid.

T *(feeling agitation and even horror, but not knowing where it comes from)*: Why don't you ask Brian how he feels before you come home and when you come home?

E *(a little confused)*: I don't know. I really don't know how you feel when you're waiting for me. I always had the feeling that I bothered you.

B *(confused, squirming in his chair)*: You have no idea. And the way you guys argue all night. How am I supposed to sleep?

E *(more attentive now)*: Brian, I really do care.

B *(angry, still shifting nervously on his chair)*: Then do something about it.

E *(calmly)*: I'll try.
B *(starts to cry)*: I'm just saying . . .
T *(feeling the distress and sadness as pressure in her head and stomach, she turns to Eric)*: Could you go closer to Brian and comfort him?
E *(first visibly surprised, and then moves closer to Brian and hugs him)*: It will be all right, Brian, everything will be all right.
T *(feels a deep sadness and numbness in her legs)*: This is hard for both of you. You've waited a long time to be able to talk like this. From now on, I think it will be easier for you to understand each other.

Eric and Brian finally have gotten closer. Brian feels that his father is finally accepting him, but only after he expressed his deep sadness. He could no longer maintain his rebellious pose and thus helped his father to confront his own sadness, despair, and anger. The therapist senses that Brian's tears are also his father's. Eric has deeply repressed his own emotions. He has been separated from his own sadness, disassociated from his agitation and fear, which is why his son expresses all of these emotions instead of him. His son's eruptions of rage were only manifestations of deep sadness and despair, and perhaps also of feelings of not being wanted and rejection. But the therapist will have to discover these repressed emotions in order to address them.

On the other side of the equation was Sonya who was now holding back her own anger and rage. These emotions probably also cover feelings of sadness, despair, and rejection, and the fear of not being wanted, which Brian also expresses in her place. Because, in fact, the two are often together so the anger between them is very pronounced. As the therapy continues, the therapist will turn her attention to Sonya in an effort to reveal the mental content that she has repressed and transferred to Brian. Brian has activated these emotions in her, unconsciously choosing to skip school and engage in destructive behavior, thus bringing enough agitation into the family system that it can no longer function. It is precisely in response to these denied and dissociated emotions that the affective psychic construct is formed. The therapist will have to address these themes, but first she must establish more functional methods of communication between the members of the family.

S *(very upset, unable to control herself anymore)*: Yes, in our house, it's all sadness and loneliness.
T *(still feeling the sadness and tears)*: You feel similar to the way Brian does, don't you?
S *(holding back her tears)*: Yes, everything fell apart when my husband got a new job. It was pretty tense before but now. . .
T *(feeling her agitation and sadness manifested as pressure in her head)*: I understand you're feeling very upset. Sometimes we feel terrible sadness, even horror, and we don't really know where these emotions come from. Maybe these emotions have roots deep in your past. *(Sonya nods thoughtfully.)* Now would be a good time to explore

these emotions and resolve them, but Brian is here today. Let's spend a little time dealing with his emotions first. There will be plenty of time for you and your husband later.

S *(looks sadly toward Brian who is still being hugged by his father)*: Brian, I know that you're suffering, though I didn't know how bad you felt. I promise that your father and I will talk about our problems from now on and not involve you in them.

B *(as if he were waking up, extricates himself from his father's embrace)*: Yeah, you know. . . when you only nag. . .

S *(still very sad)*: Brian, my nagging, as you call it, won't continue. I understand that you want us to talk in a different way.

B *(surprised)*: Yes, I just don't want to hear any more nagging because of school.

T *(feeling their distress)*: You all seem very upset. It's obvious that you want things to change and are promising to change. Now why don't we talk about how you would like things to change?

S *(sad and thoughtful)*: I think my husband and I need to sit down and have a talk. *(She turns to Brian.)* Brian, for you, I think we should just take a little time each day to talk. Maybe when you come home from school?

B *(resisting slightly, shifting in his chair)*: What are we going to talk about?

S *(decisively)*: About things, about what's happening in your life. You can tell me what you want to talk about, and I will be available for you. About school, you will talk exclusively with your father, as we agreed.

With this statement, the mother gives an indication that she understands why the problem with Brian's school had assumed such proportions. She feels her place in her son's life, wants her son to want to talk to her, but she doesn't want to talk anymore about his problems at school, because even he unconsciously realizes that he has become a scapegoat, although he cannot state that explicitly. During the first therapy session, much could be gathered by behavior. Brian was guided by hidden distress and hurt that he could not avoid but was also unable to explain, and all of this was manifested in his behavior. Brian, by misbehaving and skipping school, had achieved the goal of making his parents understand how terrible his isolation was and how much he wants someone to miss him. His mother also realizes that Brian is using his behavior as a way to get his father to return to the family, and she is prepared to confront her own pain as well her husband's. She is prepared to deal with their relationship. In subsequent sessions, they will have to speak much more about this as well as address themes from the past that have a strong influence on their present.

T *(still feeling a certain distress, probably coming from Eric, she addresses Sonya)*: Thank you, Sonya. I think Brian feels better. *(turns to Brian)* Do you feel all right?

B *(cheerfully, gesturing with his hands)*: Yes, okay, I do. But I hope you stick to it . . . *(His mother nods to him.)*

T *(turns to Eric from whom she is still feeling a sense of distress)*: How do you feel now, Eric, emotionally?

E *(uncomfortably, with a trace of disappointment in his voice)*: What I can't understand, what doesn't make sense to me is that I change jobs, I get a much higher position than my previous job, but at home things don't work out.

T *(still feeling his discomfort mixed with sadness and disappointment, and also feeling her own heart beginning to race)*: You seem disappointed. How do you feel listening to all of this?

E *(calming down a little)*: I feel like a loser, humiliated, ashamed. And I'm also mad!

T *(senses that there is a lot more hidden behind these emotions)*: Before, we said that we are going to talk a lot more about these emotions, that these feelings may be coming from much farther away, and that they are only being reawakened now. At this point, I would like you to include Brian in the conversation again.

E *(calmer now than before, but still somewhat reserved)*: Yeah, I don't know what to say, why. . . *(turns to Brian)* I don't know what to say to you. I just think it's important that we stick to our plan.

T *(wants to clear up any ambiguity)*: What if we first go over what was agreed to at the last session? That you'll drive Brian to school in the morning, that you'll be in contact with his homeroom teacher, that Brian will call you when he gets home from school, that you'll help with his homework. . .

E *(reflecting)*: Brian, I'm going to drive you to school this week too, and, if I can't, your mother will. I will be in regular contact with your homeroom teacher, and, if necessary, I'll even come to school and talk to her. You'll have lunch at school. You'll call me when you get home. Then after you talk to your mother, you'll do your homework, and then you have free time until dinner. You can talk about that with your mother. After dinner, you and I will meet, first to look at your homework and then we can chat. You won't go out in the evening until. . .

B *(shifting uneasily)*: And so on and so forth. . . until . . .

E *(calmly)*: Yes, until we can trust you again.

B *(rebellious again, looking angrily at both of them)*: And when will that be?

E *(still calmly and with an even more decisive tone)*: I hope it won't be too long, Brian, because we all want you have to more free time, but it depends on you. The moment we see that you aren't playing rough games in the park with other kids. . .

B *(challenging, looking at his parents mistrustfully)*: And how will you trust me if you don't follow me everywhere. . .

E *(pleasantly)*: Brian, it depends on you. Your mother and I want to trust you and next week we can already try, that is, if your homework is all right and you don't skip any more classes. Those are the basic conditions.

S *(decisively joining the conversation)*: Brian, we've talked about all of this. And your father and I are here for you.

T *(feeling that this statement is essential)*: All right, then, next week we'll spend more time talking about the two of you. *(She looks at Eric and Sonya.)* First, we'll check how the three of you are doing, how you're progressing, and then we'll probably ask Brian to go to the waiting room so just the adults can talk. I also recommend that you pray together, perhaps before you go to bed. Prayer will help to calm you inside and to develop more compassion for each other. Thank you. We'll see each other next week.

The therapeutic session ended with more certainty that the parents will take care of their son, Brian, and that they will take seriously his destructive behavior, which is, to a large degree, a reflection of their marital relationship. In this way, the entire family system will calm down again and achieve the permitted deviational level of behavior. Everything became clearer during this session, namely that the affective psychic construct was derived from the core affect of sadness that also generates feelings of defeat and despair. Deeper feelings lay behind these emotions, particularly the fear of rejection and abandonment. During the next session, the therapist will very cautiously attempt to uncover layers of the marital system and approach the extremely vulnerable intrapsychic level of the two spouses' experience. At the same time, the therapist senses that Brian's behavior is probably the expression of the emotions of past generations, but at this point this is only a hypothesis. The therapist will try to build the case during the next sessions.

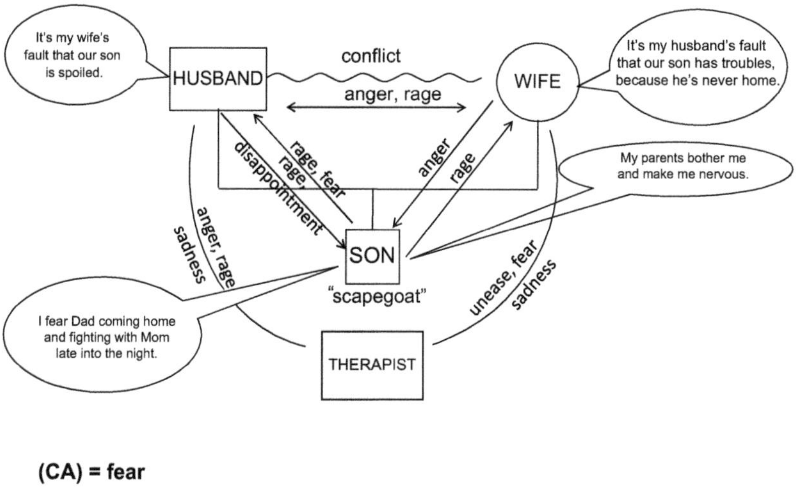

Figure 3.3 Systemic level (father, mother, son)

Figure created by Tanja Repič Slavič and Janko Slavič

At the fourth therapy session, all three family members come and it is already obvious that they are more relaxed in the waiting room. The parents appear more engaged with their son and happier in general. Nevertheless, there is a strange tension between Sonya and Eric that they cleverly conceal by being extremely attentive to Brian.

T *(feeling the greater relaxation as well as the tension between husband and wife who are avoiding each other's glance)*: How was your week? You seem more relaxed today.
S *(with satisfaction)*: Eric was home more so we had more time together. Brian worked harder, doing all his homework. As far as I know, he's no longer skipping classes.
E *(calmly joining the conversation)*: Yes, there were no problems except…
B *(irritated)*: How many times did I tell you that you don't need to talk about that…
T *(feeling a sense of tension manifested in difficulty breathing)*: Okay, Sonya was satisfied with how the week went, but you two… *(looking at Eric and Brian)* have something you'd like to talk about. You said everything went well "except"… What happened?
E *(embarrassed)*: Nothing really. Brian's phone ran out of juice and he didn't call. It's true, we really don't really use the stationary phone anymore, but he could have tried.
B *(shifting uneasily)*: Why don't you ever believe me? Mom knows.
E *(backing down)*: All right, all right, I understand. If I wanted to check, I could have also called. I did talk to your mother.
T *(looking at the three of them)*: So you had a pretty successful week? *(All three nod.)* Would you like to say anything more about it?
S *(a little uneasy)*: Yes, I think we could move on from here.
T *(feeling Sonya's impatience)*: You think we should…?
S *(looking straight ahead and then at Brian)*: Yes, I think Brian should wait outside for a while and we could talk more.
T *(feeling her impatience)*: Will you let him know that he can leave?
S *(trying to stay calm)*: Brian, would you go out to the waiting room? Your father and I need to talk about some things, and I think since they have to do only with us, you don't need to be here.
B *(looking uncertain)*: You guys aren't going to fight, are you?
S *(more decisively)*: No, we won't fight. The therapist is going to help us.
B *(bored)*: And what am I supposed to do?
E *(inserting himself into the conversation)*: There are some books outside. You'll find something to read.
B *(looking like they haven't convinced him)*: That's really boring.
E *(firmly)*: Brian, we have some things we need to talk about and you don't need to be here. You don't want to hear all of that heavy stuff, as you would call it. Everything will be okay. You'll see.
B *(looks at both of them again)*: Okay. *(goes out to the waiting room)*

After Brian's departure, the tension shifts. Eric and Sonya give the impression of being completely lost, yet another indication that they are not used to dealing with difficult emotions together. It appears that their communication is blocked by emotions that have been deeply engrained in their intrapsychic world, which is why Brian serves as a catalyst for their problems. It is easier for them to deal with their problems with him than with their own problems with each other. The therapist first addresses that theme.

T *(feels the growing tension as pain in her stomach)*: It's quite difficult to start the conversation when we no longer have a concrete problem. Your son, as we discovered in our previous sessions, plays a very important role in your relationship.

S *(thoughtfully)*: Yes, that's become clear to me now. I had difficulty understanding much of what you said, until I suddenly felt it. I realized that our marriage is at a crisis point, that we need our son to...

T *(feeling Sonya's tension and sadness manifested as a lump in her throat and difficulty breathing)*: I know this is hard for you. You really stood up for Brian once you realized what was happening. Do you want to say something about that?

S *(sadly)* I remember my own childhood, how my father and mother constantly argued and yelled. What hurt most was the terrible silence in between arguments followed by another painful eruption.

T *(feeling Sonya's fear manifested as numbness in her legs and tears in her eyes)*: You seem so sad...

S *(wiping away her tears)*: I really am sad. I'm sorry. It hurt even more when my mother packed all my things and took me to my grandmother's. The arguments continued there: first my grandparents yelled at my mother, why did she bring me again, accusing her of all sorts of things. Then my grandparents argued with each other, especially in the evening. I used to hide and cover my ears, but I still heard them. I felt completely powerless.

T *(feeling her sadness, anger, and helplessness)*: I can imagine how difficult it was for you. It must have been too much for you. You were completely alone, overwhelmed, scared, afraid of rejection, and the same kept happening: first with your parents, then with your grandparents, and now you feel something similar with your own child. I believe that all of this must make you feel terrible and even angry. How old were you when these things happened to you?

E *(interrupting the conversation)*: And now we have to talk about your problems again? Isn't it about time we stop with that? *(He looks at his wife angrily.)*

T *(turns decisively toward Eric, feeling his anger)*: Excuse me. I feel your anger and impatience. You would prefer that all of this would have been forgotten a long time ago, but it is precisely these emotions that keep reappearing and we need to address them. So I ask you to be a little patient, to try and listen to your wife's experiences, because they conceal important information, also for you...

E *(still angry)*: I always have to be quiet. *(contemptuously)* This constant repetition of the same old stuff. We never get anywhere.

T *(decisively, feeling his anger)*: I do understand that it's hard for you to hold back, but still these are your wife's emotions and they have a strong affect on her. These emotions are hers; she experienced them. You're not responsible for them. You didn't cause them, but they are sometimes awakened by you.

E *(calms down slightly)*: All right, I'll try. . .

T *(turning again to Sonya)*: Extremely painful emotions have been evoked in you, emotions that you suppressed for a long time, hoping that they would never come back. You probably made up your mind a long time ago that you would no longer feel such sadness, desperation, the sense that you don't matter, the fear of rejection, the utter powerlessness.

It was clear from the start of these interactions that Sonya—from whom these destructive and painful emotions, this extraordinary sadness, were erupting—had experienced difficult circumstances in her childhood. It was also clear that, as a result of these experiences, she had developed an extremely strong affective psychic construct intended to permanently conceal these emotions. Nevertheless, they keep finding expression with her husband who is apparently a suitable recipient for them. When the couple is together, the emotions are intensively evoked and they are also transferred to their son who has become her (and their) identified patient. With the father's absence, the son began to experience these emotions more drastically and this has caused imbalance in the entire family system.

On the other hand, Eric contributes his own share of destructive and painful emotions, though thus far he has been successful at concealing them during therapy. When his wife begins to discuss these emotions, both hers and unconsciously his as well, he protests without really knowing why. Unconsciously, he fears a catastrophic experience and indeed begins to sense it through his feelings of distress and anxiety, which up until now had been transferred through projective and introjective identification first to his wife and then his son.

S *(very agitated)*: I remember very well. I was 5 years old. I was at my grandmother's, crying uncontrollably behind the living room curtains because my mother, grandmother, and grandfather were arguing, and I heard them say that I wasn't really theirs, that even before the wedding they had said that my father wasn't the right man, and that they wouldn't be able to take care of me. At that moment, I decided I wouldn't feel anything anymore, because it just hurt too much.

T *(feeling flooded with a variety of emotions, but especially shame and fear)*: Can you talk a little bit more about these painful emotions?

S *(crying)*: I felt completely unwanted. I wondered why I had ever been born. At that moment, I didn't even believe that my mother was really my mother.

T *(the sadness, sense of rejection, despair, and shame is manifested in difficult breathing)*: It must have been horrible for that little girl to hear all those arguments. You must have felt that you were passed from hand to hand, and nobody wanted to take you in, to accept you, that you weren't loved.

S *(crying even more, speaking through her tears)*: Yes, I felt as if they were rejecting me, as if I didn't belong anywhere. . .

T *(feeling her deep sadness and desperation manifested in increasingly shallow breaths)*: Did you tell your parents that?

S *(calming down a little bit)*: No, never. Later, they calmed down a bit, especially after my grandmother and grandfather died rather suddenly. But I couldn't even cry at their funerals. And then life just went on.

T *(feeling her fear, sadness, and numbness)*: You were left completely alone with your pain and your deep sense of rejection and abandonment. That seems so unfair, and now the terrible realization that your son is experiencing a part of the same thing. Certainly, you never wanted anything like that to happen.

S *(forcefully)*: Yes, and I'm going to fix it. We have to. *(She turns to Eric.)* He really doesn't deserve this.

T *(looks at Sonya and Eric compassionately)*: Have you shared these emotions with Eric yet?

S *(tears streaming down her cheeks, glances at Eric with slight annoyance)*: I've tried many times and then I just gave up. I really don't want to talk to him about it anymore. It's too painful.

T *(feeling her deep sadness and paralysis)*: So many uncried tears and no one with whom you can share them. It just keeps being repeated generation after generation: first your grandparents, then your parents, now you. . . Perhaps you could tell Eric what you're experiencing, the emotions that keep being repeated, hurting you more each time. *(turns to Eric)* I know it's hard to listen because your wife's emotions trigger anxiety and distress in you, but still if you could just try to let your wife share these emotions with you.

At this point in the therapy session, it is important for Sonya to tell and for the husband to listen, not only because it is her story, but because the therapist feels that much of it is also repeated between them. Sonya and Eric awaken in each other painful emotions that neither realized cause so much distress. Still less do they realize that these emotions have become part of their mental structure and thus a necessary part or constitutive element of the relationship that they have built together. The core emotions of sadness, fear of rejection, and abandonment that the wife has spent her life suppressing, denying, and disconnecting herself from, still belong to her. The therapist does not yet know what it is in the husband that evokes them. It is also clear that the wife has developed an affective psychic construct around these unacceptable affects that are reawakened in her relationship through projective and introjective identification. This is why the wife doesn't dare to fully express them.

S *(very cautiously, fearfully)*: You know *(she turns to her husband)*, when you switched jobs and were always away from home, I started to feel that you didn't want me anymore. I felt neglected. I felt that your job meant more to you than I did, than your family did, and somewhere deep inside of myself, I felt like I did when I was with my grandparents, when I had to fight for my emotional survival.

T *(feeling a sense of horror manifested in tightness in her throat)*: Which would mean . . .?

S *(sitting very uncomfortably, like her son was before, as if she were in great distress)*: Which would mean that I am completely unnecessary, unwanted. I've started to wonder why I even got married, since there is no room for me in your life. . .

T *(feels her distress and disappointment)*: You are so disappointed. I see in your eyes an enormous amount of distress and anxiety.

S *(frightened)*: What I feel is fear. . . yes, even terror. . . the feeling of being unwanted and rejected is so terrible for me. *(She begins to cry loudly.)*

T *(turns to Eric)*: Could you comfort her?

E *(confused)*: Of course. *(He tentatively hugs Sonya.)*

T *(pauses a moment during which she feels sadness and distress, and then turns to Sonya)*: Could you tell me how you feel right now?

S *(wiping her tears, still in her husband's embrace)*: Your new job completely threw me off balance. Just tell me that I'm still yours.

E *(in amazement)*: But I can't believe this. You don't even know how much I need you, especially now, when I'm at a sort of crossroads, when so much is demanded of me.

T *(feels his anxiety and fear)*: Can you talk to Sonya a little more about those feelings?

E *(slowly releases her from his embrace)*: I have many times, but she doesn't understand.

T *(feeling his embarrassment, anxiety, and shame)*: Why don't you try now? Maybe this time it will be different.

E *(closing in on himself)*: Oh, I don't now, what good would it do?

T *(feeling his distress, anxiety, and isolation)*: Maybe you wouldn't feel so alone. . .

E *(disappointed)*: I don't need understanding. I've always been alone. I don't see any point in telling Sonya about my emotions, because she already is so sad and she also feels completely alone. Why would I burden her with my problems?

In this dialog, it has become increasingly clear that Eric is also extremely hurt by the loneliness he feels with his wife. Because he cannot tell her his feelings and blames them on her vulnerability, the therapist senses that he was probably also wounded in a similar way as his wife, that he had a similar childhood experience as she did. They connected with each other on the basis of this emotion without fully realizing it. Feelings of extreme loneliness and isolation, containing far more destructive feelings of rejection and not being wanted, paradoxically allowed for the two to establish a relationship with the unconscious aim of redemption and overcoming them, even though both of them have suppressed, denied, and disconnected themselves from these emotions for a long time.

It is also becoming increasingly clear that the husband has developed, in reaction to this core affect, his own affective psychic construct and a rationalized defense mechanism that triggers constant conflict so he can continue to deny, suppress, and dissociate himself from unacceptable affects. This protects him from the invasion of unacceptable emotions, which he transfers through the mechanism of projective and introjective identification onto his wife. Put another way, he functions in a way that she is made to experience his emotions, which overlap with her own emotions in a very complex way. In this case, it is a true vicious circle ceaselessly repeating old patterns of feeling, thinking, and behaving that are only confirmed with each repetition. This leads to the further entrenchment of their method of affect regulation, which ends up creating a more restrictive and distorted experience of the self and others. It could even be said that their interpretation of reality is colored above all by their fear of loneliness, being unwanted, and rejection. These feelings are then additionally confirmed by their experience of each other. Thus, they are constantly returning to these extremely painful emotional states, which they do not know how to resolve.

T *(feeling their anxiety and fear, her heart beats harder)*: When do you have these feelings?

E *(uncomfortably, with a sense of resistance)*: But how does that. . .

T *(feeling his resistance as pressure in her chest)*: I understand that this is very difficult for you. It is difficult to open old wounds that you were convinced you had put behind you a long time ago.

E *(calmer now)*: Yes, I really don't know why I need to go back and remember all of that.

T *(persisting because she feels that Eric needs to reach back into his own past in order to resolve the painful experiences that are now being reawakened with his wife)*: What is the most painful thing you can remember, an emotion that never lets you go?

E *(tentatively)*: There were a lot of them. I don't know what you want to hear.

T *(feeling his anxiety as tightness in her stomach)*: Can you confront these emotions, for example, loneliness and the fear of not being wanted, and remember when you first felt them?

E *(thinking deeply)*: Yes, let me try to remember. I don't know when I first felt lonely. I felt it most when I was 7 years old and I had to go to school and my parents had just got divorced. I never saw my father again after that. I didn't even know where he was. Sometimes I really missed him. But what could I do if he didn't want to see me?

T *(feeling his sadness, tears, and numbness)*: And how was that for you? The divorce, your absent father? You were alone. . .

E *(having difficulty holding back his tears)*: Even before he left they always argued. What remains with me the most is once when my father yelled at the top of his lungs at night. He said that he doubted I was really his. That hurt me so much. Then all the yelling and arguing with my mother. Sometimes I wanted them to divorce. I hoped it would end and then at least my mother would be with me, and that's what happened.

T *(feeling anger, sadness, numbness, which causes her to breathe shallowly)*: I sense how terribly this must have hurt you. What happened next?

E *(wiping the tears from his face as Sonya leans in toward him)*: I'm sorry. I'm really all right. It's just that these memories. . . Yes, then my mother took me to my grandparents. She visited occasionally. Then when she got remarried, we lived together again.

T *(still feeling sadness and anger as numbness in her legs)*: And how did you feel when they divorced, when your mother sent you to live with your grandparents, and then when she remarried?

E *(still sad but somehow calmer)*: Nobody understood me when my parents argued, how horrible it was for me, what unrelenting fear I felt. Then they divorced and my mother took me away. Then I felt unwanted, that my father didn't even think. . . I felt rejected. I didn't even know if my grandparents wanted me. They didn't know how to say anything nice about my father and they always compared me to him.

T *(feeling anger as pressure in her chest)*: And you couldn't talk to anyone about it?

E *(angry and sad at the same time)*: No, there was no one for me to talk to. I cried a lot in secret. And I also got angry, provoked other people. I fought at school, didn't do the work. I know what you're going to say, but my son is in a completely different situation.

T *(still feeling angry)*: All that is left from those experiences is anger.

E *(surprised)*: Anger? I wasn't even allowed to be angry. That was totally forbidden. But on the other hand, it's true that I decided I wouldn't feel anything anymore, because it hurt too much. Yes, I still feel angry, but I suppress my anger.

T *(feeling the husband relax)*: It's really incredible how similar your childhood experiences are. You were both lonely, misunderstood, had feelings of deep sadness and desperation, feelings of not being wanted, fear of rejection. You had to suppress all those emotions because otherwise you wouldn't have survived. You sensed that. Only anger remained, which is, in fact, positive. But you were attracted to each other because of these shared feelings. You built your relationship on those emotions although you did it completely unconsciously. Now you have the possibility of finally resolving these emotions, of liberating yourselves from all of this. You can help each other now and then you'll have the possibility of really living together, really sharing a life.

E *(even more amazed now)*: Yes, it's true. I can hardly believe it, but if I think about it, of course it's true.

S *(excited)*: I'm sorry, but I also can't believe it, how everything has been repeated this way.

T *(feeling their amazement and excitement)*: I can tell this makes you excited, especially since both of your feel how true it is. I must say to both of you that these emotions are very old and that they were only rarely evoked in you, but they were carried over to you by your parents and you also felt the same way with your grandparents, and now these emotions are embodied in your son who reactivates them again.

E *(excited)*: Yes, this is amazing. I simply can't believe that we are passing this legacy on to him. *(He nods thoughtfully.)*

T *(feeling a growing sense of guilt and shame)*: Your son has sent you a very loud reminder about what emotions you are hiding inside of yourselves. Of course, that doesn't excuse you for not caring for your son the way you should, but now at least you understand why, because nobody took care of you when you were children. Your son is the first person who has the possibility to receive your love and care, and I think you are both inclined to give it. This subject, which is very painful and very important, has only been slightly explored today. We're going to talk about it a lot more in future sessions. I would recommend that the two of you pray about this, because prayer will change your state of mind and make you more receptive to risking more and to trusting more.

E and S *(nodding and speaking with satisfaction)*: Yes, we will try.

Both Sonya and Eric came to a fundamental realization during this session about why their relationship has evolved in such a sad, sometimes distressed, and often painful way. This represents an important beginning for them. First, they must take care of their son, making certain that he is no longer the recipient and carrier of the emotions they received from their parents, and even from their grandparents. They have the opportunity to stop a generational compulsive transfer of pain and trauma to subsequent generations. In this way, they can liberate their child from these painful emotions and they will also help themselves by tackling the core affects that were transferred from generation to generation through projective and introjective identification, and finally have control over them.

Once they do this, Sonya and Eric can finally confront the problems and psychological complexes that they have been transferring to each other, emotional problems that came from their own personal histories. They will also have to confront themselves and how, each on their own and also together, they create an emotional atmosphere that becomes a dumping ground for the unresolved mental content of the other. The therapist will have to be very attentive to their necessary internal boundaries. She will have to force them to face their own affects that they each unconsciously project on to the other. In this process, it will be crucial to constantly remind them that these emotions come from deep generational complexes that were never addressed, much less resolved.

The therapist also will have to address the affective psychic construct, the primary defense mechanism of denial, disassociation, and suppression that blocks the free flow of information, functional communication, and appropriate responses to life challenges. In short, it prevents the couple from ordering and regulating their marriage and developing appropriate parenting methods. Up until now, the therapeutic process has been conducted on the systemic, interpersonal, and intrapsychic levels of Sonya and Eric's experiencing and function, and much has been accomplished given the number of therapy sessions. Nevertheless, the therapist must not become complacent, because cognitive acceptance does not mean emotional integration, which is crucial for real change and transformation. For this reason, the therapist must persistently return to all three levels of experiencing and make connections between them in terms of the core affect or affects, while also seeking solutions on all three levels. In relational family therapy, only this complex integrating process can offer lasting solutions.

T *(feeling that Sonya and Eric are ready to talk to their son)*: I think it's time that we call Brian back in. Who will go get him? You? *(She turns to Eric.)*

E *(enthusiastic)*: Of course, though I am not sure exactly what to say to him.

T *(feeling his uncertainty)*: What do you feel you should say to him?

E *(uncertain)*: Well, I could say that we had talked a lot, confronted some painful issues, and are trying to resolve them.

T *(feeling his fear)*: You're a little afraid right now. You're not sure that this is what Brian wants to hear.

E *(thoughtfully)*: Yes, I didn't know I was so helpless.

T *(feeling his helplessness)*: When you were growing up, what would you have wanted your father to say to you when things were bad between your mother and father? Or when he left, of course if he was there, because despite it all you want to be present in Brian's life.

E *(still pondering)*: I really don't know. I would like to tell him that I will always be his father, that I support him, stand by his side, that I love him, and that his mother and I will do everything we can to get along better so he will feel better too.

T *(feeling that the father is ready to address his son)*: That sounds good. So call him in.

E *(when the son is back in the therapy room)*: Brian, thank you for waiting for us. Your mother and I talked a lot and decided that we are going to change things at home. We love you and whatever happens, we will also be with you. We will always be your mom and dad.

B *(confused)*: Yeah, and...

E *(decisively)*: That means that we will all try to understand each other better, to have a nice home and family.

B *(worried)*: All right. Just so you won't be pestering me all the time.

S *(joining the conversation)*: Brian, I also want to say that we are going to do everything we can to make our family more pleasant and that everything will be different if you also do what you're supposed to do. Your dad and I will try to get along better and to take care of you the best we can, but you will also need to cooperate.

B *(shifting nervously)*: And you won't cry anymore, nag, and constantly talk on the phone.

S *(decisively)*: Brian, I know all of that bothers you a lot. We talked about it with the therapist, and your dad and I decided that from now on we are going to do everything we can to make things better for you.

B *(still nervous)*: And when you have problems, and when you start crying?

S *(she leans in toward him and speaks softly)*: Look, Brian, we talked about a lot of things today, and I really do think it will get better.

T *(feels the son's sense of guilt)*: You can also tell him that it's not his fault.

S *(first a little surprised and then able to relax)*: Brian, I promise that I'm going to take care of you, that I'll always be your mom, and, it's true, none of this is your fault.

B *(still nervous)*: Then why are you constantly blaming me?

S *(with understanding)*: It will be different from now on, Brian. We're all going to work on it. I promise you again that when I'm in a bad mood, I won't take it out on you but I'll talk to your dad directly.

B *(calmer now)*: Okay. *(turns to his father)* And you too, you have to stop giving me such a hard time...

E *(startled)*: Brian, you know that my work is very demanding, but I'll try to be more relaxed when I'm at home. *(He looks at his son.)* We won't just talk about school and homework.

B *(still not trusting his father)*: What if you're in a bad mood?

E *(decisively)*: I'll also try to be pleasant to you and deal with everything else with your mom.

B *(calmer)*: But if you're not home very much, it won't work, and if Mom will keep asking you stuff...

E *(even more decisively)*: Brian, today we talked about things and I really do think it will be different from now on. Your mom and I are going to make a real effort.

B *(becoming rebellious again)*: Yeah, and school and homework, you know how you hassle me so much...

E *(stares at him)*: Brian, we'll keep our word. Your mom and I will work out our problems with each other.

B *(much calmer now)*: And if I do something wrong, you're not going to mess with me?

E *(decisively and with understanding)*: Brian, sometimes I don't like the way you talk, and we can discuss that in the future, but not today. I promise you we'll talk about a lot of things in the future and I will also care about how you feel.
B *(happily)*: Can we go home now?
T *(feeling that Brian's concerns have been addressed)*: Yes, of course, we'll see each other next week. Thanks so much for today.

To summarize, in this therapy session, all of the family members confronted the fundamental premises of family relations and realized how closely they are connected with old or inherited patterns of behavior, emotions, and reflection that had been established in previous generations. The parents saw how Brian's absenteeism from school and his inappropriate behavior are only symptoms of and at the same time a compromise for his parent's conflict. Brian is using his behavior to demonstrate in the most graphic way possible destructive feelings of being unwanted and fear of rejection, in short the core affects that permeate the parental relationship. In other words, we could say that Brian's truancy reflects his fear of rejection—in this case, fear of being expelled from school—an emotion that is painfully present in this family, also in previous generations.

Once the symptoms on the systemic level have been analyzed and treated and it is concluded that the affective psychic construct is based on the core affect of fear of rejection, the therapist must cautiously and compassionately probe the interpersonal marital conflict that has deep roots in the intrapsychic structure of each of the spouses and powerfully

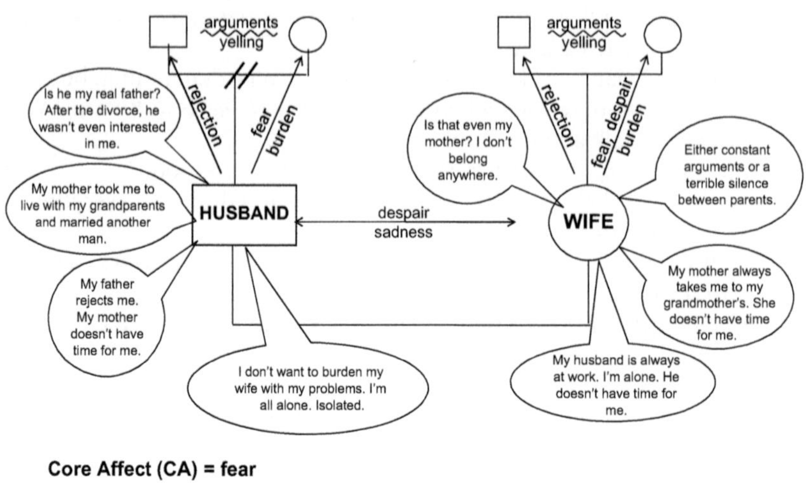

Figure 3.4 Interpersonal (husband – wife) and intrapsychic level (childhood)

Figure created by Tanja Repič Slavič and Janko Slavič

influences interactions throughout the entire system. This conflict functions for both as the affective psychic construct that protect them from vulnerability, which is expressed as a fear of exposure and contains a whole array of defense mechanisms, including disassociation, repression, rationalization, and the mechanism of projective and introjective identification, which externalizes unacceptable intrapsychic content.

In subsequent chapters, we will deal with the basic reciprocal marital relationships that are presented, maintained, and confirmed through unconscious processes of projective and introjective identification and repetition compulsion. We will show that only by integrating these two mechanisms into the systems dynamic that is made possible by the core affect can we completely explain marital interactions, their dynamics and complexes in what are sometimes extremely painful and traumatic relationships. The integration of reciprocal dynamics into systemic rules transformed therapeutic practice and insight into marital therapy and created a new and fresh integrative psycho-organic relational approach.

4 Relational Family Therapy and the Marital Relationship

Relational models (Bruschweiler-Stern et al., 2010; Cooper, 2000; Cummings & Davies, 2010; Donavan, 2003; Fishbane, 2013; Fosha, 2009; Johnson & Whiffen, 2003; Lachkar, 2004; McCormack, 2000; Mitchell, 1988, 2000, 2002; Poulton, 2013; Ringstrom, 2014; J.S. Scharff & Scharff, 2000, 2006, 2014; Siegel & Solomon, 2013; Solomon & Siegel, 2013; Solomon & Siegel, 1997; Summers, 1994) strongly suggest that the relationship, or attachment to others, is inherent to our psycho-organic system. This theory shows the internal representation of individuals, objects, relationships, or experiences, and particularly the core affect, that becomes part of our intrapsychic or psycho-organic structure. Children who are often left alone have no internal images of their mother, which makes them cry. When the mother's image is internalized, children can handle the mother's temporary absence, since the internalized image promises her return. This is referred to as affect regulation, a function vital for healthy growth and development (Beilock, 2015; Fonagy et al., 2007; Fosha, 2009; Schore, 2003, 2012). In adults, the internalized psycho-organic or maternal image includes both a real maternal image from various periods in a child's life, as well as an abstract image formed under the influence of cultural stereotypes and myths about motherhood (Kim et al., 2014; Lachkar, 2004; Pines, 1999).

To determine what experiences, genetic predispositions, psycho-organic states, affects, and people have most influenced a child's life, it is crucial to consider the child's age when certain events occurred. How an individual interprets these experiences is also of great consequence. For example, a child experiences a mother differently than an adult does. A child's intrapsychic system, psycho-organic status, is a mixture of affects and internalized views of the self and surroundings. It also reflects the relationship between the child's self and the mother's intrapsychic image, as well as all affects between mother and child (Bruschweiler-Stern et al., 2010; Lassiter, Czerny, & Williams, 2015; Poulton, 2013; Stern, 2004, 2010). Relational theory also emphasizes that our intrapsychic world is a blend of relationships and affects between individuals. This is the foundation for the affective psychic construct, which suppresses threatening and traumatic affects. It is also the birthplace of the affect regulation mechanism, which regulates our perceptions, experiences, psycho-organic system, and behavior in the future. Therapists slowly work to reveal all of these levels as they look for the core affect, the cornerstone of our functioning.

4.1 Relational Marital Therapy

Relational marital therapy—or model—deals with our earliest relationships and seeks in them the basis for all further relations; this search is colored by the affects and psycho-organic states (Schore, 2003, 2012; Siegel, 2010, 2011; Siegel & Solomon, 2013) that are imprinted into the human psyche early in development. The relational marital model also assumes that affects are always reciprocal, or that affect always seeks relationship. In relational family and marital jargon this means that we will always seek out others who match the psycho-organic, intrapsychic representations of our parents who made the deepest imprint on our early sensory experience and psycho-organic state. The reference here regards core affects formed through relationships between children and their significant others during youth, clarifying why these affects are also so binding. Furthermore, these core affects, which are a constitutive part of every relationship, positive or negative, promise a sense of belonging, vitality, and an intrapsychic experience of the self. An individual's sense of self is founded on relationships with others and on the affect that permeated these relationships (J. S. Scharff, 2010; J. S. Scharff & Scharff, 2014).

It follows that all intimate relationships, those rooted in romantic infatuation as well as those linked in any way with closeness, are always about the self-affect-object-psycho-organic relationship. More than a decade ago, Mahler (1974) pointed out that only when we have successfully concluded the developmental stages of separation and individuation can we establish love relationships. We are then able to truly love and share intimacy with others—and not just projections or reflections of ideas and emotions—only after we have established boundaries and become autonomous individuals in touch with our true selves. We all strive to establish a certain balance between needing to be a part of something larger and needing to feel as unique as possible. In other words, we are constantly battling between being together and being separate: we try to establish equilibrium in our intrapsychic system in order to balance our interpersonal and psycho-organic family systems. By doing so, we maintain the affective psychic construct (Robins, 2010; Ringstrom, 2014).

The level to which each partner is able to separate from his or her own family of origin has critical impact on the quality of their relationship and therefore represents one of the essential themes in the therapeutic process. A warm and loving relationship and early developmental dyad with one's mother paves the way towards a healthy couple's relationship (Cooper, 2000; Dicks, 1967; Johnson, 2014; Johnson & Whiffen, 2003; Lachkar, 2004; McCormack, 2000). What happens when the initial connection with the mother is not warm and loving? What happens when children feel they are a burden to or rejected by their mother? Even in these cases, children will always strive to accept and feel accepted, knowing they cannot change or reject their own mother. Hence, they will internalize their mother's rejecting love and try to retain her image in their psyche (J. S. Scharff, 2010; J. S. Scharff & Scharff, 2006, 2014). The rejection experienced continues to split off into parts deeply suppressed within their internal world. The newly formed suppressed elements become unconscious mental content and constitutive parts of the individual's mental structure (Cummings & Davies, 2010; Givelber, 1990; Siegel, 2007,

2010, 2011). This structure is the foundation of right hemisphere communication between individuals. When their psycho-organic structures are similar, two people can become passionately attracted to each other. Mental structures therefore encompass psycho-organic states and affects that facilitate the affective psychic construct and the mechanism of affect regulation (Schore, 2003, 2010, 2012; Siegel & Solomon, 2013).

All meaningful early childhood experiences leave a mark on children's intrapsychic systems, including their needs, and their parents' reactions and feelings toward them (Bruschweiler-Stern et al., 2010). This process unfolds through projective and introjective identification on intrapsychic, interpersonal, and psycho-organic systemic levels. Children's intrapsychic worlds are developed, fulfilled, and systemized based on these experiences and affects, and all in very different ways. Thus, the affective psychic construct is a creation rooted in suppressed, split-off, and denied affects that are continuously reawakened through interpersonal relationships (Cvetek, 2009; Repič, 2008). Neglected children may develop a lack of self-confidence and a sense of unworthiness, both of which are a reflection of their powerlessness. To the contrary, they perceive their parents as all-powerful, and they may develop a sense of supremacy. The individual's psyche or self develops on the basis of this unconscious content in which both extremes are observable. Arrogant and snobbish behavior denotes the presence of a grandiose self; at the same time, internal content that makes such individuals feel uncertain and unsure of themselves is also detectable, and yet they manage to successfully conceal it (Carlson & Sperry, 2010; Siegel & Solomon, 2013; Silverstein, 2007).

A partner who feels like a victim of abuse will also experience hateful, aggressive, and destructive elements; however, they will also split off and suppress them (Pines, 1999; J.S. Scharff, 2010; Siegel & Solomon, 2013), and project them into their interpersonal world of relationships. In most cases, individuals who perceive themselves as victims of abuse are only able to see one side of the story. An example of this is the configuration of paranoid personalities, where feelings of aggression are completely denied and projected onto others. Hence, such individuals experience themselves as victims and see others as aggressive, hurtful, envious, and evil. The way they perceive others is in line with their own deeply suppressed unconscious feelings of aggression, rejection, and suffering (McCormack, 2000; Poulton, 2013). In other words, they see through the eyes of their own intrapsychic structure the anger, fear, envy, hate, and malice that they experience in interpersonal relations (Cvetek, 2009; Fosha, 2009; Pines, 1999; Ringstrom, 2014; J.S. Scharff, 2010).

In some ways, the feeling of infatuation is an unconscious choice that lines up with the suppressed and fragmented elements of their self (Clulow, 2005; Cummings & Davies, 2010; Dicks, 1967; Lachkar, 2004; Siegel, 2011). It is always a reflection of intrapsychic, interpersonal, and psycho-organic systemic dynamics. Once a person begins to express their partner's projected suppressed content, their partner no longer has to feel the uncomfortable elements in their own mental structure. For example, a woman who has felt unloved her entire life will end up choosing men who are unable to provide her with the love she yearns for. Her affective psychic construct is shaped by feelings of inadequacy and lack of love. By choosing a man who cannot provide her with these feelings, she is able to put the blame on her partner and project her own feelings of incompetence onto him.

Similarly, a self-conscious man develops an affective psychic construct to project onto his partner, hence perceiving her as critical and judgmental. Through projective and introjective identification, he will blame her for his own destructive feelings of insecurity. Both partners are thus able to maintain their ingrained affects and psycho-organic system through a newly formed relationship: one in which the woman criticizes her partner's inability to show her love and in which the man feels misunderstood by his partner. It is easier to endure a relationship in which one blames the other person for feeling bad, rather than confronting those emotions and admitting that they are a part of one's personality structure.

4.1.1 *Valency*

An individual's ability to accept certain projected mental content involves the concept of valency (D. E. Scharff, 1992; J.S. Scharff, 1989; J.S. Scharff & Scharff, 1998, 2006, 2014). Individuals will identify with parts of the sender's self, for example, with the affect of anger. D. Scharff and J.S. Scharff apply the theory used by Bollas, which hypothesizes that valence parts actively seek their counterpart through the messenger by identifying with them. Bollas' (1987) concept of "extractive introjection" defines an intersubjective process in which individuals penetrate others, extracting and adopting certain elements of their mental atmosphere. They take on the "victim's" ideas, emotions, and mental structure. Bollas refers to an example of a woman who fails an exam, feeling as though the reasons are unjustified. Her partner is equally as frustrated, and she begins to feel robbed of her right to feel upset. In other examples, Bollas refers to an individual who takes on parts of others' psyches, leaving them feeling empty and hopeless. Extractive introjection unfolds through projective identification.

Feelings of suppressed or denied elements are especially negative when partners have not differentiated from their traumatic childhood experiences of rejection and suffering. Furthermore, since people tend toward denying any negative feelings, they have all the more reason to find a partner who will express these negative emotions instead of them (Lachkar, 2004; Pines, 1999; J.S. Scharff, 2010; J.S. Scharff & Scharff, 2006, 2014). Interpersonal and psycho-organic systemic elements thus pervade the entire family, forming the affective psychic construct, which protects the system from negative emotions. Moreover, most affects are reinforced through repetition compulsion. Infatuation is a consequence of people discovering their own intrapsychic structure suppressed in someone else, thus bringing two individuals closer together. Sometimes infatuation may be exaggerated, destructive, or even abnormal, but it is always possible to decipher unconscious elements that cause the reaction. Once two people have established such an intense relationship, they unconsciously encourage each other to express suppressed or forbidden elements of their mental structures through valency (Fosha, 2009; Lachkar, 2004; J.S. Scharff, 2010; J.S. Scharff & Scharff, 2006, 2014).

When this happens, both partners are able to criticize each other and control the fragmented parts of their self in the other person. According to the relational family systems model, this process also enables both parties to resolve the deeply rooted core affect each of them carries in their psycho-organic structure. A newly established relationship gives hope to both partners that they will be able to resolve negative emotions. If both partners are differentiated and integrated, they are able to perceive and experience each other as their complementary part, thus valuing each other's existence (Catherall, 2004; Siegel & Solomon, 2013). For example, a detail-oriented husband who thrives on order and neatness will find joy in his spontaneous wife. In contrast, the wife will appreciate her husband's attentiveness and organizational skills. Their complementary intrapsychic structures bring the two together in accordance with the dynamics and concept of valency.

Romantic infatuation, in opposition to the common idea of loving yourself before you love another, is a quest to find someone who knows how to react to the personal view we have of ourselves. The more negatively we view ourselves, the sooner the other person will become infatuated through projective and introjective identification. People are quick to identify their missing part within and then to seek it in others. Once in love, they project the missing part onto their partner on the basis of valency and through projective and introjective identification (Fosha, 2009; Lachkar, 2004; McCormack, 2000; J.S. Scharff, 2010; J.S. Scharff & Scharff, 2014).

4.1.2 Projective and Introjective Identification

Relational dynamics demonstrate the mechanism of projective and introjective identification, through which partners project split-off parts of their affects, objects, and self and transfer it onto the other. The process goes in both directions. Each uses the other as a means of expressing suppressed and denied elements (J.S. Scharff, 2010; J.S. Scharff & Scharff, 2014). This enables them to maintain and reinforce their affective psychic construct. Paradoxically, they also try to dissolve it at the same time. This process reveals a dynamic intrapsychic and interpersonal conflict. For example, women who have internalized their traumatic childhood experiences and see them as a relationship between victim and aggressor will always perceive themselves as victims. They divide this conflict into two parts: one belongs to them and the other to the aggressor. Later in life, they project the suppressed parts of the aggressor onto their partners. Their internalized childhood conflicts thus become the central issue in their adult partnerships. These women need evil, hateful, and aggressive men on whom they project their unconscious, suppressed hatred. The valency between them is powerful and enables an interpersonal relationship (J.S. Scharff & Scharff, 2014).

Friends and family often have trouble understanding why gentle women choose aggressive and violent men. However, it is their internalized conflicts that prompt them to do so. By projecting the split-off and suppressed aspects of their selves onto their partners, these women reinforce the primary affective psychic construct from their pasts. At the same time, their male partners internalize their own agonizing childhood conflicts, and project their counterpart—the victim aspect—onto women. Thus, they are able to experience and control their split-off parts and reinforce the affective psychic construct. This process usually happens between undifferentiated individuals who evoke early childhood experiences in their partners so as to transfer affects and perceptions into the romantic relationship (Dicks, 1967; Donavan, 2003; Lachkar, 2004; MacFarlane, 2004; McCormack, 2000; J.S. Scharff & Scharff, 2006, 2014; Siegel & Solomon, 2013; Solomon et al., 2001).

Projection is a primitive and unconscious need. People are usually unable to see their partner's true behavior because they perceive it through their own projections. For example, a woman may perceive a man as aggressive and violent, even when he is not. Similarly, a man can perceive a woman as a victim even when she is not one (Lachkar, 2004; J.S. Scharff, 2010; Siegel & Solomon, 2013; Solomon et al., 2001). Because their intrapsychic structures are complementary, both partners will continuously force certain projections of psycho-organic content onto the other (Schore, 2003, 2012). This is the principle of valency. We seek partners who hold the complementary elements to our suppressed and split-off content. We identify with the elements our partners have projected onto us through projective and introjective identification. These dynamics result in further repetition compulsion as both partners unconsciously strive to maintain and reinforce their split-off parts in the other, thus perpetuating the affective psychic construct and the affect regulation mechanism.

Projective and introjective identification is essential to relational theory. It contributes significantly to understanding infatuation and the dynamic of couples' relationships and interactions (Donavan, 2003; Fosha, 2009; Framo, 1992; Lachkar, 2004; McCormack, 2000; Scharff, 2010; J.S. Scharff & Scharff, 2014). For instance, women project their denied, split-off, and suppressed objective imagery, including aggressive, parental, and authoritarian mental content and experience, onto their partners. Men then internalize these projections and identify with them, thus creating a strong affective psychic construct. These men begin to perceive themselves as their partners perceive them. Similarly, women identify with characteristics their partners have projected onto them. They may begin to see themselves as victims and feel helpless or infantile, which is a direct reflection of their partner's split-off mental structure. Both partners externalize their own unconscious internal conflicts, which are then transferred onto the interpersonal relationship. Couples' conflicts are thus a repetition of the internalized conflict carried by both partners. The more two partners are undifferentiated, the greater their infantile needs and the more intense their conflicts (Donavan, 2003; Lachkar, 2004; McCormack, 2000; Pines, 1999; J.S. Scharff, 2010; J.S. Scharff & Scharff, 2006, 2014).

The principle of valency explains how projective and introjective identification pushes a couple to mutually project their suppressed elements onto each other. For example, a woman may be in denial about her need to feel independent—this was probably an interpersonal and systemic dynamic in her family of origin—and builds her affective psychic construct around that idea. She then projects that need onto her partner, causing him to present himself as more independent than he might feel. On the other hand, this man has suppressed his need for dependency and intimacy, hence creating his own affective psychic construct and projecting it onto his partner. She then presents herself as more dependent than she might be in reality. The mechanism of projective and introjective identification makes each of the partners fit for accepting each other's projections. This manifests in many relationships where both partners feel the need to seem pleased with the roles they play. However, they are often filled with pain and unhappiness.

In some cases, women completely lose their sense of reality and clear-sightedness in the process of internalizing their partner's projections. Similarly, men can become dominant to the point where they expect another to fulfill all of their needs and desires (Low, 1990; J.S. Scharff, 2010; J.S. Scharff & Scharff, 2006, 2014). These dynamics originate in their psycho-organic system of their families of origin. Some women will endure abusive relationships because they create their mental construct by eliciting abusive affects from their partners. Most of these women grew up believing that being loved means they must split off their feelings of power and subjugate themselves by suppressing any strong feelings of independence, self-confidence, and emotions such as anger. In reality, however, they were forced to act independently. This is why they are attracted to vulnerable and immature men who portray themselves as strong on the outside, a characteristic that attracts them through the principle of valency.

Women who get involved with abusive men are fooled by the illusion of a new beginning, and that the man who loves them is gentle and vulnerable, rather than abusive. However, these men's vulnerability and victimization have been split off from their personality and instead they embody abusive behavior. The couple creates and becomes addicted to a destructive cycle that is reinforced by the projective and introjective identification of affects. They both feel hurt, but the defense mechanisms they use to battle their pain are very different. According to Murray Bowen (1978), people tend to fall in love with those who share the same levels of differentiation yet utilize different behavioral styles and defense mechanisms to cope. Defense mechanisms such as projective and introjective identification are behaviors that protect people from confronting and experiencing high levels of anxiety. The principle of valency brings together couples with complementary styles of behavior. Men seek women with the same level of differentiation, similar psycho-organic structure, yet different defense mechanisms, and vice versa. For example, women with histrionic tendencies or those who express their emotions dramatically and in extreme ways will find themselves with partners who are extremely detail-oriented and who hide their emotions through ritual behaviors. Women who experience phobias as a means of coping with painful emotions might seek men who deny their fears and anxieties by engaging in risky adventures or extreme sports.

4.1.3 The Principle of Complementarity

Defense mechanisms and characteristic behaviors enable people to cover up their internal emotions. For example, some partners can portray themselves as dependent, while others reflect independence and autonomy. Some behave actively, and others passively, some are more rational, others more emotional, etc. In other words, people have complementary defense mechanisms or models that are deeply rooted in the interpersonal and systemic dynamics of their primary families. The following are a few examples (Pines, 1999; J.S. Scharff, 2010; J.S. Scharff & Scharff, 2006, 2014; Siegel & Solomon, 2013):

a) One partner is dominating and aggressive while the other is subordinate and masochistic;
b) One partner is helpless and needs someone to take care of him or her while the other seems omnipotent;
c) One partner is emotionally removed while the other requires substantial emotional attention;
d) Both partners strive to have a sense of power and control, each in their own way and from their own perspective (Pines, 1999; J.S. Scharff, 2010; J.S. Scharff & Scharff, 2006, 2014).

All couples have unique emotional and rational characteristics of interacting, as well as conscious and unconscious, and internalized, suppressed, and projected psycho-organic content (Schore, 2003, 2012). Although some of these relational elements may seem unclear, we are able to identify them by paying attention to the partners' emotional dynamic (Lachkar, 2004; Siegel & Solomon, 2013). Differentiation enables people to experience true intimacy—one in which both partners feel happy and connected, and are at the same time autonomous individuals. These couples feel close to each other and mutually encourage each other's personal growth. However, if partners' levels of differentiation are low, any attempt to establish autonomy will be seen as a threat to the relationship. One or the other partner will feel hurt and react by trying to cause pain or withdrawing. They may have frequent outbursts of anger or rage, and experience painful emotional content that hinders healthy and functional communication. Low levels of differentiation cause emotional insecurities and prevent individuals from accepting responsibility for feeling endangered or unprotected (Catherall, 2004; MacFarlane, 2004; Siegel, 2011).

Taking full responsibility for feelings of vulnerability, uncertainty, and fear can be difficult for couples. It is common for them to blame each other instead. They convince themselves that their partner is the one who needs to change in order to resolve their own negative emotions (Donavan, 2003; McCormack, 2000; Meissner, 1978; Siegel & Solomon, 2013). People are unable to wholly fulfill their undifferentiated partner's unconscious infantile needs. Hence, unsatisfied partners experience pain, despair, disappointment, frustration, hate, and ongoing relational struggles. The relationship dynamic becomes a constant battle as neither partner is willing to let go of their position. In addition to a difficult atmosphere, the partners experience an ongoing codependency. Even the smallest struggle can turn into an extremely painful dispute with catastrophic consequences. Although these partners may claim they cannot live without each other, their existence together is characterized by deep hurt (Johnson, 2014; Pines, 1999). Not being able to differentiate also makes it difficult to separate from the family of origin, which has a strong impact on future romantic attachment.

In the families of origin, undifferentiated individuals were responsible for taking care of their family psycho-organic system and maintaining its homeostasis. Hence, it is hard for them to develop their own independent personality. Their emotional energy is focused on their family, so they developed an autonomous self. Unconsciously, they remain loyal to their psycho-organic structure of their family of origin. To let themselves get completely attached to their partner would give them the feeling that they have betrayed their own family (Boszormenyi-Nagy & Ulrich, 1981; Porges, 2009). For example, men from such backgrounds feel the need to visit and call their mother frequently and to regularly spend time with her even when their wives disapprove. However, the fact that they disapprove and yet remain in the relationship implies that their level of separation is as low as their husband's. These women are equally undifferentiated, although the ties to their own families may not appear strong. Based on the principle of valency, these women have the unconscious need to stay with their husbands (J.S. Scharff, 2010).

Neglected children also grow up not knowing how to differentiate from their families. As adults, they expect their romantic partners to provide them with everything they were denied as children, to love and care for them. Unfortunately, they usually look for what they need in the wrong place, because no one can make up for their childhood losses (Boszormenyi-Nagy & Ulrich, 1981; Catherall, 2004; MacFarlane, 2004; Robins, 2010). Neglected individuals may find partners who seem attentive and caring but in reality may not be. Thus childhood traumas of neglect are only recreated. Not only are their partners unable to provide them with the unconditional love for which they yearn, but they trigger old traumatic emotions. The failure of differentiation from their families of origin thus manifests in their romantic choices. The childhood experience generates the affective psychic construct. As adults, they carry and hold on to the most problematic emotions they experienced as children (Bitter, 2014; Cummings & Davies, 2010; Gehart, 2016).

Couples find each other based on their levels of differentiation. For example, undifferentiated men seek out women with equally low differentiation levels. They seek out conflicting, stressful, and traumatic relations that are similar to those they knew as children, especially from their relationship with their parents (Cummings & Davies, 2010; Pines, 1999; Siegel & Solomon, 2013). This dynamic guides them in establishing romantic relationships. Internalized objects also known as pathogenic introjects are a result of childhood relationships with each of their parents, as well as of their parents' marital relationship. Romantic imagery passes on through the generations, is a reflection of the romantic relationships between the two parents, and includes intrapsychic imagery or their psycho-organic structure. For example, women who experienced their father being unfaithful to their mother and their mother's pain internalize the role of the betrayed victim and the affect of betrayal. This becomes the foundation of their affective psychic construct. It influences the romantic relationships these women seek out as adults, causing them to take on two different roles: both victim and betrayer. They may act out both roles at once, not realizing the paradox of the situation. Women like this may be unfaithful yet jealous at the same time, ascribing and projecting their own elements of betrayal onto their partners (Cummings & Davies, 2010; Johnson, 2014; Pines, 1999).

Pathogenic introjects and unconscious motivations explain specific types of behavior that are otherwise difficult to comprehend. For example, it may seem incomprehensive that people fall in love with partners who are seemingly unsuited for them. It can be hard to grasp why people may insist on staying with partners who make them miserable. However, such partners are the perfect targets for their suppressed psycho-organic content. By staying with them, these individuals are able to ascribe their own issues to their partner rather than confronting their painful internal self. Both concepts help explain obsessive love and infatuation in which partners become each other's drug. Obsessive relationships can have immense emotional power, often making people think and behave irrationally. Despite their terrible pain, fury, disappointment, and endless conflict, such people will continue to believe they are madly in love and incapable of ending a relationship, regardless of how painful or destructive it may be (Beilock, 2015; Catherall, 2004; MacFarlane, 2004; McCormack, 2000; Pines, 1999).

4.1.4 The Mystery of Intimacy

Relational theory puts forward two essential characteristics of romantic relationships: right hemisphere communication and projective and introjective identification (Schore, 2010, 2012; Siegel, 2007, 2010, 2011; Siegel & Solomon, 2013).

4.1.4.1 People actively, albeit unconsciously, seek romantic relationships. Childhood experiences, especially those of rejection or denial of the love for which we yearn, have a significant influence on who we choose as romantic partners. Relational theory emphasizes that we re-experience the same feelings in adult relationships, manifested through intrapsychic, interpersonal, and psycho-organic systemic dynamics. We continuously reenact those experiences through projective and introjective identification and the principle of valency (J.S. Scharff, 2010; J.S. Scharff & Scharff, 2014; Schore, 2003, 2012).

4.1.4.2 Marital and partner relationships are object-relational. They are deeply connected to childhood experience, including how we perceived our parents' relationship. So, falling in love and choosing a life partner is not coincidental, but deeply based in our psycho-organic experience from our childhood. We seek out partners who give us hope that they might match our internalized experience, especially the elements for which we yearn most powerfully. This unfolds through the principle of valency. With our partner's help, we are able to recreate experiences similar to those from our childhood. Projective and introjective identification enables our partner to give us hope that they may satisfy our unfulfilled childhood needs. This hope, in turn, inspires feelings of excitement and euphoria, love, and happiness—in other words, infatuation. Soon, we have fallen in love (Poulton, 2013; J.S. Scharff, 2010).

4.1.4.3 Unfulfilled needs reflect introjections people have adopted from their parents. Couples' introjections are complementary; both partners fulfill each other's unconscious complementary needs, thus creating a set of unwritten rules, such as: "I will express your anguish, if you calm me down," or "I will think of you, if you express my emotions" (Lachkar, 2004; Poulton, 2013; J.S. Scharff & Scharff, 2014; Siegel & Solomon, 2013).

4.1.4.4 Levels of differentiation reflect the individual's ability to love and function in romantic relationships. These levels depend on their childhood psycho-organic experiences, especially the systems' needs that impelled them to take on certain roles in order to preserve systemic balance (Catherall, 2004; Fishbane, 2013; Panksepp, 2009; Poulton, 2013). These roles and experiences also provided the foundation for the affective psychic construct. Despite the fact that we leave our families of origin, as adults we tend to follow the models from early childhood using repetition compulsion. The affective psychic construct thus remains continuously active, regardless of our physical and mental setting (Kim et al., 2014; MacFarlane, 2004; McCormack, 2000).

Children are able to separate from their family of origin if they grew up in a healthy, loving, and accepting family environment, and with parents who cultivated healthy relationships. As differentiated individuals, such individuals will be able to establish loving intimate relationships as adults. However, if parents were constantly conflicted, frustrated, or hurt, children grow up with low levels of differentiation and this leads them to develop immature relationships. Couples who have equally low levels of differentiation express highly intense emotions, both positive and negative. They often get lost in a cycle of obsessive attachment (Clulow, 2005; Siegel, 2010, 2011; Siegel & Solomon, 2013).

4.1.4.5 People become attached and fall in love with partners whose levels of differentiation are similar. Partners' levels of emotional maturity are usually very similar, although they may utilize different, and sometimes opposite, spectrums of defense mechanisms; i.e. victim and abuser, masochist and sadist, etc. This manifests through the principle of valency. Hence, we are able to trace certain levels of pathology or dysfunction in people whose partners are equally dysfunctional (Fishbane, 2013; Johnson, 2014; Lachkar, 2004; Pines, 1999; Poulton, 2013). This is a reflection of affective reciprocation between intrapsychic and interpersonal relational dynamics learned in their psycho-organic experiences in their families of origin.

Our romantic image is always a result of positive and negative childhood experience, although the negative has a stronger influence on our choice of partner. In fact, romantic relationships offer a chance to resolve past negative emotional experiences. We try to find romantic partners with whom we are able to resolve early traumas, based on our personal romantic image and the principle of valency. This is why we fall in love with those who share similar negative characteristics as we do with our parents (Beilock, 2015; Cummings & Davies, 2010; Donavan, 2003; Fosha, 2009; Hendrix, 1992; Hendrix & Hunt, 2004; Johnson, 2014; Lachkar, 2004; McCormack, 2000; Siegel & Solomon, 2013).

For example, women may appear to want a loyal and trustworthy husband but end up with one who is unfaithful just as their own father might have been. Of course, these women do not wish to recreate the same traumatic experience, but they are unconsciously convinced that only men similar to their fathers are able to provide the loyalty they yearn for so much: the trust of an untrustworthy "Don Juan." The paradox of these women is that they fall in love with men similar to their fathers, although it is the opposite of what they truly yearn for: someone who loves and accepts them, and who is faithful, unlike their father. They want handsome men who love women and who women are attracted to; they also want them to be faithful, loving, and trustworthy. Only a faithful "Don Juan" can give a woman what she and her mother never had. For these women, finding a man that *may* be able to provide them with love gives them a sense of control, even though in the end he may be unfaithful and incapable of resolving unconscious childhood traumas. In short, people repeat familiar patterns from their childhood, hoping that the issues they faced back then may get resolved (Johnson, 2014; Lachkar, 2004).

People often end up choosing partners who are the exact opposite of their parents with whom they have unresolved relations. For example, men who witnessed their mothers being unfaithful may seek women whose core value is loyalty. In this way, they can either enjoy her loyalty or choose to be pathologically jealous, constantly accusing her of cheating. Only when these women continuously prove their fidelity will the men's childhood traumas begin to heal. Through their wives' fidelity, such men are able to live without having to experience the pain their fathers endured (Johnson, 2014; Lachkar, 2004; Pines, 1999; Siegel & Solomon, 2013).

We are always attracted to people who fit our romantic image in a certain way. The foundation for this is the dynamic of valency. The people we are attracted to may fit our romantic image in their personality traits, physical appearance, social background, and often in their way of thinking, feeling, and behaving. When we meet people who have specific characteristics, we project our romantic imagery onto them. Romantic imagery is made up of systemic intrapsychic images, the self, the parents, and the relationship between the two (Johnson, 2014). If the people upon whom we've projected our image reciprocate by projecting their imagery onto us, we identify with each other's affects through projective and introjective identification (J.S. Scharff & Scharff, 2014). This makes us fall in love.

When two partners identify with each other, they often feel as though they have known each other for a lifetime (Donavan, 2003; Fosha, 2009; Hendrix, 1992; Hendrix & Hunt, 2004; Johnson, 2014; Lachkar, 2004). This happens because they play such important psychological roles in each other's lives; falling in love with someone makes us feel as though we have discovered an eternity of deep psycho-organic states overshadows all other experience. Being in love makes us feel complete and invokes the same psycho-organic state we used to feel as children with our mothers (Cummings & Davies, 2010; Fosha, 2009; Schore, 2002, 2003; Siegel & Solomon, 2013). Infatuation makes people feel they have found eternal, true love and that they will never again have to feel sad, alone, or abandoned. It makes it seem as though our affective psychic construct has dissolved. Love makes even the darkest parts of our life seem brighter and gives it purpose (Donavan, 2003; Johnson, 2014; Lachkar, 2004; Pines, 1999; Siegel & Solomon, 2013). As a result of these feelings, it is all the more brutal and destructive when romantic loves begins to perish. It puts both partners in a difficult position: if they want to recreate true love, they have to start all over again.

At that point in a relationship, partners have to work through the mechanism of projective and introjective identification, as well as their affective psychic construct that is tainted with painful affects that erupted after the period of infatuation. In order to resolve their problem, they must address the entire range of family psycho-organic experiences of relations because these are the foundation of all adult relationships. Hence, relational family therapy focuses on exploring the dynamics of family configurations. When it comes to intimacy and infatuation, it looks closely at right hemisphere communication and the early formation of psycho-organic states. In fact, psycho-organic states are the model for all further relational dynamics. Relational family therapy delves into family foundations to seek solutions to current issues. The affective psychic construct and affect regulation are rooted in the core of family systems, causing members of a family system to reflect their deepest dynamics.

Intimacy is a deep interpersonal relationship between two people who have chosen to create a life together. It involves the dynamics of both partners, including how they mutually accept and understand each other. It offers a chance for both partners to begin exploring and resolving their difficult childhood experiences, and also enables them to explore and establish existential relevance. Our unconscious plays a very important role in this process. Falling in love is a strong emotional and organic experience that transcends our normal capacities of perception. Rather than occurring in the logical sphere of the cortex, it involves electric activity in the limbic system—the location of strong emotional impulses (Fosha, 2009; Pines, 1999; Schore, 2003, 2012; Siegel, 2007, 2010, 2011; Siegel & Solomon, 2013). Right hemisphere communication and projective and introjective identification is what awakens our impulses. Additionally, it is what restores the most primary aspects of psycho-organic states in our mental construct, reestablishing them through intimacy in our adult lives.

Although in many cases the choice of certain romantic partners seems illogical, it is, in fact, an intelligent, albeit unconscious, choice. It allows an individual to find the significant other best suited to rectifying unresolved childhood issues by engaging the core affect and affective psychic construct. Once someone has found such a partner, a romantic spark is reawakened and experienced, spreading euphoria and vibrancy throughout their body. These choices are sometimes dangerous, especially when the attachment transforms into physical, emotional, or mental abuse. However, even in these cases, the choice is intelligent as it gives new hope to repair, and not only repeat, old traumas (Hendrix, 1992; Hendrix & Hunt, 2004; Johnson, 2014). Abusive relationships can only be resolved if the abusers confront their actions and accept full responsibility for them. Victims must also confront own unresolved issues and learn how to recognize and avoid people who may abuse them, even though they are probably the most appealing to them (Cummings & Davies, 2010; Pines, 1999; Schore, 2003, 2012). Past experiences and significant subjects in our intrapsychic structures become the fundamental themes of our interpersonal connections (Johnson, 2014; Lachkar, 2004). Romantic relationships provide the arena for the affective psychic construct to reveal itself in all its strength. In its essence, it decelerates healthy functioning. Infatuation is not a relationship in itself. The intimate relationship develops after two people begin to discover not only what brought them together, but also what makes them belong together. The partners' main issues usually remain the same as when they first became a couple, even after years of hurting and disappointing each other when they feel as though their problems will never end. By this point, their intrapsychic constructs have fully evolved. Unresolved childhood conflicts is what brought them together through projective and introjective identification, and this often makes their relationship all the more painful and complex (Cummings & Davies, 2010; Donavan, 2003; Hendrix, 1992; Hendrix & Hunt, 2004; Lachkar, 2004; McCormack, 2000; Siegel & Solomon, 2013).

Relational family therapy views intimacy as a replica of the relationship people had with their parents as children in their psycho-organic family system. Both partners are thus presented with another chance to resolve unresolved content from their primary family backgrounds. Hence, a relationship between two people that started out as euphoric infatuation may become painful over time. The core mental content that brings them together is hidden during the period of infatuation. Later, it provides the fundamental conflicts of their relationship. Sometimes, individual partners are able to stop blaming themselves as well as each other. Once partners overcome the need to put blame elsewhere, they become much more susceptible to taking responsibility for their part in the marital conflict. This is an important step in resolving couples' problems, especially since these conflicts are so often permeated with themes from their families of origin.

Relational issues are an attempt to repair, manage, and transcend old conflicts rooted in our infantile relationships with our parents (Hendrix, 1988, 1992; Hendrix & Hunt, 2004; Johnson, 2014; Siegel & Solomon, 2013). These conflicts are transferred into a couple's intimate atmosphere and interpersonal relationship, and consequently their intrapsychic space. Partners re-experience old anxieties, pains, and frustrations in newly formed intimate relationships. They attempt to resolve their old intrapsychic problems by bringing them into the interpersonal marital arena (Donavan, 2003; Hendrix, 1992; Hendrix & Hunt, 2004; Johnson, 2014; Lachkar, 2004; McCormack, 2000; Siegel & Solomon, 2013; Solomon et al., 2001). Relational family and couples therapy delves into such issues, taking into account all mental and biological components, as well as integrating systemic, interpersonal psycho-organic, and intrapsychic levels. All three levels display core affects, establish systems of affect regulation, and maintain an affective psychic construct that hinders healthy functionality. We will take a closer look at these dynamics in the following pages.

Sabina (S) and Kieran (K) came to therapy because Sabina felt their relationship had reached a dead end and therapy was their only chance to save their two-year-old marriage. They first sought advice on how to change each other, rather than themselves. The therapist (T) introduced them to the therapeutic process, in which they will need to learn how to feel and listen to each other rather than try proving which of them is right or wrong. By their fifth therapy session, the couple was able to take a closer look at their relationship and the hidden energies fueling their distressed relationship. The therapist had to be very active in trying to deter the couple from falling back into their habitual ways of speaking to each other in a demeaning and shaming manner. They began recognizing that their patterns of feeling, thinking, and acting are rooted in dynamics from their families of origin. They began to realize how they would enact these patterns when they were yearning for compassion and understanding from each other, usually causing the opposite effect.

Sabina and Kieran have no children, mostly because Sabina does not want to bring a child into their conflicted relationship. Sabina believes their children would end up as victims of their perpetual arguing. Both partners have good jobs and are respected for their intelligent and responsible work ethic. They are both working towards saving up enough money to move into a more comfortable housing situation and raising a family after they have resolved their problematic relationship. They both strive to achieve high goals at work and to create a better career in order to then be able to enjoy life to the fullest. They both come from families that thrived on feeling and presenting themselves as prestigious or elite. They both grew up feeling neglected, especially at times when their parents' relationship was at a point of no return or threatened by the possibility of divorce. In fact, their parents would often threaten each other with divorce, bringing up the subject of adultery, mainly to accuse or shame each other.

T *(experiencing pressure in her head and burning stomach pain):* There seems to be quite a bit of tension between the two of you today.

S *(very upset):* Well, it's no surprise. It's pointless. We just fight and yell at each other more and more. Kieran completely lost it this week and finally left me all alone.

K *(angrily):* What was I supposed to do? Honestly, I can't put up with your negativity anymore.

T (*experiencing their rage as pressure in the chest*): Can you tell me where this frustration and rage comes from?

K (*yelling*): It's too much! All she does is accuse and insult me! It's a nuthouse! Even the neighbors are scared at this point!

S (*sarcastically*): Oh, you poor thing, you have such a terrible wife.

T (*feeling shame and contempt*): The distress you two are experiencing is not easy. There are so many deep wounds hiding beneath it. They bring up so much disappointment, anger, rage, shame, and hatred.

K (*seeming genuinely embarrassed*): I really am ashamed of your yelling—our entire neighborhood has to listen to it.

S (*angry and contemptuous*): You go ahead and apologize to all of our poor neighbors. And while you're at it, tell them what a pig you are! Oh, I should probably apologize to all of the pigs for saying that, shouldn't I?

T (*experiencing terror and shame, her face flushing hot*): Excuse me, when the two of you express your most painful emotions like this, by continuously shaming and insulting each other—

K (*angrily interrupting*): She keeps on insulting me! Every step of the way!

S (*contemptuously*): You poor thing.

T (*adamantly*): You are both extremely distressed and terrified about what's going to happen. The ways you express this is a reflection of what is truly hurting you deep inside, and it leads to you to cause even more pain for each other.

S (*contemptuously*): So what am I supposed to do with him, poor thing, so scared of me. . .

K (*appearing hurt and hopeless*): And this is supposed to be a relationship. If you're that upset, why don't you just divorce me?

S (*erupting sarcastically*): Yeah, and then what are you going to do? You can't even iron your own shirts! Are you going to move in with your mommy? You poor little boy, you can't survive a day on your own. And then that woman will have to come to you, right? You probably deserve each other.

The first few therapeutic sessions revealed how hurt, shamed, and degraded both partners feel. They are unable to address, let alone resolve their feelings, as they are too frightening. They threaten their core psychic structures, which are already weak and vulnerable. Their emotions and affects emanate from their early developmental years and have become the core of their affective psychic construct and their affect regulation style. When these affects reawaken in their relationship, they are unable to manage them. Instead, both partners' affects manifest through anger, rage, and shaming; each concealing their true affects that are too painful to address. It is as if the couple has an unwritten pact to do this. Through projective and introjective identification, the couple is able to avoid facing uncomfortable affects. Instead, they do each other the service of carrying and maintaining each other's unacceptable mental content. This is also the reason they persist in their relationship, despite its destructive nature.

The therapist must gently explore these deep and painful affect, the first step being to address their intrapsychic and interpersonal boundaries in order to help them take full responsibility for their own emotions, thoughts, and actions. The process will help the partners to contain their own mental content, thus being able to resolve it with the therapist's help, rather than project onto the other.

T (*experiencing the strong pressure of the couple's rage, shame, and demeaning behavior*): Both of you are deeply hurt and are experiencing terror, disappointment, and despair. These emotions have haunted you for a long time. Because of this, you reenact familiar scenarios. In order to understand each other, I'd like you both to contain yourselves for a while. Try focusing on the fact that you each have your own, specific feelings. Your partner may have caused them, but they are yours and belong only to you. Shall we give it another try? (*Both nod. The therapist senses that they are more relaxed.*) Sabina, can you calmly tell us what happened and what it was that hurt you so much?

S (*appearing hurt*): I waited for him like we agreed. But he keeps doubling his own workload and spending time with that secretary of his.

K (*scornful*): You're disgusting!

T (*experiencing a feeling of disgust towards him*): Just a moment, Kieran. (*Kieran restrains himself.*) You were worried. Your husband wasn't there, and you were afraid something might have happened to him. Then you became furious, enraged, and he began to disgust you.

The therapist is going out on a limb here, taking an emotion from the husband through projective and introjective identification, and trying to clarify where this deep affect is actually coming from.

S (*angrily*): Yes! He really disgusted me! And then when he finally came home, I just lost it.

T (*experiencing terror manifested as tension in her chest*): Sabina, it must have really been terrible, right? You were so furious, and then your anger turned into disgust. (*Kieran is trying very hard to hold back and not interrupt.*)

S (*angrily*): Yeah, something like that.

The therapist senses that the affect of disgust had been present for most of her life, and is being reawakened in her marriage. Sensing terror behind the disgust, the therapist must figure out where these affects are really coming from, and which one of them is holding on to them.

T (*still experiencing terror and disgust, trying to put it all into words*): What if we tried to figure out where this disgust is coming from. Where have you already experienced this feeling?

S (*tears filling her eyes*): Well, we used to always wait for my father to come home and it took forever before he would show up. That's when feelings of disgust hit me.

T (*sensing a deep sadness and loneliness manifested as numbness in her legs and throat*): So, when your father didn't come home, you must have suppressed feelings of disgust, and might have experienced a sense of deep sadness. Perhaps feelings of being in the way, worthless, even abandoned?

S (*crying*): Yes, I know all of those feelings. . .

T (*sensing a terrible loneliness*): What did you do with all those terrible feelings? Were you able to talk to anyone about them?

S (*wiping her tears; Kieran turns to face her for the first time*): Well, for the longest time I tried not to feel anything. And I slowly became kind of numb. . .

T (*feeling contempt*): And you probably despised your father.
S (*with a look of consternation*): Well, despised is a harsh word. I was always afraid of feeling that. I was afraid I'd lose him completely if I did. But, to be honest, even just thinking about him back then makes me despise him.
T (*sensing Kieran is losing hope*): It seems that the only thing left between you and your father is contempt, as if it's the strongest feeling you have towards him. What do you feel when you are afraid you're husband is not coming home? Can you tell him?

At this point in the therapeutic process, it is important that the therapist includes Kieran once again so as not to lose him completely. All intrapsychic themes are transferred onto the interpersonal and systemic level. Transference makes the therapeutic process more lucid and offers a better chance of resolving the affective psychic construct. In this case, the construct is permeated with disgust and contempt: deep, suppressed, and split-off emotions that the therapist had been picking up on. With his behavior, Kieran triggers these emotions in his wife. In order to respond more functionally, Sabina will have to accept the uncomfortable emotions she avoids and locate them where they belong.

S (*reluctantly*): Well, he knows already. It's pointless. He'll just accuse me of... well, of I don't know what.
T (*experiencing a sensation of fear manifested as stomach pain*): I understand that you are frightened, that this is a very delicate subject for you. What would happen if you gave it a try? What are you most afraid of?
S (*calming down*): Well, I'm scared he won't understand me. He'll just shame and degrade me.
T (*stomach pain subsiding*): Well, it is scary. Especially since you are so used to experiencing that kind of reaction.
S (*turning slowly towards her husband*): Kieran, when you're not home, for whatever reason, I feel neglected. I feel like I don't mean anything to you. And then all of these old feelings come up, like they did back at home.
T (*facing Kieran*): What are you feeling now that your wife is openly expressing her painful emotions?
K (*looking at his wife directly*): I don't know what to say. You know I'm not doing this on purpose.
T (*turning towards Sabina and experiencing her distress*): What feelings would you like your husband to understand the most?
S (*timidly*): I want him to know how much I miss him, and how worthless I feel when he's not around. That's why I get disgusted.
T (*sensing Kieran is feeling calmer*): Can you accept that?
K (*sighing*): I understand. But I want you to understand me, too. (*looks at the therapist*) I can feel, I can understand that you're scared and

you miss me, but I didn't know. You don't know how scared I am, driving home every night, not knowing if you're going to be all upset again when I come home. Sometimes I'd rather just stay at work.

T (*sensing they are both frightened, turns towards Sabina*): Sabina, we'll get right back to you. Kieran, where do you think this fear is coming from?

Knowing it is difficult for both of them to speak about their vulnerability, the therapist guides them gently, making sure they both understand what's being triggered in their significant other, what they may or may not be thinking and feeling. In order to explore and face these hurtful affects, as well as share them and ultimately change them, the first step for the couple is to find a middle ground and understand each other's pain. They will have to accept the fact that they unconsciously reawaken hurtful emotions from each other's childhood in order to avoid these painful and traumatizing affects. Their early childhood affects are dangerous and create the affective psychic construct that manifests through their conflicts. Paradoxically, their affective psychic construct seems safe, as it guarantees that their relationship will continue. This is why they recreate these constructs in many of their interactions.

K (*mortified*): Well, it was also terrifying for me, waiting for my father to come home. Sometimes it took a couple of days. My stomach would ache. I didn't even want to see him when he came back! I would hide and pretend I was asleep. Ugh, I hate thinking about those times.

T (*sensing deep sadness as a personal countertransference affect*): You must have experienced a lot of distress. It was so horrible for you—you would hide, rather than see him! What would happen once he returned home?

K (*quietly, agonized*): Usually there would be a huge argument. My mom would go completely crazy. She would blame him for all sorts of things, yell at the top of her lungs. My father would mock her and that made her even more upset. It would all go on until the early morning hours when they were too exhausted to go on, but they would pick up as soon as they woke up. Sometimes we couldn't wait for him to leave again, but then it would be even worse when he returned again.

T (*feeling contempt for Kieran's father*): What did you feel through all of this? Did you start hating your father?

The contempt the therapist feels towards Kieran's father is a countertransference. The therapist goes out on a limb and delicately vocalizes this emotion, similar to how she expressed the emotion of disgust earlier.

K (*taking a moment to think*): Yeah, I think we all began to despise him, but we never dared to say that to each other.

T (*empathically, but still feeling the sense of contempt*): And how is it—hating your own father? How does it feel to have a relationship with your father that is based on hate?

K (*sad and also angry*): It's terrible. I'm ashamed of feeling that way, but I can't help it. I was ashamed when my mother screamed the way she did.

T (*feeling shame manifested as pressure in the chest*): You were frightened and shocked. You must have felt ashamed that your mother was unable to have more self-control and that your father made fun of her and shamed her. That's probably why she began to hate him.

K (*surprised*): I hadn't thought about it that way. In truth, she still hates him today, and I have those feelings every now and then.

T (*empathically, still feeling a sense of shame*): It must be horrible to feel such awful emotions. Worse still, they keep coming up in your relationship with your wife—you also feel ashamed when she yells. Could you ask her how she experiences you in those difficult moments? (*Kieran looks timidly at his wife and then back at the therapist.*)

At this point in the therapeutic process, Kieran and Sabina have revealed painful emotions that had hitherto been suppressed and denied. However, they are both beginning to realize that they are reliving these same emotions in their marriage. They have split off their most unbearable emotions and projected them onto each other. Furthermore, their whole relationship is rooted in these destructive and painful affects of shame, disgust, and contempt. On the surface, they each experience feelings of anger, rage, hate, and humiliation, but these emotions are a defense against more catastrophic emotions. It is becoming clearer that shame and anger reside at the very core of their mental structures, and that their affective psychic construct is founded upon these core affects. This ends up manifesting in contempt. There are probably deeper levels of affects hidden behind these emotions, perhaps including a fear of worthlessness and an even deeper fear of abandonment. These are the affects that both partners have managed to deny and split off, unconsciously projecting them onto each other. At this point, the goal of therapy will be to help Kieran and Sabina express and share these affects, as well as to find their meaning and place. In fact, these affects belong in their past and yet have became a constitutive part of their developing mental structures and thus part of their relationship.

S (*facing Kieran, appearing embarrassed*): You know, I feel so ashamed to be listening to all of this. I know that I yell, I know that you feel disgust, and that's a really difficult emotion for me—it makes me feel terrible and guilty. But I had no idea you were afraid to come home! And I'm going to go ahead and say this too: I feel terrible that you're scared of me. In fact, I feel really bad for you.

T (*feeling a sense of shame and contempt*): This is why you probably start feeling contempt. Perhaps you feel that Kieran is not manly enough, the way you are experiencing him now. (*turning towards Kieran, sensing his shame*) You must also feel terrible and ashamed, especially when Sabina yells at you and you feel like she doesn't understand anything, like she can't deal with anything. Then you start humiliating and shaming her in those moments, and Sabina doesn't let you get away with it. That's how the two of you continuously share each other's most painful and destructive emotions. Somewhere, on an unconscious level, you feel like you wouldn't even have a relationship without these feelings. How is it for you both to hear all of this?

Suddenly their deepest affects, formative to their relationship, are revealed to be an extremely powerful connecting element between them. The dynamics of their attraction begin to be revealed. The therapeutic process demonstrates the connecting valency of their mental structures. It explains why Kieran and Sabina need each other so much: their connection lies in their core affects. In a way, they bring each other to life. They give each other the chance to live through the other's emotions, to feel the affects that they had denied and split off a long time ago because they were too painful. Now they are able to give them to each other, while still managing to avoid dealing with them on their own. At the same time, they both need these affects in order to establish a relationship in the first place; these are their earliest, most important, and fundamentally connecting affects. The therapist's main job at this point is to explain to them why it is so dangerous to make changes in their relationship. Only after they understand this, will they be able to give themselves and each other a chance to risk something new.

S (*in tears*): Well, now I feel ashamed, because I am repeating my mother's story all over again. When she yelled at my father, degrading and humiliating him, I swore that I would be a completely different person, that I would never shame or humiliate my own husband.

K (*sadly, yet adamantly*): I also decided I would never neglect my own wife, like my dad neglected my mom.

T (*sensing sadness and despair manifested as numbness in her legs*): Both of you are literally re-experiencing stories from your childhood. You've both become very sad now. I feel despair and helplessness, and I think these emotions have even deeper roots!

It becomes even more evident that their feelings of contempt and affects of disgust are hiding an even deeper affect that has been concealed until now. The therapist senses the couple began feeling sad for reasons other than the realization that they are recreating their childhood stories. It seems their feelings of rage, their affect of shame, and their affective psychic constructs are concealing deeply rooted intrapsychic affects. The therapist senses that the hidden emotions include a catastrophic intrapsychic affect of fear—the fear of being worthless and of abandonment. These are the foundation of the affective psychic construct that prevents the deeper affects from reaching consciousness. It also creates their affect regulation style that leads them to have continuous conflicts on the interpersonal level. It prevents them from making healthy and functional judgments and setting appropriate intrapsychic and interpersonal boundaries. The therapist will address these affects, well aware that the Sabina and Kieran will most likely resist.

K (*upset and slightly angry*): It's not that bad, and anyway what does any of this matter? They're old stories we can't do anything about now.

T (*experiencing tension in her head and chest*): We've touched on something very painful.

K (*getting more upset and angry*): What does it mean anyway? I'm not trying to contradict you, but. . .

T (*sensing escalating anger manifested as pressure in her chest*): Are you feeling angry? It seems as though something else is hiding behind all of these feelings, something much deeper.

K (*still angry, shifting in his chair*): Don't you get it? If your wife was constantly humiliating you and doing everything she can to shame you, you wouldn't be happy either. Anyway, you two can talk about that without me! (*staring angrily at his wife and avoiding the therapist's eyes*)

S (*gesturing angrily*): See? You're accusing me again! The best way to defend yourself is to attack! Just like last week! I can't ever really trust you. I must be crazy to still be with you! And all of this makes it even more painful. . . (*looking at her husband with contempt, and covertly at the therapist*)

T (*feeling rage from both partners*): All of these emotions are coming up and I am not able to understand all of them, or to protect you and give you more security and empathy. In fact, maybe I'm just making it worse, exposing you even more, rubbing salt in your wounds. That's why you're angry with me. But now that we're talking about all this, can you tell me what else you are feeling?

The therapist is sensing anger and reluctance through countertransference, that each partner has turned and begun to perceive the therapist as someone from their past. They each continue to focus on the other, humiliating and shaming each other, and actually doing everything to let their partner do so in return. But they are unaware of it. It is the fundamental task of the therapist to recognize and evaluate this process, and help them put an end to this vicious circle. At this point, the only source of their relationship is shame and degradation, which distances and connects them at the same time.

S (*crying*): I don't know. I'm starting to feel completely helpless.

T (*sensing a deep sadness manifested as numbness and pressure in the chest*): Where is this helplessness coming from? Where have you felt it before? Have you felt the way you do here somewhere else?

S (*wiping her tears*): I always felt completely helpless at home. There was no way out and no way to fix anything.

T (*sensing terror, still feeling numb*): What were you most afraid of then?

S (*sobbing*): That I would be left alone, that I was just in the way.

T (*sensing a powerful fear of abandonment*): You were afraid that you might be completely abandoned. And now you feel the same when you're waiting for your husband to come home?

S (*speaking through her tears*): Yes.

T (*sensing a deep sadness and the numbness beginning to subside*): Was there no one who could console you? No one you could turn to? No one to give you the empathy you needed?

T (*turns towards Kieran briefly, sensing his restlessness, then back to Sabina*): Would you let your husband comfort you? Let him reassure you he is still here and is going to stay.

S (*still crying inconsolably*): He's never done that before. It's like he's not even here.

The more the therapist addresses these painful affects, the more distressed and anxious the couple seems. The therapist knows they are on the right path, and empathically continues, risking even more. The therapist understands that sadness and despair were simply concealing the other more powerful affects that are now being evoked. She senses this is the path to the core affects of fear of abandonment and worthlessness. It is imperative for Kieran and Sabina to participate in these moments. They each need to experience that they can find the right response to their distress. They need to show each other that there is an alternative resolution, and by becoming conscious of their deepest affects, they will experience resolutions on an interpersonal level. This is the only way they will be able to address their affective psychic construct and all its hidden painful affects, including worthlessness and the fear of abandonment. Basically, they are striving to establish a new relationship, one free of shame and humiliation, emotions that are only there to protect them from even more destructive and unbearable affects. If they are successful, then they will finally feel understood in this new relationship and that will further enable them to take chances and risk new things.

T (*sensing sadness and despair manifested in pressure in the throat and tears*): I understand your sadness and despair. There really wasn't anyone there to comfort you and give you hope. How can you let your husband comfort you now, if you don't even know if he can? If he can't, you would lose your last hope. I know it's a huge risk to take, but do you think you could just try and let him comfort you? (*At first Sabina is cautious, then she nods in agreement. Kieran gently hugs her and she leans into him. The therapist senses her own distress subsiding.*) That was a big risk for you, Sabina. How do you feel now?

S (*tears trickling down her cheeks as Kieran gently tells her that everything will be all right*): Better, so much better. . .

T (*turning towards Kieran and feeling her body calming down*): How is it for you? What are you feeling?
K (*calmly*): Well, I understand Sabina very well. I also never felt consoled or comforted. Everyone would just yell at me when I was upset. They didn't put up with my crying.
T (*sensing his distress rising*): So you also risked quite a bit now as well. You accepted her tears, her sadness. In a way, it is your sadness too.
K (*uneasily*): Yes, I hate sadness and tears. I hate feeling so helpless and powerless.
T (*sensing Sabina often cries instead of him*): So perhaps you transfer your sadness onto Sabina and she cries instead of you?
K (*perplexed*): I don't understand that.
T (*sensing feelings of guilt*): Well, it's not a conscious process. What do you do when you're feeling sad or hopeless?
S (*joining in*): Whenever I feel like he's sad and I ask him about it, he starts insulting me.
T (*sensing fear manifested as numbness in her hands*): And that makes you cry, perhaps out of despair and fear?
S (*still in Kieran's embrace, looking up into his eyes*): Yeah, you really do everything to make me feel—I know you don't mean it—I just give up and feel like you've abandoned me…
T (*experiencing pain in her stomach, turns to face Kieran*): What if you were to look inwards, toward your sadness and despair? What's hiding behind all of that?
K (*deep in thought, Sabina gently removes herself from his embrace*): Well, I feel guilty. I had no idea I make Sabina feel that way. I just feel attacked and so I try to defend myself.
T (*still sensing guilt, tears well up in her eyes*): Yes, it's very difficult to be in touch with yourself in those moments and to recognize that it's your sadness and your despair. There's other emotions hiding behind these…
K (*thinking out loud*): Other emotions, yes. Well, it was always like that at home.
T (*sensing anger manifested as anxiety and pain in her stomach*): Your father was always attacking, and your mother yelled and cried. They didn't know how else to handle their problems. What about you?
K (*calming down*): My father never apologized—we gave up on hoping that he would. All that was left was anger.
T (*still sensing anger and sadness*): He never apologized. What were you afraid of most? What did you think would happen in that fear?
K (*cautiously*): Well, that someday my father would get so angry that he would just pack up and leave.
T (*sensing despair, tears well up in her eyes*): And you would be left alone.
K (*still cautiously*): Yeah, that he would just… and my mother would…
T (*sensing terror and anxiety*): You were terrified of being abandoned.
K (*Sabina gently leans in towards him*): Well, in a way, he had abandoned us long before that. He never understood us. It was almost as if we

didn't belong to him. Whenever he would take us places we were scared he might just leave us there. Because that's what he did when he was angry. . .

T (*still sensing terror and experiencing stomach pain*): This feeling of terror and worthlessness, this horrible fear of abandonment, it made you numb yourself completely. That way you never had to feel the fear. It was too painful for you.

K (*with deep sadness, slowly calming down as if a load has been lifted from his shoulders*): Yeah, something like that.

T (*sensing his calmness*): You have risked a lot today as well. (*looking at Sabina and Kieran*) This can be a new hope for you both: hope that you can manage and hope that things can be different. I suggest you both hold onto that hope, be brave, and let yourself take more risks. We are going to have to finish for today. I'm going to ask you to be gentle with each other. If difficult subjects come up and you feel overwhelmed by them, try holding onto them, and we'll discuss them here together.

S and K (*both nod in agreement*)

T (*sensing the two have calmed down*): Thank you, both. I'll see you next week!

In the following sessions, the therapist must address other subjects hiding behind their fear of abandonment and worthlessness—the affects that create their affective psychic construct of contempt, sadness, and despair and define their affect regulation style. These reciprocal dynamics mutually influence and maintain each other. Their parents' threats of divorce and accusations of adultery shaped Sabina and Kieran's core affects and penetrated deep into their intrapsychic structures. To this day, those affects unconsciously pervade their interpersonal experience and intensify an already pained relationship. The therapist will have to be

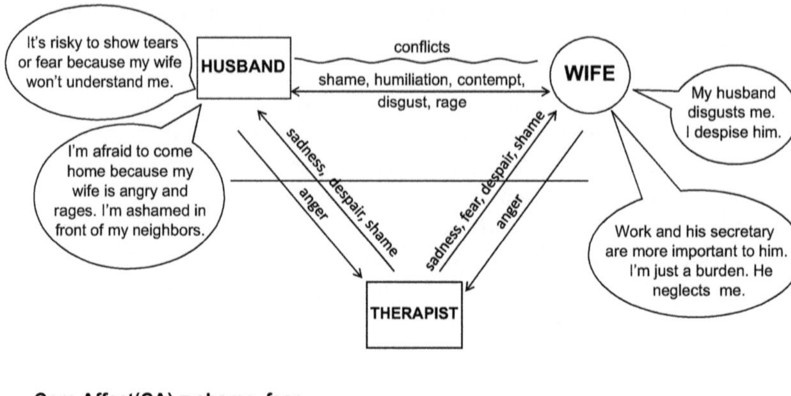

Figure 4.1 Interpersonal level (husband – wife)

Figure created by Tanja Repič Slavič and Janko Slavič

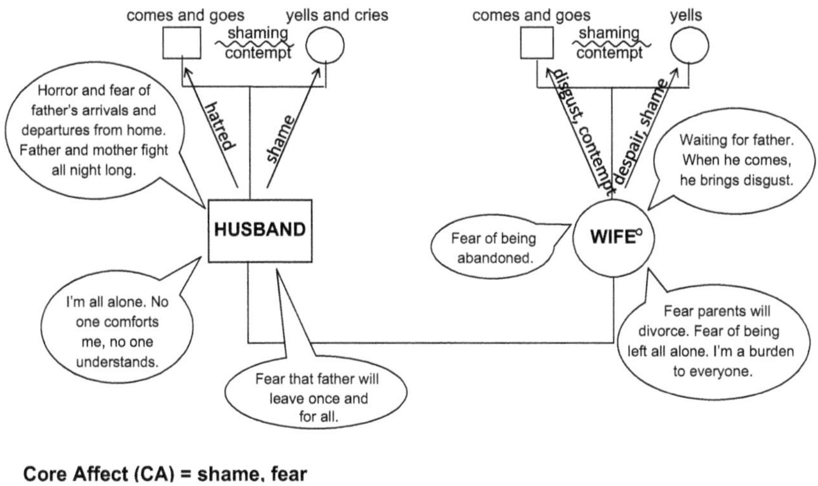

Figure 4.2 Intrapsychic level (childhood)

Figure created by Tanja Repič Slavič and Janko Slavič

extremely careful and actively pay attention to their interactions in order to prevent them from hurting each other even more. This will only be possible if they are able to listen to and hear each other, giving each other the support and empathy they need. This will enable them to approach each other and speak about their most painful and intimate experiences.

Breaking established patterns of communication is a therapist's greatest challenge. The partners need each other precisely because of their most painful emotions. This is what gives them a sense of livelihood and brings freshness to their relationship. However, they end up getting caught in their old ways that unconsciously promise them a relationship, regardless of how painful it may be, and a sense of safety and belonging. The ongoing painful conflicts create their affective psychic construct. On the surface, they manifest through affects of rage, humiliation, and degradation—all serving to protect the partners from experiencing their true fears of worthlessness and abandonment. In addition, these emotions establish their affective psychic construct and determine their affect regulation.

4.2 The Fundamental Concepts of Relational Marital Therapy

The rationale of relational marital therapy holds that individuals deal with conflicts rooted in the frustrated and threatening environment in which they grew up by later forming intimate relationships that match the models of the core psycho-organic experiences from their families of origin. The basis for this lies in the core affect that is often concealed by the affective psychic construct. When the distress level of individuals, couples, or an entire family is too high, or if they are fearful of confronting these painful themes, projective and introjective identification becomes the main mechanism. It usually gets acted out in one of the following three ways (Fishbane, 2013; Geher & Kaufman, 2013; Johnson, 2014; Poulton, 2013; Siegel & Solomon, 2013):

4.2.1

Individuals fall in love with people who remind them of the parent with whom they had an unresolved relationship. This predetermines a relationship between their psycho-organic systems of affect regulation, a consequence of exceptional valency and right hemisphere communication between the two partners rooted in their psycho-organic states (Fishbane, 2013; Rothschild, 2006; Schore, 2003). This is the domain of implicit memory. The two experience an extremely strong attraction, but it may soon result in complications and conflicts. These are revealed once the feeling of infatuation begins to subside.

4.2.2

By means of projective and introjective identification, individuals unconsciously force their partners to react in a way similar to how their parents did (J.S. Scharff, 2010; J.S. Scharff & Scharff, 2014). This is defined as the mechanism of induction, which actually forces recipients to react based on the sender's split-off mental and psycho-organic states. Recipients then behave in precise and specific ways in line with senders' perceptions and ways of reacting.

4.2.3

People project their intrapsychic romantic imagery based on their psycho-organic states (Fosha, 2009; Schore, 2003, 2010, 2012). By projecting it onto their partners, they start perceiving them as they did their parents, despite the fact that they may have nothing in common with them (Givelber, 1990; Hendrix & Hunt, 2004; Lachkar, 2004; Poulton, 2013). Nonetheless, a core affect similar to the one that once pervaded their families of origin and shaped their affective psychic construct is definitely present.

Emotions established through intimate relationships are extremely powerful; they are very uncommon in other types of relationships, such as those between friends, coworkers, or neighbors that lack the closeness that comes with intimacy. Our romantic partners are capable of generating powerful positive feelings in us. They are also able to have an equally strong negative effect. For example, small disagreements can seem much more intense in romantic relationships, being anchored in the deepest complexities of our relations. Relational family therapists believe that romantic relationships and marriages are battlefields between two family structures. Each family sends their representatives to fight for its morals and values, thus creating a war for family power within the romantic relationship. Relational family therapists try to help couples recognize and address their distorted views of each other, which have been tainted by their family's beliefs. Therapists teach couples basic regulatory systems that can help to manage difficult affects and determine their affective psychic constructs.

For example, therapists can help women recognize that their partner's anger and rage may, in fact, be hiding their vulnerability. Partners have to learn that some feelings cover up deeper emotions, ones they may not want to acknowledge. They suppress, deny, split off, and project their hidden emotions onto each other, thus taking on roles as carriers of their partner's most painful affects. For example, a wife who experiences her husband's anger, may, in fact, be denying her own. Through therapy, couples can learn how to recognize these patterns and create a safer, more integrated image of themselves, their relationship, and their partner. They no longer need to perceive their partners as different or threatening.

Once couples learn how to address these issues and work together to improve their relationship, they are able to resolve their own individual intrapsychic difficulties. However, this does not mean they are able to fully overcome their infantile needs and desires. This is only possible once two people have established a healthy and functional intimate relationship. Only then are they able to tolerate each other's infantile needs and even fulfill them (Carlson & Sperry, 2010; Cummings & Davies, 2010; Donavan, 2003; Lachkar, 2004; McCormack, 2000; Pines, 1999; Poulton, 2013; Solomon et al., 2001).

Once partners have learned to accept each other, they are able to fully embrace themselves as well, including all the suppressed, denied, and split-off parts they have tried to ignore and project onto each other. Full acceptance of a significant other—including their infantile needs and desires—demands empathy and reciprocity. This means each partner must fully empathize with their significant other and feel what their partner feels. This can be dangerous for undifferentiated couples without strong systemic intrapsychic boundaries. It means they have to dissolve their own core affective psychic construct that has protected them for so long. This process can be extremely difficult. These individuals usually feel unsafe and mentally dependent. In order to feel what their partners feel, they must deny their own emotions. The capacity to actively listen to an intimate partner and express empathy is a manifestation of autonomy, as well as an act that facilitates autonomy (Donavan, 2003; Fishbane, 2013; Geher & Kaufman, 2013; Lachkar, 2004; McCormack, 2000; Pines, 1999; Siegel & Solomon, 2013; Solomon et al., 2001).

4.3 Ten Premises Used by Relational Marital Therapists

The following enumerates the fundamental premises relational family and couples' therapists have to bear in mind and address while working with clients (Fishbane, 2013; Johnson, 2014; Poulton, 2013; Ringstrom, 2014; J.S. Scharff & Scharff, 2006, 2014; Siegel & Solomon, 2013):

4.3.1

Relational marital therapists believe that interpersonal and intimate relationships provide one of the best chances to rectify unresolved experiences and intrapsychic dynamics, including psycho-organic states. They take into account that affective psychic constructs and affect regulation form at a very young age and help individuals to avoid facing non-transferable and painful issues from their childhood (Bruschweiler-Stern et al., 2010; J.S. Scharff & Scharff, 2014; Siegel & Solomon, 2013).

4.3.2

People choose their partners based on the unconscious forces of their intrapsychic dynamics rather than with logical thought processes. These choices depend on the valency with the psycho-organic states of others. Unconscious right hemisphere communication levels determine this valency, and they are fueled by projective and introjective identification, which simultaneously substantiates affect regulation (Fosha, 2009; Poulton, 2013; J.S. Scharff & Scharff, 2014; Schore, 2003, 2012). Unconscious repetition compulsion of old established patterns plays a large part in the process that culminates in the choice of a partner.

4.3.3

When people fall in love and choose their partners, they transfer their intrapsychic structures to the interpersonal level and later to the systemic level. Individuals choose romantic partners with whom they re-experience emotions, affects, and psycho-organic states from their childhood. Establishing romantic relationships gives people a new chance to free themselves of their past issues and conflicts that were transferred onto them by their parents. Partners entering intimate relationships carry and connect to their parents' most significant characteristics, including their relationship, as well as the core affect of the family system (Gehart, 2016; Hendrix, 1992; Hendrix & Hunt, 2004; Siegel & Solomon, 2013).

4.3.4

Negative characteristics have a stronger influence on people choosing romantic and marital partners than positive ones, especially in extreme cases of obsessive love or infatuation. This is because the wounds and lack of positive emotions from their past need healing. Healing is the essence and purpose of every relationship, albeit on an unconscious level (Hendrix, 1992; Hendrix & Hunt, 2004; Johnson, 2014; Siegel & Solomon, 2013). People's intrapsychic distress is reawakened in order to present the opportunity to heal on the interpersonal and systemic levels. At the same time, this distress reciprocally impacts the entire relational system.

4.3.5

The more traumatic the intrapsychic childhood wounds are, the stronger romantic infatuation will be, and the closer the similarity is between the partner and the parent who traumatized them. This is because romantic relationships promise resolution on an unconscious level. People can fall in love multiple times until they find the right person to help them. However, some are unable to establish such a relationship at all (Lachkar, 2004; McCormack, 2000; Schore, 2003, 2010, 2012). Couples will continuously recreate the intrapsychic imagery, including their psycho-organic states from their past in their newly established relationship, and will help each other maintain it at all costs.

4.3.6

Intimate relationships always reawaken primary psycho-organic states, including all corresponding affects, both negative and positive. These create the most unique vibrations and sensations (Fosha, 2009, Siegel & Solomon, 2013). In a way, they recreate the symbiosis children once had with their mother. They create a complete connection or enmeshment, without boundaries for autonomy. We are unable to fall in love with two people at once. Once we fall in love and re-experience our blissful primary symbiosis, it triggers our hope and expectations that our significant other will fulfill our psycho-organic infantile needs (Hendrix & Hunt, 2004; Pines, 1999; Poulton, 2013).

4.3.7

Our intrapsychic romantic imagery dictates with whom we fall in love. This imagery includes our psycho-organic states, the intrapsychic states of our parents, and their relationship. People in love often feel as though they have known each other forever. This is because we recreate our strongest childhood experiences while in love. People often feel as though their significant others are the only ones who mean anything, and without whom we would be unable to go on. Hence, infatuation is timeless (Hendrix & Hunt, 2004; Pines, 1999; Robins, 2010). It follows that one of the most important roles for therapists is to help couples shed light on the strong connections they have to their past experiences and psycho-organic states, as well as recent experiences, and whatever conflicts are part of them.

4.3.8

Only when couples realize their roles can they recognize that their choice to fall in love was unconscious, mutual, and complementary. By doing so, they give each other the chance to express their most fundamental mental content and themes. They recreate this content, and it becomes the cornerstone of their future conflicts. This can be painful and detrimental, but partners take this risk in order to repair the most vulnerable parts of their psycho-organic states (Cummings & Davies, 2010; Fishbane, 2013; Robins, 2010; Schore, 2003, 2010).

4.3.9

In order to begin the therapeutic process, individuals must first understand the connection between their unresolved childhood experiences and the problems they encounter in their adult lives. This makes it easier to accept responsibility for their part in their relational conflicts (Cummings & Davies, 2010; Hendrix & Hunt, 2004; Poulton, 2013; Robins, 2010). It can also help them turn current problems into opportunities for personal growth and relational progress. It gives couples the choice of deconstructing their affective psychic construct, which hinders healthy and functional communication.

4.3.10

In order to make romantic love last, couples must be able to attune to their partner's needs and emotions and express true empathy, as well as provide whatever they expect and desire from one another. People's expectations and desires emerge from the attachment they have with their partner and their mutual dynamic, as well as the connection between their relationship and their unresolved childhood experiences. These dynamics facilitate the possibility of personal and relational growth. It is the partners' individual mental progress that enables their relationship to mature (Cummings & Davies, 2010; Fishbane, 2013; Johnson, 2014; Pines, 1999; Pines & Aronson, 1988; Robins, 2010).

To conclude, all types of love and infatuation have unique emotional and psycho-organic dynamics. These arise from interactions between conscious and unconscious elements as well as suppressed and projected parts of our psycho-organic states. This happens on an interpersonal level. The imagery created by both parents and their relationship strongly influences the components that enmesh to create a new, complex, and often tragic picture. This imagery is unique to each individual relationship. There are many factors that influence our choice of romantic partner. Our decisions depend on our surrounding environment, our social and cultural setting, and even our genetic predispositions. It also depends on who is available at any given moment and how available we are ourselves. Logical thinking, social beliefs, pressures from our family system and its needs, as well as our spiritual expectations and romantic ideals also contribute to our decisions (Johnson, 2014; Pines, 1999). However, it is our unconscious psycho-organic content that has the greatest impact on our choices.

Related research shows that our expectations of romantic relationships and our romantic ideals strongly influence our experience in romantic attachment (Cummings & Davies, 2010; Lachkar, 2004; Morrow & O'Sullivan, 1998; Siegel & Solomon, 2013; Solomon et al., 2001). Some people believe in romantic destiny: they are either destined to a single person or they expect to be alone forever. For these people, the connection between their happiness in the first stages of their romantic relationship, and their will to maintain it, is much stronger than with those who do not believe in romantic destiny. Those who have believe in destiny use strategies to avoid relational strife. They feel responsible for relationships falling apart and justify their responsibility by believing it was not meant to be from the very start. In contrast, people who do not believe they are destined to a specific partner believe a successful relationship depends on how they cultivate and develop it, and to what extent. They approach romance with caution and use a certain amount of judgment. They apply more tact and critically assess the relationship as they are convinced that this is the only way to build a good relationship. If their relationship doesn't succeed, they do not necessarily believe there was something wrong with it from the very beginning (Cummings & Davies, 2010; Knee, 1998; Poulton, 2013; Robins, 2010).

Romantic ideals and relationship expectations thus strongly influence the way relationships evolve. The question is whether or not they can influence or predict with whom we fall in love and why. Research regarding this subject is too scant to establish a unified answer to the question. However, the best answers to the fascinating question of romantic infatuation can be found in clinical theories that elaborate on these dynamics. Each theory uses its own terminology in defining people's intrapsychic romantic imagery or psycho-organic states or systems. However, all of them presume people fall in love with those who remind us of both or one of our parents—usually the one with whom we have unresolved issues. This involves our psycho-organic state and core affects such as anger, fear, rage, humiliation, or shame. These characterize us and create our destructive personality elements as well as our affective psychic construct. The more unresolved these dynamics are, the more intense our experience of infatuation—in the form of euphoria when infantile needs are met, or to the contrary, extreme frustration when these needs are neglected or unsatisfied as they were in the past (Pines, 1999). Following a short period of infatuation, partners begin to experience the dark forces of their past, elements that have haunted them since their childhood and that they will have to confront if they want to maintain a comfortable relationship and avoid excessive pain (Cummings & Davies, 2010; Gottman & Silver, 2012; Johnson, 2014; Robins, 2010).

Our parents are complex people with both positive and negative characteristics. This is why our childhood relational experience is also multifaceted and complex, creating complicated intrapsychic romantic models. This explains why we can become attached to multiple people. People are able to create unique models of interpersonal interactions with different romantic partners. They can fall in love with someone who fulfills their fundamental need for safety. Once that need is met, people can fall in love with someone else who might fulfill some other need, perhaps the need for drama and excitement. Sometimes people are unable to see their loved ones for who they really are. Instead, they fall in love with their own projection of their intrapsychic romantic model, thus forcing their significant other to react to their projections (Lachkar, 2004; McCormack, 2000; Pines, 1999; Robins, 2010; Siegel & Solomon, 2013; Solomon et al., 2001). This holds especially true for people who fall in love based on physical attraction rather than a deeper synchronic mutuality on emotional, cognitive, and spiritual levels. Such partners will either separate or, due to codependency, remain together in distressing relationships.

Despite the unique model of each romantic relationship, they all share a similar dynamic of continuously battling forces, some working towards symbiosis between lovers and others striving for independence and individuality. The forces that strive for symbiosis are founded on our yearning to connect and unite with someone. They are a reflection of the symbiosis we once had with our mother. The forces encouraging our individuality are rooted in our desire to do something unique and important that would give our life meaning. When people fall in love, the forces of symbiosis take over. After a certain amount of time passes, perhaps weeks, months, or even years, the forces of individuality grow stronger. Relationships that remain stuck in the cycle of striving for symbiosis can become very strenuous. Partners lose their sense of self and their personality, which should be separate from their significant other (Bader & Pearson, 1988; Bruschweiler-Stern et al., 2010; Cummings & Davies, 2010; Geher & Kaufman, 2013; Hendrix, 2008; Johnson, 2014; Pines, 1999; Robins, 2010).

An intimate relationship balances the individual's need for closeness, intimacy, and security, as well as the need for independence, self-realization, and autonomy. In relationships where people are able to maintain a spark of romance and intimacy, partners are able to feel comfortable and safe in their independence. Intimacy does not pose a threat and is not perceived as a danger (Cummings & Davies, 2010; Robins, 2010; Siegel & Solomon, 2013). Falling in love and maintaining romantic attachment has very positive effects on people. People in love feel more in touch with their ideal selves, and thus feel better about themselves. Hence, love positively affects all individuals and their emotional state and is a valuable life experience. It is up to us to decide which script we choose to follow in finding romantic partners, including how, when, and why we make our choice—regardless of our genetic predispositions, childhood experiences, physical appearance, personality, or perceptions of others, ourselves, and the concept of love in general.

In the following pages, we will provide an example of relational marital therapy and work with Anja (A) and Miha (M), an unmarried couple. According to Anja, they came to therapy because of their difficult and painful relationship arguments, which had to do with Miha's indecisiveness. Anja felt hopeless and sad. At their initial session, the therapist (T) asked both of them about their plans for the future. Miha began to seem very uncomfortable, especially regarding the subject of marriage. Miha's comments about making rash decisions seemed to upset Anja very much. They had been together for two years and had begun to feel helpless and disappointed as they were unable to agree on basic matters. They both felt that they still loved each other very much but knew they couldn't go on this way. Anja was the one to suggest they should try therapy as their last chance to make things right. Miha was reluctant initially but then realized this really was their only chance. The following is a transcript of their second therapy session. They both arrived seeming upset and uneasy.

T (*sensing agitation*): At our previous session you two became very uneasy and upset. It seems as though you are still upset, as though it has continued throughout the week.

A (*angrily*): If only he could decide what he wants! Waiting forever seems so pointless to me.

M (*seeming hurt*): If only you had a little more patience. You only think of yourself. You think you're so important. I'm the one that has to do everything—but I have to do it your way.

A (*lost in thought*): Well, maybe I do expect too much from you. But it's hard waiting and waiting.

T (*sensing fear manifested as pressure in the throat and chest*): Are you afraid that he will never make up his mind?

A (*sadly*): Yes, I am scared. I never used to be. I used to have hope somehow. But it's harder now, and that's why I get angry.

T (*sensing fear, sadness, and apathy*): Yes, it is humiliating having to wait constantly, and that's what makes you angry. Then you get scared that he may never make up his mind or that he may simply leave forever.

A (*sadly*): Yes, I am scared.

M (*upset and jumping in*): But you do know I love you and that I won't leave you.

T (*sensing fear manifested as pressure in her stomach*): Just a moment, Miha. This is how Anja feels whenever you can't decide. Are you willing to accept that?

M (*reluctantly*): Well, I understand that's how she feels. But I'm not *leaving*, I just need more time.

T (*sensing a looming fear manifested as pressure in her head*): You are both upset for your own reasons, but your mutual fear connects you. You are both afraid of losing each other, yet at the same time you are afraid of being too close to each other.

The therapist senses their fear, which is the core affect upon which they have built their relationship. Their fear both unites them and distances them at the same time. It is the affect the therapist decides to explore. The therapist focused on the systemic and interpersonal levels of their relationship during their first session. The couple talked about their constant bickering regarding their different tastes in lifestyles, apartment options, and with which of their parents they would feel most comfortable living. The therapist soon realized all of their disagreements lead back to their fear of intimacy and their fear of making the decision to get married and spend the rest of their lives together. In fact, fear is the foundation of their psychic structures, serving as a pathway for them each to protect themselves from being vulnerable, but it has resulted in two years of relational strife. The therapist sets out to explore the deeper levels of their intrapsychic experience in hopes of finding the reasons Miha and Anja are unable to agree. There is insufficient insight on the systemic and interpersonal levels as to the true cause of their inability to understand and come together when it comes to a decision about getting married.

A (*agitated*): I don't understand that. (*Looks at Miha*): I'm always trying to accommodate you. But every time we start talking about the apartment and where we're going to live, we get into a fight.

M (*angry*): That makes me so mad. I'm always accommodating!

T (*sensing a deep uneasiness manifested in trembling hands*): Fear and anger keep appearing and you don't even know why. Could you talk to each other about that?

A (*timidly*): Miha, whenever you can't or don't want to talk about the apartment, when you say we have plenty of time to figure it out, and you say we have plenty of other things to talk about before we move, I get scared because I don't know if you're really up for it...

M (*trying to conceal his anger*): You know, there are so many things we need to do before that.

T (*sensing his coercion and experiencing as pressure in her head*): It sounds like you feel Anja is trying to force you into something...

M (*calmer*): Yeah, I often feel like she wants everything at once, like there's no room left for me...

T (*sensing distress manifested in difficult breathing*): It's almost as if you are suffocating.

A (*agitated*): I'm not trying to...

T (*feeling lightheaded*): Anja, I know it must be difficult for you to hear this. Could you try to hold on for a moment so we can see what is happening in Miha? He seems flooded with feelings of anger and coercion. (*Anja nods.*)

The therapist is still trying to help them resolve their issues on an interpersonal level. However, it is becoming clear that Miha's anger and feeling of being forced into something stems from deeper levels of his mental content. Although the therapist has sensed this for a while, it is important to collect enough material to discover his core affect and go deeper into Miha's intrapsychic structure. The therapist senses that Miha has felt these emotions before, that they are what comprise Miha's affective psychic construct. He is unconsciously afraid of the danger that would come with the emergence of these deeper emotions and fears of intimacy. It is easier for Miha to express the affect of anger and resent being forced into something he does not want. This allows him to conceal other emotions that might be too delicate and painful. Anja feels it is unfair that Miha is making her feel as though she is forcing him into making decisions that ultimately belong to him. Anja is also hiding a deeper affect of fear, perhaps the fear that she is not important enough. The therapist will address this later in the therapeutic process. Anja and Miha enable each other's affects to be evoked on a regular basis, almost as though they need each other to tease out their most painful emotions in order to maintain their relationship.

T (*sensing distress and a deep countertransference of sadness*): Miha, when Anja wants to talk to you about your future, you begin feeling as if you're being pushed into something. You feel suffocated as if there's no room left for you. When has that happened before? Can you remember feeling that way in your past?

M (*thinking, then answering slowly*): When I was 4 years old, my dad died and my mom and I were left alone. It was difficult for us. My mom became very attached to me. She was very good to me and did everything she could for me. She would often say I am the only reason she was still alive. She followed me everywhere...

T (*feeling anger towards his mother and sensing guilt*): She was good to you and did everything for you. She sacrificed for you and it would feel unfair now if...

M (*lost in thought*): Yes, she gave me everything. I can't just leave her now...

T (*empathically, after regulating the anger to you*): She became very attached to you and probably still is. She gave you everything, took care of you, loved you. It is kind of similar to Anja who now feels as though it is unfair that you cannot make up your mind...

M (*reluctantly*): Yeah, but this is completely different. I'm not trying to hurt anyone.

T (*still sensing distress and realizing that it is imperative to differentiate between her own emotions and those sensed through countertransference*): I'd like for us to be on the same page now. Your mother did everything she could possibly do for you, perhaps too much, which is why you feel scared it would be unfair to her or hurt her to move out. However, we are not talking about what your mother did for you, here we are discussing your experience and your feelings. How does it make you feel that your mother couldn't live without you, that you mean so much to her?

M (*relaxing slightly*): I really don't want to be unfair or hurt anyone, and I do think my mom became too attached to me. I often felt forced into, well, I suppose that's the wrong term... All I knew was that it meant a lot to her that I got good grades, that I was happy, that I am at home with her. Even after I grew up, she is always happiest when I am with her...

It is becoming clear that Miha feels this pressure to stay at home deep down in his intrapsychic structure. Having been her emotional partner growing up, he now feels obliged to stay loyal to his mother. The therapist senses the fear of intimacy is connected to Miha's unconscious fear that the suffocating atmosphere he experienced as a child will be repeated. He was his mother's only son and she used him as her sole emotional support. It is too early in the therapeutic process to touch on this subject because Miha is still very sensitive and filled with feelings of guilt that connect him to his mother. First, they will have to resolve the affect of feeling pressured and forced into something. This is extremely frightening for Miha and he will need to feel safe in order to address the subject.

T (*feeling lightheaded*): This flood of emotion makes it difficult to figure out what's what. It's hard to understand the difference between someone loving you, and when they need you or cannot live without you.

M (*pensively*): I never really thought about it that way. . .

T (*sensing this is where the core affect of fear is hiding*): And if you imagine it, what do you think would happen to your mother if you were to get married?

M (*worried*): I'm afraid, she might. . . Well, she likes Anja but I'm afraid she won't really feel like it's worth it. She might think it's pointless. . .

T (*sensing anxiety and worry*): It seems as though you still feel forced into something. What would happen if you were to talk to her about it?

M (*still worried*): We did talk, and I felt like she still cared. She told me to decide on my own, that I don't need to keep living at home. Sometimes it's almost as if she's talking me into leaving, and other times I feel like she doesn't want me to, as if she would be happier if I stayed. I'd rather not talk about this anymore, you understand though. . . (*timidly looking at Anja every now and then*)

T (*sensing anxiety manifested as pressure in her head and chest*): It looks as if you're stuck. You are not sure what to do so everything will be okay. It's hard to imagine that you and your desires are the most important in all of this. And there's also Anja who wants you all to herself. (*At this point, Miha seems very distressed and starts withdrawing. The therapist looks at Anja.*): We'll come back to this later. Anja, how do you experience Miha's distress when he is divided in this way?

Miha is giving clear signals that he no longer wants to discuss this matter. He feels very vulnerable, especially with Anja. The therapist empathically accepts his reluctance and senses there is a strong defense mechanism related to these emotions that is protecting his affective psychic construct. Miha has suppressed, denied, and split off his deep-rooted affects, and is now transferring them to Anja through projective and introjective identification. She responds with fear, anger, and resentment at being in the way, although these are actually Miha's emotions. His reluctance indicates that the therapist will need to make a safer place for him so that he will take the risk of exploring his deeply rooted vulnerability. Hence, the therapist decides to address Anja's vulnerable intrapsychic content, which manifests itself in their interpersonal relationship.

A (*cautiously*): Well, we've tried talking about this so many times, and then we always pull back. It's just too painful.

T (*sensing fear manifested as numbness in her leg*): What do you feel during these arguments?

A (*timidly*): Just thinking about it makes me frightened. Then I get angry. I don't want to feel humiliated anymore. Then I start feeling as if I'm in his way. . .

T (*empathically, sensing fear*): What happens then? How do the two of you cover up these emotions, at least on the outside?

A (*ashamed*) Well, first we both get angry and hold grudges, then we calm down and wait for each other to reach out, wait for the other one to call or send a text message. After that, we're fine again. Sometimes we fight again right afterwards because we expect too much from each other. It can last for quite a while, but eventually everything is back to where it started because Miha is incapable of coming to terms with. . . Ugh! I don't even know why I persist. It's so humiliating, but I also don't think I can go on without him. . .

T (*sensing shame manifested as flushed cheeks as a countertransference reaction*): This makes you feel ashamed, almost as though you are begging him, forcing him into something. You feel humiliated?

A (*showing her despair*): Exactly! It's terrible, really, it's as if I'm imposing on him. . .

T (*still sensing shame and despair*): And when you're sick of it all, and you feel completely humiliated, and you're just about to give up, that's when he approaches you again.

A (*angrily*): Yes! I feel so humiliated! I've promised myself I won't let it happen again so many times and that I'm not going back. . . But then some invisible force draws me back to him.

Anja has now embarked on a journey through her intrapsychic world. The therapist senses that her painful affects emerge from childhood and come to life in her relationship with Miha. These affects are probably stronger and more painful than those she would feel if Miha rejected her. The principle of valency ensures that both partners find each other attractive due to the experiences and mental structures they share. These unite them, enable their affect regulation, and secure their relationship, which is why the two continuously evoke these affects on the interpersonal level. The intrapsychic space gives life to their affective psychic construct, which in turn influences the way they regulate their affects. Their disagreements and painful arrivals and departures conceal and protect their hidden, suppressed, and split-off unconscious affects. The relationship Miha and Anja established brings these affects to life on a regular daily basis through projective and introjective identification and repetition compulsion. This entire dynamic gives them hope that their early childhood traumas will be resolved in a positive and healthy manner.

T (*sensing distress and shame along with a feeling of intrusiveness and humiliation*): All of this must be terrible for you. So much humiliation, so many feelings of shame, and the feeling that you're in his way, imposing yourself on him. Did you feel that way growing up?

The therapist wants to help Anja evoke her childhood memories and affects so she can recognize the suppressed mental content that is reappearing in her intimate relationship. The therapist will help Anja to recall the first time she felt these emotions that have become a constitutive part of her intrapsychic structure through projective and introjective identification and repetition compulsion. This will help Miha to recognize himself in her experience, and at the same time learn how to empathize and approach his own unresolved mental content.

A (*deep in thought*): I remember when I was still very young, I woke up in the middle of the night and heard my parents yelling in their bedroom. I ran over and saw my mom crying and my dad yelling at her. I didn't know what was going on. I only remember walking over to my dad and asking him to stop. . .

T (*feeling dread and numbness*): And how did you feel?

A (*her fear turning into dread*): I was terrified. I was shaking. I don't know how I calmed down. I kept crying and begging. I remember doing that a lot, especially when my dad would come home late and they argued. I would always go to him, beg him to stop. . .

T (*still sensing dread*): Did your parents comfort you?

A (*disappointed*): Sometimes, not often though. I would grab my dad's hand and try to drag him into the living room.

T (*feeling distress*): How did your parents respond?

A (*humiliated*): Sometimes they would both attack me, tell me not to get involved. They would push me away and I would run and hide in my room, covering my ears. Sometimes my dad would come with me to another room and listen to me. He'd try to explain how impossible my mom was and then she'd come into the room and say bad things.

T (*sensing shame manifested in flushed cheeks and a lump in the throat, along with anger towards the father*): How did it make you feel to be stuck between them, trying to mediate their arguments? When your father didn't protect you? When your mother spoke to you in a bad way?

A (*ashamed*): I felt as though I was in the way, and I felt guilty—as though they were fighting because of me. Sometimes they'd even say so: that if I weren't born they wouldn't have gotten married. . . (*hanging her head in shame*) And I was ashamed that I took my dad away from my mom.

T (*sensing more shame*): You felt ashamed because your mother told you that you're on your father's side, and you felt guilty for imposing yourself onto him. But none of it was your fault! Those were their problems. How unfair for a little girl to have to experience something like that, when she really deserved love, protection, and gentleness.

A (*starts crying*): I want to stop trying to remember all of this. (*Miha approaches and hugs her, then suddenly moves away, almost with a jerk.*)

T (*sensing distress*): Anja, this is very upsetting for you. You are overwhelmed by emotion. And Miha, what happened? Why did you move away so suddenly?

A (*crying even more*): He hates it when I cry.

M (*angry and distressed*): I know it is hard for you, but you can't change the past.

T (*sensing his anger and distress as tears in her eyes*): Anja, your parents never comforted you. Instead, you had to comfort them. We will come back to this painful subject. But let's first take a look at what emotions this evoked up in Miha. Miha, what was it like for you growing up?

This interaction was essential in revealing which affect has been concealed and causes both of them immense pain. Miha has trouble tolerating Anja's tears and sadness, which makes her afraid that she will be abandoned. These are the precise affects that both have suppressed and split off a long time ago with projective and introjective identification. Now they are projecting them onto each other, provoking them in very specific ways and reenacting old scenarios. The therapist will use this example as a point of reference in further discussions, mainly because it demonstrates the core affects that maintain their affective psychic construct.

M (*very sad*): Yeah, my mother cried a lot. I never knew how to comfort her.
T (*feeling sadness and anger*): You felt so powerless when she cried. You must have experienced a lot of her sadness. You were probably also angry with her.
M (*angrily and sadly at the same time*): Well, to be honest, yes. I was often mad at her, but I wasn't allowed to show that. I would just be sad with her and try to make her feel better, but she just kept on crying.
T (*feeling distress and shame, which is a countertransference, and must be differentiated from what is personal*): What did your mother do when she was this sad? (*feeling that she might have hugged him and kept on crying*): How did she act towards you when she was in such a bad place?

The therapist is taking a risk by asking this question and senses that Miha and his mother went through similar interactions. When Miha sensed Anja needed a hug, just as his mother once did, he would pull away, afraid of the closeness that he used to feel with his mother. The therapist sensed many painful affects hiding beneath Miha's interaction with Anja when he was unable to comfort her and accept her sadness, and the therapist continues to explore them.

M (*upset*): She would hold me tightly and tell me how hard it was for her and how I'm all she has, how she couldn't live without me. . .
T (*sensing distress and shame*): How did that make you feel? What emotions did that evoke in you?
M (*still upset*): Well, I was always uncomfortable when she hugged me, especially when she cried because. . .

T (*sensing dread, even terror*): You must have felt terrible.
M (*shifts restlessly*): It was suffocating.
T (*still sensing dread and terror*): If I'm understanding correctly, her hug filled you with dread and fear. Perhaps it was invasive.
M (*uneasily*): Yeah, I can still see her now, crying. It got a little better as I grew up.
T (*sensing distress, a feeling of paralysis, and the mother's exploitation*): Did your mother learn how to respect your boundaries?
M (*still upset, embarrassed, and ashamed*): When I got older, she distanced herself a little bit, but it was awful when she'd hug me in front of my friends. She'd give me a really big, strong hug, and kiss me. I was so embarrassed when she did that. I was so ashamed. . . (*putting his head down*)
T (*sensing anxiety and shame*): You felt ashamed in front of your friends and guilty for rejecting her love.
M (*distressed*): Yes, it was horrible. I would feel ashamed at first and then guilty. I just wanted everything to get better. Then when she rejected me I got angry.
T (*feeling sadness and anger and a sense of paralysis*): Were you ever able to tell her how this makes you feel?
M (*holding back his anger*): Sure, I tried, many times. But she would always remind me of all the things she had done for me. She said I was ungrateful, not even wanting to hug her.
T (*realizing that this scenario is repeating itself in his relationship with Anja*): It sounds very much like what's going on between you and Anja right now. How does that make you feel?
M (*pauses to think*): Well, it's similar in a way, except that Anja is my girlfriend and not my mother.
T (*sensing distress and feeling numb*): That's true. These feelings belong to the relationship you have with your mother, but they're repeating themselves in your relationship with Anja: feelings of possessiveness, suffocation, almost as if you're trapped all over again. Meanwhile, all Anja really wants is to be with you as much as possible, to feel you, touch you, hug you. . .

After these painful affects have been revealed, the therapist's job is to evaluate them and place them into their present context. This is not where they belong, but they have been triggered in their relationship. The suppressed, denied, and split-off affects brought them together and they have transferred them to each other through projective and introjective identification. Now they have fully reemerged, gaining new dimensions. On an unconscious level, the two need each other intensely in order to avoid having to address this painful mental content. Their arguments conceal the unacceptable hidden affects created by their affective psychic construct. It appears that the affect of shame is concealing other emotions, such as feeling unneeded, being forced to do something unwanted, possessiveness, and loss of autonomy. In short, what has been revealed is the fear of intimacy.

A (*begins speaking without having to be prompted*): That's all I really want. It's hard to hear how difficult it's been for you. I understand now.

T (*sensing almost unbearable anxiety*): Anja, it must have been hard waiting, but you did. It must be upsetting realizing you've become such a deep part of Miha's experience. Thank you, we'll come back to this in a bit. *(turning towards Miha)* Anja just saved you from having to express how you're feeling or having to explain it to her. How are you feeling now? Could you tell her?

Here, the defense mechanism of avoidance again brought up the true affective psychic construct. Anja managed to help Miha avoid expressing himself, at least for the moment. In a way, she was protecting them both. Had they continued on this path, Anja might have condemned Miha's mother for his inability to be intimate and at the same time avoided having to face her own painful affects. They both could have continued to be caught up in the hurtful conflicts that allow them to avoid their true mental content.

M (*thoughtfully*): I don't understand what happens to me when Anja comes closer or wants to hug me. . .

T (*sensing a paralyzing fear*): What are you afraid of? What would you call this distress, the one that is emerging now?

M (*uncomfortably*): It's always hardest when she cries. I start feeling angry. . .

T (*sensing anger, sadness, and helplessness*): That's when Anja evokes the same feelings you had when your mother was sad.

M (*nodding, still upset*): Yeah, I can't stand tears. . .

T (*still sensing sadness mixed with anger*): What if you were to accept her feelings of sadness? You're a grown man now.

M (*calming down*): I guess I would have to face my own sadness. . .

T (*sensing a deep sadness*): Can you tell me more about that?

M (*sadly*): Well, I was always alone, feeling sad and hurt because my father was gone. And I was angry that I was left alone with my mom. I mean, it was nice, but also. . .

T (*sensing his distress*): What else?

M (*timidly*): Suffocating. Something inside me, a pressure I can't name. I felt so anxious. I wanted to run away.

T (*sensing a growing uneasiness*): Do you experience these feelings with Anja now?

M (*lost in thought*): Yeah, especially when she cries, and when she starts talking about a wedding or planning it. (*looking at Anja*) Anja, you know I love you, but it feels so suffocating when you start talking about weddings and apartments. You cry and you get angry, and I feel I have no space left, you weigh me down and I feel I've been forgotten. You get so possessive.

T (*sensing Miha has let a load off his shoulders*): You get scared, almost terrified that you'll be lost in the shuffle and lose your freedom, lose yourself. If I'm understanding correctly, something is shifting within you right now—perhaps you feel hopeful that things can be better if you actually face your fears. (*Miha inhales deeply and nods in agreement. The therapist turns to Anja.*) Thank you for waiting. It must have been difficult listening to how Miha experiences you. How do you feel?

A (*upset*): Well, normally I'd be crying now, but I'm actually feeling very angry. (*The therapist feels her anger.*) When he acts like this, we start fighting. Then he withdraws, and I feel humiliated, ashamed of being in the way, as if I'm forcing myself onto him. (*calming down*) I just want to be with him and love him, and I want to feel loved by him too.

T (*feeling an almost unbearable sense of discomfort manifested in difficulty breathing*): So you are experiencing the same emotions you did as a child—when you begged to be heard and weren't, and you felt ashamed, angry, and unneeded. And all you ever wanted was for your father to talk to you, and for your mother. . .

A (*upset*): Yes, that's all I wanted, all I needed. It's like that now too. All I want is for him to make up his mind.

T (*feeling a growing anxiety*): Waiting is hard. You never know how long it's going to last or if it will get any better. You just keep waiting and waiting. . .

A (*slowly calming down*): I've told myself so many times I won't wait anymore—but I cannot bring myself to leave. It's hard to admit. It's almost as if I needed this to happen all over again.

T (*feeling anger*): You're angry that it's happening again. As if you needed these feelings of shame and the fear of being abandoned. . .

A (*angrily*): Yes, I'm angry. At the same time, I see now that I may have another chance. (*looking at Miha*) I think we're going to have to talk about all of this.

T (*realizing they are starting to hear each other more, despite the feelings of fear, uneasiness, and restlessness*): I'm sorry to say that we have to finish up for today. You both took big risks. You discovered some new things, and now you will able to embark on a new path. I want you both to try to stay hopeful and to pray you can endure for a little longer. That is the only way we can resolve the issues that are tearing you apart and making you feel so exposed, vulnerable, and hurt. Do you think you will be all right? (*They both nod yes.*) Thank you.

In a way Anja and Miha's therapeutic process had only just begun. Their pain and fear of intimacy and vulnerability was powerful. The couple was definitely compatible in their complementary intrapsychic needs that so conditioned their interpersonal relationship. However, their therapy sessions had taken place on a cognitive level, and neither of them felt truly connected because they were both so hurt. Anja was

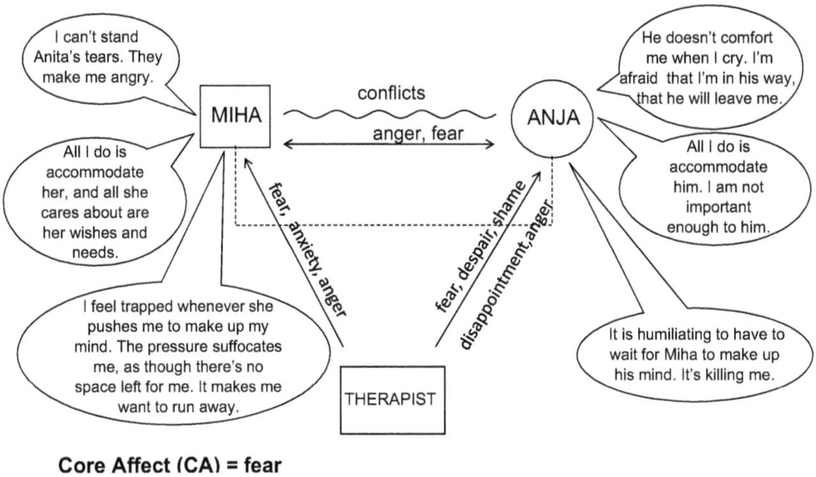

Figure 4.3 Interpersonal level (the relationship between Anja and Miha)

Figure created by Tanja Repič Slavič and Janko Slavič

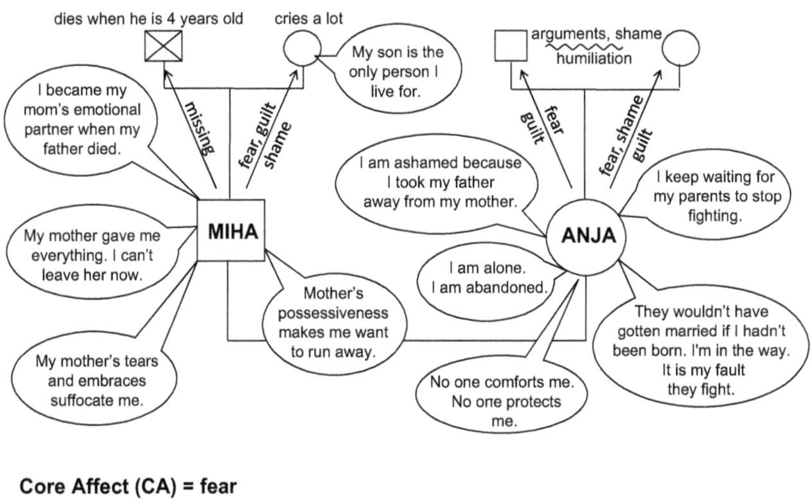

Figure 4.4 Intrapsychic level (Anja's and Miha's childhoods)

Figure created by Tanja Repič Slavič and Janko Slavič

afraid of being a burden and feeling worthless, fearing that Miha doesn't love her enough to stay. Miha, on the other hand, felt that Anja's need for closeness and intimacy would get in the way of his independence. They had both experienced the emotions now resurfacing in their romantic relationship in their childhood with their parents. The therapist's task in the following sessions will be to continue tracing the emotions that lead to the core affects. By doing this, Miha and Anja will be able to dismantle their defense mechanisms, especially the projective and introjective identification that has enabled them to suppress their core affects and transfer them onto each other.

They will both have to face the most painful of their childhood emotions and thus "take back" their own affects. They will need to address these emotions, express them, give them meaning, and understand how they affect their current relationship. They will have to confront the affects that create their relationship, including their conflicts. These affects belong in their past, yet unconsciously create their binding relationship. They are the foundation for the way Miha and Anja regulate their own affects, which simultaneously affects their views of each other. They seek new affects based on their affect regulation mechanisms, and this in turn leads them to new complications and relational strife. They will need to come to terms with their fear of intimacy, which serves as a way to avoid feeling exposed and vulnerable. This is a fear from the past and should not be a part of their present or future. They will both have to realize that they recreate their fear in order to preserve the type of relationship they knew in the past. The fear will begin to subside once they come to terms with it.

In the next chapter, the concept of the intrapsychic structure and its dynamics, which have defied change in psychological paradigms, will be examined. The concept of intrapsychic structure is a controversial subject in classical instinct-oriented and behavioral models as well as in psychoanalysis. Relational models and clinical practice have introduced new findings into this area. Scientists have drawn on analytic and therapeutic work and come to recognize the natural tendencies of human beings to seek attachment, a relationship. Namely, they have established that from the earliest stages of life, relationships with significant others drive, constitute and determine our mental structures.

Research on children and their relationships with their parents reveals above all the extraordinary loyalty children have towards their parents. This has led to additional insights into the mother-child relationship, which deeply affects the development of all children. The mother-child relationship is the fundamental vector shaping how children form their future relationships. All the mental and psycho-organic content that researchers have observed on the systemic and interpersonal levels has proven to be equally present in intrapsychic structures. These discoveries are the foundation of the relational model, which integrates all three levels—intrapsychic, interpersonal, and systemic—into the innovative theory that is known as relational family therapy.

5 Systemic Dynamics in Relational Theories

This chapter will address the intrapsychic and interpersonal levels of human perception, feeling, and experiencing, and will attempt to disclose the developmental palette of intrapsychic psycho-organic structures. The development of these structures is founded on our experiences of relationships with significant others in early childhood in the primary family system (Cummings & Davies, 2010; Ringstrom, 2014; J.S. Scharff & Scharff, 2014; Siegel & Solomon, 2013). Relational models and theories do not explicitly refer to the system, but rather implicitly apply it. Similarly, systems theory does not explicitly mention intrapsychic and interpersonal dynamics, mechanisms, and configurations, despite the fact that they form the foundations for the system and the relationships encompassed in it. And yet systems theory cannot explain even the most basic systemic characteristics without them. It is impossible to define, clarify, and validate the core of the human psyche without the integration of these three levels—intrapsychic, interpersonal and systemic—for they provide the cradle for the most deep-seated experiences of interpersonal relationships.

This chapter will present the modern analytical relational model developed by Mitchell (1988, 1993, 2000, 2002) and integrate systemic and relational theories in an innovative psycho-organic paradigm known as the relational family model. The relational-systemic configuration is innate to the human psyche or psycho-organic system of our experiences. Thus, integration is not only possible, but necessary in order to fully understand humankind and the intrapsychic, interpersonal, and systemic structures that are intrinsic to each human being.

Psychoanalysis also has seen changes in its paradigm. Boundaries regarding the human psyche were redefined and reframed in psychoanalysis, which indelibly influenced theory and clinical practice (Mitchell, 1988). We can say that in analytic theory, the mind went from being merely a set of existing structures, the source of which is the individual's internal organism, to being secured within relational patterns and intrapsychic structures that are the result of relationships, the very foundations of modern psychoanalytic reasoning. In response, Mitchell (1988, 1993, 2000, 2002) developed an integrated relational model that combines three relational theories that interrelate and understand interpersonal relationships as constitutive components of human psycho-organic development.

Mitchell (1988, 2000, 2002) integrated object relations theory, self-psychology, and interpersonal analysis and called the combined theory relational theory. The relational model, similar to the social theory of the mind, is not an exclusive domain in psychoanalytical theory. Interpersonal theory, object relations theory, and self-psychology, and their conglomerate—the relational model—are only a selection from an even wider array of theories of the mind, all of which share certain elements (Mitchell, 1988, 2002; Mitchell & Black, 1995). Anthropologists in the late nineteenth and early twentieth centuries assumed that humankind had developed along one dimension: specifically, that physical attributes, and the human brain as the most important among them, developed in response to adaptations necessary for survival. These adaptations increased cognitive capacity, which in turn enabled the development of culture and other areas of social exchange (Mitchell, 1988). During the last few decades, research, particularly fossil research, has revealed that different human attributes developed simultaneously and that cultural relationships are not only the result of more developed brains but also played a significant role in the development of the cerebral cortex. This means that prehistoric mankind gradually developed various forms of social exchange, such as collaboration, reciprocal sensitivity, perhaps even empathy (Mitchell, 1988, 2000, 2002; Robins, 2010; Siegel & Solomon, 2013).

These social impulses caused natural selection to lean in the direction of a larger cerebral cortex. According to previous theories, humankind first developed and then entered into social and cultural interaction. Today, however, it is unequivocally accepted that human development is both a natural social product and the result of interpersonal relationships (Mitchell, 1988, 2000, 2002; Robins, 2010; Schore, 2003, 2010, 2012). It is simultaneous and reciprocal construction and integration that enables the ongoing development of cultures as well as of the human brain. It can even be argued that the human brain could not function without culture (Mitchell, 1988, 2000, 2002). Similar advances have also been made in the field of linguistics. Language had long been understood as distinct from experiencing, and of secondary importance. According to this theory, the individual lived in a world of experiencing that was then translated into language or a communication tool such as social media that conveys interaction. But now the boundary between experiencing and communicating has come under question because experiencing is what structures the foundation of communication, and this means that experience is social and interactive by nature (Mitchell, 1988, 2000). Preverbal communication precedes learning to speak, and nonverbal communication is extremely important in all relationships. Once semiotic communication develops, we can recall both verbal and preverbal dimensions of experiencing, although we can only experience and speak of them in the socially modeled system (Mitchell, 1988, 2000, 2002; Mitchell & Black, 1995; Schore, 2003, 2012; Siegel, 2007, 2010, 2011).

The apex of the linguistic revolution in the 20th century is marked by the realization that meaning is not only something spoken or reflected through language, but also includes what is created on the basis of language (Mitchell, 1988, 2000). Meaning is not something innate that simply is described with words because an experience only gains meaning on the basis of language, that is, of the spoken word, which incorporates both meaning and experience. It follows that our individual experience is social by nature (Mitchell, 1988,

2000, 2002; Robins, 2010). The relational model in psychoanalysis is guided by this realization and posits that the mind is always relationally oriented (Mitchell, 2002). Sullivan (1972) and Fairbairn (1958), the most important advocates of relational theory, claim that Freud concentrated on the wrong unit for observing social life, namely on the individual mind and the individual's mental structure rather than on the interactional field. Freud, along the lines of the anthropologists and linguists of the 19th century, placed the mental content of the individual beyond social experience and even in opposition to the social environment (Mitchell, 1988). He understood the individual as being divided between innate instincts and social norms, between nature and culture. According to this theory, meaning is biologically inborn in human physiology. It would follow that the human mind and its content seeks expression in the wider social environment by absorbing culture, learning public and social language, and taming and channeling instincts (Mitchell, 1988, 2000, 2002; Schore, 2003, 2010, 2012; Siegel, 2007, 2011).

The relational model—along with models put forward by modern anthropologists and linguists—proposes that the human mind is simultaneously a product and active constituent of the cultural and linguistic matrix in which the individual lives. Meaning is not predetermined, but emerges from the relational matrix. Thus, the relational field is a constitutive element of human experience (Mitchell, 1988, 2000; Robins, 2010). More radically, from the relational point of view, the mere idea of the mind as a meaningful unit of research is questionable. From birth onwards, the human being is in constant interaction with others and primary experience is being built on the basis of these primary relationships. The representation of the self, or the intrapsychic image of the self, formed by each of us is a secondary construction that is then placed within a more fundamental and flexible interactional reality. We organize our encounter with the world in order to preserve the necessary and comfortably functional activities in a world in which objects are either controllable or uncontrollable, near or far. Above all, it is vital that the individual preserves connection with others (Bruschweiler-Stern et al., 2010; Cummings & Davies, 2010; Maroda, 2010; Mitchell, 1988, 2000, 2002; Robins, 2010; Sullivan, 1940).

5.1 Stern's Research

Stern, in a synthesis of his research on children, determined that a child's consciousness and activities are essentially socially wired (Bruschweiler-Stern et al., 2010; Stern, 1985, 1995). A child's world is in many or indeed all respects social to the point that almost everything the child does, feels, and perceives occurs in relation to others. Due to memories, we are rarely really alone. This is particularly true of the first six months of life. The idea that being with others is the subjective reality of the child is very convincing in this respect (Stern, 2010).

Consolidating the research and clinical practice of other authors, Stern puts forward an exceptionally empirical view into child development. This development is summarized below:

5.1.1 *From 0–2½ Months*

During the first weeks of life, eating, sleeping, crying, and being soothed are the child's principle activities. The main interactive task during this period is the regulation of an infant's eating, sleeping, and waking, which will deeply impact the affect regulation system and the affective psychic construct. Primary activity cycles and social exchanges take place around and during these activities. Social and affective exchanges, such as parental smiles and baby talk, are instruments for regulating and cueing these events (Bruschweiler-Stern et al., 2010; Stern, 1985, 1995). It is the regulating and adjusting of these activities, the orchestrating of a rhythm to the feeding, sleeping, and soothing cycles, that is essential to the infant's development, enabling the reciprocal empathy and harmony co-created between the mother and child. Reciprocity in the mother–infant dyad promises a satisfying interaction, healthy child development, and healthy mothering. This marks the onset of the core affect and the psycho-organic state as well as a link to organically implicit memory saturated with organic and sensory components. It encompasses simple physical touching, hugging, gentleness, caressing, etc., all of which are the first and most significant responses a mother can give to her infant, and vice versa. These sensations create the content of core affects that are based on psycho-organic states (Fosha, 2009; Schore, 2003, 2010, 2012; Siegel, 2007, 2010, 2011).

How well a mother is able to read and respond to her hungry infant is crucial. For instance, is she able to quietly collaborate while letting her infant proceed voraciously? When the infant is partially sated, does the mother know how to provide enough stimulation to maintain an effective feeding rhythm? Does she know how and when to cuddle and caress her infant? Does she correctly read the signs of satiety her infant gives and respond appropriately? The same processes take place in connection to the sleep cycle. How a mother responds to her child's needs—with sensitivity, too much or too little control—how she calms her infant to sleep, attunes to her infant's rhythm, and senses the temperamental fit between them is all determinative. Can the mother stay internally calm while adjusting to her infant's cycles, or does she lose control or react with discontent, exaggerated affect, or strangeness (Bruschweiler-Stern et al., 2010; Stern, 1985, 1995, 2004, 2010)? These early experiences become deeply embedded in the infant's mental structure and psycho-organic states and are the makings of implicit memory that will unconsciously guide the child through life and especially into adulthood with the choice of intimate partners. This choice is determined by valency in right hemisphere communication, the foundations for which were established in the mother-infant relationship (Kim et al., 2014; Maroda, 2010; Schore, 2003, 2010, 2012).

As the regulatory processes of feeding and sleeping are routinely broken, the baby will cry and it is up to the parents to repeatedly try and rectify the situations that arise. This cycle is the mechanism of affect regulation in its essence. How well parents manage to comfort and calm their infant during these windows of time and how they react and respond to their infant's crying is crucial. Do they become agitated, angry, or apathetic? Do they respond with exaggerated concern? Do they ignore their infant or leave her or him to cry for extended intervals of time? Or do they respond to their infant's needs with sensitivity, spontaneity, creativity, and flexibility (Bruschweiler-Stern et al., 2010; Stern, 1985, 1995, 2010)? To a large degree, this parental feedback conditions the creation of the operative mechanism of affect regulation. For instance, if parents force food upon children in infancy, these children will most likely experience discomfort later in adulthood when others are too forceful or manipulative. They may build an affective psychic construct that seeks resolution to their psychological issues through food. Food may assume the symbolic form of emotions, and as such, the element and object against which they struggle. When they feel the pressures of the outside world, they may experience a loss of appetite. Furthermore, food may become the instrument through which they self-regulate. Specifically, food becomes the only source of control over the outside world and the dangerous emotions that are in it. Anorexia, which is ultimately a control system over the outside world, is the most extreme example of this, with food becoming the symbol through which anorexics reject everything the outside environment has to offer.

Anorexia is a terrifying example of dysregulation. Those suffering from anorexia perceive their bodies as an extremely vulnerable instrument, exposed to outside influences that must be consistently rejected and refused. Because of their damaged self-image, they will always see their own bodies as disgusting, revolting, and unacceptable. Excess weight is horrific to them, and this is despite the actual reality of being extremely underweight. Starvation and food deprivation are demonstrations of a total rejection of outside influences. The consequences of anorexia on the organism can be catastrophic because of ongoing malnourishment and induction of vomiting whenever the minimal amounts of food consumed lead yet again to feelings of loss of control, in the world and of the self (Bruschweiler-Stern et al., 2010). In contrast, for children whose only connection with the outside world came through feeding, food becomes a symbol of attachment. It generates a specific dynamic that gets expressed in the growing affective psychic construct. These individuals tend to overeat and automatically turn to food, a symbol of satiation, when they feel depressed or under stress. This process may even escalate—for example, in the case of bulimia—to the point that the food ingested cannot be metabolized. Those suffering from bulimia cannot digest the influences, events, and emotions generated by the outside world. In response to excessive amounts of food—symbolizing the despised, formidable, and uncontrollable elements in the environment—these individuals artificially prompt the body to vomit (Bruschweiler-Stern et al., 2010; Fonagy et al., 2007; Fosha, 2009; Schore, 2003, 2010, 2012; Siegel, 2007, 2010, 2011).

Food thus reflects the early interactions between children and parents and forms the foundation of psycho-organic systems as well as the affect regulation system. In this context, the consumption and non-consumption of food encompasses dimensions of early relationships in western civilization and creates the alarming combinations of anorexic and bulimic symptomatic personalities. We might even go so far as to suggest that the worst disorders of modern society are evident in the symptomatology of eating, and thus in the symptomatology of disordered relationships in the earliest stages of child development. These are diseases of the body itself. The body, which tells only the truth and never lies, falls ill when it cannot heal itself. The body will always protest when the mind can no longer control inner turmoil, and will react to anything of significance that transpires in our conscious and unconscious worlds.

5.1.2 From 2½–5½ Months

The next stage in child development is face-to-face social interaction without toys or other objects (Bruschweiler-Stern et al., 2010; Stern, 1985, 1995, 2004, 2010). The infant is now entirely adjusted, both by design and default, to demonstrate full social and affective capacities in face-to-face play as well as in prompting the parents to respond. Marking essential elements of play, the infant's innate preferences at this time are oriented towards the human face, voice, touch, and movement. Nothing compares with these stimuli in terms of attracting and holding the attention of the infant whose nervous system at this age is designed and developed for face-to-face play. The social and affective behaviors used to regulate face-to-face interaction, including control of the gaze, responsive smiling, and vocalizing, are developing and maturing. The affect regulation mechanism is acquiring its basic characteristics, and its fundamental structure—including the defense mechanisms available during this developmental stage—and the affective psychic construct are being formed. The infant's behaviors are still very fragile, and face-to-face interactions at these early stages involve the determinative interaction between two people, that is, between parent and infant (Bruschweiler-Stern et al., 2010; Stern, 2004, 2010).

These interactions are about control and the will to contribute to the initiation, maintenance, adjustment, termination, or avoidance of face-to-face engagement. This marks the onset of the mutual regulation of social interaction of individual psycho-organic states (Stern, 1985, 1995, 2010). However, the infant at this stage is still very limited in movement and, since crawling or walking away is not yet an option, is basically at the mercy of the environment. The infant's hand-eye coordination is also not yet developed enough to promote interest in the world of inanimate objects in the near proximity. By nature, the infant at this stage is almost a prisoner of face-to-face communication (Bruschweiler-Stern et al., 2010; Stern, 1985, 1995, 2004, 2010). Infants are dependent upon right hemisphere communication and the mechanism of projective and introjective identification that facilitates connection with the mother. Infants are also reliant on the mother's capacity and communication skills, that is, on how well she can read and understand her child's desires and needs and how well she can respond and help. Her infant may trigger her own unresolved psycho-organic states, which will cause her to misunderstand or even reject her own child. The mother needs to be able to regulate distressing emotions that the infant cannot control and therefore "gives" to her. She must process them and return them in a digested and manageable form to her infant (Bruschweiler-Stern et al., 2010; Fosha, 2009; Maroda, 2010; Schore, 2003, 2012; Siegel & Solomon, 2013; Stern, 2004, 2010).

The feeding and sleeping processes of regulation by now have become routine. The action and desire for connection have now passed to face-to-face play and interaction. The same interactional themes that were observable during the feeding process in the preceding months are now noticeable in play. If the mothering was over-controlling during feeding, a similar pattern of intrusive or overregulation may emerge in face-to-face interaction. This may be seen by her initiation of most of the face-to-face dialogs. In this case, it is the mother who dictates and adjusts the intensity of interaction when she feels that it has climbed too high or fallen too low in order to satisfy her sense of connection. If the infant decides to avert his or her gaze, the mother may choose to seek out and reestablish a mutual gaze, thus ignoring the child's desire to interrupt it. Later, she may end the mutual gaze when she chooses to, which may be a rebuff of the infant's needs or will (Bruschweiler-Stern et al., 2010; Stern, 1985, 1995, 2010). Consequently, the affect regulation system is developing according to the mother's desires rather than the infant's. When right hemisphere communication between mother and child fails to transpire according to the infant's needs, the infant is compelled to adjust to the mother at a very early stage. This generates a specific and painful psycho-organic state, including corresponding affective psychic constructs that emerge in order to fend off the painful affects.

Human eyes are one of the most sensitive organs in the human body. Our eyes reflect the deepest layers of our experience: fear, horror, disappointment, anger, rage, jealousy, and sadness, as well as happiness, joy, desire, satisfaction, and love. Basically, all these emotions and core affects are the nuclei of psycho-organic states. During this stage of infancy, the eyes are an exceptionally constructive organ of the developing mind, as well as of the developing psycho-organic states and affect regulation mechanism. Eyes, in addition to bodily awareness, are the primary instrument for perceiving and organizing the surrounding environment (Stern, 1995, 2010). If parents behave intrusively and fail to allow an infant to express their own needs and will through gaze, this child may also avoid eye contact later in adulthood. These experiences, subsequently fortified by the affective psychic construct, create the circumstances whereby some people experience life situations and human intimacy as intrusive and threatening (Siegel, 2007, 2010, 2011; Siegel & Solomon, 2013). In other words, it is possible for children to learn very early in their lives that their needs are insignificant. They may even feel ashamed for having needs at all. Moreover, their own needs will trigger a foreboding sense of imminent rejection. Children may deal with such emotions by convincing themselves that they must first see to the needs of others and only then dare hope that they might be noticed and have their own desires and expectations fulfilled.

Such children will literally scan their surroundings and evaluate if everything is taken care of. They will silently hope to be noticed. If they remain unnoticed, they will begin the familiar process of disappointed self-blaming and underestimating themselves, thereby continuing to create and consolidate their fragile self-esteem (Siegel, 2007, 2010, 2011). The affective psychic construct directed and guided by the mechanism of affect regulation becomes well-developed in such cases. It should be evident by now what is meant by the continuation of issues—such as over-caring mothering, indifference, or control—as opposed to the discontinuity of forms of interaction—such as feeding, sleeping, and face-to-face play (Beilock, 2015). In such cases, new forms of interaction simply cover up the same issues at each developmental leap of child psycho-organic developments (Bruschweiler-Stern et al., 2010; Stern, 1985, 1995, 2004, 2010). The situation comes to fruition in adulthood, especially in intimate relationships, where such individuals tend to either conceal their shame or trigger it in others.

5.1.3 From 5½–9 Months

This stage is characterized by mutual play, or joint object play, where the parent and baby will play together with some object. Such activities become the main interaction during this stage. The child has by now acquired better hand-eye and hand-to-hand coordination, and, along with these skills, a keen curiosity in the world around. How parents and child adjust and attune their direction, timing, space, focus, production, development, change, and disengagement of play is utterly crucial during this phase. It has the same significance as feeding, sleeping, and face-to-face play did in the previous months (Beilock, 2015; Bruschweiler-Stern et al., 2010; Johnson, 2014; Schore, 2003, 2010; Stern, 1985, 1995, 2004, 2010).

Intrusiveness takes on a new form in this phase. Perhaps a parent, the mother in this example, imposes too many limitations or control over her child's play, which encourages and then maintains a corresponding psycho-organic style of affect regulation and affective psychic construct. The situation might be as follows: the child is happily engaged with one toy when the mother decides that a different toy is better, more stimulating, educational, or pleasing for whatever reason. So the first toy is taken away and the mother's alternative is offered. The child may accept the alternative toy, explore, and thereupon lose interest in it and seek a third option. The mother may feel that the child has not spent enough time with this second toy and try to re-engage the child's focus and interest, perhaps demonstrating an aspect of the toy that had gone unnoticed. She may persist in her efforts to trigger her child's curiosity and fascination and entirely miss picking up on his or her signals of disengagement and boredom. The child's effort to satiate the mother's needs that do not match his or her own desires or needs also goes unnoticed (Bruschweiler-Stern et al., 2010; Stern, 1985, 1995, 2004, 2010). The child will first respond with confusion, then frustration, perhaps even a moment of anger. If the mother still doesn't notice, the child will yet again learn that his or her needs and desires are of no importance in new situations.

On the basis of right hemisphere communication and projective and introjective identification, parents thus convey to children that their desires are inappropriate, wrong, or even unworthy. In the earliest stages of development, these children learn what their parents want and need as well as how to adjust and adapt to their parents in order to secure the basic attention they need in order to survive (Schore, 2003, 2010, 2012; Siegel, 2010, 2011). The influence exerted upon the child, who is expected, for example, to play with toys that bear a specific significance to the parent, may even be deliberate. Such toys might be geared to encourage some future professional orientation. Sometimes parents—as a result of their own unarticulated anger and rage, hatred, and aggression—allow their child to play with toys that instill fear and distress, and expose them to danger. These are affects that will fortify a particular type of affect regulation and affective psychic construct. Inappropriate films and children's television programs that portray violence and aggression may have a similar effect. All this can have a deep impact on children because they are not capable of absorbing, still less of processing, cruel and aggressive emotions during the early stages of psycho-organic development (Siegel & Solomon, 2013). Children learn basic models of aggressive behavior through these experiences. They absorb these experiences and view the only appropriate response as anger and frustration, even when dealing with feelings of sadness and disappointment.

Parents who overtly discipline their children for playing with a particular toy for too long, forcefully taking away the toy, yelling, insulting, and sometimes even striking the child, can have a catastrophic impact on their child's development. These children will evaluate their surroundings fearfully, shrinking away from taking any initiative. Feelings of uncertainty will emerge, especially the sense that any independence is threatening to the parents, and consequently to them, because their needs and desires are not in accord with those of their parents. Efforts to over-control a child's play are essentially the same as over-regulation of face-to-face play and interactions during the first months of life. It is of utmost importance who initiates or terminates interaction, when, and why. At this phase, the psycho-organic relationship between parent and child is more established and vibrant. Exaggerated forms of interaction can be more easily distinguished, such as unresponsiveness to the child, neglect, and providing an unstructured environment, one without rules and regulations, where anything goes (Bruschweiler-Stern et al., 2010; Stern, 1985, 1995, 2004, 2010). All interactions, and especially the emotions they trigger, become deeply anchored and consolidated in the child's psyche, thus forming the psycho-organic state that can continue to have a catastrophic impact on development. How children learn to regulate affect will be steeped with these affects, and they will also shape the affective psychic construct.

5.1.4 From 9–12 Months

Two major psycho-organic developmental events mark this period: attachment and intersubjectivity. Towards the end of the first year, children begin to demonstrate very clearly the behaviors characteristic of attachment and separation from their parents. This process is accelerated by their growing mobility. It is increasingly possible for children to move away from and return to the parent, first crawling and then walking. The attachment patterns established between parent and child during this phase are considered one of the best predictors of the quality of the parent-child relationship, as well as an extraordinary reflection of the psycho-organic state and the affect regulation system that is forming at this time (Bruschweiler-Stern et al., 2010; Fosha, 2009; Schore, 2003, 2012). The clinical view into the theme of attachment applies to a wide range of potential clinical problems, not just to those directly related to attachment and the parent-child connection, but also other deep and long-term consequences (Bruschweiler-Stern et al., 2010; Stern, 1985, 1995, 2004, 2010) on further development, especially as concerns the selection and building of intimate relationships (Siegel & Solomon, 2013).

How parent and child negotiate the comings and goings, the moving away and returning that inevitably occurs, provides the raw material of the child's mental life and lays the foundations for the child's interactive and interpersonal relational style to parents and others throughout life. Children whose parents evade them to the point that the children are fearful and in tears while searching for them will have difficulty leaving their parents because they will fear that the parents may never return. Similarly, children whose parents do not allow them to roam freely will feel that their independence to come and go as they please is forbidden. Afraid of hurting their parents' feelings, these children will also feel apprehensive about leaving. In adulthood, they will regularly feel that they are doing a disservice to their parents, that they are neglectful and rejecting, that they do not demonstrate enough respect and attention. This is a manifestation of the affective psychic construct that developed during those early stages of development. These intense deep-rooted psycho-organic states and their corresponding affect regulation systems are created at this early stage and consolidate into binding constitutive elements of the developing mental structure of the child (Bruschweiler-Stern et al., 2010; Schore, 2003, 2012; Siegel & Solomon, 2013; Stern, 2004, 2010).

Such children learn early on that their need for independence is insignificant and threatening to their parents. Fear and the sense of restriction can sometimes make these children turn to drastic measures when growing up, such as running away from home in order to temporarily break free from the constraints of the parental relationship. Other interactions, such as establishing relationships with others, will also be marked by the core affect of fear, sometimes also by neglect, terror, and feelings of lack of control. Thus, basic relational interactions with parents, along with the emotions generated, repeat in adulthood because similar emotions are reawakened in relation with the other. Similar patterns emerge, and unpleasant and threatening emotions are transferred to the other. Emotions and interactions might be only slightly reminiscent of the relationships and interactions from childhood but are interpreted and perceived in a way that makes them seem identical. This is how such children inadvertently become entangled in similar relationships, tainted with a sense of neglect or rejection, when they become adults. In general, however, many such individuals remain unaware that it is their own deep-rooted feelings that lead them to seek out others who behave comparably to their parents and evoke similar emotions, and that they are thus co-creating these later relationships (Beilock, 2015; Schore, 2003, 2012; Siegel, 2010, 2011; Siegel & Solomon, 2013). This is how the mechanism of affect regulation and its corresponding affective psychic construct lead to the painful repetition of old emotions and affects and the inability to separate from old behavioral forms that are not only extremely charged with affects from childhood, but are also unconscious and therefore even more difficult to manage.

In addition to separation, other forms of behavior can have a determinative impact on attachment, such as affect manifestation, seeking out comfort, the relationship to helping others, and collaboration. These forms of behavior involve core affects that form the basis upon which the psycho-organic system is built, and as such they mark all subsequent interactions and further enhance the significance of the interactions in the parent-child relationships

(Bruschweiler-Stern et al., 2010; Kim et al., 2014; Stern, 2004, 2010). They permeate our relationships with others, characterize how we approach and enter intimate relationships, and dictate how we maintain relationships with others. For instance, if the affect of fear promises a real relationship, we will instill fear and terror in others or seek out others who will evoke these kinds of destructive feelings in us. Despite the pain and distress of such interactions, they promise connection or a relationship, and so they can only be relinquished with great difficulty.

Intersubjectivity is another important concept that characterizes this stage of development (Bruschweiler-Stern et al., 2010; Stern, 1995, 2004, 2010). Children come to realize that their mother experiences the world and them differently from the way they do. They realize that the contents of mind may be the same or different, but that even if they are not the same, they can be brought into alignment and connected. Thus, the core affect of fear and danger can connect, or affects of contempt and shame, or feelings of aggression and self-destruction. All of these pairs can become complementary elements of mutual connection and, in certain cases, are fundamental to the creation of the affective psychic construct and the affect regulation mechanism. These processes take on many forms, all of which indicate the presence of intersubjectivity, including social referencing, affect attunement, joint attention getting, and the reading of the other's intentions. What matters is that a connection be negotiated between parent and child through which the child joins and shares the universe of mental phenomena. This connection continues to determine all interpersonal interactions: what is considered public, what must remain private, what happens but is not talked about, and what can be shared and thus triggers the creation of intimate relationships. The negotiation and development of intersubjectivity between parent and child provides a fascinating and rich perspective (Bruschweiler-Stern et al., 2010; Stern, 1985, 1995, 2004, 2010).

At this stage in life maternal over-regulation appears in a number of formats. Perhaps the mother will set limits on her child's exploration and, in terms of the experience of emotion, perception, and intention, will distance herself from her child by primarily satisfying her own needs and desires. Thus, she neglects her child's need for attachment. In terms of intersubjectivity, some parents make deliberate decisions regarding their child's emotional and general psycho-organic experiences: namely, which emotions are legitimate and shareable and worthy of response and which are not. In other words, they decide which of their child's experiences will be thwarted and which encouraged. For instance, if a child experiences too little excitement and enthusiasm about something that the over-regulating mother feels ought to be perceived as more exciting, she may demonstrate a modifying and escalated attunement to show the level of excitement or enthusiasm she expects from her child. In order to fully share the experience, the child will manifest a false reaction. Such a mother is being insensitive to her children's indications of what they would like to share (Bruschweiler-Stern et al., 2010; Stern, 1985, 1995, 2010). These children may later seek out false reactions in relations with others. They may become involved in insincere relationships founded on a false self that is guided by the mechanism of affect regulation in attunement with the affective psychic construct, and this will only reinforce this painful psycho-organic state (Schore, 2003, 2010).

Parents who interrupt or terminate the expression of their child's wishes or need for a certain type of play that is not in accord with their own preferences, who show emphatic enthusiasm or pressure their child to play in a particular way even when that the child declines or resists are considered over-controlling. For example, over-controlling parents might hug and tickle children when they don't want to be hugged or tickled. Once again, the parents' wishes and needs are in the forefront, while the children are compelled to adapt because their parents' disappointment would be too unsettling. These children may become over-accommodating in adulthood; for instance, they will settle for entertainment that doesn't actually entertain them or will feign satisfaction when feeling apathy or discomfort. Such individuals accept the will and preferences of others because they fear rejection and isolation.

5.1.5 From 18–24 Months

There are two significant psycho-organic developmental leaps that occur during the second year: language learning and an increase in physical capacity and mobility (Bruschweiler-Stern et al., 2010; Stern, 1985, 1995, 2004, 2010). In a clinical sense, learning language is very much like learning to play with objects. Both occur regardless of parental input. All the same, normal circumstances in which parents collaborate, help, and adapt their responses to their child's desires, sensitivities, and abilities provide richer interaction. There exists a clinically revealing triad between child, parent, and the world that establishes and fortifies the psycho-organic state, the style of affect regulation, and also the affective psychic construct. Just as it is possible to observe this triad with real objects at 6 months, between 18 and 24 months, the triad becomes discernible with "sound objects" or with words. Again, similar interpersonal themes of over-control and neglect, negotiated and structured differently at different stages can be observed at this stage (Bruschweiler-Stern et al., 2010; Stern, 1985, 1995, 2010). Maternal or parental intrusiveness or lack of adaptability also can have a strong impact on children at this stage during which everything is directed towards a particular manner of speaking, thinking, and behaving. Children with over-controlling or neglectful parents will not develop into full and healthy individuals. Rather, as a consequence of a faulty parental presence, they will develop a false self that is a typical reflection of a particular style of affect regulation (Beilock, 2015; Schore, 2003, 2012). This will then manifest in specific aspects of the affective psychic construct.

Parents who are attentive to their children, collaborate with them, and encourage their spoken expression by being attuned and responsive not only stimulate the development of linguistic capacity but also build a relationship. With the help of linguistic capacity, children begin to understand that speech is a tool with which it is possible to resolve emotional problems, conflicts, and complex relations with and in their environment. In contrast, children's strongest mode of communication is the expression of conflicted emotional affects at the level of behavioral reactivity. Rather than articulating complicated and sometimes conflicting emotions, they will act them out impulsively in various ways. For instance, children might angrily throw toys and other objects, yell and cry, throw themselves on the floor, writhing or biting various objects that happen to be nearby, stubbornly go to sulk in a corner or under a table, or run around wildly.

At a later psycho-organic stage in development, these individuals may respond to distress in similar form especially when establishing intimate relationships. This response corresponds to the style of affect regulation and the functioning of the affective psychic construct developed in childhood. For instance, a husband might respond to the distress caused by his wife with sulking and silence. He may hold a silent grudge for days or weeks, feeling that a terrible injustice had been done to him and that his wife doesn't understand him. He will come and go without letting his wife know where he's going, how long he'll be gone, or when he'll return. He will evoke deep distress and disappointment in his wife, thus transferring to her the emotions he used to feel when confronted by the inappropriate responses of his parents. In all likelihood, however, she won't be able to understand his emotions in the midst of his confusing silence, much less to accept his behavior.

Parents who are in healthy emotional attunement with their children will notice their distress and recognize an overwhelming emotional state from their behavior. They will help their children use words to express their difficulties. These children will gradually recognize and then consolidate the sense that their parents take them seriously and that their problems deserve their parents' attention, that their desires and needs are valued. Entirely different emotions will accrue to children whose parents do not pay attention to them, who neglect, push away, and punish them when they behave in disharmony with the parents' beliefs and emotional expectations. These children soon begin to feel they are a burden to their parents. They close themselves off or draw attention by acting out with exaggerated and even vulgar forms of behavior. If the parents respond with harshness and threats, these children may seek attachment and connection precisely in these forms of parental response (Siegel, 2010, 2011). They may repeat inappropriate behavioral models simply because they have learned that it promises parental attention.

Such a situation may lead to habitually bad behavior and reactions within the married relationship. Even in this context, cruel physical behavior may promise the strongest and sometimes only connection between spouses. Such relationships are full of anger, rage, and hatred, covert shame and contempt. These emotions form the very essence of attachment in such relationships, and at the same time they co-create a mechanism of affect regulation based on the psycho-organic state and corresponding affective psychic construct. Children who are often the victims of such bad behavior learn that this kind of response and interaction secures connection with their parents. This explains why they may also engage in such behavior, choosing friends whom they may treat harshly or friends who will treat them harshly.

The next developmental psycho-organic change in this phase of childhood is increased mobility and physical capability, which requires the establishment of limits (Bruschweiler-Stern et al., 2010; Stern, 1995, 2004, 2010). At this stage, children have the ability to hurt themselves and others. In addition, the social environment begins to expect that parents will have taught their children basic social norms. Frequently, parents find it challenging to set limits because it is difficult to control the interaction and behavior of children. Setting limits is not merely a matter of establishing and enforcing rules, but, in fact, requires the negotiation of forms of behavior through direct interaction with the children. In most instances, both parents and child are on shaky ground. Children at this stage are highly active, creative, and spontaneous, which can present parents with very unsettling situations. This stage is perhaps the most challenging to parental skills (Bruschweiler-Stern et al., 2010; Stern, 1985, 1995, 2004, 2010). If parents are not able to regulate their children, then the children will lack basic good judgment and may develop self-destructive behavior or the lack of healthy boundaries and care for the self and the body. This may generate a dysfunctional style of affect regulation that will facilitate the development and consolidation of the affective psychic construct.

If children at this age fail to develop a basic psycho-organic and social sense and compassion for others, and are unable to develop intrapsychic boundaries within the framework of the limitations imposed by their parents, it is likely that they will later be unable to control their impulses because of insufficient affect regulation. These impulses are not only expressed through inappropriate behavioral models such as "being right at all costs" or "it's my way or the highway" or "my needs are the most important, so I must take care of myself first before looking to others," but also through what are called internal boundaries. For instance, such individuals may be unable to assess their situation and react on the basis of their present sense of being, which may be enthusiasm, satisfaction, the promise of pleasure, or alternatively anger, aggression, rage, and revenge. Internal boundaries enable us to apply good judgment, to establish to what extent we should let others come close as well as to whom, why, and about what we should speak. These boundaries also mark and differentiate between whose feelings are whose, where they come from, and where and to whom they are intended.

Parental resolve in relation to their children is particularly important. Clear boundaries and limits concerning behavior teach children initial behavioral structures. This facilitates not only the recognition of what is allowed and what is not, what is good, acceptable, desired, intentional, and what is not, but also by having clearly defined behavioral structures children begin to feel safe and secure. In short, the establishment of boundaries teaches children a system of self-regulation (Bruschweiler-Stern et al., 2010; Schore, 2003; Stern, 2004, 2010). Unpredictable and impulsive parents who constantly change the rules of behavior make their children feel that nothing is permanent or reliable. These children lose their sense of safety and security in their parents, and this can lead to inadequate forms of affect regulation. Rapid, unpredictable, and constant changes without clear criteria for making them leave lasting consequences in children. Even in adulthood, they may be afraid of any rapid change, which will trigger feelings of alarm, fear, danger, and threat, all of which influence the formation of the mechanism of affect regulation and the affective psychic construct. Above all, these individuals may come to fear spontaneity and creativity, and therefore find it difficult to take risks, an essential aspect of any healthy intimate adult relationship.

The basic elements of psycho-organic development are comprised of continuous and recurring themes that remain present throughout life (Bruschweiler-Stern et al., 2010; Fonagy et al., 2007; Schore, 2003, 2010, 2012; Siegel & Solomon, 2013). The forms of these themes transform and are reestablished with each qualitative developmental leap, engendering new behavior, new ways to interact, and new ways of repeating old themes. Each developmental stage sees old themes repeating in new forms (Bruschweiler-Stern et al., 2010; Stern, 1995, 2004, 2010). It is thus understandable why these themes reemerge in adulthood without our awareness. This occurs aided by mechanisms of projective and introjective identification, right hemisphere communication, and repetition compulsion, although Stern does not necessarily refer to these mechanisms as such. However, it seems impossible to fully understand the transference and establishment of these interactional models in the psyche of a child without taking into account these basic unconscious relational mechanisms, which are also the constitutive mechanisms of core affects, psycho-organic states, affect regulation, and affective psychic constructs. All these mechanisms are interconnected and mutually conditioned.

Couples, for instance, may have difficulty recognizing how they reenact old painful scenes, repeating the themes and basic emotions that permeated their childhood and youth. Yet, anything else would risk losing the other. The most painful and traumatic feelings and affects are not only the most binding and require unconditional loyalty, but they are also the strongest constitutive material of the psyche itself. This is why abuse, especially sexual abuse, makes such a strong impact on the human psyche. Individuals who have been abused repeatedly seek out—precisely on the basis of the abusive affect—similar situations and people with whom the abuse can be repeated (Fishbane, 2013; Poulton, 2013). Each time, this takes place with renewed hope that the abusive affect will be resolved.

Nevertheless, regarding the relational configuration or interaction with others as the basic unit of study does not entirely eliminate nature at the expense for nurture. On the contrary, the relational connection interrupts the apparent exclusivity between nature and nurture. Social relations are no longer seen as merely a supplement springing from biological functions such as sexuality and violence. Rather, social relations are viewed as biologically and genetically intrinsic facts, as fundamental motivational processes. Even sex and violence are no longer considered aspects of instinct, which in itself carries meaning, but as strong physiological responses that play out in a biologically mediated relational field, and as such, they acquire their meaning from a deeper relational matrix (Cvetek, 2009; Fonagy et al., 2007; Mitchell, 1988, 2000, 2002; Mitchell & Black, 1995; Repič, 2008; Schore, 2003, 2012).

No relational theorists view the child as a "blank slate" upon whom external events and other important characteristics are forcibly imprinted. Early and also later relationships are numerous and complex. Children not only perceive them but they also experience them through their physiological responses, which are conditioned by constitutional characteristics and temperament. Responsiveness and talents are thus processed, divided, reassembled, and organized into new and unique models that shape the individual's life. The research of Bowlby (1982), Stern (Bruschweiler-Stern et al., 2010; Stern, 1995,

2004, 2010), and many others conveys that it is best to understand relationships as being both fostered from the outside and grounded in the genetics and physiology of human experiencing. This is how we transcend the apparent exclusivity of nature and nurture. Studies of cognitive development and the way children think and organize experience continue to provide new insights on how children process and reorganize early relational experiences (Beilock, 2015; Bruschweiler-Stern et al., 2010; Fonagy et al., 2007; Fosha, 2009; Mitchell, 1988, 2000, 2002; Mitchell & Black, 1995; Schore, 2003, 2010, 2012; Siegel, 2007, 2010, 2011).

The following sections will present a description of the fundamental tenets of object relations theory, self-psychology, and interpersonal theory, which together form the psycho-organic relational model. However, first we must provide a brief survey of the basic psycho-organic mechanisms mentioned in the previous chapters as they affect all intrapsychic processes: namely, the mechanism of projective and introjective identification, repetition compulsion, and the mechanisms of affect regulation, core affect, and the affective psychic construct. These unconscious mechanisms, or forces, enable us to transfer our psycho-organic content—the core affect, psycho-organic states, affect regulation, and affective psychic construct—to significant others, thus compelling them to repeat established patterns of behavior, feelings, and cognition, which are then reinforced through repetition compulsion. These processes transpire via right hemisphere communication and explain why spouses find themselves repeating established patterns of behavior, feelings, and cognition, regardless of how destructive they are. The process allows them to maintain the familiar atmosphere and promise of a relationship, and to remain part of the relational configuration that constantly regenerates between them. Also, while relational theory may not specifically refer to these mechanisms, it does apply them implicitly.

5.2 Basic Relational Mechanisms

The projective and introjective identification mechanism involves an intrapsychic, interpersonal, and also systemic psycho-organic process. For instance, the mother, father, child, or partner—the giver—projects, by attributing split-off and denied affects, psycho-organic states, and internal images of the self to the recipient, as well as internalized forms or relationships with others (J. S. Scharff, 2010; J. S. Scharff & Scharff, 2006, 2014). This psycho-organic content is then forced via the repetition compulsion mechanism onto the recipient who must identify with it. Classical analysis refers to this process as the dynamic of transference and countertransference. This is a process that specifically transpires between the analyst and the individual. However, as this process is explicitly based on instinctual forces, where there is no room for the relationship, our model leans more towards the relational concept of projective and introjective identification that is based on affect and that provides better foundations for the transference of psycho-organic content. In other words, it is about the projection of intrapsychic content, such as psycho-organic states and core affects, as well as aspects of the self or object onto the other. Introjective identification, which continues the psychological process, is an integral part of projective identification. The individual internalizes certain aspects of the other, takes them on as part of their own self, securing them within through the mechanism of repetition compulsion. Introjective identification is in this respect a reflection of projective identification (Sandler & Perlow, 1987; J.S. Scharff, 2010; J.S. Scharff & Scharff, 2006, 2014; Schore, 2003, 2010, 2012).

Projective and introjective identification and repetition compulsion create intrapsychic, interpersonal, and systemic psycho-organic dynamics. This means that they also determine the affective psychic construct and affect regulation. When senders transfer their own split-off intrapsychic parts to others, the recipients usually adopt and identify with the content. There are other cases in which the psychological process remains at the level of projection without affecting the recipient. By acting in certain ways, senders persistently "invite" recipients to offer their services as "dumping grounds." Recipients, in turn, may choose to react to this or refuse it. For example, senders who have a distorted self-image will perceive others through the same distorted perspective, although they may not even be aware that their own self-image is distorted. If recipients have a secure self-image, they will not identify with the senders' distorted imagery, and will recognize to whom it belongs (J.S. Scharff & Scharff, 2014). However, if recipients struggle with their own self-image, they are more vulnerable, and thus more susceptible to a sender's projections. Their affective psychic construct is predisposed to projections, and reinforced with mechanisms of repetition compulsion, affect regulation, and affective psychic construct.

People with poor or fragile self-images are more prone to providing an anchor for senders' distorted self-imagery and their affective psychic construct. As a result, such recipients start to feel uncomfortable and perceive themselves as unattractive. Their levels of anxiety rise. When senders experience a recipient's discomfort, they can identify with their struggle, and may, in fact, learn how to face their own issue of feeling unattractive (McCormack, 2000; J.S. Scharff, 2010; J.S. Scharff & Scharff, 2006, 2014; Schore, 2003, 2010, 2012). This interpersonal and intrapsychic process is best portrayed in situations where both parties feel unsure of their self-image. Senders try to regulate their anxiety by denying and splitting it off, then projecting it onto another. By doing so, they feel they can control it better. Recipients take over the projection and feeling of anxiety, which goes hand in hand with their own unacceptable and negative self-image.

The mechanism of projective and introjective identification stems from right hemisphere communication, which is based on valency and repetition compulsion. It helps clarify how people can become "dumping grounds" for others, absorbing their split-off emotions. This often happens in mother-child relationships or between partners. The principle of valency helps explain how two very different people can be attracted to each other, or why parents may encourage their children to remain dysfunctional. These concepts clarify why parents may try to prevent their children from growing up, blame them for their own unresolved emotions, or use their children to regulate their own dysregulated affects. They are thus able to maintain their own denied, suppressed, and split-off psycho-organic content. Together, affect regulation and consequently the affective psychic construct resulting from the core affect enable this process. These relational mechanisms point to concepts such as separation, individuation, and differentiation that are essential for maintaining healthy relationships (Fishbane, 2013; Poulton, 2013; Siegel & Solomon, 2013). People who have trouble differentiating often hold distorted perceptions and affective psychic constructs of each other.

Partners can usually detect each other's levels of valency and responsiveness to projections. They often elicit them from each other unconsciously, while consciously perceiving this feeling as love and harmony, or the feeling that they complete each other (McCormack, 2000; J.S. Scharff, 2010; J.S. Scharff & Scharff, 2006, 2014; Siegel & Solomon, 2013). They are actually creating a deeply engrained affective psychic construct and manner of affect regulation. It is particularly noteworthy that projective and introjective identification, as well as repetition compulsion are not only defense mechanisms, but also the foundation for psycho-organic development. The goal of good mothering is to support and project loving emotions, gentleness, and acceptance onto children. In turn, they will transfer their own unresolved emotions, especially difficult affects, onto her. The "good enough" mother then metabolizes and regulates these affects and returns them in a processed form that is more acceptable for her children. For example, a mother accepts and processes her children's feelings of anger, unease, and anxiety. By doing so, she frees her children from such destructive emotions and teaches them how to process emotions in a functional manner. However, she must first feel her children in all of their difficult affects, which is accomplished through right hemisphere communication and projective introjective identification. When mothers are unable or unwilling to accept their children's unmanageable emotions, children quickly begin to feel guilty and ashamed of their own needs. They close up internally and develop specific affective psychic constructs.

5.3 Object Relations Theory—The Relationship of Intentionality

Object relations theory holds that the individual is intentionally oriented toward others. This theory contends that people develop intense psycho-organic attachment because they deeply yearn to relate to others. The relationship is considered a basic phenomenological fact, which the clinical situation can always trace. Individuals seek out and maintain relationships with intrapsychic images that have been created on the basis of psycho-organic relationships with significant others (Schore, 2003, 2012). They maintain these relationships at all costs, and on the grounds of projective and introjective identification and repetition compulsion, they repeatedly renew them on an intrapsychic level, as well as in interpersonal and systemic psycho-organic relationships, where these attachments are most evident. The individual will strive to preserve the relationship with another simply because this is a survival mechanism (Carlson & Sperry, 2010; Fosha, 2009; Mitchell, 1988, 2000, 2002; Schore, 2003, 2010, 2012) with an emphasis on psycho-organic states. The individual's family of origin provides the grounds for survival and the relationships that are the fundamental constitutive elements of the individual's emerging psyche. These relationships provide the intrapsychic images that make the deepest impact on psychic development. Individuals therefore cannot survive without psycho-organic relationships (Maroda, 2010; Ringstrom, 2014).

Families provide the space where we are able to first experience the extensiveness of relationships. We develop a fundamental psycho-organic mental structure, equipping ourselves with whatever we need to enter a wider social spectrum. Our primary relationships play an essential role in the creation of our core affect. We internalize these relationships through projective and introjective identification (J.S. Scharff, 2010; J.S. Scharff & Scharff, 2006, 2014), and they determine our further growth and development. We continuously reinforce our primary relationships via repetition compulsion because this gives us a sense of belonging. Moreover, this provides the foundation for our affective psychic construct, a result of our core affects, and determines how we regulate affect. This strong dynamic is a synthesis of our earliest affects, imagery, experiencing, and psycho-organic states. All of these deeply impact our lives: we remember them implicitly and explicitly, and use them as a foundation for interpreting and building our present experiences (Bruschweiler-Stern et al., 2010; Poulton, 2013; J.S. Scharff, 2010).

Fairbairn's (1952, 1958, 1963) object relations theory provides a well-developed model to describe how people seek relationships by regenerating the intrapsychic imagery absorbed from their parents through introjective identification. These internal images become a part of their interpersonal sphere and a constitutive element of all interpersonal relationships. We then create and recreate this imagery in our most intimate relationships.

Fairbairn began researching these dynamics with children from abusive relationships. He discovered the astonishing loyalty children have towards their parents. In contrast to more traditional theories, which suggest that we all have an innate need to seek comfort and minimize pain, Fairbairn found that abused children remained completely loyal to their parents, despite being abused. The children rejected their foster parents, no matter how kind, loving, and caring they were. Despite their pained relationships, they displayed unconditional attachment to their biological parents (Fairbairn, 1952, 1963).

Fairbairn came to the following conclusion: if the libido really did seek comfort, the objects of comfort or discomfort could be replaceable based on whether or not they actually offered comfort. However, loyalty presents a fundamental connection with others. In this context, children remain loyal to their parents' introjected intrapsychic imagery because it provides that connection, albeit through multilayered trauma (Fairbairn, 1952, 1958, 1963). Hence, children continuously come back and seek the core affect created through that relationship and its intrapsychic imagery. As adults, they recreate this core affect for themselves and in relationships with others. This is because the deeply engrained mental content and its imagery are what enables them to establish the relationship they could not live without. Even as adults, they rediscover, seek, and recreate similar affective content in their inter-relational configurations and do so in newly established interpersonal spaces via projective and introjective identification (J.S. Scharff, 2010; J.S. Scharff & Scharff, 2014). They then consolidate it through repetition compulsion. Their affective psychic construct is created in this space. It enables their split-off, suppressed, and unacceptable mental content to remain concealed.

Further development of this research reveals that these dynamics are not only a characteristic of abusive relationships and psychopathology, but that they are also present in completely healthy and functional relationships. We repeatedly seek relationships that connect to our core affect, where we can bring our intrapsychic images to life. We constantly transfer these into our interpersonal and systemic psycho-organic relations through projective and introjective identification. The imagery and affects are a reflection of our parents' relationship, which has deeply characterized our existence. Viewed in this regard, psychopathology can be understood as a need to repeat our painful experiences by feeling the same painful emotions and establishing the same self-destructive relations. However, Fairbairn (1952, 1958, 1963) points out it is difficult to square this with the hypothesis that humankind has a hedonistic need for comfort. If we truly strive only to find comfort, one would think we would simply resolve and let go of early psycho-organic childhood issues. Instead, we continue to systematically restore them throughout our lives (Poulton, 2013).

To approach this question, Freud developed the concept of repetition compulsion, which emphasizes our loyalty and psycho-organic attachment to objects from our early years, even our most painful affects. Initially, Freud combined this idea with the principle of comfort (Freud, 1900/1958), proposing that our libido, which manifests through psychopathologic torment, is our punishment for the unacceptable desires we have. In time, he altered this theory and pointed out that our libido follows certain clichés of our primary attachments, such as the mother (Freud, 1921/1955b). According to this new theory (Freud, 1920/1955a, 1923/1961a, 1927/1961b), torment signifies the characteristic of our mental functioning that is the derivative of our death drive, although this explanation was unsatisfactory to many theorists (Schore, 2003, 2010, 2012; Fonagy et al., 2007; Fosha, 2009; Maroda, 2010; Mitchell, 1988, 2000, 2002; Poulton, 2013).

Fairbairn (1952, 1958, 1963) approached the topic in a more economic manner, altering the fundamental hypotheses: the libido does not seek comfort; rather it seeks an object. He came to the conclusion (Fairbairn, 1958) that the basic need of children is to find connection as opposed to comfort. If parents provide comfort, children will grow up using it as a tool for interacting with others. If parents provide mostly painful experiences, children will not seek comfort in their relationships with their parents, rather in connecting with others, and they will grow up seeking interaction with significant others through pain itself. Painful emotions will guide them in their search for intimate connection and will manifest later in their relationships, although not consciously. These individuals will seek others who they find attractive and who they believe will fulfill their deepest needs. After a period of time, they will realize their partners are unable to do so, but they nevertheless persist in maintaining a relationship because the pain itself makes them feel deeply connected (Beilock, 2015; Poulton, 2013). Such individuals are willing to sacrifice everything to keep their relationship, even accepting self-destructive humiliation characterized by shame, anger, and contempt.

Feelings similar to those from childhood psycho-organic experiences dictate that such individuals remain loyal in relationships—no matter how painful—until they are filled with the fear of being abandoned or completely lost (Fairbairn, 1958; Fosha, 2009; Maroda, 2010; Schore, 2003, 2012). They will consider leaving the relationship only at this point, the fear of abandonment compelling them to walk out on their partners to avoid feeling abandoned themselves. According to Fairbairn (1952), the human experience revolves around the motivation to pursue and maintain intense emotional connections with others. So repetition compulsion refers to more than just the application of one's libido to an object. Rather, painful experiences and self-destructive relations are a means of preserving our experience of early attachment to significant others and intrapsychic imagery (Fairbairn, 1952). These transfer consecutively onto new interpersonal relations through projective and introjective identification, thereby generating new dimensions of systemic complexity. Children learn basic methods of connection through the family models they know. Through introjection we adopt models, psycho-organic states, intrapsychic imagery, and affects, which we then hold and carry throughout the rest of our lives (Poulton, 2013; Ringstrom, 2014; Schore, 2003, 2010, 2012; Siegel, 2007, 2010, 2011; Siegel & Solomon, 2013).

For example, in some families sexuality is the fundamental component of emotional connection. In other families it might be outbursts of anger or perhaps depressive yearning. These emotions all play an important role in forming the mental structures of children, characterizing them deeply and predisposing them to establish relationships through repetition compulsion. Our families of origin provide us with certain fundamental positive values as well. Some of these include honesty, integrity, participation, morals, values, and religious views. According to Fairbairn (1952), parental pathology is what children connect with most, internalizing it, as it is the core where children feel their parents are emotionally most present. Again, the most intense affects provide the foundations for our mental structures. Affects can vary in amplitude and intensity and are interchangeable later in life. Certain situations can bring new affects to life and replace others. Children who were raised by depressed, masochistic, or sadistic parents grow up to become like their parents and thus nourish a strong attachment to them. The complex dynamics of various emotional experiences and their manifestation is the model upon which people build new relations. It follows, therefore, that we sometimes experience others changing drastically in short amounts of time without understanding why (Maroda, 2010; Ringstrom, 2014; Robins, 2010; J.S. Scharff, 2010; J.S. Scharff & Scharff, 2006, 2014).

Internalized affects or psycho-organic content are what guide us in our interpersonal worlds. Sometimes these affects emerge without our control, especially when it comes to deeper mental issues or trauma. They erupt repeatedly and in various relational configurations. Fairbairn's (1952) theory states that the foundation for pathology is not trauma, memory, or impulse, but rather the relationship between the self and its identification with representations or the intrapsychic imagery of the parents. This imagery does not exist on a conscious level, nor is it connected with other experiences of the self. According to Fairbairn, psychopathology is not structured on the basis of conflicts between instincts and defense mechanisms, rather the breach between remaining loyal to others and to the various dimensions of human personal relationships with others (Fairbairn, 1952, 1958, 1963). This generates a strong affective psychic construct that protects individuals from being too vulnerable and guides them to project their split-off parts outward (J. S. Scharff & Scharff, 2014).

To reject the psycho-organic attachment we have to our intrapsychic imagery would mean complete isolation from any intense human connection. We would have to reject our family, which is, of course, impossible. Even when people consciously decide to leave their family of origin, emotionally or even physically, they will always carry with them the intrapsychic images and affects experienced in their primary connections, although they may not realize it. The affects and images will emerge in their adult life through intimate connections with others. People cannot simply free themselves from this imagery by making the choice to leave their family behind. This, in fact, necessitates a thorough restructuring of the psyche. This process is usually very frightening, and it makes people feel isolated and lonely because they feel they are no longer loyal to their family's fundamental psycho-organic, intrapsychic imagery and emotions, which the parents created through their style of relating (Cummings & Davies, 2010; Poulton, 2013; Ringstrom, 2014).

Losing and letting go of those emotions can make people feel like they are no longer in a relationship or that they have ceased to exist. Sometimes even the thought of this loss can make people feel deeply depressed. Experiencing different emotions, even feeling open to joy and true intimacy with others, causes people to feel they have lost the connection to their inner objects, which used to provide the sense of belonging despite the fact that they were manifested through sad or painful childhood experiences. The interpersonal and systemic perspective emphasizes that children learn deep, binding relational models that are imbedded in individual organic structure and also their family of origin, where these primary relationships are developed. These relational models are also a matter of survival that represent the promise for all relationships with others (Beilock, 2015; Fishbane, 2013; Geher & Kaufman, 2013; Johnson, 2014; Poulton, 2013; Ringstrom, 2014; Schore, 2003, 2010, 2012; Siegel & Solomon, 2013).

5.4 Self-psychology—The Relationship Implication

Philosophers traditionally differentiated human intelligence from animal intelligence on the basis of the capacity to reflect (Mitchell, 1988, 2000; Clulow, 2005; Siegel, 2007, 2010, 2011). Human beings with self-awareness are able to develop and maintain self-esteem, and this plays a significant role in subsequent relationships with others, the choices they make, and how they experience the world. Often the development of self-awareness is considered automatic like the maturation of the body or as a natural result of our experiences like cognitive functioning. However, psychoanalysts are increasingly convinced that the development of self-awareness is a complex process embedded in a multi-layered psycho-organic structure, and that it is the main motivational factor that makes human beings deeply dependent upon each other. Theorists of self-psychology claim that the establishment and maintenance of personality or identity are the primary and highest human motivations and that this presupposes certain interpersonal relationships that are critical for cognition and are the central psychological elements in the building of self-awareness (Beilock, 2015; Clulow, 2005; Mitchell, 1988, 1997, 2000, 2002; Schore, 2003, 2012; Siegel, 2010, 2011).

In this chapter, we introduce two very important elements of human consciousness that contribute to difficulties in the development of self-awareness—time and its complexity. Human consciousness functions within time: the flow of thoughts, emotions, sensations, and desires is in constant circulation. Everything that constantly changes is imperfect at specific moments. Moreover, the moment we attempt to conceptualize and define something that is changing, it is already different, and yet a stable frame of reference that transcends changeable discontinuity is necessary as a way of ordering experience (Clulow, 2005; Mitchell, 1988, 1997, 2000, 2002; Siegel, 2007, 2010, 2011). Put another way, children slowly learn who they are, how they fit into their psycho-organic states of their family of origin, and how to become accustomed to the complex external world and to the equally complex world of their own consciousness, which is replete with so many processes, particularly projective and introjective identification and repetition compulsion (although some self psychologists do not recognize these mechanisms). Nevertheless, as we have already concluded, these two complex mechanisms represent the dynamic by which emotions are established and without which it would be impossible to understand the self. All of the components of a healthy psycho-organic life should be gradually acquired in early childhood and youth. These components include a stable and integrated representation of the self, object constancy, and the flexible regulation of self-esteem (Clulow, 2005; Siegel & Solomon, 2013).

In the opinion of most modern psychoanalysts, children acquire these components through the formation of relationships within their psycho-organic experiences of their family of origin. The organization of children's experience is built on the basis of relationships with the mother and father in the family of origin and the parents' relationship with each other, as well as on the basis of the entire collective experience of the core psycho-organic relationships (Clulow, 2005; Siegel & Solomon, 2013) that prevail in the family and are transferred to children through projective and introjective identification and repetition compulsion. And this establishes and reinforces the affective psychic construct, which is derived from the core affect and the affect regulation style. Self-knowledge develops from birth onwards from parental recognition and acknowledgement. Children begin to learn about themselves in the reflections of their parents' eyes and words. The family also provides a mirror because of the sense of belonging. The growing self-awareness (their intrapsychic image of themselves) of children is always a reflection of the relationships that prevail throughout the entire family or the relationships and emotions that are created and mark family members in the deepest sense. This phenomenological unit of the self (Robins, 2010) is acquired during the years of development through the mechanisms of projective identification and repetition compulsion. The theory of self-psychology claims that the pursuit and maintenance of the reflexive stability of intrapsychic imagery of the self are innate and represent the central motivational force that drives us to relate with others (Beilock, 2015; Clulow, 2005; Fosha, 2009; Mitchell, 1988, 1997, 2000, 2002; Schore, 2003, 2012).

The definition of the primacy of relationships is also a central theme of self-psychology. Mahler and Loewald's theory understands the child's ego as something that springs from a psychic union with another. For Mahler (Mahler, Pine, & Bergman, 1975), the healthy development of the self depends on a mother's ability to care for her child: from her emotional contributions and from her cooperation that allows her child to experience a symbiotic union from which follows the gradual articulation of the self, followed by differentiation and periodic returns to the mother. Loewald (1971) also emphasizes parental organization and the processing of children's experiencing, which enables children to learn through identification until they are able to do things by themselves. Bion (1967) goes even further, defining the maternal embrace and emotional support of the child as essential for the metabolizing of children's emotions, which in contemporary terminology is known as the psycho-organic state (Schore, 2003, 2010, 2012). The concept of "containment" is used as a description of the maternal capability of "holding" a child emotionally and physically. With this concept, Bion explains the complex mechanism of maternal behavior with her child, which takes place on the basis of projective and introjective identification. The mother, for example, takes in the child's angry emotions that cannot be processed alone and are thus upsetting. When the child is angry or upset, the child's emotions move into the mother and become a part of her (J.S. Scharff & Scharff, 2014).

The mother holds these emotions and becomes the "container" of her children's unprocessed emotions, processing them instead in a way that peacefully addresses them and calms her children. Children will always try to project unprocessed emotions that cannot be mastered onto the mother, which marks the beginnings of affect regulation and the development of the self-regulation of affect (Fosha, 2009; Schore, 2003, 2010, 2012). In contrast, a mother may respond with anger to her children's emotions and ultimately block anger in her children, causing them to feel unwanted, fear, and even rage. Namely, children will suppress the emotions that are not acceptable to the mother. This is how children learn that there are parts of them that are unacceptable. Later in life, it will be difficult for them to express these emotions, as well as their needs and desires, because they fear that their mother will humiliate or even reject them as a result of their inappropriate behavior and emotions. Such children will direct feelings of shame and contempt at themselves and in adulthood will project these emotions onto others, above all onto those with whom these now grown-up children have intimate relationships. Future partners then become the "dumping grounds" for unresolved feelings of shame and contempt, emotions that were never processed and therefore repressed, only to rise to the surface in adult relationships. Throughout life, there will be an ongoing and powerful effort to transfer the emotions that cannot be tolerated, let alone processed, onto significant others (Clulow, 2005; Siegel, 2007, 2010, 2011; Siegel & Solomon, 2013).

Particularly noteworthy are two contemporary psychoanalysts, Winnicott (1988) and Kohut (1984), who have a similar way of describing the development of the self or the psycho-organic, intrapsychic imagery of the self.

Winnicott claims that the establishment of a firm sense of self is the principle achievement of normal early development. And yet some individuals only seemingly become full-fledged personalities and do not have the experience that leads to a true and serious sense of self. Winnicott (1971, 1988) conceives of children as slowly beginning to realize their own needs. The key to satisfying these needs is a suitable environment and above all the mother's ability to intuitively perceive her children's needs using the mechanisms of projective identification and repetition compulsion. Winnicott (1988) calls this mechanism the transmutation process, a process through which the mother models her children's affects and desires and makes certain that her children's needs are fulfilled. Above all, children need a suitable environment where they feel they belong, an environment that to a large degree is created by the father and mother. A child's experience is a condition that vacillates between desire and satisfaction, between the desire for the maternal breast and the moment when it appears. Children believe it is their desire itself that produces the breast that is the object of their desire. The same applies to a blanket or a toy, which, from the perspective of children, are the products of their creativity (Clulow, 2005; Siegel, 2007, 2010, 2011; Siegel & Solomon, 2013).

The mother's adaptation to her children's desire creates what Winnicott (1988) calls the moment of illusion. According to Winnicott (1988), in the earliest months of life, a good enough mother is invisible. It is precisely this invisibility that allows children to feel perfect mastery of the world, which Winnicott characterizes as a state of subjective omnipotence. Children experience this period as omnipotence because everything they experience appears to be a product of their own creativity. This sense of omnipotence enables them to develop a healthy childish self, which, in this context, means a complex unified intrapsychic self-image. In this period of early childhood, children hardly see the mother as a person. Rather, she is the one who brings the world to the children, the invisible fulfiller of all their needs. Later, children will notice her more, but even then the main role of the mother is to reflect the children's image to them. The mother's role therefore is known as containing the child. This maternal capability provides a mirror image that tells children who they are and what they are like. Winnicott (1988) theorizes that children's first developmental psycho-organic task is to develop a sense of self. The mother plays a very specific role in this process, providing experiences that enable children to feel emotionally safe and accepted, which in turn allows for the development of the healthy childish self (Carlson & Sperry, 2010; Clulow, 2005; Robins, 2010).

Kohut (1984) similarly claimed that an individual does not suffer because of conflicts or the inability to satisfy basic instincts or the failure of defense mechanisms, but rather because of the deficit of a true and strong sense of self. This leads to a lack of cohesion, integrity, and complexity in the intrapsychic image of the self. As a result, such individuals are extremely vulnerable and their self-confidence wavers (Clulow, 2005; Siegel, 2007, 2010, 2011; Siegel & Solomon, 2013). Both Winnicott and Kohut developed their theories on the basis of their clinical work, from which a number of fundamental questions emerged, such as: How does a cohesive and stable sense of the self develop? How is it preserved? How do these same processes produce a distorted self-image?

Kohut (1984) theorized that the intrapsychic image of the self develops on the basis of specific relationships that he called "selfobject" relations, in which the parents not only serve as objects for their children's needs and desires, but also play a narcissistic role. This occurs through the mechanism of projective and introjective identification and repetition compulsion, which reinforce the intrapsychic image in the psycho-organic structure. Kohut does not explicitly name these mechanisms but, like Winnicott's, his theories implicitly rely on them. Kohut's early formulation of his theory included two specific functions of the selfobject: mirroring children's spontaneous and grandiose experiences and enabling children to idealize their parents (Kohut, 1984; Siegel, 2011).

The sense of self, or the actual self, develops on the basis of these two basic functions or experiences, in which the parents idealize and admire their children, and conversely children see their parents as ideal and worthy of admiration. Gradually, these narcissistic experiences transform into a more realistic and measured self-image. In later psycho-organic development, Kohut and his followers and other analysts of self-psychology put an increasing emphasis on the function of the selfobject and specifically on the empathic function of parents who are attuned to their children's experience from the very beginning of life and thus know how to value and mirror them (Clulow, 2005; Schore, 2003, 2010, 2012). Relationships within the psycho-organic experiences of individual family are therefore of critical significance to the developing child (Kohut, 1984). Although Kohut and other relational theorists do not explicitly refer to the family system, their theories implicitly represent it as a fundamental element of functional development. Children who do not conceive of relationships as a safe place in which the self can be tested, in which needs and desires are recognized by others, and in which to find a reflection of the self in others will never develop a strong sense of self (Clulow, 2005; Johnson, 2014; Siegel, 2007, 2010, 2011; Siegel & Solomon, 2013).

All of the emotions or psycho-organic states that children cannot test with others and thus do no not learn how to process will become part of their unconscious world. These emotions or psycho-organic states will be repressed and later split off, in other words, recognized in others, but not in themselves. So for example, children whose parents did not teach them how to deal with anger will suppress anger and later in life find ways to establish relationships in which they can cause their significant other to feel and process their anger. In intimate relationships, they will project anger onto their partners but will themselves always fear anger and all subjects that cause it. Their partners will become angry instead of them and unconsciously reinforce the conviction that anger is unacceptable (Johnson, 2014; Siegel & Solomon, 2013).

In short, self-psychology concludes that the relationship to the other is primary and individuals who suffer as a result of an undeveloped and disorganized self will spend their lives in search of the self, using others as selfobjects to replace crucial parental functions that were absent in their childhood (Clulow, 2005). For Winnicott (1988) and Kohut (1984), the establishment of the reflexive stability of the self is the central motivational force of human experience. Relationships with others and roles that are played with others provide the primary context of human experience (Clulow, 2005; Siegel & Solomon, 2013). These are roles that are played in the family psycho-organic system and mark the self of the child or, better put, establish it and give it life energy for survival and healthy development. A healthy family and a functional relationship between the parents are both central elements for the maturation and development of every human being and also for the entire family system (Beilock, 2015; MacFarlane, 2004).

D. W. Winnicott (1988) was one of the first theorists of relational theory who dedicated a special place in his work to the dialog between religion and psychoanalysis and defined a mental space for religious experience. He strived to bridge the gap between external and private worlds, between the subjective and the objective. In this context, he proposed a third dimension of human experience, the so-called potential interpersonal mental space that always exists between two people and is a space of new, not yet processed, creativity and dialog. This psycho-organic relational space of creativity emerges on the basis of mutual enrichment and is in its essence also open to transcendence. In this mental space, relationships with others internalize our reality and our external lives encounter and complete the reality of others. This is the arena of interpersonal relationships in which we are repeatedly enmeshed when we strive to establish and preserve the division between internal and external reality, while at the same time maintaining a connection between them. It is therefore a psycho-organic relational space that is neither entirely external nor entirely internal; these two worlds are constantly merging in the so-called transitional phenomenon, which vacillates between the subjective and what is perceived as objective. These worlds and the transitional phenomenon merge together on the basis of creativity, games, arts, knowledge, and above all religion and religious experience (Siegel, 2007, 2010, 2011).

The interaction between our personal psycho-organic reality and experiences with real objects is always a risky one. There is risk in the creativity that intimacy triggers, in a relationship that is legitimate and real and at the same time dreamlike, illusory, and full of longing for what is new, different, higher, and more fulfilling. This is also a space of culture, which in its essence is always a repetition of childish creativity and games with the fundamental goal and purpose that the self is transcended in this potential mental space and an interactive relationship with the other is established. A true relationship provides a way out of the old world of repetition and maintenance of affective psychic constructs. This can only happen if a third space opens in place of the old mutuality of two. From the psychological religious perspective, this third space is potential mental space and one of religious experience, which in addition to culture, science, and art, represents one of the most sophisticated efforts to bridge the gap between the subjective and the objective. This potential psycho-organic relational space of creativity and transcendence is where religious experience is at its most essential and fully defined. However, these epistemological dimensions belong more to the domains of philosophy and theology than to the subject of this book. Suffice to say that the religious experience or the very idea of God is something deeply engrained in the child's mental structure and one of the most essential dimensions of the psyche (Siegel, 2007, 2010, 2011).

The religious phenomenon also plays an important role in the relational family model and indeed in every effort that carries risk and strives to transcend the conflicts that are also only a part of the interpersonal potential and psycho-organic space. The creativity it risks strives to transcend the restrictive aspect, or the interactional phenomenon. The religious experience provides, for example, couples with the possibility of greater openness and creativity, not limited to the conditions of conflict. In this potential psycho-organic relational space, the couple can embark upon a new path in a very concrete way and a third party, God in the religious sense, will enter their relationship.

5.5 Interpersonal Psychoanalysis—The Relationship Concept

The relationship concept or the theory of interpersonal psychoanalysis assumes that the primary motivating force of human development is the establishment and building of relationships with others and that this is how people are shaped. In short, people are made to be interlinked (Bruschweiler-Stern et al., 2010; Cummings & Davies, 2010; Fonagy et al., 2007; Fosha, 2009; Mitchell, 1988, 2000, 2002; Schore, 2003, 2010, 2012; Stern, 2004, 2010). This implies that personality is generated from the emotions or psycho-organic states that we experience in connection with others. Whatever is missing in a relationship is not integrated into the mental structure. In short, the fundamental relationships learned in the psycho-organic experiences within the family—and especially the corresponding affects such as fear, anger, shame, etc.—mark us forever. These core affects are imprinted on us through the mechanisms of projective and introjective identification. Because we constantly repeat and reinforce these affects, they become the cornerstone of right hemisphere communication and are further consolidated with repetition compulsion. These affects promise us relationships with others (Bruschweiler-Stern et al., 2010; Maroda, 2010; Schore, 2003, 2010, 2012; Siegel & Solomon, 2013). Relationships, together with affects, affective psychic constructs, and methods of affect regulation, attach us to each other, while at the same time acting as the fundamental motivating force behind human development (Montgomery, 2013).

This so-called psycho-organic mutual space between the self and the other, which is also a space of creativity, is a space where relationships develop and where the attachment between two people creates something new, something that hitherto did not exist (Bruschweiler-Stern et al., 2010; Siegel, 2007, 2010, 2011; Stern, 2004, 2010). If the partners' selves are not differentiated in a relationship and there is no psycho-organic attachment between their deepest emotions or affects, then rather than creating a new space, they will look for a connection with split-off and denied parts of the self (J.S. Scharff & Scharff, 2006, 2014; Schore, 2003, 2012). This means that, through projection and identification, they will try to force each other to play certain roles from their pasts and will expect each other to regulate painful and unprocessed affects. They will strive to maintain a psycho-organic attachment to the emotions that feel familiar and that they remember from the atmosphere of their family of origin (Carlson & Sperry, 2010; Catherall, 2004; Cummings & Davies, 2010; Johnson, 2014; MacFarlane, 2004). We first seek out a partner on the basis of valency, or right-hemisphere communication, which draws us to the person whose core affect provides the best match. When two individuals find each other in this way they fall passionately in love, though this does not necessarily mean that functional communication or a healthy relationship will develop between them (Cummings & Davies, 2010; Siegel & Solomon, 2013).

For example, the couple might awaken in each other unconscious feelings of psycho-organic attachment on the basis of fear and anger. On the conscious level, the two constantly avoid these emotions. One of them fears the anger of the other while the other will be constantly angry because their partner appears to be retreating in fear. This kind of relationship will be characterized by a discomfort that is assuaged by retreat, which in turn triggers anxiety and fear of abandonment, which in turn will incite attacks and accusations from the one who feels abandoned. The cycle continues, triggering more fear and causing even deeper withdrawal until the terror of rejection reaches a peak. A period of tenderness and caution often follows at this point in the cycle. If children are included in this dynamic—and they almost always are—they will become carriers of fear and anger, victims of the ongoing anxieties that will be expressed in a variety of behavioral, emotional, and cognitive disturbances (Beilock, 2015; Catherall, 2004; Cummings & Davies, 2010; MacFarlane, 2004; McCormack, 2000).

Interpersonal analysis researches both intrapsychic affective and interpersonal psycho-organic relationships (Bruschweiler-Stern et al., 2010; Cummings & Davies, 2010). An effort is made to discover the relationship between the imagery of the self, objects, and affects that create and express a psycho-organic attachment between the self and the object (Schore, 2003, 2010, 2012; Siegel, 2010, 2011; Siegel & Solomon, 2013). On the interpersonal level, the latter is comprised of a relationship between the images of the self and the object in connection with intrapsychic images of the self and the objects of the other, which create affects in the very complex dynamics of relational configurations. Relational configurations are defined as the complex dynamic of mutual affective overlapping on the intrapsychic and interpersonal levels, as well as on all systemic levels of psycho-organic states through projective identification. Bowlby's concept of attachment (Bowlby, 1980, 1988) assumed an even wider meaning in terms of the human relationship being the foundation for thinking about human beings. Bowlby wanted to preserve Freud's biologically rooted explanation of motivation in the same way that Freud had respected Darwin's theory as a basic scientific framework. In doing this, Bowlby came to the realization that Freud's assumption—that the basic human motivational force is the struggle for survival and comfort—is too narrow; a child's survival is not only dependent on physical needs such as food, warmth, etc., but also on the presence and attention of the mother, without which the child would not survive (Schore, 2003, 2012; Siegel, 2006, 2010; Siegel & Solomon, 2013).

From the beginning of their lives, children are very strongly inclined toward psycho-organic attachment with their mother; and during the critical early years, this attachment provides one of the most fundamental stimuli that children long for both on the emotional and behavioral level. It is not so important what the mother does or how she does it, but simply that she is present (Bruschweiler-Stern et al., 2010; Fosha, 2009; Stern, 2004, 2010; Winnicott, 1988). The mother does not gain in importance by satisfying her children's needs, but simply by being with them (Mitchell, 1988, 2000; Mitchell & Black,

1995). Bowlby (1980) came to a similar realization in connection with his research into instinctual behavior in animals, recognizing that a complex system of behavior is needed for survival (Bowlby, 1969). This system has a hierarchy of internal controls and feedback with the following five components of instinctual responses: suckling, cuddling, laughing, crying, and following. Together, these serve to establish a strong mother-child attachment, and only this attachment to the mother's presence ensures survival. These five components directly mediate the child's attachment to the mother, which is the exact opposite of Freud's traditional approach that only the oral quality of the child enables attachment and determines the later development of affective attachment. It is possible to locate similar components in all other relationships, especially intimate ones in which two people mutually create, ceaselessly reawaken, and constantly repeat (Montgomery, 2013; Robins, 2010).

A married couple will, for example, "suckle" each other, nourish each other, laugh together, all of which awakens a deeper dimension of mutual joy and happiness. The two cuddle each other and cry together, and this in turn means that the couple empathizes most with each other, desires each other most, and also follows each other. The attachment or seeking of connection in any close relationship triggers the ability for attachment without words, the ability to summon each other through wordless dynamics. In the intrapsychic field, this is known as the attachment between the self and the object, which on the basis of internalized interpersonal relationships, creates a dynamic that the couple returns to their interpersonal relationship. The form of psycho-organic attachment with the other is thus always dependent on the original attachment to the mother. The intrapsychic form of attachment will be established between partners on the basis of negative and positive feedback (Clulow, 2005; Siegel, 2007, 2010, 2011).

Bowlby describes the child's psycho-organic attachment to the mother as "an archaic heritage" that was imprinted in the genetic code of each human fiber from the very beginning (Bowlby, 1980). This attachment is not the result of biological needs as articulated in theories about instinct, but rather is constructed as part of the intrapsychic structure (Bruschweiler-Stern et al., 2010; Cummings & Davies, 2010) in the same way that a bird might build a nest (Mitchell, 1988, 2000). By nature, children desire their mother and father because this desire is deeply etched in their mental structure. Children want a family and will always search for one. This is true even if they never had a real family or experience of what a family means; its model is present in their unconscious world. The same is also true of the mother and the father whom the children will always look for and miss when they are not there. The downside is that, as a result of projective and introjective identification, the children will search for the image of their family of origin regardless of how stressful and full of pain and anxiety the family experience may have been. The family represents primary psycho-organic attachment and the core affect on which the mental structure is built is part of this. Moreover, this core affect will be constantly reinforced through repetition compulsion, and this in turn strengthens the affective psychic construct.

In short, Bowlby (1969, 1973, 1980), who built his theory on a wide specter of empirical research on the separation of offspring in animals, proved that psycho-organic attachment is primary and is not established merely as a secondary function derived from the need to satisfy physiological needs (like the oral instinct). The most important proof that the relationship between mother and child is of paramount importance to the child's survival is confirmed by the most recent research in the field (Bruschweiler-Stern et al., 2010; Stern, 1985, 1995, 2004, 2010). This research reveals that if the child's relationship with the mother were truly based on merely instinctual needs, the child would have to learn to communicate with the mother. The child would learn this only gradually so that the child's needs, for example for food, could be satisfied by another person who would be essential and therefore interesting because of that. It follows that the relationship with the mother would be less natural than instinctual, and secondary social relationships would be sufficient. However, as already mentioned, research in the field of child development shows that from the beginning of life the child actually seeks a close relationship with the mother (Fosha, 2009; Maroda, 2010; Mitchell, 1988, 2000, 2002; Robins, 2010). Children are born into a psycho-organic system of relationships, born into a family, and regardless of how stunted that family may be, it provides the first path to the other(s) and represents the fundamental psycho-organic and social cell in which development occurs.

In contrast to the traditional theories that children are oriented inward at the beginning of life, in a sort of autistic phase, and only later gradually become oriented toward the external social world, contemporary researchers are discovering that all children possess mechanisms of functional perception at birth. This means that children have an interest in other people shortly after birth. In other words, they very quickly enter into the world of interpersonal relationships. So, for example, the human voice is the aural stimulus that first attracts infants' attention. Research shows that infants will instinctually turn toward a person who is speaking. The human face is also one of the strongest visual stimuli for newborns. Even before infants are able to actually see, they turn toward faces. During the first weeks of life, the eyes of infants do not behave as we would expect, focusing only on the nearness of the maternal breast, but actually seek out her face (Bruschweiler-Stern et al., 2010; Stern, 1995, 2004, 2010). On the basis of these stimuli, infants create the basic psycho-organic state that will later guide them in adult intimate relationships (Montgomery, 2013; Schore, 2003, 2012).

Researchers continue to be amazed by the quality and complexity of infants' interactions with other people and also by the responsiveness and the initiative they are capable in these interactions. Specifically, there is a transfer of affects that are exchanged in the interpersonal field and are the foundations of the mechanism of projective and introjective identification. By three months, infants are well-equipped with a wide repertoire of reactions with which they can independently include and exclude the mother. All of these simple but also complex interactions prove that children have a strong inherent predisposition (Bruschweiler-Stern et al., 2010; Stern, 1985, 1995, 2004, 2010), which enables them to be active and responsive, and to distinguish between the important people in their lives and strangers. Similarly, by the end of infants' first weeks of life, the mother's face is a point of reference. If the mother's face is covered or she speaks with a different voice, infants become agitated. By the eighth day of life, infants can differentiate between a pillow permeated with the smell of their own mother's milk and one permeated with the milk of another woman, and will always turn their faces toward their mother's pillow. By the fourth week of life, infants will move their hands differently toward their mothers than they do toward their fathers (Bruschweiler-Stern et al., 2010; Mitchell, 1988, 2000; Stern, 1995, 2004, 2010). This research shows that a feeling for family awakens very early in infants, or more accurately a feeling for the father and mother who together create the family atmosphere.

All of this proves that a child is equipped at birth with the capabilities of direct human-to-human interaction, already making use of projective and introjective identification or right hemisphere communication. In other words, this type of interaction is not learned. Infants are already physiologically and psychologically prepared for the sociability that allows participation in a system of family relationships. This sociability is not only a tool on the basis of which a certain goal is achieved, for example the reduction of tension and enhancement of comfort and safety, but it is in itself a condition for development and a goal of development (Bruschweiler-Stern et al., 2010; Stern, 1995, 2004, 2010). Children are driven toward sociability. Just to be in a relationship or to observe a relationship is one of the strongest elements in children's ability to solve problems and function in general (Bruschweiler-Stern et al., 2010; Mitchell, 1988, 2000, 2002; Stern, 1995, 2004, 2010). To observe a father doing his work or in relationship with the mother, to be present in the mother's relationship with the father, that is to be an active participant with both parents, provides the foundation of the relational structure of children's experiencing. Human beings will always strive to create a similar feeling as the one that permeated original relationships made in early childhood and reinforced in adulthood. They will try to awaken these same feelings in all relationships with others, especially intimate ones.

The research described above was completed by Bowlby's theory of attachment (1980), which explored integral psycho-organic instruments and models that govern psycho-organic attachment even in newborns. Every primary psycho-organic attachment or relationship assumes motivational elements in the organism and is thus understood as a survival instinct. However, Bowlby and other relational theorists do not understand the dynamic of psycho-organic attachment as an innate mechanism in the same way that Freud did (Freud, 1912/1957). By definition, attachment is an interaction, and this is already very different from Freud's concept of instinct. Bowlby's (1980) motive for attachment is also different. Psycho-organic attachment is an internal integral model of interaction as described by researchers of childhood development. At the same time, attachment spurs human beings to search for connection with others because of the connection itself, interaction for the sake of interaction, not in order to channel something else through it (Bowlby, 1980). Using the language of Fairbairn (1958), the libido seeks no other comfort but the object. This is a crucial conclusion. What is important therefore is someone, the other, who does something. Also, what the other does and at the same time the understanding of the whole event becomes exceptionally important (Schore, 2003, 2010, 2012). The other therefore is not merely a tool for mastering an anxious internal condition, but the exchange with the other and attachment to the other fulfills the most fundamental mental need and reality in and of itself. This, of course, has an influence on all further psychology theory (Mitchell, 1988, 2000, 2002; Montgomery, 2013).

Thus, the psycho-organic system of family relationships represents children's most fundamental need; children are born for sociability, coming to life in relationships, developing within them, and achieving perfection, whether they are permeated with emotions such as acceptance, love, and desirability, or with rejection, abandonment, and the feeling of not being wanted. The most frequent core affects are shame, anger, and fear. This indicates that human beings can also be deeply hurt in a psycho-organic system of relationships and that this hurt can become the fundamental atmosphere equated with closeness. It is precisely the primary relationship that is most important because children develop within a family, and the family is the fundamental cell in which they realize themselves fully and come to life with others. These primary relationships along with their core affects, which in many ways are based on internal images or psycho-organic states, are critical because of the functional and pathological experiencing of the self and others in later life. Regardless of whether these relationships are loving or painful, they promise connection and psycho-organic attachment, without which human beings cannot live. For this reason, these early relationships will provide a pattern throughout life (Cummings & Davies, 2010; Siegel & Solomon, 2013).

Conclusion

Relational family therapy is based on the relational configurations of psycho-organic structure, which by definition has three dimensions: the self, the self-other, and the affective psycho-organic relational space between the self and the other. From this perspective, it is impossible to conceive of the psychological meaning of an individual—on the intrapsychic, interpersonal, or systemic level—without a sense of the individual's self-other relationship. In this context, it is also impossible to conceive of a self that would be isolated outside of the relational matrix, or of a self or individual in the psycho-organic sense of dynamics, without considering the affective relational space in which the self and the other are in interaction, with the self and others connecting in an organic system. All of this means that we are attached to each other, enmeshed, individual subjective experience merged with mental worlds that are articulated in a particular way through the family system, which in this case represents a fourth dimension in the configuration of mutual relationships. All four dimensions contain an intrapsychic, interpersonal, and organic systemic level. All four dimensions overlap and intermingle with each other. At the same time, each intrapsychic unit represents the entire system in which the intrapsychic elements—the self, the other, and the affect created between them—complete the whole. Therefore, it is not only intrapsychic content and objects, or only disassociated parts of the self or affects, that are projected outward, but also a whole complex system of relationships that create an affect between them, and this affect in turn creates the entire psycho-organic system with its specific pattern of relationships.

Relational family therapy is directed toward all of these aspects on all levels. It seeks out psycho-organic problems on all dimensions and tries to resolve them, above all on the systemic level. It is a progressive process that takes into account all dimensions of experience and all levels of interpersonal interactions. If it is not possible to find a solution on the systemic level, the therapist looks for a solution to the problem on the interpersonal level and finally on the intrapsychic level where there is a similar configuration of self and other and the affects that are created in the psycho-organic relational space between them. Deeper searches will be similar to the therapist's efforts on the systemic level where there are more selves and others and mental spaces between them that together create the entirety of the family system with all the categories that comprise and represent that system. The relational family therapy model deliberately seeks out and researches all the places where problems have both their roots and their resolutions, namely on all three levels: systemic, interpersonal, and intrapsychic. This involves the discovery of the systemic, interpersonal, or intrapsychic affective psychic construct and its resolution, because the affective psychic construct maintains a specific pattern of relationships within the system and requires for its existence and growth a specific type of problematic behavior.

Relational family therapy is based on five fundamental mechanisms. The first are projective and introjective identification and repetition compulsion, two unconscious forces that allow an individual to transfer mental content onto the other and to compel the other to repeat settled patterns of behavior, emotion, and cognition that are then reinforced through repetition compulsion. This process is usually reciprocal and is always expressed in the form of right hemisphere communication, especially between individuals in intimate relationships on the basis of the valency that attracts them to each other. Ultimately, both partners repeat established patterns of behavior, emotions, and cognition even if they are destructive because this enables the preservation of a familiar and domestic atmosphere and promises a relationship. They remain part of the psycho-organic dynamics of the relational configuration, which has been internalized. Specifically, it is the internalization of the implicit memory of the first sensation—the touch of parents—that creates the psycho-organic state. This is exceptionally binding in human beings, especially when it comes to psycho-organic attraction and the establishment of intimacy.

We always look for or create the same feeling, affect, or psycho-organic state on the basis of which we can once again create a relationship with others, even if it is destructive. Without relationships, human beings cannot live. Thus, we unconsciously use mechanisms that enable the transfer of fundamental affects, psycho-organic states, and internalized and reinforced objects and object images. Specifically, these dynamic processes enable the development of the self, that is the development of intrapsychic images, core affects, and psycho-organic states, which is why they are of such essential importance in the construction and reinforcement of the human psyche. The relational family therapist focuses on the strongest mental dynamics such as those that are apparent in the mechanism of projective and introjective identification. What is at play here are intrapsychic, interpersonal, and systemic psychological processes, for example, when the mother, father, child, or partner, the so-called sender, projects split-off and denied internal aspects of the self, internalized forms of the other, or indeed a whole system of relationships onto the other or, in this case, the so-called recipient. Then, using repetition compulsion, the sender forces the other to identify with these projections. This is an extremely powerful kind of right hemisphere communication.

This process involves the projection of intrapsychic content, affects, psycho-organic states that take place on the intrapsychic, interpersonal, and also systemic levels. An essential constitutive part of projective identification is the introjective identification that continues the psycho-organic process by which, as stated above, the recipient internalizes certain aspects of the other into the self. This is then reinforced through repetition compulsion. Thus, an identified patient is often designated and becomes the main source of regulating unacceptable affects in the family and subsequently in relational family therapy.

This family scapegoat is always the result of compromises throughout the entire family. Usually, this person is the carrier of deeply rooted marital conflicts that were not addressed and are too painful for the couple (or parents) to address. Parents then transfer unacceptable and painful affects and destructive content onto the child who becomes the carrier of unresolved psycho-organic content and thus reestablishes systemic balance that may have been threatened or disrupted because of marital conflict.

Projective and introjective identification together with the mechanism of repetition compulsion create an intrapsychic, interpersonal, and systemic dynamic, which also represents an exceptionally strong system for regulating affects. When senders attribute split-off intrapsychic parts of the self to the other, the other is compelled to identify with these aspects or parts. If the other does not identify with the projected mental content, the psychological process remains on the level of projection and has little influence on the recipient. The essence of this process is that senders, through knowledge and behavior, send a constant "invitation" to recipients who can respond to the call and thus become a "dumping ground" for the senders' projections, or not. If senders have a distorted self-image, they usually deny it and instead develop an interest in the image of the other, which they will begin to perceive as distorted. If recipients have a secure self-image, they will not identify with the projections of the sender or will feel that there is something wrong with the sender's self-image. But if recipients are concerned about their own self-image, they will be very vulnerable to the projections, and, aided by the mechanism of repetition compulsion, will create a foundation in their own fragile and uncertain self-image on which the sender's distorted self-image will find fertile ground.

As a result of this process, recipients will feel very uncomfortable, perceiving themselves as unattractive, and their anxiety will increase. Senders will observe recipients' discomfort and will identify with their struggle, and they perhaps will even learn how to confront their own problems of unattractiveness. The interpersonal and intrapsychic process can thus be observed at the point where senders and recipients regard their own self-images with uncertainty, and unconsciously and persistently search in each other for a way to regulate difficult affects. Senders will try to resolve their anxiety in such a way that they will deny or disassociate these feelings and will project them onto recipients where they can be controlled. On the other side of the equation, recipients will accept the projections or emotions because they match their negative and unacceptable self-image. In this way, the mechanisms of projective and introjective identification and repetition compulsion clarify how in the relationship between partners or the mother-child relationship, both parties can become a "dumping ground" for split-off aspects or affects of the other. At the same time they answer the question of why partners who are seemingly very different have a valency that attracts each other. On the systemic level, they also answer the question of why parents try to maintain a dysfunctional child, why they don't let that child grow up, and why they always blame their unresolved emotions on this family scapegoat, failing to address their own split-off, repressed, and denied psycho-organic content.

This process occurs as a result of the following three dynamics: the core affect, affect regulation, and the affective psychic construct that is built from the core affect. The relational family therapist must dedicate special attention to these mechanisms, as they are essential to the establishment and ultimately the resolution of painful psycho-organic content. At the same time, these three mechanisms together with the two discussed in the previous paragraph reveal the crucial importance of separation, individuation, and differentiation in every healthy relationship. When senders and recipients are undifferentiated, a distorted comprehension and recognition of the other takes place. A romantic relationship is initially established because partners intuitively, on the basis of right hemisphere communication, perceive the responsiveness or valency in the other, that is, the acceptability of the projections with which they attract each other. On the unconscious level, this explains certain emotions such as harmony or love—the sense that two people complete each other—and the creation of a deeply anchored affective psychic construct as well as the mechanism of mutual affect regulation.

The affective psychic construct contains a cognitive, behavioral, and emotional configuration as well as an organic component. All of these elements are based on the core affect generated by the most significant experiences in childhood, or on traumatic events such as abuse, which will persist in a variety of later relationships and thus be reinforced in the mental structure, becoming an essential part of it. For this reason, the affective psychic construct also represents the deepest connection or attachment as it pertains to primary relationships or physical, sexual, cognitive, emotional, and mental abuse. It is a complex defense mechanism that creates a defensive wall around the fundamental mental structure of the self, the object, and the affect, together with the organic components, and thus protects the self from additional injury. This defense mechanism enables the individual to split off, dissociate, suppress, and deny painful and traumatic psychic content and blocks further invasions of painful emotions such as sadness, hurt, loneliness, abuse, rejection, abandonment, fear, etc., at least temporarily calming and quieting these feelings.

The affective psychic construct therefore contains all the defense mechanisms such as disassociation, denial, rationalization, etc., which prevent the individual from directly confronting psychological problems or trauma, and encourage the use of the mechanisms of projective and introjective identification to transfer them to others. Thus, this content is repeated in relationships with new people. Because of this, it is necessary for the therapist to unearth the affective psychic construct as it blocks healthy and functional communication. Problematic behavior in the family that emerges from these psycho-organic configurations both leads the affective dynamic of the distorted regulation of affects and continually influences ongoing affect regulation. It could be said that it comprises an integrated method of affect regulation, which also includes organic components and all of the sub-elements such as the hormonal system, the system for regulating organic tensions, relaxation, and initiative, and cortical and subcortical connections between the limbic system and cortical cognitive functions. This integrated method of affect regulation enables "switching" between physical and cognitive processes and between the parasympathetic and sympathetic nervous systems, indicating a fundamental mutuality between affect regulation and problematic behavior instigated, caused, and maintained in the other. The core affect that was created on the basis of the primary relationship with the mother and father in early childhood and represents the constitutive primary relationship is unconsciously sought with similar people in similar situations so that it can be repeated, acted out, and developed.

In the creation of relational configurations such as the core affect and the affective psychic construct, abuse of all kinds has particular significance, as abuse shapes the psycho-organic structure in a very forceful way, establishing an extremely strong affective psycho-organic attachment between the abuser and the victim. For this reason, the victim of abuse will, precisely on the basis of this brutal and forceful relationship, unconsciously search for new situations of abuse and for similar relationships in which they will again be abused. For this reason, the relational family therapist will use the relational approach with victims of abuse to understand the essence of this dynamic and to draw on new methods to resolve the painful and complex cycle. The core affect and the affective psychic construct connected to it maintain the entire family system in its dysfunction, and that takes place primarily on the systemic level where both are engrained. The essential task of the therapist is therefore to discover as early in the process as possible the affective psychic construct. In general, both its latent and visible symptoms appear as a sort of compromise, for example, phobias, psychosomatic illnesses, drug and alcohol abuse, unfeeling parents, or a complete inability and unwillingness to have a healthy functional relationship. It is possible to locate in these compromises the core affects such as anger, rage, horror, shame, and anxiety that characterize the relationship but have their roots somewhere else and are carried into the new relationship from a different situation.

The relational family therapist first tries to find a solution to the compromise in which the affect is contained on the psycho-organic systemic level of the family. If it is not possible to find a solution and the system does not relax and become more functional—on the emotional, cognitive, behavioral, and finally organic levels—then the problem is deeper. The therapist must then search for a solution on deeper levels of the system. The therapist will dig down to the interpersonal level and finally to the intrapsychic level of experience and the perceptions of individual members of the system.

The therapist will also search for the affective psychic construct that is the driving force in each of the dysfunctional relationships because that represents the compromise that is necessary for the survival of the individual, couple, or family system. This is why it becomes an essential constitutive part of the method of affect regulation that guides the individual in the relationship where a new affective system and its many dimensions have been created. Individual members of the system may deny or become disassociated from the painful parts of their mental and/or organic structures but will transfer these feelings onto others in the system through the mechanism of projective and introjective identification.

At the beginning of a relationship, the individual will think and feel that it is a completely fresh and different situation but will soon realize that the affective relationship is very similar to the one experienced in early childhood psycho-organic development. It may be the consequence of trauma that with all its graphic power promises belonging and connection, precisely based on the affect that is most deeply imprinted in the individual's psyche. The same affect will be expressed differently in each individual and in individual relationships within the system. We must also consider intergenerational affective complexes as well as biological or organic pathological elements that can have a crucial influence on dysfunction and the method of affect regulation in both individual members and the whole family system. From this perspective, the search for the affective psychic construct that prevents healthy functionality is based on the affect itself. The therapist will sense this in the clinical environment and search for its roots in all layers of the mental experience of individual members on the systemic, interpersonal, and above all intrapsychic levels.

The core affect that usually appears in the psycho-organic systemic or interpersonal field as a disproportionate response to certain behavior of a partner, child, or whole family system leads the therapist to continually search until all components that make up the affect are found. This is why the historical aspect and the intrapsychic world that carries the basic outlines of the affective, organic and implicit world of experience are so important. Already in childhood, the relationship with the mother on a purely organic level creates the essential elements of the psycho-organic state and core affects that only later acquire cognitive, behavioral, and emotional components of experience. All of this psycho-organic content unconsciously leads to the promise of psycho-organic attachment, relationship, and with it belonging, without which we cannot survive. The relational family therapist addresses these themes with keen attention, seeking out the fundamental psychological problem and its solution, in particular the early relationships that powerfully influence the individual, couple, and family system on the personal, interpersonal, and intrapsychic levels. Particular affects, patterns of behavior, and structures of perception characterize the individual, couple, and family system on all of these levels of experience. For this reason, the relational family therapy considers and integrates the three levels into a new systemic whole, where the essential psycho-organic relational space is also one of religious experience.

References

Bader, E., & Pearson, P. T. (1988). *In quest of the mythical mate: A developmental approach to diagnosis and treatment in couples therapy.* Philadelphia, PA: Brunner/Mazel.

Beilock, S. (2015). *How the body knows its mind: The surprising power of the physical environment to influence how you think and feel.* New York, NY: Atria Books.

Berman, R. (2014). *Permission to parent: How to raise your child with love and limits.* New York, NY: Harper Collins.

Bion, W. R. (1967). *Second thoughts.* London: Heinemann.

Bitter, J. R. (2014). *Theory and practice of family therapy and counseling* (2nd ed.). Belmont, CA: Brooks/Cole, Cengage Learning.

Blatt, S., & Layton, P. (2009). A structural-developmental psychodynamic approach to psychopathology: Two polarities of experience across the life span. *Development and Psychopathology, 21*(3), 793–814.

Bollas, C. (1987). *The shadow of the object: Psychoanalysis of the unthought known.* New York, NY: Columbia University Press.

Boszormenyi-Nagy, I., Grunebaum, J., & Ulrich, D. N. (1991). Contextual family therapy. In A. S. Gurman & D. P. Kniskern (Eds.), *Handbook of family therapy* (Vol. 2, pp. 200–238). New York, NY: Brunner/Mazel.

Boszormenyi-Nagy, I., & Krasner, B. R. (1986). *Between give and take: A clinical guide to contextual therapy.* New York, NY: Brunner/Mazel.

Boszormenyi-Nagy, I., & Ulrich, D. N. (1981). Contextual family therapy. In A. S. Gurman & D. P. Kniskern (Eds.), *Handbook of family therapy* (pp. 159–186). New York, NY: Brunner/Mazel.

Bowen, M. (1978). *Family therapy in clinical practice.* New York, NY: Jason Aronson.

Bowlby, J. (1969). *Attachment and loss: Vol. 1: Attachment.* New York, NY: Basic Books.

Bowlby, J. (1973). *Attachment and loss: Vol. 2: Separation: Anxiety and anger.* New York, NY: Basic Books.

Bowlby, J. (1980). *Attachment and loss: Vol. 3: Loss: Sadness and depression.* New York, NY: Basic Books.

Bowlby, J. (1982). Attachment and loss: Retrospect and prospect. *American Journal of Orthopsychiatry, 52*(4), 664–678.

Bowlby, J. (1988). *A secure base: Parent-child attachment and healthy human development.* New York, NY: Basic Books.

Bradshaw, J. (1988). *Bradshaw on: The family: A revolutionary way of self discovery*. Deerfield Beach, FL: Health Communications.

Bradshaw, J. (1996). *Family secrets: The path to self-acceptance and reunion*. New York, NY: Bantam Books.

Bruschweiler-Stern, N., Lyons-Ruth, K., Morgan, A. C., Nahum, J. P., Sander, L. W., Stern, D. N. S., . . . Tronick, E. Z. (2010). *Change in psychotherapy: A unifying paradigm*. New York, NY: W. W. Norton & Company.

Carlson, J., & Sperry, L. (Eds.) (2010). *Recovering intimacy in love relationships: A clinician's guide*. New York, NY: Routledge.

Cashdan, S. (1988). *Object relations therapy: Using the relationship*. New York, NY: W. W. Norton & Company.

Caspar, F. (1995). *Plan analysis: Toward optimizing psychotherapy*. Seattle, WA: Hogrefe & Huber Publishers.

Caspar, F., Rothenfluh, T., & Segal, Z. (1992). The appeal of connectionism for clinical psychology. *Clinical Psychology Review, 12*(7), 719–762.

Catherall, D. R. (Ed.) (2004). *Handbook of stress, trauma, and the family*. New York, NY: Brunner-Routledge.

Chiron, C., Jambaque, I., Nabbout, R., Lounes, R., Syrota, A., & Dulac, O. (1997). The right brain hemisphere is dominant in human infants. *Brain: A Journal of Neurology, 120*(6), 1057–1065.

Chu, J. A. (1991). The repetition compulsion revisited: Reliving dissociated trauma. *Psychotherapy: Theory, Research, Practice, Training, 28*(2), 327–332.

Clulow, C. (2001). Attachment theory and the therapeutic frame. In C. Clulow (Ed.), *Adult attachment and couple psychotherapy: The 'secure base' in practice and research* (pp. 85–104). New York, NY: Brunner-Routledge.

Clulow, C. (2005). Partnership and marriage. In E. Rayner, A. Joyce, J. Rose, M. Twyman, & C. Clulow (Eds.), *Human development: An introduction to the psychodynamics of growth, maturity and ageing* (pp. 213–230). London: Routledge.

Colapinto, J. (1991). Structural family therapy. In A. S. Gurman & D. P. Kniskern (Eds.), *Handbook of family therapy* (Vol. 2, pp. 417–443). Philadelphia, PA: Brunner/Mazel.

Cooper, S. H. (2000). *Objects of hope: Exploring possibility and limits in psychoanalysis*. Hillsdale, NJ: The Analytic Press.

Cummings, E. M., & Davies, P. T. (2010). *Marital conflict and children: An emotional security perspective*. New York, NY: Guilford Press.

Cvetek, R. (2009). *Bolečina preteklosti: Travma, medosebni odnosi, družina, terapija* [Pain of the past: Trauma, interpersonal relationships, family, therapy]. Celje: Društvo Mohorjeva družba, Celjska Mohorjeva družba.

Dallos, R., & Draper, R. (2005). *An introduction to family therapy: Systemic theory and practice* (2nd ed.). Maidenhead: Open University Press.

Dicks, H. V. (1967). *Marital tensions: Clinical studies towards a psychological theory of interaction*. London: Routledge & Kegan Paul.

Donavan, J. M. (2003). *Short-term object relations couples therapy: The five-step model.* New York, NY: Brunner-Routledge.

Dutton, D. G. (2007). *The abusive personality: Violence and control in intimate relationships* (2nd ed.). New York, NY: Guilford Press.

Fairbairn, W. R. D. (1952). *Psychoanalytic studies of the personality.* London: Routledge.

Fairbairn, W. R. D. (1958). On the nature and aims of psychoanalytic treatment. *International Journal of Psychoanalysis, 39,* 374–385.

Fairbairn, W. R. D. (1963). Synopsis of an object relations theory of the personality. *International Journal of Psychoanalysis, 44,* 224–225.

Feinstein, S. G. (2013). *Secrets of the teenage brain: Research-based strategies for reaching and teaching today's adolescents.* New York, NY: Sage.

Feldman, L. B., & Pinsof, W. M. (1982). Problem maintenance in family systems: An integrative model. *Journal of Marital and Family Therapy, 8*(3), 285–294.

Fishbane, M. D. (2013). *Loving with the brain in mind.* New York, NY: W. W. Norton & Company.

Flannery, R. B. (1992). *Post-traumatic stress disorder: The victim's guide to healing and recovery.* New York, NY: Crossroad Publishing.

Fonagy, P., Gergely, G., Jurist, E. L., & Target, M. (2007). *Affect regulation, mentalization, and the development of the self.* New York, NY: Other Press.

Fosha, D. (2009). Emotion and recognition at work: Energy, vitality, pleasure, truth, desire, and the emergent phenomenology of transformational experience. In D. Fosha, D. J. Siegel, & M. F. Solomon (Eds.), *The healing power of emotion: Affective neuroscience, development & clinical practice* (pp. 172–203). New York, NY: W. W. Norton & Company.

Framo, J. L. (1992). *Family of origin therapy: An intergenerational approach.* New York, NY: Brunner/Mazel.

Fredrickson, B. L., & Losada, M. F. (2005). Positive affect and the complex dynamics of human flourishing. *American Psychologist, 60*(7), 678–686.

Freud, S. (1955a). Beyond the pleasure principle. In J. Strachey (Ed. & Trans.), *The standard edition of the complete psychological works of Sigmund Freud* (Vol. 18, pp. 7–64). London: Hogarth Press. (Original work published 1920).

Freud, S. (1955b). Group psychology and the analysis of the ego. In J. Strachey (Ed. & Trans.), *The standard edition of the complete psychological works of Sigmund Freud* (Vol. 18, pp. 65–143). London: Hogarth Press. (Original work published 1921).

Freud, S. (1957). On the universal tendency to debasement in the sphere of love. In J. Strachey (Ed. & Trans.), *The standard edition of the complete psychological works of Sigmund Freud* (Vol. 11, pp. 177–190). London: Hogarth Press. (Original work published 1912).

Freud, S. (1958). The interpretation of dreams. In J. Strachey (Ed. & Trans.), *The standard edition of the complete psychological works*

of Sigmund Freud (Vol. 4–5, pp. 1–621). London: Hogarth Press. (Original work published 1900).
Freud, S. (1961a). The ego and the id. In J. Strachey (Ed. & Trans.), *The standard edition of the complete psychological works of Sigmund Freud* (Vol. 19, pp. 12–59). London: Hogarth Press. (Original work published 1923).
Freud, S. (1961b). The future of an illusion. In J. Strachey (Ed. & Trans.), *The standard edition of the complete psychological works of Sigmund Freud* (Vol. 21, pp. 3–56). London: Hogarth Press. (Original work published 1927).
Gehart, D. R. (2016). *Theory and treatment planning in family therapy: A competency-based approach.* Boston, MA: Cengage Learning.
Geher, G., & Kaufman, S. B. (2013). *Mating intelligence unleashed: The role of the mind in sex, dating and love.* New York, NY: Oxford University Press.
Givelber, F. (1990). Object relations and the couple: Separation-individuation, intimacy, and marriage. In R. Chasin, H. Grunebaum, & M. Herzig (Eds.), *One couple, four realities: Multiple perspectives on couple therapy* (pp. 171–190). New York, NY: Guilford Press.
Goleman, D. (2006). *Social intelligence: The new science of human relationships.* New York, NY: Bantam Books.
Gostečnik, C. (2004). *Relacijska družinska terapija* [Relational family therapy]. Ljubljana: Brat Frančišek in Frančiškanski družinski inštitut.
Gostečnik, C. (2007). *Relacijska zakonska terapija* [Relational marital therapy]. Ljubljana: Brat Frančišek in Frančiškanski družinski inštitut.
Gostečnik, C. (2010). *Sistemske teorije in praksa* [Systemic theories and practice]. Ljubljana: Brat Frančišek in Frančiškanski družinski inštitut.
Gostečnik, C. (2015). *Inovativna relacijska zakonska terapija* [Relational paradigm and clinical praxis]. Ljubljana: Brat Frančišek, Teološka fakulteta in Frančiškanski družinski inštitut.
Gottman, J., & Silver, N. (2012). *What makes love last.* New York, NY: Simon & Schuster.
Gurman, A. S. (Ed.) (2008). *Clinical handbook of couple therapy* (4th ed.). New York, NY: The Guilford Press.
Gurman, A. S., & Kniskern, D. P. (1991). *Handbook of family therapy* (2nd ed.). Philadelphia, PA: Brunner/Mazel.
Guttman, H. A. (1991). Systems theory, cybernetics, and epistemology. In A. S. Gurman & D. P. Kniskern (Eds.), *Handbook of family therapy* (Vol. 2, pp. 41–62). New York, NY: Brunner/Mazel.
Haley, J. (1976). *Problem-solving therapy.* San Francisco, CA: Jossey-Bass.
Haley, J. (1987). *Problem-solving therapy* (2nd ed.). San Francisco, CA: Jossey-Bass.
Hecker, L. L., & Wetchler, J. K. (2003). *Introduction to marriage and family therapy.* New York, NY: Haworth Press.
Hendrix, H. (1988). *Getting the love you want.* New York, NY: Henry Holt and Company.
Hendrix, H. (1992). *Keeping the love you find.* New York, NY: Pocket Books.

Hendrix, H. (2008). *Getting the love you want: A guide for couples*. New York, NY: Henry Holt and Company.
Hendrix, H., & Hunt, H. (2004). *Receiving love: Transform your relationship by letting yourself be loved*. New York, NY: Atria Books.
Johnson, S. M. (2014). *The love secret: The revolutionary new science of romantic relationships*. London: Hachette.
Johnson, S. M., & Whiffen, V. E. (Eds.) (2003). *Attachment processes in couple and family therapy*. New York, NY: Guilford Press.
Kerr, M. E., & Bowen, M. (1988). *Family evaluation: An approach based on Bowen theory*. New York, NY: W. W. Norton & Company.
Kim, S., Fonagy, P., Allen, J., & Strathearn, L. (2014). Mothers' unresolved trauma blunts amygdala response to infant distress. *Social Neuroscience*, *9*(4), 352–363.
Klein, M. (1940). Mourning and its relation to manic-depressive states. *International Journal of Psychoanalysis*, *21*, 125–153.
Klein, M. (1946). Notes on some schozoid mechanisms. *International Journal of Psychoanalysis*, *27*, 99–100.
Klein, M. (1948). *Contributions to psychoanalysis*. London: Hogarth Press.
Klein, M. (1962). *The psychoanalysis of children*. Oxford: Grove.
Klein, M. (1975). *Envy and gratitude and other works 1946–1963*. London: Hogarth Press.
Knee, R. C. (1998). Implicit theories of relationships: Assessment and prediction of romantic relationship initiation, coping, and longevity. *Journal of Personality and Social Psychology*, *74*(2), 360–370.
Kohut, H. (1984). *How does analysis cure?* Chicago, IL: University of Chicago Press.
Lachkar, J. (2004). *The narcissistic/borderline couple: New approaches to marital therapy* (2nd ed.). New York, NY: Brunner/Mazel.
Lassiter, P. S., Czerny, A. B., & Williams, K. S. (2015). Working with addictions in family therapy. In D. Capuzzi & M. D. Stauffer (Eds.), *Foundations of couples, marriage, and family counseling* (pp. 389–417). Hoboken, NJ: John Wiley & Sons Inc.
Lebow, J. (2003). Integrative approaches to couple and family therapy. In T. L. Sexton, G. R. Weeks, & M. S. Robbins (Eds.), *Handbook of family therapy: The science and practice of working with families and couples* (pp. 201–228). New York, NY: Brunner Routledge.
Loewald, H. W. (1971). Some considerations on repetition and repetition compulsion. *International Journal of Psychoanalysis*, *52*(1), 59–66.
Levenson, E. (1983). *The ambiguity of change: An inquiry into the nature of psychoanalytic reality*. New York, NY: Basic Books.
Lewis, J. M. (1997). *Marriage as a search for healing: Theory, assessment, and therapy*. Philadelphia, PA: Brunner/Mazel.
Low, N. S. (1990). Women in couples: How their experience of relationships differs from men's. In R. Chasin, H. Grunebaum, & M. Herzig (Eds.), *One couple, four realities: Multiple perspectives on couple therapy* (pp. 249–268). New York, NY: Guilford Press.
MacFarlane, M. (2004). *Family treatment of personality disorders: Advances in clinical practice*. Binghamton, NY: Haworth Clinical Practice Press.

Mahler, M. S. (1974). Symbiosis and individuation: The psychological birth of the human infant. *The Psychoanalytic Study of the Child, 29*, 89–106.

Mahler, M. S., Pine, F., & Bergman, A. (1975). *The psychological birth of the human infant: Symbiosis and individuation*. New York, NY: Basic Books.

Main, M., & Goldwin, R. (1996). *Adult attachment scoring and classification systems*. Berkeley: University of California.

Maroda, K. J. (1994). *The power of countertransference*. Northvale, NJ: Jason Aronson.

Maroda, K. J. (2010). *Psychodynamic techniques: Working with emotion in the therapeutic relationship*. New York, NY: Guilford Press.

McCormack, C. C. (2000). *Treating borderline states in marriage: Dealing with oppositionalism, ruthless aggression, and severe resistance*. Northvale, NJ: Jason Aronson.

McCormack, C. C. (2004). An object-relations approach to the treatment of personality-disordered marriages. In M. M. MacFarlane (Ed.), *Family treatment of personality disorders: Advances in clinical practice* (pp. 71–113). Binghamton, NY: Haworth Clinical Practice Press.

Meissner, W. W. (1978). The conceptualization of marriage and family dynamics from a psychoanalytic perspective. In T. J. Paolino & B. S. McCrady (Eds.), *Marriage and marital therapy: Psychoanalytic, behavioral and systems theory perspectives* (pp. 25–88). Oxford: Brunner/Mazel.

Minuchin, S., & Fishman, C. H. (1981). *Family therapy techniques*. Cambridge, MA: Harvard University Press.

Mitchell, S. A. (1988). *Relational concepts in psychoanalysis*. New York, NY: Basic Books.

Mitchell, S. A. (1993). *Hope and dread in psychoanalysis*. New York, NY: Basic Books.

Mitchell, S. A. (1997). *Influence and autonomy in psychoanalysis*. Hillsdale, NJ: The Analytic Press.

Mitchell, S. A. (2000). *Relationality: From attachment to intersubjectivity*. New York, NY: The Analytic Press.

Mitchell, S. A. (2002). *Can love last? The fate of romance over time*. New York, NY: W. W. Norton & Company.

Mitchell, S. A., & Black, M. J. (1995). *Freud and beyond: A history of modern psychoanalytic thought*. New York, NY: Basic Books.

Montgomery, A. (2013). *Neurobiology essentials for clinicians: What every therapist needs to know*. New York, NY: W. W. Norton & Company.

Morrow, G. D., & O'Sullivan, C. (1998). Romantic ideals as comparison levels: Implications for satisfaction and commitment in romantic involvements. In V. C. de Munck (Ed.), *Romantic love and sexual behavior: Perspectives from the social sciences* (pp. 171–199). Westport, CT: Praeger Publishers/Greenwood Publishing Group.

Nelson, T. S. (2003). Transgenerational family therapies. In L. L. Hecker & J. L. Wetchler (Eds.), *An introduction to marriage and family therapy* (pp. 255–296). Binghamton, NY: Haworth Clinical Practice Press.

Ogden, T. H. (1979). On projective identification. *International Journal of Psychoanalysis, 60*(3), 357–373.

Ogden, T. H. (1982). *Projective identification and psychotherapeutic technique.* New York, NY: Jason Aronson.

Ogden, T. H. (1986). *The matrix of the mind.* Northvale, NJ: Jason Aronson.

Ogden, T. H. (1994). *Subjects of analysis.* Northvale, NJ: Jason Aronson.

Ogden, T. H. (1997). *Reverie and interpretation: Sensing something human.* Northvale, NJ: Jason Aronson.

Panksepp, J. (2009). Brain emotional systems and qualities of mental life: From animal models of affect to implications for psychotherapeutics. In D. Fosha, D. J. Siegel, & M. F. Solomon (Eds.), *The healing power of emotion: Affective neuroscience, development & clinical practice* (pp. 1–26). New York, NY: W. W. Norton & Company.

Pine, F. (1990). *Drive, ego, object, and self: A synthesis for clinical work.* New York, NY: Basic Books.

Pines, A. M. (1999). *Falling in love: Why we choose the lovers we choose.* New York, NY: Routledge.

Pines, A. M. (2001). The role of gender and culture in romantic attraction. *European Psychologist, 6*, 96–102.

Pines, A. M., & Aronson, E. (1988). *Career burnout: Causes and cures.* New York, NY: Free Press.

Pinsof, W. M. (1995). *Integrative problem-centered therapy: A synthesis of family, individual, and biological therapies.* New York, NY: Basic Books.

Pinsof, W. M., & Lebow, J. L. (2005). *Family psychology: The art of the science.* New York, NY: Oxford University Press.

Porges, S. W. (2009). Reciprocal influences between body and brain in the perception and expression of affect: A polyvagal perspective. In D. Fosha, D. J. Siegel, & M. F. Solomon (Eds.), *The healing power of emotion: Affective neuroscience, development & clinical practice* (pp. 27–54). New York, NY: W. W. Norton & Company.

Poulton, J. L. (2013). *Object relations and relationality in couple therapy: Exploring the middle ground.* New York, NY: Jason Aronson.

Racker, H. (1968). *Transference and countertransference.* New York, NY: International Universities Press.

Repič, T. (2006). Avtonomija in intimnost v družini kot dejavnika tveganja za spolno zlorabo [Autonomy and intimacy in the family as risk factors for sexual abuse]. *Psihološka obzorja, 15*(1), 111–125.

Repič, T. (2008). *Nemi kriki spolne zlorabe in novo upanje* [Silent screams of sexual abuse and new hope]. Celje: Društvo Mohorjeva družba, Celjska Mohorjeva družba.

Ringstrom, P. A. (2014). *A relational psychoanalytic approach to couples psychotherapy.* New York, NY: Routledge.

Robins, S. P. (2010). *Exploring intimacy: Cultivating healthy relationships through insight and intuition.* Lanham: Rowman & Littlefield Publishers.

Rothschild, B. (2000). *The body remembers: The psychophysiology of trauma and trauma treatment.* New York, NY: W. W. Norton & Company.

Rothschild, B. (2003). *The body remembers casebook: Unifying methods and models in the treatment of trauma and PTSD*. New York, NY: W. W. Norton & Company.

Rothschild, B. (2006). *Help for the helper: The psychophysiology of compassion fatigue and vicarious trauma*. New York, NY: W. W. Norton & Company.

Rothschild, B. (2010). *8 keys to safe trauma recovery*. New York, NY: W. W. Norton & Company.

Sandler, J., & Perlow, M. (1987). Internalization and externalization. In J. Sandler (Ed.), *Projection, identification, projective identification* (pp. 1–11). Madison, CT: International Universities Press.

Scharff, D. E. (1992). *Refinding the object and reclaiming the self*. Northvale, NJ: Jason Aronson.

Scharff, D. E., & Scharff, J. S. (1987). *Object relations family therapy*. Northvale, NJ: Jason Aronson.

Scharff, J. S. (1989). *Foundations of object relations family therapy*. Northvale, NJ: Jason Aronson.

Scharff, J. S. (1992). *Projective and introjective identification and the use of therapist's self*. Northvale, NJ: Jason Aronson.

Scharff, J. S. (2010). An object relations approach to intimacy: Loss and recovery. In J. Carlson & L. Sperry (Eds.), *Recovering intimacy in love relationships: A clinician's guide* (pp. 127–148). New York, NY: Routledge.

Scharff, J. S., & Scharff, D. E. (1994). *Object relations therapy of physical and sexual trauma*. Northvale, NJ: Jason Aronson.

Scharff, J. S., & Scharff, D. E. (1998). *Object relations individual therapy*. Northvale, NJ: Jason Aronson.

Scharff, J. S., & Scharff, D. E. (2000). *Tuning the therapeutic instrument: Affective learning of psychotherapy*. Northvale, NJ: Jason Aronson.

Scharff, J. S., & Scharff, D. E. (Eds.) (2006). *New paradigms for treating relationships*. Lanham, MD: Jason Aronson.

Scharff, J. S., & Scharff, D. E. (2014). *Psychoanalytic couple therapy: Foundations of theory and practice*. London: Karnac Books.

Schore, A. N. (1994). *Affect regulation and the origin of the self: The neurobiology of emotional development*. Hillsdale, NJ: Lawrence Erlbaum Associates.

Schore, A. N. (2000). Attachment and the regulation of the right brain. *Attachment & Human Development*, *2*(1), 23–47.

Schore, A. N. (2002). Dysregulation of the right brain: A fundamental mechanism of traumatic attachment and the psychopathogenesis of posttraumatic stress disorder. *Australian and New Zealand Journal of Psychiatry*, *36*, 9–30.

Schore, A. N. (2003). *Affect regulation and the repair of the self*. New York, NY: W. W. Norton & Company.

Schore, A. N. (2010). Relational trauma and the developing right brain: The neurobiology of broken attachment bonds. In T. Baradon (Ed.), *Relational trauma in infancy: Psychoanalytic, attachment and*

neuropsychological contributions to parent-infant psychotherapy (pp. 19–47). New York, NY: Routledge.
Schore, A. N. (2012). *The science of the art of psychotherapy*. New York, NY: W. W. Norton & Company.
Sexton, T. L., Weeks, G. R., & Robbins, M. S. (Eds.) (2003). *Handbook of family therapy: The science and practice of working with families and couples*. New York, NY: Brunner-Routledge.
Shur, R. (1994). *Countertransference enactment: How institutions and therapists actualize primitive internal worlds*. Lanham, MD: Jason Aronson.
Siegel, D. J. (2003). An interpersonal neurobiology of psychotherapy: The developing mind and the resolution of trauma. In D. J. Siegel & M. F. Solomon (Eds.), *Healing trauma: Attachment, mind, body, and brain* (pp. 1–56). New York, NY: W. W. Norton & Company.
Siegel, D. J. (2006). An interpersonal neurobiology approach to psychotherapy: Awareness, mirror neurons, and neural plasticity in the development of well-being. *Psychiatric Annals, 36*(4), 248–256.
Siegel, D. J. (2007). *The mindful brain: Reflection and attunement in the cultivation of well-being*. New York, NY: W. W. Norton & Company.
Siegel, D. J. (2009). Mindful awareness, mindsight, and neural integration. *The Humanistic Psychologist, 37*(2), 137–158.
Siegel, D. J. (2010). *The mindful therapist: A clinician's guide to mindsight and neural integration*. New York, NY: W. W. Norton & Company.
Siegel, D. J. (2011). *Mindsight: The new science of personal transformation*. New York, NY: Bantam Books.
Siegel, D. J., & Solomon, M. F. (2013). *Healing moments in psychotherapy*. New York, NY: W. W. Norton & Company.
Silverstein, M. L. (2007). *Disorders of the self: A personality-guided approach*. Washington, DC: American Psychological Association.
Slipp, S. (1988). *The technique and practice of object relations family therapy*. Northvale, NJ: Jason Aronson.
Slipp, S. (Ed.) (1993). *Curative factors in dynamic psychotherapy*. Northvale, NJ: Jason Aronson.
Slipp, S. (1996). *Healing the gender wars: Therapy with men and couples*. Northvale, NJ: Jason Aronson.
Solomon, M. F. (1992). *Narcissism and intimacy: Love and marriage in an age of confusion*. New York, NY: W. W. Norton & Company.
Solomon, M. F. (1994). *Lean on me: The power of positive dependency in intimate relationships*. New York, NY: Simon & Schuster.
Solomon, M. F. (2009). Emotion in romantic partners: Intimacy found, intimacy lost, intimacy reclaimed. In D. Fosha, D. J. Siegel, & M. F. Solomon (Eds.), *The healing power of emotion: Affective neuroscience, development & clinical practice* (pp. 232–256). New York, NY: W. W. Norton & Company.
Solomon, M. F., Neborsky, R. J., McCullough, L., Alpert, M., Shapiro, F., & Malan, D. (2001). *Short-term therapy for long-term change*. New York, NY: W. W. Norton & Company.

Solomon, M. F., & Siegel, D. J. (Eds.) (2013). *Healing moments in psychotherapy*. New York, NY: W. W. Norton & Company.

Solomon, M. F., & Siegel, J. P. (1997). *Countertransference in couples therapy*. New York, NY: W. W. Norton & Company.

Sperry, L. (Ed.) (2004). *Assessment of couples and families: Contemporary and cutting edge strategies*. New York, NY: Brunner-Routledge.

Steinberg, L. (2014). *Adolescence* (10th ed.). New York, NY: McGraw-Hill.

Stern, D. N. (1985). *The interpersonal world of the infant: A view from psychoanalysis and developmental psychology*. New York, NY: Basic Books.

Stern, D. N. (1995). *The motherhood constellation: A unified view of parent-infant psychotherapy*. New York, NY: Basic Books.

Stern, D. N. (1998). *The birth of a mother*. New York, NY: Basic Books.

Stern, D. N. (2004). *The present moment in psychotherapy and everyday life*. New York, NY: W. W. Norton & Company.

Stern, D. N. (2010). *Forms of vitality: Exploring dynamic experience in psychology, arts, psychotherapy and development*. New York, NY: Oxford University Press.

Sullivan, H. S. (1940). *Conceptions of modern psychiatry*. New York, NY: W. W. Norton & Company.

Sullivan, H. S. (1972). *Personal psychopathology*. New York, NY: W. W. Norton & Company.

Summers, F. L. (1994). *Object relations theories and psychopathology: A comprehensive text*. New York, NY: Analytic Press.

Umbarger, C. C. (1983). *Structural family therapy*. New York, NY: Grune and Stratton.

van der Kolk, B. A. (1994). The body keeps the score: Memory and the evolving psychobiology of posttraumatic stress. *Harvard Review of Psychiatry*, *1*(5), 253–265.

van der Kolk, B. A. (1996). The body keeps the score: Approaches to the psychobiology of posttraumatic stress disorder. In B. A. van der Kolk, A. McFarlane, & L. Weisaeth (Eds.), *Traumatic stress: The effects of overwhelming experience on mind, body and society* (pp. 214–241). New York, NY: Guilford Press.

White, J., Klein, D., & Martin, T. (Eds.) (2015). *Family theories* (4th ed.). Thousand Oaks, CA: Sage Publications.

Winnicott, D. W. (1971). *Playing and reality*. New York, NY: Basic Books.

Winnicott, D. W. (1984). *Deprivation and delinquency*. London: Tavistock Publications.

Winnicott, D. W. (1986). *Home is where we start from: Essays by a psychoanalyst*. New York, NY: W. W. Norton & Company.

Winnicott, D. W. (1988). *Human nature*. London: Free Association Books.

Index

For Product Safety Concerns and Information please contact our EU
representative GPSR@taylorandfrancis.com
Taylor & Francis Verlag GmbH, Kaufingerstraße 24, 80331 München, Germany

www.ingramcontent.com/pod-product-compliance
Ingram Content Group UK Ltd.
Pitfield, Milton Keynes, MK11 3LW, UK
UKHW021502240926
475702UK00035B/204
* 9 7 8 1 1 3 8 6 8 6 1 8 2 *